THE RUGBY REBELLION

The Divide of League and Union in Australasia

Sean Fagan

LONDON LEAGUE PUBLICATIONS LTD

THE RUGBY REBELLION:
The Divide of League and Union in Australasia
© Copyright Sean Fagan

Foreword © Tony Collins, Introduction © Ian Heads.

The moral right of Sean Fagan to be identified as the author has been asserted.

Front cover photos: Dally Messenger, New South Wales versus Great Britain (rugby league) 1910, R.A.S. Challenge Shield

A CIP catalogue record for this book is available from the British Library.

This book was originally published in Australia in July 2005 by RL1908. This edition first published in Great Britain in November 2005 by: London League Publications Ltd, P.O. Box 10441, London E14 8WR

ISBN: 1-903659-25-6

Cover design by: Stephen McCarthy Graphic Design
                                        46, Clarence Road, London N15 5BB
Original cover design: Kylie Prats, Brevier Design
Editor: Kim Dixon
Index and statistics: Luanne Fagan
Typesetting and layout: Best Legenz
Photo editing: Kim Dixon
Development of this edition: Peter Lush

Printed and bound by: Antony Rowe Ltd, Eastbourne

FOREWORD

In March 1907 a letter arrived completely out of the blue at the office of
the Northern Union secretary Joseph Platt. It was from an obscure New
Zealand rugby player, A.H. Baskerville. He asked the Northern Union (NU)
leaders if they would be prepared to host a tour by southern hemisphere
players. It signalled the start of a movement that would spread from New
Zealand to Australia and turn the world of rugby upside down.

As *The Rugby Rebellion* makes clear, Baskerville's letter was merely the
tip of an iceberg. Down under, rugby union had been wracked with
conflict since the turn of the century. In Australia, relations between
rugby's middle-class administrators and working-class players had been
stretched to breaking point and there was an increasing dissatisfaction
in both countries with the Rugby Football Union (RFU) and its
uncompromising attitude towards those who disagreed with its policies.
Baskerville's announcement of a professional All Black tour to the
NU was the spark that lit the blue touch paper of a full scale rugby
rebellion.

Amazingly, this is a story that has never before been told in full. With
this book Sean Fagan has filled a cavernous hole in the history rugby
league, and indeed world sport, by writing the first fully researched and
comprehensive account of the birth of rugby league down under.

What a story it is. The players and officials who founded the game
took considerable personal risks. The whole weight of official sport, not
just rugby union, was against them because they challenged the amateur
ethos of the times. Because of the RFU's ban on anyone who played
NU football, there was no going back if the venture failed. It took guts,
determination and a faith in the new game for the pioneers to succeed.

Sean Fagan himself is a pioneer. Rugby league history in Australia
has usually been written by journalists, unlike here in Britain where
there has been a thriving community of historians since Robert Gate
and Trevor Delaney blazed a trail of immaculately researched books
in the 1980s. Like Gate and Delaney, Sean has set a new standard of
research and presentation that future league historians will now have to
match. Along the way he has uncovered much that is new, unravelled old
mysteries and set the facts straight on numerous controversial issues.

Why should events that took place 14,000 miles away and 100 years
ago be of interest to rugby league supporters in Britain? The answer is
simple. Without rugby league's expansion into the southern hemisphere,
the history of the game in Britain would have been radically different.
The impetus that international tours have given the game and the boost
that overseas players brought to clubs would never have been available.

Without the links to Australia and New Zealand, it is probable that
rugby league would have remained locked into the north of England,

trapped in a single country like the nationally-limited sports of Gaelic football and Australian Rules. It may well still have been called the Northern Union too - it was only after pressure from the Australians that the NU changed its name to the Rugby Football League in 1922. Most importantly, the game's advance down under demonstrated that it is not a 'northern sport' which cannot grow outside of the counties of its birth. After all, there is almost nowhere further 'down South' than Australasia.

And, as *The Rugby Rebellion* makes clear, the Northern Union's split from the RFU was itself an event of international importance. Not only was the progress of the NU being watched closely by rugby players and officials down under, but the treatment of the northern clubs by the RFU was mirrored by the behaviour of the 1899 and 1904 British rugby union tourists towards their Australasian hosts. As readers will notice, the Reverend Mullineux's snobbish disdain for Australians seems to be a direct reflection of the Reverend Frank Marshall's attempts to curb the influence of working-class rugby players in the north of England before the 1895 split. And of course the RFU was determined to 'throttle the hydra' of Northern Unionism wherever it reared its head.

One of the book's great strengths is that it shows how much in common there is between league in Australia and Britain. The influence of Widnes émigré Tom McCabe cannot be underestimated. The tours to and from down under helped to cement the sport's appeal and influence across the hemispheres. And as the book makes clear, the game in both countries was born in opposition to the discrimination and social exclusivity of the rugby union authorities. Both wanted to give working-class players the opportunity to make the most of their football talents, unhindered by the prejudices of social class or status.

These shared values date back to the earliest years of the game - when the 1914 British Lions tour manager John Houghton was asked why the tourists played matches in remote country towns in New South Wales and Queensland, he told the press that 'their mission was to propagate their game of [rugby league] football because they believed it was the people's game'. When the 1946 Lions arrived in Sydney, *Rugby League News* welcomed them with the declaration that 'rugby league, with justifiable pride, always emphasises the fact that it is the most democratic of sports'.

This book is as important to the history of rugby league in Britain as it is to the game's history in Australia. It is a shared history that belongs to every rugby league supporter, wherever they may be in the world. It is common to hear people in Australian rugby league quote the old Chinese proverb 'let those who drink the water remember who dug the well'. Now, at last, this magnificent book tells us the full story of those who dug deep and true to establish the greatest game of all in Australia.

Tony Collins — October 2005

INTRODUCTION

If you would understand anything, observe the beginnings — Aristotle

As the early years of the 20th century unfolded, the city of Sydney must have been an enthralling place to live for anyone who cared about that notable English export – the game of rugby, which had arrived in the colony in the 1860s and gained a powerful foothold. From perhaps late 1905 the air of Sydney's winters in sporting clubs and pubs would surely have crackled with rumour and debate. In rugby's world muttering unease and discontent was abroad. The 15-man game, its coffers full from the great crowds its men and its teams could draw, was seen to be treating its players less well than they deserved. In England, such a climate had led directly to the Great Split of 1895, and the establishment of the game first known as `Northern Union' - the (eventual) 13 man version of rugby that was to become… rugby league. In Sydney town, the question hung over it all: was it possible that the recent history of England's North would repeat itself in Australia?

This remarkable time, when any sportswriter worth his salt would surely have been glad to be alive, is the backdrop for Sean Fagan's brilliantly researched book: *The Rugby Rebellion: The Divide of League and Union*. Library hours beyond counting, in which Fagan studied in the finest detail the documentation and media coverage of the times has produced a book of immense value to both codes. It is also in its unfolding way, a thrilling tale – of an uprising by footy-playing working class blokes dismayed they were not getting a `fair go' from those who ran their game, and the result of that anger. The stunning outcome of the events of those long ago years was the formation of a new game, rugby league (1908) and a chastened and bitter rugby establishment left to rail against the `new professionalism' and the loss of champion players to the game that had arrived from Yorkshire and Lancashire without even (as yet) a rule book. The bitterness between the codes lived on for years, and maybe there are still pockets of it remaining even now. But today, at last, with a comfortable pathway existing for players back and across between the games, the relationship could be fairly called `robust rivalry' — with genuine mutual respect existing between the two different brands of rugby…. and both doing well.

It is therefore a happy time for Fagan to tell his story. In it as he recounts the detail of rugby's beginning, and captures the ebb and flow of Sydney life back then, he skillfully pieces together the jigsaw of what went right…or wrong – depending on which way you may wish to consider it. Heroes/villains abound: the great Herbert Henry `Dally' Messenger, rugby's pride and champion player of his time, who agreed in August 1907 to join the new game (once his mum had given him the nod) and thus made rugby league possible; James Joseph Giltinan, son of a coachbuilder, cricketing umpire, entrepreneur and the driving force in the breakaway; Victor Trumper, cricket's magnificent `bird in flight', one of the greatest of all batsmen, a key figure in it all via his support for the new game; in Wellington, New Zealand, Albert Henry Baskerville (or Baskiville), a young man of rare vision who constructed the first New Zealand (rugby league) tour of England (1907-08) and by bringing his Kiwi team to Sydney en route, gave Australia its chance; the imposing James Joynton-Smith, rugby league's benefactor and saviour in 1909 when he bankrolled the signing of the Wallabies of 1908 – at a time when league was looking decidedly shaky; Chris McKivat – vice captain of the Wallabies and a great halfback whose decision to sign Joynton-Smith's contract, led to teammates doing the same. McKivat remains one of the great heroes/villains of the time – a monumental figure in the story of both games.

These men and so many others dance across the pages of Fagan's book. Mysteries of early years are explained....then here and there new unanswered questions emerge to fill the space. The impression is of a (sporting) world in turmoil, of intrigue that would do Agatha Christie proud – and of a fabulous sporting story. In some cases friendships of a lifetime were split forever because of what took place. Many years later the Super League raids and resultant `war' (from 1995) had the same effect. But what happened back in those early years of the 20th century added up to be a far bigger and more influential shaper of history even than the Super League battle – with all its greed and false promises and awfulness.

In his book Sean Fagan has added positively and importantly to the story of the two rugby's in Australia and this scholarly work deserves to be highly valued by both codes. His timing is impeccable – to research and write such a book on the very edge of the 100th anniversary of the Great Divide....that long ago time when rugby wars broke out in Sydney...... and changed forever the sporting winters of Australia.

Ian Heads – Winter 2005
(This was the Foreword to the Australian edition)

ABOUT THE AUTHOR

Sean Fagan first became involved with rugby league when he played for the Fairfield RSL junior club (Parramatta district) in the early 1970s. Towards the end of the decade he began attending club matches across Sydney, particularly Lidcombe and Cumberland Ovals, though Manly was his favourite team (and still is). At high school he took up rugby union (the school did not offer League) and continued to play until the mid-1980s with a local club. The Northern Eagles merger in 2000 saw him (momentarily) lose interest in modern rugby league, and he turned to the game's history for enjoyment. This led to the launching in 2001 of his acclaimed web site RL1908.com and a new career as a writer. Having a background in both codes sparked his wider interest in how rugby split in Australia, and was played in the 1800s. Sean lives in north-western Sydney with his wife and two children.

CONTENTS

Professional football cannot live here
unless a miracle happens. *The Arrow*

CHAPTER ONE

A GRAND OLD GAME
IS KING FOOTBALL

WHEN FORWARDS WERE ARISTOCRATS

The big club matches were played upon the boundless Moore Park. With surging, and sometimes yelling crowds hemming in the players, as though the battle were one of fisticuffs instead of a friendly game of football.

This was Sydney club rugby in the late 1870s. Spectators freely entered the open parkland outside the Sydney Cricket Ground (SCG) and stood along the touchlines marked out by low cut grass.

Rugby was purely amateur, more because of its cultural setting within the colony's upper classes, than any formal rules. The teams came from gentlemen's social clubs and private schools. Club competitions were not played; the teams issued invitations to each other to arrange matches. Players did not have specialised positions and if team training sessions were held at all, they were for fitness, not strategy or coaching.[1]

Concepts such as playing to attract fee-paying crowds and compensating footballers for travelling expenses — (issues that would

Rugby in the 1870s – scrummaging battles were the centre-piece of rugby football.

become pivotal in the early 1900s) — were unheard of. The players made their own way to the field, paid for their own jerseys and boots, and took part for the enjoyment of the game and to make use of their leisure time.

Rugby's purpose was to 'try the muscles of the men's bodies, and the endurance of their hearts, to make them rejoice in their strength.'[2] For the youth of the upper classes this exercise may have provided some use — testing their personal and team reactions in the heat of battle.

For the working classes, who laboured six days a week and had no free time for sport, physical activity was their daily routine. Rugby was of no consequence to the greater population of Sydney. If they cared at all, their only awareness of its existence came from scant reports in the city's newspapers.

This was when the forwards, rather than the backs, were the aristocrats of the game. Twenty men a-side in cricket kit put their heads down and tried to carry the position by brute force, and 'when to pass the ball was to label oneself an imbecile.'[3]

Like all forms of football, the objective of rugby was to drive the ball through the other team's goal. The centre-piece of the game was the scrummaging battles. It is why men played the game, and where most of their time on the field was spent.

Thirteen of the twenty players were forwards, whose business was to batter their way through the opposition with the ball at their feet. There were no scrummages in the modern manner, either set or loose. The forwards faced each other, standing upright, like two moving walls, and by sheer kicking one line forced the ball and themselves through the other. The attackers would then attempt to dribble the ball downfield in a 'forward rush' toward the opposition's goal.

'There was no planned method of getting the ball out to the backs,' recalled a player from that time. 'If it came out, it came out, but it might come out anywhere. It was not the business of the forwards to put it out, but to push it through.'[4]

Heeling the ball backwards was practically never done. It was thought to place the forwards in front of the ball, leaving them in an off-side position. The 'back division,' outside the scrum, comprised quarterbacks (immediately behind the scrum), halfbacks and fullbacks — it was their job to collect the scraps. When the ball was expelled from the scrum, they raced to gain possession and then, by a drop or punt kick, return it back up field or through the goals. A further option was to run and attempt to carry the ball over the goal line for a touchdown.

The passing game was rarely contemplated or attempted — most considered throwing the ball away when confronted by an opponent as cowardly. The only skills employed by a running back were the hand-off (palming-off a defender) and dodging (side-stepping).

Each team came with its own on-field umpire to observe the game — players appealed if they saw a breach of the laws. No penalties (free-kicks) were given for breaking a rule, the ball would be brought back and play restarted. It was a matter of personal and team discipline to play the game as gentlemen and with honour. As in cricket, frivolous appealing and trying to deceive an opponent or umpire for an advantage was frowned upon. If found necessary, the captain issued a reprimand to a player for his unsporting conduct. Any disputes between the teams were resolved solely between the two captains, though not always amicably (some gave up an argument just so the game could continue).

Points were only scored by kicking a goal — from a drop-kicked field goal or a place kick taken after either a mark (fair catch) or the gaining of a 'try at goal.' Once a player touched the ball down behind an opponent's goal line, their team could have a 'try at goal' place kick. The player carried the ball back into the field (in line with where he touched down) and then placed and held the ball in the position for the kicker. Though points were awarded for a missed 'try at goal,' they only counted in matches where no goals were scored.

When a player carrying the ball was tackled to earth or held (so that he couldn't pass), he hurriedly called 'Down!' and put the ball on the ground in front of himself. A scrummage was then formed and play would continue.[5]

The game itself emanated from Rugby School in England and was spread by former pupils who were employed in positions of influence in the colonies, many as school principals. Interest also grew following the publication of *Tom Brown's Schooldays,* a book by Rugby School 'old-boy' Tom Hughes, which included a lengthy and enticing narrative of a rugby match.

Rugby was a game for the players, not spectators. With the ball hidden from view for so much of the game, rugby had no prospect of ever rivalling cricket, pedestrianism (professional athletics) or rowing for the interest of Sydney spectators.

No one minded though. It was a sport played by the upper classes purely for their own challenge and enjoyment — attracting crowds was irrelevant.

THE SOUTHERN RUGBY FOOTBALL UNION

Rugby in NSW was controlled by the Southern Rugby Football Union (SRFU), which was formed in 1874 by ten of the city's seventeen rugby clubs. Preferring to use 'Southern' as its descriptor instead of Sydney or

The Sydney University F.C. - at the Albert Ground (1878).
Captain Ted Raper is holding the ball.

NSW, the SRFU implied it was the antipodean equivalent or branch of the Rugby Football Union (RFU) in England.

The SRFU made it plain that all its member clubs could only play rugby football by the rules laid down by the RFU and English Public Schools. The SRFU sought to portray its status, and rugby's, as superior to that of their competitor, the Melbourne-born 'Victorian rules' game.

The Australasian colonies were part of the British 'nation,' and one of the most prominent national games was rugby. Most of the inhabitants, apart from the indigenous populations, thought of themselves as 'colonial Britishers.' 'Home' was England, Wales, Scotland or Ireland. It was important to many rugby followers in the colonies to maintain the link to England's RFU.

However, far from dominating football in the colonies, by 1877 the SRFU still controlled only half of the sixteen rugby clubs in Sydney and a handful of clubs in rural NSW. Apart from in New Zealand, the code did not exist.

During that season matches between Wallaroo, University of Sydney, and the Waratahs began to attract crowds of up to 6,000 to the open fields of Moore Park — but the increase in interest brought problems. Larrikins amongst the spectators were more intent on disrupting play than watching it. Some citizens, objecting to the use of the public park for rugby matches, exercised their common right to freely walk across the field any time they pleased. The solution would be to move to an enclosed ground, but the hiring fees incurred would mean having to charge patrons an entry fee to cover the costs.[6]

In August, 1877, the SRFU held some matches at the Albert Ground in Redfern — a ground that had successfully hosted large crowds at inter-colony and international cricket matches. But, unlike cricket, the SRFU quickly found that spectators were not willing to pay money to watch rugby. *The Sydney Mail* said there was no problem with the venue, rugby just wasn't worth paying to watch. 'After a brief experience of the pleasures of a clear field at the Albert Ground, our football players have been compelled to return to Moore Park. Unless some plan can be devised which will make the thing pay, the public do not appear to care for paying to see the game as played here. Until the game becomes livelier and less risky the public are not likely to give a substantial proof of their appreciation of football by paying to witness it.'[7]

THE CALL FOR A NATIONAL FOOTBALL CODE

While rugby had its strongest support in Sydney and the major centres of New Zealand, in the rest of the Australasian colonies 'football' meant Victorian rules. Perceived as less violent, it found favour as it did not possess (to anywhere near as much) rugby's tedious scrummaging that delighted few spectators and many footballers. This view was growing even in NSW and New Zealand. The danger loomed that rugby could be replaced by either Victorian rules or some new football code utilising hybrid rules.

The rise of Victorian rules coincided with the first calls for the formation of an Australasian commonwealth (comprising the mainland colonies together with New Zealand and Tasmania). One newspaper asked, 'Why shouldn't we have uniform national rules for our football, and why shouldn't the rules be designed for our conditions?'[8]

In the summer months cricket ably met both these demands and even provided for international contests against England. However, in winter, no football code gained universal support. The prospect of a national football game could only come from the creation of hybrid rules or one code dominating all the others in popularity.

Late in the 1877 season the SRFU received a proposal from Melbourne suggesting that a 'football' contest be played between NSW and Victoria using mixed rules. The match could provide an opportunity to develop a set of rules to appeal to both colonies. The SRFU rejected the plan outright, saying that if they played anything other than rugby, the RFU in England would be forced to sever all connection with them.

The principal supporters of this view were the founders of the Wallaroo club, William 'Monty' Arnold and his brother Richard (a former student of Rugby School). They reminded the members of the SRFU that its sole objective was to play rugby football.

Not all SRFU officials and clubs agreed. Many argued that the Union should bow to the demands of Australian footballers and spectators, even if it meant ending the association with the RFU in England. The Waratahs club openly pushed for the elimination of scrummaging and the introduction of a limit on how far a player could run with the ball — two primary attributes of Victorian rules.

To demonstrate their case, the Waratahs contacted the Carlton F.C. (Victorian rules) in Melbourne and arranged an inter-club contest. Held at the Albert Ground, the clubs played two matches, one rugby and one Victorian rules, to compare codes in the hope of reaching some common rules. The Waratahs involvement received the sanction of the SRFU, but many of its committee members, particularly the Arnolds, were far from pleased.

'By far the largest number of [paying] spectators that were ever present at a football match in NSW watched these matches with great interest,' reported *The Sydney Mail*. A crowd of 3,000 paid to watch the rugby match, won by the Waratahs 'two goals to nil.' Two days later, 1,500 went through the gates to see Carlton score a 'six goals to nil' victory in the Victorian rules match.[9]

That 3,000 patrons paid to attend the rugby match suggests that playing rules were not the sole reason club contests could not attract paying crowds. The SRFU and newspaper columnists attributed the size of the crowd to the novelty of the match. But apart from one side consisting of Melbournians, there was nothing unusual in two teams playing rugby. The Sydney public had actually demonstrated they were more interested in rivalry, in this case inter-colonial, than changes in the playing rules. Club rugby, built on exclusive gentlemen's clubs and private schools, offered no rivalry for the general community — at least none they were prepared to pay for.

ABOLISH THE SCRUM

With rivalry overlooked as a factor, the dissatisfied clubs and press continued with their push to improve the SFRU's playing rules. In the wake of the Carlton F.C. visit, the Waratah and University clubs proposed the elimination of scrummaging to the SRFU. In effect, it was a proposal to join with Victorian rules.

The majority of city clubs favoured the change. Only Wallaroo and a few others stood against it. However, the country clubs, all formed by ex-Wallaroo players, were staunch supporters of rugby and their votes ensured it was rejected.

Frustrated by the SRFU's decision, a group of Sydney footballers and supporters formed the NSW Football Association (NSWFA) to play Victorian rules. They were soon joined by the Waratahs who eventually gave up seeking to introduce reforms to the SRFU from within.

The loss of the Waratahs and the formation of the NSWFA had an impact upon the SRFU. The Union acknowledged that improvements to rugby had to be made if it were to thwart the challenge from Victorian rules and attract paying spectators.

Ensuring it did not put at risk its association with the RFU, the SRFU went as far as it could with 'local interpretations' of rugby's playing rules.

Edicts were issued that the scrum should only be a means to restart play and not be the game itself. Open play using backs who would run, pass and kick, or forwards dribbling or passing the ball downfield in a rush, were to be encouraged. Endless scrummaging battles were to be avoided. Teams were standardised at 15-a-side [by the RFU].

While rugby did improve somewhat as a spectacle, it did not deliver the expected increase in crowds at fee-paying matches. The SRFU moved a match between Wallaroo and University from Moore Park to the adjacent SCG. Despite being barely a few minutes walk from where 6,000 usually watched these clubs, only 500 were prepared to pay the entry fee of a shilling.[10]

For most Sydney people rugby continued to provide little interest. While some clubs adopted the name of a suburb, they were still membership based gentlemen's clubs. A local man had no automatic right to make an application to join. He had to 'be nominated by a member before the Committee proceeds with election.' Members had to be of an acceptable standard and could be fined or dismissed for 'behaving in an ungentlemanly manner.'

FIRST INTER-COLONIAL RUGBY MATCHES

In 1879, the Victorian [Rules] Football Association (VFA) introduced inter-colonial matches between Victoria and South Australia. Held in Melbourne, the game attracted 10,000 paying spectators. Two years later, the VFA and NSWFA organised the first NSW v Victoria matches under Victorian rules in Sydney. Even though the home team was facing (and duly received) a thrashing, over 5,000 people paid to witness the SCG contest.

It was thought that the SRFU, in the face of such a disparity in the willingness of football patrons to pay, and seemingly with no hope of its own inter-colonial matches, would concede to the Victorians and introduce hybrid rules. However, Richard Arnold suggested that the SRFU should ignore the Victorians, and look to the other major Australasian colony, New Zealand. Arnold revealed that he was in regular correspondence with New Zealand rugby enthusiasts who 'unanimously upheld the Rugby Union rules, in spite of two or three attempts to introduce Victorian rules.'[11]

New Zealand had taken up rugby in 1870 and the game was thought to be of a standard comparable to NSW. Canterbury and Wellington formed governing bodies in 1879, with Otago and Auckland following soon after. These provincial Unions organised inter-regional representative games, leading to a steady rise in public interest. The SRFU followed Arnold's suggestion and began negotiations. Loyalty to

New South Wales team to New Zealand (1882)

Back Row: C A H McClatchie, C Hawkins.
Middle Row: M H Howard, R W Thallon, H B Fligg, C Jennings, W Glynn,
H M Baylis, R B Hill, G C Addison.
Front Row: G W Graham, Z C Barry, G W Walker,
E J Raper (c), G Richmond.

the RFU also held the possibility of future tours from a Home nation or a combined British team, something the Victorian game could not offer. Unexpectedly, NSW's first inter-colonial opponents were not New Zealand, but Queensland.

Victorian rules was the dominant code in Brisbane, with rugby not appearing until 1879 when occasional games were played. This was still the case in 1882, when Brisbane's four football clubs played nineteen Victorian rules matches and a mere three under Rugby rules. Late in the season, Pring Roberts, secretary of the Brisbane club, wrote to the Wallaroo club in Sydney challenging them to a rugby match.

Given rugby's minimal presence in Brisbane, the match could have passed quietly, but the inter-colonial aspect attracted much wider attention. Calls were made in Brisbane, led largely by club officials who favoured Victorian rules, for the Brisbane team to be styled as 'Queensland' and for matches to be played under each code.

The Wallaroos handed the matter over the SRFU, and suggestions were made in the press for rugby and Victorian rules to share the costs so that a true football challenge could be held between the colonies. The NSWFA offered to pay half the costs of bringing the Queenslanders to Sydney. Rather than respond to the NSWFA, the SRFU contacted the Brisbane club and told them they would cover the entire costs provided they agreed to only play rugby. The Brisbane officials accepted.

In both cities it was decided that the teams should be representative, and players were selected from the various clubs. In what became the first ever inter-colonial match, NSW (who adopted heather green as their colour) defeated Queensland (wearing red and black) 28–4 in front of 4,000 paying spectators at the SCG.[12]

The unexpected match against Queensland spurred the SRFU to complete negotiations for a tour of New Zealand. At the end of the 1882 season a 16–man NSW team travelled across the Tasman, taking five days to reach the neighbouring colony. Captained by University's Teddy Raper, each of the players had to contribute £5 towards the cost of the tour before they were allowed to board the ship. The Wallaroo members of the team were given honour caps by their club, with a silhouette of a wallaroo on the front. NSW won four of its seven matches against New Zealand provincial teams

The styles of rugby being played in the two colonies had evolved differently. Encouraged to play open football in Sydney, the NSW players now encountered the older and less sophisticated 'all-forward' game. They subsequently claimed that their visit introduced the passing-game to the New Zealanders.[13]

QUEENSLAND'S FIREFLIES AND WANDERERS

Monty Arnold, keen to keep inter-colony matches going with Queensland, accompanied a NSW team to Brisbane in 1883. Under the guidance of Fred Lea, an Englishman educated at Allesley College near Rugby, the Queensland team were far more formidable. The Queenslanders, despite Arnold taking on the role of sole referee, were able to defeat NSW 12–11 with a last-minute goal from a try. A great crowd of 3,500 attended the Eagle Farm match.

The win over NSW gave rugby in Brisbane a huge boost, with many footballers wanting to try 'the only sport in which Queensland can compete with the other colonies.' With Brisbane having only enough men for four football clubs, the preferred option was to simply increase the number of rugby games scheduled for the next season. However, news broke that a 'Queensland Football [Victorian rules] Association' was to be formed for 1884 and rugby would not be permitted to be played.

The rugby supporters reacted by creating the Northern Rugby Football Union (NRFU). Their first decision was to form two clubs — Fireflies and Wanderers — to play rugby in 1884.[14] Brisbane could not sustain two football codes, and after the SRFU and NRFU agreed to make the NSW v Queensland matches an annual fixture, rugby gained the ascendancy.

Yet again, while both footballers and spectators desired a more open form of football, it was the attraction of annual inter-colonial matches that caused the greatest shift in support.

IN THE INTERESTS OF PURE SPORT

When a New Zealand team came to Sydney in 1884 they defeated NSW three times with an improved version of their own passing game. As one player put it, 'They had brought it up to a science, while we had only jogged along in our own little fashion.'[15] The tourists (who wore blue jerseys) were unbeaten in their eight matches in NSW, scoring 167 points for, with only 17 against.

The matches against NSW were all played at the Agricultural (Society's) Ground under clear skies, attracting an average crowd of 4,500 paying spectators. The attendance brought significantly higher gate-takings than any previous rugby matches in Sydney, and it was now clear that people were prepared to pay to watch rugby if at the inter-colonial level.

Interestingly, none of the money from the matches went to the SRFU — it was all given to the tour's private promoters, a Dunedin businessman and a Canterbury Union official. The SRFU had not only

The Queensland team that visited Sydney in 1882

Back Row: Tom Bond, Henry Pritchard, Arthur Hickson, Pring Roberts, Jack Burrell.
Middle Row: Tom Welsby, Fred Hardgrave, H Stokes, Jack Blake, Jim Boyd.
Front Row: Frank Baynes, Arthur Feez, Arthur Cutfield, Ted Markwell, Hugh Mcintosh,
J E W Townson.

undertaken to hand all profits to the promoters, but also to pay all hotel and travel expenses for the team, including to and from New Zealand.

Despite the tour clearly being a money-making exercise for the promoters, the players received nothing. One of the first New Zealanders selected, Bob Whiteside, 'the most dangerous scoring player in the colony,' was dropped from the team after 'requesting terms' for his involvement.[16] No law existed that prevented players being paid, but in 'the interests of pure sport,' it was frowned upon by most — the inference being that a man could be paid to perform to his best or his worst, and therefore, one could never be assured that the final result was legitimate.

The inter-change of visits between NSW and New Zealand (repeated again in 1886), together with the annual matches between Queensland and NSW, resulted in the rugby and Victorian rules codes permanently going their separate ways and ending the calls for a hybrid game.

While the Victorians were now isolated from serious inter-colonial competition, their game was not lost from the northern colonies. Their continued presence would remind rugby's officials that their game must find wider public appeal.

By the mid-1880s another factor appeared — working-class men gained a half-day holiday on Saturday afternoons. With their new-found free time, young men looked for cheap entertainment. Playing football, whether rugby, soccer or Victorian rules, suited this need perfectly. The strong working-class communities in Sydney and Auckland favoured rugby.

In England, particularly Yorkshire, the increasing number of working-class players led the RFU in 1886 to introduce regulations ensuring ideals of amateurism were maintained. Such laws had been unnecessary when rugby was the domain of the upper classes, but attitudes were changing as footballers eyed the monetary practises used in the soccer code and began to make similar demands on their rugby clubs. Soccer had been overrun by 'professionals,' and the RFU feared their sport would go the same way. They were 'determined to throttle it [professionalism] before it is big enough to throttle them — no mercy but iron rigour will be dealt out.'

The rule changes declared illegal any payment, either in cash or in kind, to footballers for playing or training. They also forbade the employment of a player in any capacity by his club or by any member of the club. This decree displeased the clubs and working-class footballers in the North of England.[17]

In the colonies the paying of footballers was practically unknown, so the news passed with little impact.

A BRITISH TOUR AND 'PROFESSIONALISM'

In cricket, payments to professional players were an accepted practice — Australian players shared the often bountiful profits of their tours to England amongst themselves. Professionals and amateurs played alongside each other in the same teams.

By 1887, speculators in England and the colonies contemplated following cricket's lead and undertaking international rugby tours. It would be easy money, particularly as the new RFU rules meant the players couldn't (openly) demand a share.

The first rugby tour to Australasia came from a British Isles team (predominately English players) in 1888. Almost immediately afterwards, a New Zealand team toured Great Britain.[18]

The British team's tour was organised by cricket professionals Arthur Shrewsbury and Alfred Shaw who, as sponsors of a recent English cricket tour to Australia, suffered heavy financial losses. While in Australia they observed that Victorian rules matches in Melbourne were capable of producing large gate-takings with crowds of up to 20,000. They sought to restore their finances by undertaking a football tour of the colonies, playing both codes.

The RFU refused to sanction the tour as it was arranged by entrepreneurs and was clearly a money-making venture. The Union was further displeased that the team would be playing against Victorian rules clubs. Despite its stance, the RFU did nothing to stop players becoming involved.

While some of the 'gentlemen' players could afford to make the trip, the bulk of England's best rugby players (particularly the forwards) came from the working-class counties of Yorkshire and Lancashire. They could not afford to make the tour and give up their employment. Other players sought a price for their inclusion.

The promoters overcame the problem by offering prospective members varying amounts of grossly inflated 'expenses money,' with England's rugby and cricket captain Andrew Stoddart topping the list at £200. Although it was an open-secret that payments were being offered, the RFU preferred not to act.

However, after the team sailed for Australia, the RFU banned one player as a 'professional' — Jack Clowes of Halifax. He was exposed by the Dewsbury club seeking to overturn a loss in a Yorkshire Cup match he had played in. Dewsbury officials had cleverly ensured their representative in the tour, Angus Fraser, stood down from the match. Clowes' so-called crime was accepting £3 to buy a suit for the tour. The RFU's ban meant anyone in Australia or New Zealand playing with or against Clowes would also be declared professional. He did not play a match on the tour.

No doubt when the tourists were in Australasia, Clowes' inability to play raised questions concerning the RFU's rules of amateurism. The Unions in the

England's Andrew Stoddart – a member of the 1888 British team that toured the Australasian colonies.

colonies, who were making local-rule interpretations and chasing gate-money, believed themselves to be applying the principles of amateurism in a manner suiting local conditions. The RFU had always seemed to condone acts necessary to advance the sport, which supported the activities of the SRFU. However the treatment of Clowes appeared to indicate a much tougher stance.

In Auckland, the public's need for a win against the British was so strong the local Union stretched amateurism to its limit. The home team resided in a hotel in the week leading up to the match, and they spent all their time in intensive training to ready themselves. Their 'win-at-all-cost' attitude proved so successful that they dished out to the British their heaviest defeat of the tour.[19]

As predicted, the tourists made more money from Victorian rules than rugby. The first rugby match against NSW attracted a crowd of 6,000, a good result by Sydney standards, but it was easy to see why the British played more games under Victorian rules. Crowds over 25,000 watched them in Melbourne.

When the team returned to England, some of the clubs in the Northern counties were so sure that their players would be expelled as 'professionals' they refused to let them play. Not wanting to ban fine Southern gentlemen, such as Stoddart, along with the other players, the RFU solved its dilemma by having each man sign a declaration that they had received nothing other than mere expenses. They even went so far as the remove the ban on Clowes.

To many the episode reeked of RFU hypocrisy, more so when it was learned that the RFU had sanctioned a tour of a New Zealand Maori team, set to arrive in England in late September 1888.

THE 'NEW ZEALAND NATIVES' TOUR

By proposing an all-Maori team instead of a New Zealand representative team, the venture was clearly shown to be aiming at a wider audience and producing a profit. The tour was organised and captained by Joe Warbrick, who had played for New Zealand in 1884 against NSW in Sydney. His business partners in the tour were Thomas Eyton, the tour's promoter and treasurer, and James Scott, team manager. They formed a reasonably talented combination of players that included the few Maoris who had already played for provincial teams or New Zealand. One notable inclusion was Thomas Ellison, a high points-scoring forward who became the first Maori to practise as a solicitor in the colony.

The team also included Joe Warbrick's four brothers. All apparently deserved selection in their own right. Billy Warbrick in particular was a fine footballer, and would prove to be the team's best player by the end of the tour.

The tour was not authorised by any of the New Zealand rugby bodies, who had doubts that the players were amateurs. However, each provincial Union agreed to play matches against the Maori team and share the gate-takings with the organisers. The RFU's sanction to the tour, and the New Zealand authorities tacit support, appears to stem from the side being all-Maori.

When, at the last moment, the team was altered to include five white players and styled its name as the 'New Zealand Natives Football Team,' the tour suddenly became a threat to the rugby establishment. The players were all required to sign statements declaring their amateur status before the team could sail for England.

The Natives stayed in Britain for six months, winning 49 of the 74 matches played. Wearing a black playing strip, with a silver fern badge, they performed a haka before each match as part of the entertainment. The team spent the bulk of its time playing clubs in Yorkshire and Lancashire, where it found much support. However, in the South of England the Natives were accused of being professionals and criticised

The New Zealand Native Team that visited England and Australia 1888/89

Back Row: T Eyton, R Maynard, C Goldsmith
Third Row: Lawlor (coach), D Stewart, W Nehua, H Lee, G Williams, J Rene, Karauria, W Warbrick, Ihimaira, J R Scott.
Second Row: R Taiaroa, W Elliot, T R Ellison, J A Warbrick (c), E McCausland, W Anderson, P Keogh.
Front Row: A Warbrick, W T Wynyard, D R Gage, F Warbrick, C Madigan, A Webster.

for questionable playing methods outside the spirit of the gentlemanly game, even though they were within the written rules.

It was a difficult period in British rugby, with arguments over amateurism causing significant friction. The RFU struggled to rein in the Northern English counties and Wales, and the Natives were caught in it. Given the promoters of the Natives team were seeking a financial return, and players were going to share a quarter of the profits, it should have surprised no one.

The greatest drama of the tour came in the Natives v England match. The referee was the RFU's secretary, Rowland Hill. Three of the New Zealanders left the field in disgust at his decisions. In the aftermath Hill, through the RFU, demanded that the Natives' captain Warbrick issue an apology or the tour would be terminated. Hill even went so far as to script the words of the apology. Near the end of the tour, the visitors could not find any club in the South of England willing to play against them.

The Natives came home via Australia where they played a further fourteen matches without loss, including two wins against both NSW and Queensland. The novelty of their visit attracted much interest. The first game in Sydney (against NSW) drew 10,000 spectators, while 8,000 attended the opening Queensland match.

The team still couldn't escape drama, though. In Brisbane the players were accused of betting on themselves to lose the second Queensland match, and then attempting to ensure it happened. Nothing was ever proven, but by the end of the tour the provincial Unions in New Zealand had suffered enough pain and embarrassment to end thoughts of an official tour to England for many years to come.

NEW RUGBY ARRIVES

The British and Native teams tours had the positive effect of bringing to the colonies dramatic improvements in rule interpretations and playing techniques from Britain. These changes greatly opened up the game to players and spectators.

Forwards were now allowed to heel the ball backwards, provided they were bound to the scrum. This meant that the backs could be ready to use the ball, instead of having to haphazardly chase it to gain possession. The British team utilised structured running and passing moves amongst the backs, who now comprised six players: two halfbacks behind the forwards (formerly called quarterbacks); three on the three-quarter line (the old halfback line); and a fullback.[20]

Some of the British team, perhaps fearing their careers at home were over, decided to stay behind in the colonies. Angus Fraser, a three-quarter who had played with clubs in Wales and Yorkshire, settled in Wellington (New Zealand) where he provided valuable first-hand knowledge of the new form of rugby. Willie Burnett (from Scotland) moved to western Queensland, while 'Harry' Speakman (from Runcorn) did much to encourage the growth of rugby in Brisbane, then later at Charters Towers.

The tours exposed the inconsistent approaches taken by the rugby union bodies in both New Zealand and England. For the RFU, the tours had in effect exacerbated already growing conflicts with clubs, players and supporters in Yorkshire, Lancashire and Wales. In New Zealand, the absence of a colony-wide rugby authority had left the door open for more private ventures.

The rugby authorities' actions, at a time when the working class were starting to move into rugby in the colonies, sent out mixed messages about what payments were allowed under amateurism.

After the 1888 British and Natives tours, no further overseas visits were arranged for almost half a decade. The only inter-colonial contests were between NSW and Queensland. None of the Unions were prepared to allow any of their players to be involved in further private ventures.

THE BOOM DAYS OF COLONIAL RUGBY

In 1892, each of the colonies reconstituted the control of rugby within their domain. In Australia, the 'Southern' and 'Northern' names were discarded as the bodies became the New South Wales RFU (NSWRU) and the Queensland RFU (QRU) respectively. Across the Tasman, the New Zealand RFU (NZRU) was formed, though the Otago, Canterbury and Southland Unions remained unaffiliated for a time.

The two Australian colonies mimicked the prestigious rugby match between Oxford and Cambridge Universities in England, by awarding their representative players 'blues.' Queensland with the darker Oxford-blue coloured jerseys, while NSW implemented the sky blue jerseys of Cambridge.[21] As Wellington representative on the NZRFU, Thomas Ellison convinced the Union to adopt the black jersey and silver fern badge of the New Zealand Natives team.

The formation of the NZRU made it easier to deal with the NSWRU and QRU. With Ellison as captain, the New Zealanders embarked on their first overseas visit since 1884 when they travelled to Sydney, Bathurst, Newcastle and Brisbane for ten matches. Their return to Australia produced great interest and strong gate-takings.

New Zealand played two matches in Sydney against the NSW 'Light Blues' with a win to each side. Both were held at the SCG on sunny days, drawing around 15,000 spectators. The visitors won two easy encounters in Brisbane at the Exhibition Ground, with 8,000 on hand at both games. A deciding third match against NSW was played back in Sydney on a heavy field in poor weather. Despite the conditions, interest remained high and 20,000 attended at the SCG to witness New Zealand win 16–0. The five big matches of the tour produced an impressive aggregate crowd figure of nearly 67,000.

Though criticisms of the rules of rugby continued, the paying crowds had grown over the late 1880s and early 1890s. With 50,000 attending the three New Zealand v NSW games in 1892, the NSWRU was for the first time generating high amounts of income. The boom days of colonial rugby had arrived, and with it came money and the working-class player.

THE GREAT DIVIDE: RUGBY LEAGUE IS BORN

The rugby outposts of the southern hemisphere had read with interest the goings on in Yorkshire, Lancashire and, to a lesser extent Wales, over broken-time payments. They had heard the experiences and observations of the returning New Zealand Natives about the growing divide they were caught in during the tour of 1888/89. More recently they had heard from the men migrating to Australia and New Zealand from England and Wales. The newspapers also reproduced occasional articles from English newspapers on the looming crisis. The Australasian Unions sent letters of support to the RFU.[22]

Dependent upon their working-class players, the Northern English rugby clubs needed to find a way to compensate players for lost earnings. If they couldn't, many would turn to the Association (soccer) game which had already moved to professionalism.[23]

Whether working in the mines or the factory, workers were paid by the number of pieces or amount they produced. While they could break-up their actual work time to attend football matches on Saturday, it meant their wages would drop accordingly. For a miner it was particularly difficult — to down tools at the coal face, return to the surface, clean-up, and then travel to an away rugby fixture would cause a significant dent in his weekly earnings. When matches he played in were attracting large 'gates,' the natural question to ask was why shouldn't he share in the profits or, at the very least, be compensated for lost work time and travel expenses.

While the owners of the Northern clubs wanted to compensate players, the RFU maintained its position that such payments were acts of professionalism. The Union held the view that the Northern clubs shouldn't be operating cup trophy competitions that whip the towns and villages into hysteria and attract such big crowds. Supporters of the RFU argued that rugby was a pastime, a means of exercise and recreation, and should be played solely for pleasure. Under the RFU players could not absent themselves from work to play rugby and expect to be compensated. Dominated by the opinions of their upper class members, the RFU's attitude was that if the footballer couldn't afford to play, or to support himself when injured, then he shouldn't play at all.

The acrimonious stand-off between the Northern counties clubs and the English RFU came to flashpoint in 1895. On August 29, at The George Hotel in Huddersfield '...the clubs here represented decide to form a Northern Rugby Football Union [referred to as the 'Northern Union,' and later the 'Rugby Football League'], and pledge themselves to push forward, without delay, its establishment on the principle of payment for broken-time only.' Rugby was now divided.

The RFU's response was to embrace the fundamentals of the amateurism ideal even more vigorously. This, in their view, would expunge the stain of the working class and return the sport to its rightful owners, the English upper and middle classes. In effect, the old rugby that tolerated to a degree the 'veiled professionalism' and accommodated the needs of the working class to keep its sport together, was dead. The 'Northern Union' would offer semi-professional rugby, and the RFU and all the Unions affiliated to it would adopt the strictly amateur form of rugby.[24]

No longer were cup competitions, team training, and over-specialised player positions (particularly in the forwards) to be tolerated under rugby union. Excessively striving for a win and overtly celebrating a victory was to degrade the sport, the team, the opponents and yourself. The game was to be played by gentlemen who openly and voluntarily complied with the rules, whether the referee's whistle blew or not. In this way the sport would be a true enjoyment to all those who participated.

Despite events in England, by 1896 all the major population centres of the Australasian rugby-playing colonies operated club competitions on a premiership and cup basis. Colonial rugby shared many of the attributes condemned by the RFU. Clubs played each other in a pre-organised fixture schedule set prior to the opening round of the competition. The end-of-season prize was a cup for the successful team and gold medals for their players, all kindly donated by a local newspaper owner, ground authority or hotelier who gained by his association with football. Play had become rough and competitive as the need to win became all-pervading. Meanwhile, 'a certain class of player' regularly moved between clubs and even colonies in the search for glory and reward.[25]

The suggestion that rugby in Sydney was not as pure as it might be gained currency. Concerned at how it would appear in the eyes of the RFU in England, and fearing the increasing numbers and influence of working men in Sydney clubs, the NSWRU initiated moves to protect itself before it was swamped.

CHAPTER TWO

WHEN THE WALLAROOS RULED OUR RUGBY WORLD

GOOD PLAYERS JOINING OUR RANKS

Club rugby in Sydney had progressed little since the 1880s. After the private schools and colleges left to play their own matches, the only first-class clubs from that era still playing in the mid-1890s were Wallaroo and University. Other clubs entered each season, but found it difficult to compete with the teamwork, support and player numbers enjoyed by the two old clubs. As a result, each year new clubs would rise and fall, with few having any measure of success or longevity.

Crowds were no larger at club games, but at least patrons were willing to pay to watch matches on enclosed grounds, which greatly assisted the financial well-being of the NSWRU. The game was now faster and more entertaining, as teams sought to use their back-lines.

In 1896 the NSWRU comprised 75 clubs divided into Seniors and four Junior competitions (in status, not players' ages). Most new clubs began in Fourth Junior and progressed upwards by gaining promotion from winning the premiership. However, it was possible for a new club to enter the Seniors if they could muster sufficient footballers to play at that level (players were individually graded by the NSWRU).

The Union allowed players to join any club that desired their services, provided they paid a membership fee. In turn, each club paid an entry fee to the Union to take part in the premiership. This was an attempt to ensure that players and clubs alike were genuine about participating. All clubs, Senior and Junior, had equal voting rights at NSWRU meetings, meaning the Sydney clubs far outweighed the number of country members.

At the beginning of the season each club (and those wanting to form a new club) held a meeting in a public room of one of the city's many hotels. Aside from perhaps Wallaroo and University, the meetings determined if there was enough interest to place a team in the field. It was not uncommon for a club to disband if its prospects looked poor or insufficient players could be found.

Attempts were increasingly made to form clubs on a suburban basis instead of on social connections (such as gentlemen's clubs). This was more the case in the Junior competitions; it was harder to start a new club in the Seniors. In the seven-team Seniors competition, the three weaker clubs (Randwick, Paddington and Willoughby) were built on suburban connections, but they had no control over men from their district who found an opportunity to play with Wallaroo, University, or the other strong clubs, Wentworth and Pirates (more fondly called 'the Shoremen'). Doubts continued until the start of the season as to which clubs would take part. Many suburban clubs preferred to stay in the Juniors rather than have to confront these difficulties.

'There is very little probability of the Paddington club appearing in the field during the coming season,' reported *The Sydney Morning Herald* (*The Herald*) in its preview of the 1896 season. 'It numbers amongst its ranks some capital exponents of the game, but for some reason or other, probably a lack of interest with some of the members, and want

The Pirates F.C. – one of Sydney's stronger social-based rugby clubs of the 1890s.

of proper organisation, the play generally fell off as last season's Senior competition progressed. Two of its members intend making Western Australia their future home and, moreover, at the present time, no one feels disposed to throw sufficient energy into the movement to place the club into the competition.'[1]

In comparison, the Wentworth club secretary was full of great hope for the 1896 season. 'We haven't lost a single old member from the 1895 team, while, on the other hand, many good players are joining our ranks. We have gained Anderson and Patterson from New Zealand, G. Wheeler from Enfield, who is regarded as an acquisition, J. O'Neill, who played for the Surrey club in the First Junior competition and who gives promise of being one of the leading forwards in the colony in time. Also joining the ranks are Strachan from Willoughby, B. Gibson who comes with a reputation from the South of Scotland and F. Cahill lately from Newcastle. The club has twenty-seven names to select from. Billy Warbrick, will again be halfback and captain. He played for New Zealand throughout the English tour, and he has also represented NSW and Queensland. His brother Fred, who played for Queensland and New Zealand against this colony, will also again don the Wentworth colours this season. So you can see, in every quarter the club is much stronger than hitherto.'[2]

While stability and combination attracted footballers to stronger teams, clubs often 'touted' for a player's services. 'The practice of touting for players prevalent amongst the few powerful clubs in Sydney is deserving of severe condemnation. Its effect is to restrict the number of first class Senior teams to three or four and thereby prevent public interest,' wrote *The Referee*.[3]

THE BARRACKERS OF THE BOLLYWOGS

Not every prospective player could obtain an opportunity with one of the powerful Senior clubs. However, the Junior clubs also offered good opportunities. The suburban basis of the Junior clubs generated inter-district rivalry which attracted local support. Players became local heroes when they defeated another suburb. Many players, clubs and supporters found the Juniors far more preferable than the Senior competition which was rapidly becoming irrelevant to much of the rugby community in Sydney.

The Referee was quite candid about the situation, having no doubt that clubs, particularly in the Juniors, found work for players or paid them money as the need to win over neighbouring suburbs became all pervading:

There are many players in Sydney who offer their services to the highest bidder. It must not be thought that this is very prevalent in Senior circles. Of course we know that positions have been frequently found by influential clubs for good players, which, however is a very different thing from paying men to play; they work for their living, and generally work hard, too, where positions have been procured for them.

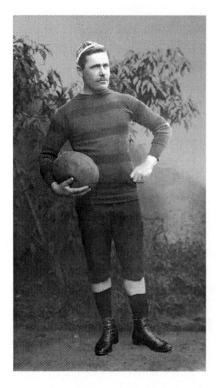

James McMahon – a popular footballer of the 1890s in Sydney and for N.S.Wales. Photographed here in his Randwick F.C. colours (indigo and gold) in 1894.

There are in different Junior grades many players of good talents who command a regular weekly stipend during winter to recompense for throwing their services with the Bollywogs of Battle Flats or some other club with no lack of enthusiastic youths to follow them on bus tops.

The barrackers of the Bollywogs throw in the threepence or sixpence weekly and thus keep in the club 'pusher,' the small deity of the moment. They 'shout' for him, give him a pair of boots, a new jersey, an honour cap, and metaphorically set him upon a pedestal for the time being. 'Pusher' can play a good game, acquit himself the sang froid of an experienced and confident hand, and can also generally manage to do something out of the box — but he is not an enthusiast, he more resembles a football parasite.

There appears to be more genuine enthusiasm amongst the Seniors than the Juniors, notwithstanding the hordes of followers the Junior teams have, and the lack of members of Senior teams. From things I have seen and heard the conclusion has formed itself in my mind that cases of professionalism are far from few amongst the Juniors. It naturally would be most difficult to prove this owning to the perversity of those whose evidence is most material; it would not suit them to open their mouths.

There are many so-called footballers about, who are coaxed into play. They pay no subscription fee and have to be supplied with boots and jersey and knickers. They give themselves the airs and graces of lordly ones, offended if they be not waited upon hand and foot by the unfortunate and misguided enthusiasts who manage some of the clubs.[4]

Sydney rugby was descending into disorder. The payment of players and other forms of professionalism, were prevalent across the Senior and Junior competitions. The win-at-all-costs attitude was turning matches into hard, rough contests. The Seniors had become a failure, with many of the colony's best players preferring to stay in the Juniors and some clubs reluctant to even take part. The move to suburban clubs threatened the dominant social clubs of the Seniors with irrelevance.

Life in the working class suburbs of Sydney revolved around community. Most men worked in their local area, socialised and met at the neighbourhood pub, concerned themselves with district issues, and they wanted to play football along such lines as well. Their communities meant as much to them as the gentlemen clubs, the University, and private school teams meant to the upper classes. Each season attempts were made to form new district clubs in the Seniors, and they nearly all failed. Most preferred playing with suburban clubs in the Junior competitions, and the standard of rugby in NSW was suffering as a result.[5]

The 'slip-shod' organisation and control of club rugby in Sydney was seen by many as unhealthy for the growth of the sport and its public role within the community.

FOOTBALLERS COMPENSATED FOR INJURY BILLS

The NSWRU dedicated the gate-receipts from the opening round of the 1896 premiership to hospital charities. Called 'Footballers' Hospital Saturday,' the entire proceeds of the Senior club matches were divided amongst the hospitals within the metropolitan area. To ensure a good gate, all Junior matches for that day '...have been declared off, such a laudable object cannot fail to meet with the sympathy and attendance of the public, independent of viewing an excellent exposition of the game.'[6]

To aid the footballers directly, the NSWRU introduced an accident insurance scheme. All (initial) medical expenses from injuries caused in matches would be covered by the Union. Schemes of up to 10s per day (for as long as a man couldn't work) were allowed under the RFU's rules — though they were rarely adopted due to the funding costs and a perception that the schemes were a means to pay footballers. Indeed, by the end of the season the NSWRU's scheme came under review because of the high number of claims for what the Union called 'trivial injuries.' The suspicion was the scheme was being 'milked' by players and club officials.[7]

The introduction of the scheme demonstrated that the NSWRU was mindful of the needs of the majority of its players. Increasingly, the game's players were working class. Without at least some relief from the full cost of medical expenses, many would have been lost to the game.

A METROPOLITAN RUGBY UNION

The NSWRU was, for the most part, a democratic body — the clubs provided delegates to the Union, who nominated and elected the governing committee from their membership. Many of these men were from the middle classes which, in Australia, was not greatly above the working class — certainly not comparable to the class distinctions in England.

However, the established members of the NSWRU were becoming concerned that a growing number of Sydney club officials on the committee would favour changes too far removed from the RFU's rules of amateurism. This would only increase, eroding the power and influence of the men who had 'owned' and controlled the NSWRU since its inception. At its very worst, it could end with the NSWRU severing its connection with the RFU.

At the 1896 end-of-season NSWRU meeting the Arnold brothers, along with John Calvert (founding president) and James McManamey, moved to ensure they maintained control of NSW rugby. They proposed: 'That it is in the best interest of football that the NSWRU dissociate from the control and management of club football, and that in future its operations be confined to the control of football throughout the colony, the promotion and management of inter-colonial matches and meetings, and to act as a court of appeal.'[8]

With just nine club delegates bothering to turn up to what was usually an uneventful meeting, the motion was passed. It was the most revolutionary change so far seen in the control of Australian rugby. The Sydney clubs would be governed by a new Metropolitan Rugby Union (MRU), which would represent them on the NSWRU. Instead of all the clubs each having a delegate on the NSWRU, they would be represented by a mere handful.

The leadership of the NSWRU had decided to sever the direct control of football in the metropolis from its responsibilities. This would ensure that the increasing compromises, straying from strict amateur practises, and the growing voice of the working classes, could only progress so far — the gentlemen founders of the game in NSW and their ideals would be protected within the NSWRU. The NSWRU could ensure they stood before the RFU as a clean body and retained overall power over NSW rugby.

SYDNEY CLUBS FIGHT TO REGAIN CONTROL

By the time the first NSWRU meeting of 1897 was held, the decision to form the MRU had become particularly heated. Held at Aaron's Exchange Hotel in the city, a large number of club representatives, footballers and club supporters gathered in expectation.

Many of Sydney's club representatives, led by Lewis Abrams and W. Speight, were incensed about the changes, condemning the decision, and seeking to rescind it. The older members of the NSWRU urged the proposal be supported.[9]

'Under the present conditions it is impossible to carry out the work of the Union,' said McManamey. 'The present scheme has been well considered, and many laborious hours have been spent on it.' McManamey spoke in his usual cool and concise manner, but his reasoning lacked sufficient substance to convince its detractors.

Monty Arnold – founded the Wallaroos F.C. and the NSWRU.

Speight's primary objection was that the current financial reserves of the NSWRU had largely been funded from the gate-takings at Sydney club matches — and this money would not be left behind for the use of the proposed MRU on the game in Sydney. Well known for 'his fiery, incoherent harangues,' he put forward that, 'There is £1,500 now in the hands of the Union, the greater part of which should be handed over to the new MRU.' He was joined by G. Vaughan who stated, 'The metropolitan clubs made most of the money in question. It should, therefore, be given to the MRU. If it is not done, I cannot agree to the proposed dissociation.'

Speight continued his attack by pointing out that the changes would result in the clubs losing their say in the running of the NSWRU. The clubs would now be represented by a handful of MRU members at NSWRU meetings, instead of each club (Senior and Junior) having a vote.

Abrams picked up the argument, cautioning that, 'The country representatives will combine and swamp the efforts of those in the city.' In other words, the Sydney clubs would have practically no say in the running of NSW rugby.

Dr Neil, speaking in favour of the formation of the MRU, said he thought the committee and Abrams had the same end in view, which is to lighten the work of the Union. He added, 'I think Mr Abrams and Mr Speight are fighting a shadow.'

Richard Arnold was surprised the metropolitan clubs did not seize the opportunity. 'The clubs will have an average net revenue between £300 and £400 a year, and they will have it all to themselves,' said Arnold. Also pointed out was that the NSWRU would have to look after the whole of the colony, and now do it without its regular income from club matches.

Given that so many of the city's rugby community favoured suburban football and participated in acts of professionalism, the NSWRU's concerns were understandable. Their dread was so strong that, rather than attempt to strike down professionalism, they preferred to simply reduce Sydney rugby's power. The rest of Sydney football, including the Great Public Schools' competition, would remain with the NSWRU.

Lewis Abrams – a strong supporter of the District Football Scheme and fought hard to improve the benefits for rugby footballers.

The debate continued at length and at times the meeting became heated and rowdy. Abrams finally concluded by saying, 'I appeal to delegates to maintain the old Union intact. For my part, I am not influenced by the question of the £1,500 in the hands of the NSWRU. That is an ulterior matter. But, I have heard no solid argument against my motion during the debate.'

The vote was held, with a resounding majority favouring the proposal to form the MRU. The fight was over. The city's clubs and players fell into line.

Interestingly, similar issues were taking shape in Wales, where many of the club footballers were working class — for a time it appeared they would join the Northern Union. The Welsh Rugby Union soon found a means to work on the edge of the RFU rules and ensure there were few complaints from players.[10]

With club football in Sydney, the NSWRU did not seem to be willing to follow in the lead of the Welsh — something that they may subsequently have come to regret. Perhaps the NSWRU were not prepared to compromise on the proper principles of amateurism and were concerned how they would be viewed by the RFU in England.

THE MAORILANDERS SMACK THE NSW BLUES

The NSWRU's finances were boosted greatly from the tour of the New Zealand team in July of 1897. Three matches against NSW attracted an aggregate attendance of 72,000 paying a total of £3,600. Unlike previous visits from New Zealand, this time the NSWRU kept all the gate-takings. The only money given to the visitors by the NSWRU was to cover their hotel bills and travelling costs.[11]

Captained by Alfred Bayly, the 'Maorilanders' included George Smith, Bill Hardcastle and Thomas Pauling — the latter two forming the front row in a 2–3–2 scrum formation. A win by NSW in the second match levelled the series at 1–1, setting up a decider in the third.

Before the third match, however, the New Zealanders went on a three week tour of NSW country centres and Brisbane. By the time they returned the city was abuzz with excitement. NSW had never beaten New Zealand in a series, nor even in consecutive matches, and anticipation was high that 'the Blues' had finally bridged the gap in the playing standards between the two colonies.

On a fine sunny day, over 27,000 flocked to the SCG to see the inter-colonial clash. *The Referee* correctly wrote that 'no greater public interest has ever clung to any other rugby contest played in the Southern Hemisphere.' At half-time the visitors were ahead by 8–3 in a dogged contest. However for 'three-quarters of the time the Welshmen played up fairly well, but in the last fifteen minutes they were overrun.' The 'superb combination of the New Zealand backs' cut NSW to pieces, scoring six tries in a 26–3 rout.

The Referee was particularly impressed, writing that '...if New Zealand be capable of improving upon it, might we advise them to seek fresh foes on English, Irish and Scotch fields.'[12] Some of the team, though, decided their next challenge was still in Sydney. In what was a not uncommon trend, New Zealand players were convinced during the tour to permanently ply their football skills with Sydney clubs. Pauling, rated 'the best forward in the team,' immediately joined Randwick. The other front rower, Hardcastle, returned to New Zealand with the team but was back in time to join the newly formed Sydney F.C. for the start of the 1898 season.[13]

Sparked by the substantial income taken by the NSWRU from the visit of the New Zealanders, the city's newspapers claimed the poor playing standard of the NSW team was due to the treatment given to the players by the Union. *The Referee* stated that future NSW teams 'must be less unrepresentative of the strength of the colony, and the men must be allowed proper travelling expenses.'[14] No doubt many of the players and supporters agreed.

TREAT YOUR PLAYERS AS GENTLEMEN

With NSW about to travel to Brisbane, to end the 1897 season with two matches against Queensland, *The Referee* again implored the NSWRU to improve the financial conditions of the players so that the best men would make themselves available to tour.

> It is to be greatly hoped that no effort to get the best possible team will be spared. It is time our football authorities recognised the fact that the players should receive proper travelling expenses. It is no use sending men away to act as representatives of the colony if they are expected to be out-of-pocket. The average footballer is not a man of independent means. In going away from home to one of the adjoining capitals to represent his colony he is necessarily put to considerable expenses. If he wishes to move about independently he has to dive into his own pocket and pay for what are legitimate charges as travelling expenses.

> If the Rugby Union can only bring itself to treat representative players with consideration similar to that of business firms it will do a good deal to uplift the standard of teams, besides opening the way for high-class players, who now see neither honour nor pleasure in being one of a touring party a second time. Treat your players as gentlemen, and you will encourage amongst the highest-class, men who play the game who desire to represent the colony away from home. If the Cricket Association of this colony did not treat its players where would the NSW cricket supremacy be? Ask the players themselves. Ask the public.[15]

Barely within days of *The Referee's* public assault on the Union, proposals were put before a managing committee meeting. James Henderson, appointed as manager of the NSW team about to depart for Brisbane, proposed that inter-colonial players be paid travelling expenses at the rate of seven shillings and sixpence (7s/6d) per day instead of the usual three shillings (3s). Henderson was encouraged to withdraw his proposal, as it would amount to professionalism. However, 'another motion, aiming at a similar end' was substituted in its place. The details of the alternative arrangement were not divulged to the press.[16]

Still not certain of what had been achieved, *The Referee* again challenged the NSWRU. In a lengthy article the writer claimed that 'it is nonsense to say that a man who accepts 7s/6d per day for personal expenses is a professional.'

The Referee claimed that the best NSW players preferred not to play instead of being out-of-pocket.

The man who represents his colony at football and thereby sacrifices his prospects of advancement in business or drains his lean purse, is simply and wholly a fool. I've been through the whole of the colonies, and have seen travelling cricket teams treated with more or less liberality — some given nothing at all, others as much as 7s/6d — and I am bound to say that the men who conducted themselves best were those who were most liberally treated.

If you treat players as sportsmen and gentlemen, you encourage the best class of man to achieve the highest success, and you'll find them in return acting as thorough sportsmen and gentlemen. Treat them as inferiors, whilst the manager, a superior sort of person, sips champagne with his cronies, and you'll find them, or most of them, act accordingly. Footballers, like cricketers, are human; to hear some persons talk of them one would think they were horses or cattle.[17]

When the NSW team returned home after defeating the Queenslanders, Henderson revealed what the NSWRU had done to improve the lot of the players — the manager had been given 'a reasonable sum to cover the players individual expenses.' It seemed everyone had a great time.

'In my opinion,' said Henderson, 'a great deal of the success of the tour was undoubtedly due to that fact (the expense account). It placed all the players on an equal footing and left them under no compliment or obligation to anybody. This innovation gives them a feeling of independence, and I feel sure if it is to be established as a custom for inter-colonial matches the football of this colony will be better represented, both as to the ability and the personnel of the team.'

When challenged that the expenses account amounted to professionalism under the rules of the RFU, Henderson stated, 'It is an absurdity to think that it has the slightest taint of professionalism about it — I am now a stronger believer in it than ever.'

NSW FOOTBALLERS PAID MONEY TO PLAY

As the Sydney clubs began their 'pipe-opening' matches of 1898, the NSWRU held their first meeting for the year. Since handing control of Sydney club football to the MRU, the meetings of the NSWRU had become fairly mundane. However, on this occasion any thoughts of any early conclusion to the meeting ended when Speight rose to his feet.

I desire to ask that a council meeting of the NSWRU be called as early as possible to inquire into the truth of certain statements reflecting on the management of the representative teams of last season. I am making no charges against any member of the management or the selection committee, but statements have been made which reflect discredit on the council as a whole, myself included.

It is for this reason that I am anxious that the council shall hold an inquiry, and prove or refute the, to my mind, most damaging statements to the best interests of NSW rugby football. A certain public player has been openly stating that he and others had received money for playing in representative matches. Perhaps this money represented only legitimate expenses, but it should be investigated. I have the names of the players who are alleged to have been paid. One of the players is willing to come forward, and depose [oust] as to the receipt of money.[18]

Though the players' names were kept confidential, the NSWRU minutes record that W. J. 'Billy' Howe, a front row forward for the Wentworth club, was the footballer who had been stating he and other NSW players had been paid.[19]

The Union set down a date two weeks later for a special meeting to inquire into Howe's comments. Langley, one of the NSW team selectors, said, 'I affirm that the selection committee is quite ignorant of any payments having been made, and I am quite anxious for the investigation to be held.'

It was soon revealed that the alleged payments were made to NSW players for the matches against New Zealand. The hurried and secretive implementation of a 'manager's expense account' for the tour to Queensland may indicate that alternatives to 'expenses' practises used for the matches against New Zealand had caused the NSWRU some concern.

When the inquiry meeting was held, with Monty Arnold as chairman, Howe came forward as promised. Speight also had a statement apparently signed by Howe, confirming the details of the payments. None of the other players were called to the meeting.

As soon as he was questioned by Speight at the NSWRU meeting, Howe withdrew all his assertions saying, 'I deny that I have received or demanded money for my services.' The signed statement was then shown to Howe. He denied having signed it.

Speight had also called a witness, George Outram, a NSW player and official from the Randwick club. Outram was a popular footballer, operating a sports store in the Imperial Arcade in the city with NSW cricketer, Syd Gregory.

Outram talked freely about Howe's statements alleging the payment of money. 'He has frequently made statements that particular players have been paid. But then, these claims are common property and I thoroughly believed them when they were made. I believe the player's assertions were made in good faith.'

Outram was then asked, 'Have you personally ever known anyone to receive payment for playing football?' When Outram could only reply with 'No, I know no footballer who has been paid,' the questioning ended. Outram was thanked by the committee for his attendance.

The Union then unanimously resolved that, 'This committee, after inquiry, find that the statements of a player as to himself and others having been paid to represent the colony are on his own admission totally untrue.'

Despite Outram's admission that payments to representative players were common knowledge, none of the other players identified by Howe were ever called to the inquiry or investigated. Nor were the nature of the payments ever examined. As Howe lived in Sydney, his only legitimate claim for expenses would have been the payment of a fare to the ground. Clearly, Howe was bragging about payments far larger than a fare.

Henderson, perhaps indicating his closeness to Howe, immediately proposed the footballer be 'severely censured' as a penalty, and the matter end there. However, Richard Arnold argued that a heavier punishment should apply. 'The player should be cited to appear before the committee,' said Arnold, 'and show cause why he should not be dealt with.' Arnold's suggestion was adopted.[20]

It would seem that players being paid was far less of a concern than a footballer publicly stating that NSW players received money. At the next NSWRU meeting, Howe again appeared and offered an apology to the Union and the selection committee. It was decided that 'a censure be recorded against the player for improper conduct in casting aspersions on the management of the Union.' A proposal 'that the player be suspended during the pleasure of the committee' was then put forward by one member. However, no one else on the committee could be convinced to go that far with the punishment.

Richard Arnold – a Rugby School 'old-boy' who became a prominent member of the NSWRU.

Richard Arnold though, speaking at the end of the meeting, said plainly, 'The record of disqualifications and censures should be taken into consideration in selecting any player to represent the colony and due weight be given to matters recorded against them.'[21]

Anyone speaking openly about the payment of money to players now knew what would befall them — the loss of any opportunity to represent the colony.

REPLACE SOCIAL-BASED CLUBS WITH DISTRICTS?

The Sydney competition of 1898 began with high hopes, as *The Daily Telegraph* put it, 'The coming season promises to be a keen one — not only keener than last, which would be saying little, but keener than for several years past.'[22] The writer was an optimist. The apparently strong Wentworth club suddenly collapsed before the season had even begun, and before long two other clubs suffered the same fate.

The season commenced with two new clubs, Sydney and Burwood, joining the Senior competition. This made the numbers a modest seven (the others were University, Wallaroo, Pirates, Randwick and Paddington). While the Sydney F.C. had been formed specifically to enter the Seniors, the Burwood club and its playing contingent had risen from the Juniors. Unfortunately, after having a bye in the first round, Burwood found it had insufficient players willing to take the field and was forced to withdraw from the competition. The MRU was then compelled into a hasty redraw of the season for the remaining six teams.

Meanwhile the Paddington club had been enduring an annual battle each season to get enough players. 'With true sportsmanlike spirit they come up as brightly as ever, looking forward each year to a better season, and can be seen indulging in hard training operations on Hampden Oval.'[23] Half way through the 1898 season they collapsed as well, forfeiting their remaining matches.

Fearing the growing number of suburban Junior clubs would soon vote to change the structure of Sydney rugby, the established Senior clubs endeavoured to get in first.

Following 'some agitation amongst the Senior clubs' the MRU formed a committee to examine the issue. The committee comprised one representative from each of the Senior clubs 'to draft alterations in the constitution to embody the clubs' views concerning the government of Senior football.' The result was the MRU changed its rules so that voting rights were split 50/50 between the Seniors and the Juniors — irrespective of how many Junior clubs there were.[24]

The MRU also became far more amenable to meeting the financial needs of the Senior clubs, granting them 7s/6d each to pay for the hiring of training quarters. Training was generally held indoors on a Wednesday evening at facilities such as Sydney Gymnasium under the supervision of a professional trainer. The MRU was cautioned by many observers that 'this is a matter in which the Union should be very careful,' as paying clubs for training was tantamount to professionalism. The clubs even obtained a 'Clubs Benefit Day' from the MRU during the season, with a series of matches held on the SCG — the entire proceeds from the gate-takings of the afternoon were devoted to the clubs' finances.[25]

None of these changes were sufficient to help the position of the struggling suburban clubs in the Seniors. The loss of Wentworth, Burwood and Paddington during 1898 again focussed attention on the financing and structure of club football in Sydney.

Darby Ryan, a member of the New Zealand team that came to NSW in 1884, was in Sydney during 1898 and suggested a solution. 'Since 1891,' said Ryan, 'a district scheme has been in vogue in Auckland, something like Electorate cricket in Sydney. It has been a wonderful success, as the public interest in the contests between the various clubs is very keen. A residential qualification is necessary for membership of a club.'[26]

The proliferation of suburban clubs in the Juniors was evidence enough of the growing preference for district football in Sydney. What it lacked was proper organisation and the ability to compete fairly against strong social clubs.

If a 'district scheme' were introduced it would require all the old clubs to be disbanded, whether suburban or social. The new district clubs would make playing in the Seniors far more appealing to younger footballers and provide more opportunities as it would remove the monopoly of the social clubs. A residential qualification would also take away any need for clubs to tout for players, and provide for a more even competition. Gate-takings would be held by the MRU for later division amongst the clubs on an equitable basis.

The idea gained favour with those who had expended all their energy and finances endeavouring to get district-based clubs into the Seniors over recent seasons. No doubt it also appealed to many who wanted to see an end to the reign of the 'cliquesters' at the established clubs.[27]

The MRU though, influenced by the leaders of social clubs, gave the proposal little consideration. They cited that as 1899 would hopefully see the visit of a team from Great Britain, it would do no good to ruin the combination skills of the best players by reorganising club teams.[28]

While 'team combination' was a strong principle of colonial rugby thinking, self-preservation of the established clubs was also undoubtedly a determining factor in their decision.

The 1890s, though, had seen the growth of workplace unions, strikes and the emergence of the Labor party on Australia's political landscape. The working class was now far more prepared to express its collective voice and seek to be involved and fairly represented in decision making. With rugby in Sydney so popular with the working classes, their demands for change would not go away.

SYDNEY WORKERS V WALLAROO GENTLEMEN

Some of the best footballers from the Juniors decided to take on the established clubs at their own game by forming the Sydney F.C. with a 'team that consists mostly of labouring men.' The playing strength of Sydney F.C. was enough to immediately challenge the social clubs for on-field supremacy.[29]

When Sydney met Wallaroo at the Agricultural Ground during the 1898 season, the match pitted the workers against the members of the city's most prestigious gentlemen's rugby club. The contest became a 'rough-and-tumble' affair. According to *The Bulletin*, it 'degenerated into little better than a slanging match, with Sydney declared the winner 15 points to 5.'

The most revealing aspect of the game was the different behaviour displayed by the teams — on the rugby field it was not necessarily the upper-class men who exhibited the most restraint. 'There were several fights, the most noticeable being when a Wallaroo man grabbed an opponent by his ears and rubbed his nose in the dirt. Both sides went in for kicking in the scrums. Sydney are probably the best disciplined crowd in the competition. They all look upon Hardcastle, their captain, as a champion of champions. His word is law both on and off the field. The Sydneys are a greatly improved team and will take a lot of beating.'[30]

TWELVE NSW PLAYERS DROPPED

The representative matches of 1898 began with 'Country Week' towards the end of the season. Teams representing the various country branches came to Sydney and played each other through the week. At its conclusion a Country team was selected for a match against Metropolis [City] at the SCG. The Country team included six players from the 'Central Western' branch Union which covered the area west of Burwood, including Parramatta, all the way to the Blue Mountains. After the match the NSW team to play Queensland was chosen.

The early game that day featured a 'Second Metropolitan XV' against 'Combined Juniors' team selected from the clubs in the Juniors. 'Combined Juniors' were beaten 18–13 despite the best efforts of promising cricketer Victor Trumper (from Newtown) who played fullback, two tries to wing-forward Dinny Lutge (Marrickville) and some fine work from Harry 'Jersey' Flegg (Adelphi) in the forwards.[31]

When the NSWRU selectors chose their first NSW team for 1898, they produced a few surprises. The first was the inclusion of New Zealand's Hardcastle and Pauling.

The more startling occurrence came from a comparison between the NSW team that played New Zealand in 1897 and the selected team — only three Blues players survived. They were the highly regarded Paddy Lane (captain of Wallaroo) and Stanley Wickham (captain of Country), along with front-row forward Norm Street (from Bathurst). None of the other Blues players appeared in any of the four inter-colonial matches played, and the Queenslanders won the series.[32]

The words of Richard Arnold from earlier in the season had obviously been adhered to. The record of censures was taken into consideration in selecting 'any player' to represent the colony. The NSWRU had effectively ensured that players would now even be reluctant to discuss with each other any payment they received, let alone talk publicly.

CHAPTER THREE

THE RUGBY REVEREND'S SERMON

REVEREND MULLINEUX'S TEAM OF GENTLEMEN

Confirmation that the 'rugby playing gentleman,' Reverend Matthew Mullineux, was bringing a British representative team out to the colonies put most rugby officials in a state of unbounded excitement. 'When I took up the honorary treasurership of the Union,' said Richard Arnold at the first NSWRU meeting of 1899, 'I had two dreams before me. The first one has been realised, for we now derive from our investments sufficient to pay administrative expenses. The second dream is about to be realised in the visit of the English team.'[1]

Mullineux initiated the idea for a tour in mid-1897. Having participated in a successful British tour of South Africa, the Cambridge University player wrote to the NSWRU seeking an invitation and terms. While Richard Arnold dreamed of bringing forth a team from 'Home,' Mullineux's letter demonstrated how ignorant Britons were of rugby in the colonies, writing 'I am sending a similar letter to Melbourne, in case Sydney is not one of the centres of rugby union.'[2]

The NSWRU duly issued the invitation, sending it to RFU's secretary Rowland Hill. A 21-man tour party of players from all four Home nations — England, Scotland, Ireland and Wales — was assembled. Officially recognised as a British representative team (but referred to by all as English), the players wore red, white and blue striped jerseys, and their off-field tour hats featured a kangaroo emblem. Since the 1870s the kangaroo had come to signify the Australian colonies (in sport and trade) and was part of an unofficial 'coat of arms.'[3]

From Mullineux's viewpoint the tour would be about popularising the game of rugby, including its finer points of good sportsmanship and sharing the amateur ideals. Mullineux issued invitations to fellow players from Cambridge and Oxford Universities and other gentlemen who met the required standards, on and off the field, and who could afford the time away from home. To encourage participation, the RFU authorised the payment of a daily cash allowance (except while on the sea) for incidental expenses.

They were not the best players from British rugby. Eleven of the fifteen Englishmen had not been selected for the England side that had recently finished 'at the bottom of the list in the internationals for the first time in many years.'[4] However, the colonial Unions pronounced themselves satisfied 'that the combination ought to be a fairly representative one of the strength of rugby at Home.'[5] They saw the tour as an opportunity to defeat the visitors and prove that rugby in Australasia was to be taken seriously. The NSWRU officials were also keen to personally impress Mullineux and his men, as representatives of the RFU and the Universities, that they were all fine British gentlemen.

The visitors would be entertained officially by the NSWRU, and also at many other dinners and functions. John Calvert, NSWRU president, encouraged his fellow committee members to contribute to a private entertainment fund in preparation for the visit.

In contrast, Monty Arnold objected to the funds that had been spent on entertaining the four regional teams that visited Sydney for Country Week in 1898: 'I find that 626 drinks were paid for by the Union — this shows that the entertaining of country teams has been vastly overdone.'

Meanwhile, the auditors closely examined the Union's own entertainment accounts for the 1898 season: 'We must reflect upon the absence of necessary vouchers and receipts, and criticise the extravagance of the Union, chiefly in regard to matters of entertainment.'[6]

The Reverend Matthew Mullineux – brought a British team to Australia in 1899.

NSWRU AND NZRU SQUABBLE OVER THE BRITISH

As the hosts of the British team, the NSWRU controlled all match and tour arrangements and were responsible for all expenses. The QRU and NZRU had to negotiate financial terms with the NSWRU to secure matches.

The NSWRU recognised that the longer the visitors were away from Sydney, the less the Union's overall income would be. The terms it sought with the other colonial Unions required that it be compensated for the lost income. A short visit to Brisbane was readily agreed to with the QRU, however the more remote New Zealanders (five-days sailing from Sydney) found negotiations with the NSWRU far more demanding.

The NZRU sought to host a two-match visit. The NSWRU reasoned that by giving up two (at least) Sydney matches to allow Mullineux's team to visit New Zealand, it would miss out on a further £1,200. Reducing the Sydney matches also meant that if any 'gates' were ruined by poor weather, the NSWRU had less opportunity to recover the lost income.

The NSWRU advised the NZRU they would consent to the visit if they guaranteed £400, covered all accommodation costs and paid for the team's return trip to and from Sydney. They also proposed that a series of Test matches between 'Australasia and England' be played in Sydney and stipulated to the New Zealanders 'that her best players should come over here at the expense of the NSWRU to take part.'[7]

The NZRU, who had nothing like the financial resources of the NSWRU, could only offer a share from the matches in New Zealand. No agreement was reached, and the British visit to New Zealand was abandoned. The New Zealanders wondered what the point of affiliation with the Unions under the RFU was if decisions were to be made solely on financial grounds.[8] Seemingly oblivious to the offence it was causing across the Tasman, the NSWRU even proposed to host a New Zealand v Britain match in Sydney and split the gate with the NZRU.[9]

Incensed at their treatment, the New Zealanders decided not to send any players to Sydney for the Australasia team. This had the immediate 'peculiar effect of causing several New Zealanders to come across on their own accord and play in the Senior competition, where no doubt some of them will show sufficient form to warrant their selection against England.'

The newspapers expressed disappointment at the NZRU's decision not to send players to Sydney, stating that an international match between the combined colonies and England 'with New Zealand unrepresented is absurd from a purely football point of view.' *The Herald* added that 'this means the matches will be "Australia" instead of "Australasia" and that the team will only consist of NSW and Queensland players.'[10] The fall-out from the NSWRU's treatment of the NZRU was the collapse of significant work and efforts that were in train to form an 'Australasian Rugby Football Union.'

In New Zealand concern was growing over the playing rules of rugby. Many thought the game ought to be made more safe to play and attractive to watch. Others urged for the formation of a combined Australasian Union representing all the colonies, suggesting it would have a far greater voice with the RFU and the International Rugby Board (IRB). An Australasian Union could standardise playing rules across the colonies, organise a programme of regular inter-colonial matches, and represent all the Unions in visits of British teams.[11] It would also have dwarfed the comparative Victorian rules body, perhaps hindering the growth of that football code.

However, as with the political movement to form a national federation of all the colonies, the New Zealanders went their own way. For Australasian rugby it meant missing the opportunity to form a strong body that could confront common issues.

AUSTRALIA PLAYS ITS FIRST TEST MATCH

Less than a month before the first Test, the QRU wrote to the NSWRU asking what colour jersey the 'Australian' team would be wearing — the Queenslanders suggested that the home Union's colours be used. The NSWRU considered the matter and resolved: 'It was agreed that the colours of the colony in which the match is to be played be adopted with the substitution of the (Coat of) Arms of Australia as a distinctive badge instead of the colony.'

Australia's First Test Team 1899 (Sydney)

Back Row: James McManamey, James Carson (Pirates), Walter Davis (Marrickville), Alexander J Kelly (Paddington), W G Garrard (referee), William Tanner (Brisbane), William Evans (Brisbane), John Calvert (NSWRU President), H A Langley.
Middle Row: Charles Ellis (Pirates), Alfred Colton (Brisbane), Charles White (Wallaroos), Frank Row (c) (Wallaroos), Hyram Marks (University of Sydney), Robert McCowan (Brisbane), Patrick Carew (Brisbane).
Front Row: Peter Ward (Marrickville), Austin Gralton (Brisbane), Stephen 'Lonnie' Spragg (Wallaroos).

The reality was that each Union would put its own representative side into the field against the British and style its name as 'Australia.' While both formed a combined selection committee for each Test, the home Union had the balance of power. Players from the other colony were 'invited' to join in, but the 'guests' never outnumbered the hosts. This extended to the captaincy of the Australian team too, where 'Messrs Row (NSW) and McCowan (Qld) captained the teams in their respective colonies.'[12]

The first Test was the biggest match of the tour. 'It was a great day, the weather being beautiful,' reported *The Referee.* 'The attendance was 28,000, and the proceeds of the match about £1,200, both records for rugby football in Australia. The aspect of the ground (the SCG) was extremely pretty, the stands being one vast array of varied colouring.'[13]

Australia won the match 13–3, with two late tries sealing victory. The British forwards seemed to fade in the final stages as the Australians enjoyed much more possession. The local players (under a New

Australia's Second Test Team 1899 (Brisbane)

Back Row: Patrick Carew (Q), Arthur Corfe (Q), Hyram Marks, Charles Ellis.
Middle Row: C Hill, Charles Graham (Q), Albert Henry (Q), Norman Street, Robert
Challoner, Stephen 'Lonnie' Spragg, Rush Nelson.
Front Row: Peter Ward, Thomas Ward (Q), William Tanner (Q), Robert McCowan (c)(Q),
Ernest Currie (Q), William Evans (Q).

Zealand referee) 'cleverly' ensured that when tackled to the ground they kept possession by quickly putting the ball down behind themselves, (instead of in front as required by the rules), and pushing it back to a team mate. This avoided scrummaging and increased the pace of the game. Even when a scrum was called, the Australian forwards gained further advantage by packing in specialised positions. This led to them winning far more ball than the British forwards who were all 'generalists' (packing according to the order in which arrived at the scrum).

The British easily defeated the Queensland-dominated Australian team in the second Test 11–0, before returning to Sydney for the remaining two Tests. The third Test proved to be a real tussle as the British forwards stood up to the local men, eventually beating Australia 11–10. The fourth Test was played in very heavy conditions which the British team found far more favourable, and they won easily 13–0. The NSWRU hadn't quite given up hopes of having an 'Australasian' side — the Australian team for the fourth Test included New Zealanders Peter Ward, Walter Davis, Jum Sampson, and Bill Hardcastle.

A COLONIAL TEAM MIGHT TOUR BRITAIN

After Australia won the first Test, great speculation arouse on both sides of the Tasman Sea that a colonial team might tour Great Britain. The NSWRU began to investigate the idea, but in New Zealand firm proposals began to take shape. Denied the chance to prove themselves against Mullineux's team, the New Zealanders were determined to proceed with a tour on their own.

In cricket, the bi-annual interchange of tours between England and Australia had become well entrenched by the time of the initial rugby Test. So it was not surprising that rugby writers and supporters predicted a similar future for football.

The Referee pondered the future of Australian rugby.

Will the history of international football resemble that of international cricket? Will it attain the same significance, the same popularity? One naturally enough frames these questions, and answers in the same breath — let's hope so! But cricket and rugby football differ in one great point, and that difference will, I feel sure, in a large degree, tend to make the meetings of Australia and England at football far fewer than has been the case at cricket. The rules of the Rugby Football Union absolutely debar professionalism in any form, and although at cricket in Australia amateurs are allowed loss of salary and other incidental expenses, such is not permitted in football.

Whether so rigid a law of this character is a beneficial one for Australian football or otherwise is scarcely worth discussing at the moment, but it is the law here, in England, and in New Zealand, and in every Union that is affiliated to the English Rugby Union. Therefore, should the success of Australia in last Saturday's match prove, as was the case in cricket, the forerunner of a visit by an Australian team to England, the Australian players must, under present law, go purely as amateurs — to receive merely travelling expenses.

Under such circumstances I feel tolerably sure that anything approaching the full strength of Australian football could not be banded together for such a trip, entailing an absence of at least eight or nine months. But this makes a problem to be tackled by football legislators of the future, so let it pass on to them.[14]

Meanwhile in Wellington, New Zealand, William 'Mac' McKenzie, a member of the NZRU teams that toured NSW and Queensland in 1893 and 1897, put forward a proposal to his colony's Union on 'behalf of a friend who is anxious to know the conditions upon which a team could tour Great Britain under the auspices of the NZRU.' McKenzie's proposed terms were circulated amongst the local Unions and each was asked to express its opinion.[15]

Thomas Eyton, promoter of the 1888 New Zealand Natives team, remarked in detail in *The Auckland Sporting Review* about the difficulties such a tour would face. Eyton obviously spoke from his experiences of the 1888 tour and his particular knowledge of the clubs in the Northern English counties. He laid out an itinerary that could be adopted by any willing promoter. 'The tour should, I think,' said Eyton, 'commence at Sydney, where the team would gain form and combination, tour Britain and should end at Sydney, Queensland and New Zealand.'

Eyton cautioned, though, that matches in the North of England had to be carefully selected as many of the areas were poor and only small admission charges could be set. He also identified that the largest problem was to how to ensure that such a tour would be viable for the working-class players. 'It seems a pity,' said Eyton, 'if the Unions cannot relax the rules in favour of teams going on an extended tour of eight months. Bare expenses would, of course, be paid, but there are numerous petty wants of a man, especially when travelling, and he would like to use spare time for some site-seeing on his own account. I doubt if there is one of the front rank players in New Zealand — if chosen to go on a tour — able to provide himself with pocket money, without which it would be found that the team would naturally be very discontented.'[16]

Most agreed that if a colonial team (combined or separate) were ever to visit Great Britain, it would have to follow the arrangements of the touring Australian cricket teams where the players shared the profits. Professionalism, in some form, would have to be allowed if rugby tours were to become a reality. Of course, that was all on the presumption that such a tour could produce sufficient income to, at the very least, cover costs.

Unable to find a ready solution that fell with the rules of the RFU, the idea of colonial teams touring Great Britain was shelved.

SOME MANLY ADVICE FROM THE REVEREND

Towards the end of their tour the British footballers were entertained at a banquet dinner conducted by the MRU in Sydney. Asked to speak at the official function, Mullineux decided it was time he offered 'a few words of manly, straightforward advice to the audience and to footballers generally.'

As the 'reverend gentleman' came out to the colonies under the auspices of the English RFU, he believed it was his obligation to see that the rules of that body were being strictly observed in every respect by the colonies' Unions. Throughout the tour he had for the most part preferred to remain silent about his views. The banquet gave him an opportunity to get his message across to city's rugby community.

'From the manner in which we have found rugby played in Sydney,' said Mullineux, 'it is very evident that there is good reason for our

Members of the Great Britain team during their 1899 tour to Australia
(Matthew Mullineux holding the ball).

dissatisfaction as English representatives.' The 'feeling' at the banquet became 'quite warm' when Mullineux spoke out about 'pointing' and 'tricks' in use in Sydney rugby and a number of contrary views were expressed. 'Pointing' was a word given to describe practices outside the rules (or even their spirit or intent) and employed to gain a winning edge over an opponent.[17]

Mullineux restated his views in an interview with a reporter from *The Australian Field*. 'I am most anxious that it be made very clear and be fully understood that in speaking out I have but one object to serve — the promotion of a better spirit in the ranks of the representative footballers of this colony' said Mullineux. He gave examples of what he, as 'the RFU's representative,' saw as not 'good sport.' This included 'pushing a man at the line-out instead of going fairly for the ball,' tackled players pushing the ball behind themselves, 'in the scrum they put their elbows or their hands in an opponent's face,' holding opponents without the ball, and calling after opponent's by name so that they would pass them the ball.

Mullineux saw these 'very reprehensible practices' as against the principles of the sport of rugby.

> Football is a game in which you put so much upon your honour. Only by a recollection of how a man played the game with honour, and by insisting upon such a recollection, can resort to dishonest practices be prevented.

> In football there is much that takes place that a referee cannot see clearly. So many aspects may be worked unfairly if a player is not going to act honourably. It would be far better to exclude that man from the game altogether. In cricket it is a very different thing. That game is so very open that not only the umpires, but every player and every onlooker, practically can see all that goes on, and there is not the same temptation to an unscrupulous man. If football is not played fairly and honourably it is not worth playing.

> In the country matches, and in those against the Schools, there was an absence of trickery, and a good spirit of true sport about the game as played by the opponents. Although there may be some differences as to the interpretation of rules, we are clearly of the opinion that the tone of footballers who were picked to play against us in the provinces was of a much higher order that that found in the metropolis.'[18]

Mullineux also argued against the prevalence in the colonies of rewards and competitions. 'The rugby game according to the English Union,' said Mullineux, 'is only able to maintain its high class as an amateur sport by the total prohibition of anything approaching payment or reward for services rendered.'

> Matches for prize badges, cups, etc., are not allowed under our regulations, and it has been necessary on some occasions, when a patron of the game has wished to signalise a great victory by presenting medals, to obtain the permission of the Union before they could be accepted. Wherever cups have been brought forward in England, it has had a tendency to spoil the game. But, as opinion was divided between the South and the North, Yorkshire has started the Northern Rugby Union, where they are allowed to pay players for the loss of time. Under the rules of our Union, no player is allowed a farthing over the actual railway or other travelling expenses and the bare cost of his hotel while away from home for the purpose of playing. There can be no allowance for even incidental expenses.[19]

The Australian Field reporter wrote, 'Upon this point Mr Mullineux expressed indignant surprise and much incredulity when told that our clubs in Sydney — many of them — were in the habit of paying men, not only for loss of time, but for their allegiance throughout a season. He could not think that such a thing was done with the knowledge of the Union, or that his team had been asked to play against paid members of the clubs affiliated to the Union.'

'Our Union in England,' said Mullineux, 'would certainly be very much annoyed at anything of that sort, and would not permit us to countenance it.' The reporter then continued, 'Mr Mullineux has evidently not known all that has gone on in the contest against the team he brought out, and possibly the bare and positive assertion now made, that men are paid in the rugby clubs in and around Sydney, will lead him to make an investigation. He will not have very far to go for proof.'[20]

COLONIAL RUGBY DISMISSES MULLINEUX'S VIEWS

The publication of *The Australian Field's* assertions about payments, and Mullineux's criticisms, caused much comment in the city's sporting circles. At the next MRU meeting many of the committee members voiced their disgust that such accusations could be brought forward at all. They called for the MRU to issue a denial of the charges.

Monty Arnold tried to quell the unrest by saying, 'Surely you don't want to notice all the silly things Mr Mullineux has said. Why, (referring to *The Australian Field*) as to the matter of paying players, we all know that Yorkshire and Lancashire players are paid.'

'But they don't belong to the Rugby Union,' replied E. Howe [not 'Billy' Howe].

The First Test between Australia and Great Britain, SCG, 1899.

Unable to reach any agreement, it was decided by the MRU committee to again discuss the allegations at their next meeting. However, the debate continued amongst the members on the stairs and footpaths outside. One delegate remarked that *The Australian Field's* statements might create an erroneous impression among country Unions and players. 'If,' he continued, 'we do not deny the charges, those country players naturally will conclude that the metropolitan players have got on a very good lurk.'[21]

At the opening of the following MRU meeting, Monty Arnold (as chairman) again tried to ensure the allegations quietly went away by having them referred to the NSWRU. Unable to gain enough support, he then simply said, 'Very well, then let us proceed. What is to be done?' For the next few hours the committee members voiced their disagreement over the issues.

The committee eventually resolved, 'That the Metropolitan Branch of the NSWRU has carefully considered the articles appearing in the *Field* of August 26, 1899, and point out that every safeguard has been adopted by the branch to prevent professionalism among the players. Any allegation having been proved, on investigation, to be baseless. If *The Australian Field* is in possession of information that would lead to prove professionalism, the committee would most cordially investigate such charges. The branch Union wish to draw attention to the disingenuous paragraph in the leading article, in which they put into the mouth of the Reverend Mullineux the words which must have been, in their opinion, clearly supplied by the interviewer.'[22]

Mullineux tried again to make his views clear before he left Australia, writing an open letter to the rugby community via *The Referee*:

I am sorry your committee did not ask me to meet them to discuss the charges. It would have been much easier for me to have kept silent here, and then abused the Australian style of play on my return to England, but such a course would have been very mean, and, to say the least of it, very unfair to you. I, therefore, spoke openly and plainly. I have been grossly misunderstood, and I shall be sorry to leave Australia with such a misunderstanding between myself and the Unions here.

As I came out at the invitation of the New South Wales Union, I presumed they desired me to point out any differences in the style of play here and in England, and I may add that in pointing out those differences, I spoke on behalf of the English team. We were all astonished at the system of 'pointing' in vogue here. Anybody practising such 'tricks' as we experienced would be tabooed by the best English clubs, and no matter how good a player might be he would never have the least chance of getting a place in a representative team. In condemning these 'tricks,' I spoke solely in the interests of football. That my words should cause some soreness was only to be expected, but I am quite sure that when the soreness has worn off, and my remarks are read in the same spirit in which I made them, there need be no cause for further misunderstanding.[23]

Meanwhile *The Australian Field* criticised the MRU committee for failing to act on its assertions that professionalism was rife in Sydney:

While declining most absolutely to enter into any controversy with the committee of the Metropolitan Branch upon this subject, we are certainly surprised that such direct assertions as were made in our leading columns should have been disposed of in so peremptory a manner. It is no part of our business to conduct investigations for the Union, and, as far as we are concerned, the matter will be allowed to drop for the present with the repeated assertion that the payment of players and the encouragement of a spirit of professionalism, such as is discountenanced by the English Rugby Union, is most certainly rife in clubs round Sydney.

If the committee of the Metropolitan Branch do not know that it is so in fact, then it is to be regretted that they are so very little in touch with the players over whom they are supposed to exercise some sort of control. Their guarded denial of our assertions does not disprove them. Members of the committee and other prominent rugby players have told more than one representative of this paper that they know these abuses exist — they have quoted cases — but they always find difficulty in obtaining the direct evidence. While we decline, at this stage, to go further into the matter of the payments made, we shall probably take another course before the next football season commences.[24]

The Australian Field did not take 'another course' and made no further accusations, while the MRU maintained nothing untoward was happening within the clubs it presided over.

PLAY TO THE WHISTLE

Mullineux had shown the rugby community where it was straying from the RFU's principles. The fact the officials of the MRU defended the way rugby was played in Sydney, even though it was clearly dominated by a competitive 'play to the whistle' spirit, illustrates that it was at odds with the amateur ideals of the RFU. Such play is a direct outcome of the need to win. While the professionalism accusations of *The Australian Field* were never expanded upon, proved or investigated — the symptoms of professionalism on the field existed, and they were what Mullineux was speaking out against.

When Monty Arnold, the patriarch of Australian rugby, cited payment of rugby players in Yorkshire and Lancashire, he added no comment at all about it being illegal or 'degrading.' Similarly, *The Arrow*, said Mullineux should 'open up the crusade in Yorkshire' rather than concerning himself with Australian rugby.[25]

These comments, along with the awareness of the difficulties of ever forming a strong team for a tour of England, the call to restructure Sydney club football, the creation of the MRU and the concessions made to accommodate working-class players, showed that the colony's rugby community recognised their off-field challenges.

They were also well aware of the conditions operating under the Northern Union. They could see that a rigid application of the amateur laws and principles could not work in Australian football and meet the needs of the working-class players. At some time in the future, their loyalty to the RFU would have to be examined.

They had hoped to form a stronger voice under an 'Australasian Rugby Union' to push for reforms with the RFU and IRB, but they had been undermined by the fall-out between the NSWRU and the NZRU.

Over the following months the members of the MRU committee wrangled with the call for reform of the club competition — to 'raise the tone of club football' by introducing a system of local football clubs and a rigid residential qualification for players. The problem was, though, no matter what changes the MRU introduced to control the growth of professionalism, as one English rugby writer put it, 'Wherever rugby football is the popular game of the artisan, the professional element is strong.'[26]

CHAPTER FOUR

THE BIRTH OF THE DISTRICT CLUBS

WALLAROO ARE THE PREMIERS

Wallaroo, in its thirtieth season, were declared 1899 premiership winners. The competition was called off early due to their unassailable lead at the head of the table. Suspended for long periods because of the visit of Mullineux's team and wet weather, the club competition maintained little interest. Near the end of the season *The Herald* noted that the 'matches for the Senior premiership continue to drag their weary length along.'[1]

The Referee praised the winners: 'New clubs have risen and shone temporarily only to fall back into oblivion after a few reverses, but the Wallaroos have withstood the shock of reverses, and throughout their career have proved a very difficult side to beat.'[2]

The 1899 season had seen three new clubs: Buccaneer, Marrickville and the Parramatta 'Reds.' The latter two were district clubs attempting yet again to take on the social-based clubs. Another district-based team, South Sydney, refused to step up to the Seniors, even though, as runners-up in the 1898 First Juniors, they were required to. The MRU declared South Sydney ineligible to remain in First Juniors but relented on appeal.

As had happened in previous seasons, the district clubs began to forfeit games (this time it was Parramatta) as players and their supporters became disinterested. Matches often went ahead only at the last moment when enough 'pick-up' players could be found to form a team.

The win of Wallaroo reinforced the domination that the gentlemen's membership clubs had on the Sydney competition. The drive to move to a district-club scheme across the whole competition faced the equally difficult off-field task of convincing these powerful clubs to disband. And how would the University of Sydney club fit under this scheme? The formation of clubs such as Parramatta and Marrickville, along with the popularity of suburban clubs in the Juniors, showed that despite the obvious difficulties, support for community clubs rather than a faction or 'clubbism' (as it was called), was growing. An increasing number of MRU delegates pushed for the new scheme, headed by Lewis Abrams from the Glebe club.

Wallaroo Rugby Football Club - Premiers, 1899

Back Row: not recorded.
Middle Row: G Wheeler, Charles White, 'Paddy' Lane (c), William Webb,
Stephen 'Lonnie' Spragg, A Chisholm.
Front Row: J McCormack, J Fuller, Frank Row, A G H Gardner.

Abrams was described in the press as the 'quick-stepping little figure who is as well-known in Sydney as almost any of the old city identities. In cricket he bobs up perennially, having been secretary to clubs or associations for about twenty years or more. He has worked very hard for many years in connection with cricket, and of late has buzzed about with untiring zeal in connection with the district football movement. He is not at all a popular man amongst legislators of the game — he says things that jar.'[4]

The front page of *The Referee* took up the issue late in the 1899 season stating: 'Wallaroo has done great work for rugby football in this colony. But there is still greater work ahead; if the club be unselfish. That work is the establishment of local football.'[5]

The complaint was clear. Many players and clubs alike were refusing to take part in the Seniors. Each season produced the same questions about who would be forming clubs and which players would be taking part. Coaxing players to move between clubs was uncontrolled. The 'tone' and the spirit of the premiership produced a desire to win at all costs, with consequent rough play. As Mullineux had illustrated, truly amateur sportsmen found this environment difficult.

Most working-class players disliked their lack of opportunity to participate on an equal standing. This intensified when some of their own were rewarded to play with the stronger clubs. Increasing numbers, from all classes, turned away from the Seniors or rugby altogether. The answer seemed to lie in a residentially-qualified, locally-supported club competition, where players could not be tempted to change clubs. It would open opportunities to play in the Seniors, particularly for working-class men, but they would be managed by local gentlemen and civic leaders.

THE DISTRICT SCHEME

A district scheme would be a compromise. It would answer the cry for equity between the clubs and give working-class players a say and involvement, yet it would put them in a structure where they would be unable to dominate the management committee of a club or the game. *The Referee's* rugby columnist wrote:

> I know of nothing better than the system in vogue in our cricket. Every member of a club connected with the NSW Cricket Association must pay his subscription of one guinea — he is a sportsman, loves his game, and is an ornament to it. It is the duty of the Rugby Union to insist, as the Cricket Association insists, on every member conforming to an unbending law of this character.
>
> We were told calmly a few years ago that local cricket clubs would never be able to enforce the subscription rule. But those who argued this now know better. Genuine cricketers, and I would strongly accentuate the adjective, have come forward in their hundreds, only too glad to pay such a subscription and other expenses in order to get decent cricket. And you will find too, if local football be introduced and soundly managed, that numbers of genuine footballers, who now play no more after leaving school, will continue playing.
>
> In a chat on Monday with Paddy Lane, the captain of Wallaroo, I ventured to suggest that he might do football great good by helping to introduce the new local club system for next season. He seemed impressed, felt that there is great room for improvement, but it was natural that with such feelings as he has for Wallaroo, and such genial associations, he should also say: 'I don't care to say much at present on the subject.' The future of the game of football is far dearer to us all then the fate of one or two clubs, even though, as was the case in cricket, they were once the pioneers, the fighters in the early days when the sport was in its childhood. *The Referee* feels that the time

for local football has come — it will fight for it as some years ago it fought for local cricket if a fight be necessary.[6]

The Sunday Times enthused about the prospects for the new season if the district scheme was adopted: 'The outlook for the success of the new clubs is more promising than it was at the inception of the movement in cricket. There are numerous splendid local grounds, well appointed, and the local boundaries are already defined.'[7] Adopting the cricket boundaries would allow for undivided local support between the summer and winter sports, enhancing rivalry between districts.

Most of the press called for a strong residential rule to apply to players, including *The Referee*:

Wallaroo F.C. captain 'Paddy' Lane – joined the North Sydney club under the district scheme in 1900.

Where you have local grounds, to preserve the local enthusiasm, the man who plays the game should be thoroughly a resident of the locality. The residential qualification in cricket is six months, it was originally three months. Knowing the nomadic character of a certain class of sportsmen, I favour a still longer period of residence, and, indeed, after the first season would go as far as to make it twelve months.

There is an absolute necessity of insisting upon the members of every club paying a subscription. Without the embodiment of this principle in the rules, local football may flourish temporarily, only to wither away ultimately. The permanent success of local football will to a large degree be determined by the attitude of the Union with regard to club management. Up to a certain point the Union should in future keep a strict and impartial supervision over every club, and by this means see that every member pays the recognised subscription to his club.

If the old method of allowing clubs to work on a no-subscription basis be perpetuated, football will become a semi-degraded sport. Like footballers, cricketers were once lackadaisical in regard to their subscriptions. But when local cricket came, in the cunning ones who wanted to continue playing without paying subscriptions were ousted, because there were numbers to take their places who gladly paid for the privilege of being allowed to be a representative of their locality.

There are, I have no doubt, a few cricketers of the present day whose subscriptions are paid by more affluent supporters of the club, but the cases are so few and exceptional that it is, perhaps, not to be regarded as an evil. By having the clubs managed decently, the Union will attract numbers of lusty young fellows, who, within the last two or three years, have drifted away from football, chiefly because they were not enamoured with the surroundings.

The local clubs themselves should be made self-supporting, that is the players should either train themselves, or if they must have a professional trainer, pay him out of the club funds. If the Union subsidises clubs in the future, the money should be spent solely, as in cricket, on the grounds on either their facilities or helping to maintain them. Not a penny of it ought to be expended otherwise. Football must be preserved as a pure sport, and to do so you must keep it attractive to the best class of men.[8]

One fundamental element of a district scheme that must have concerned the MRU, was the requirement to play matches on local grounds. The MRU enjoyed large gates at club matches at the big grounds in the city (the SCG and the Agricultural Ground). Would allowing the large number of matches at smaller suburban grounds, many without decent grandstands, refreshment rooms, and change rooms, reduce the revenue?

Some also pointed out that most suburban grounds were used for cricket and had a turf wicket in the centre. 'Our footballers get knocked about on these brick-like grounds, which look so green and soft. When the matches are over the players have generally a few green spots on their anatomy — green from bruises.'[9]

DISBANDING THE OLD CLUBS

The arguments continued until, just over a month before the 1900 season, the district scheme was adopted. Wallaroo officials, including Lane, fought hard to maintain the old system, but were well in the minority when the final MRU vote was taken.[10] The working-class players who would no longer be receiving 'boot money,' and who would now have to pay from their own pocket to play, had no say.

The resolution also called for the disbandment of all the existing clubs, except for the University. Wallaroo's Monty Arnold, by then called the 'father of Australian rugby,' voted in favour of the proposal but opposed disbanding the old clubs.

He argued Wallaroo should be allowed to continue to form teams for annual matches against the University, the King's School and other institutions or visiting teams. It would also be security against the collapse of the local club system. Naturally, there were players too who preferred the current system be maintained, particularly those that

thought they would lose something. Many refused to take part. One was Billy Howe, the footballer who had been censured by the NSWRU over the payment of money to NSW players two years earlier.

'If these men will not join in with their local club,' commented *The Referee*, 'they must remain on the shelf until such time as they qualify for some other club. Unless a man has strong personal reasons for holding aloof, he deserves no sympathy for his football idleness.'[11]

In the days that followed the old clubs held meetings to formalise their end, each in its own way.

The Glebe F.C. met at the local Humphrey's Hotel, where the club secretary, Joe McGraw,

Frank Row (from the Wallaroo F.C.) captained Australia in 1899.

proposed, 'That the members of the Glebe Football Club do all in their power to assist in the promotion of local football in the Glebe.'

The motion was adopted and after a few polite speeches of thanks to the club officials, it was all over.

Wallaroo held their annual meeting at the Oxford Hotel in the city. The members celebrated the club's successes from 1899, (winning the premiership and seeing Frank Row have the honour of captaining Australia in the Sydney Test matches), before moving on to discuss their future. Though disheartened, 'the recommendation was made that the Wallaroo players should give the new system a fair trial,' even though 'many ties of friendship and fellowship would be severed.'[12]

Monty Arnold had little trouble in convincing the members to keep the club going so that they could play social matches. However, within a season, interest in these occasional matches fell away. After three decades as Australia's pre-eminent rugby club, the Wallaroo reign was over.

THE FORMATION OF THE DISTRICT CLUBS

The MRU 'decided that the following be the districts, each one to provide a First, Second and Third grade team': Eastern Suburbs, Glebe, Redfern, Balmain, Newtown, North Sydney and Western Suburbs. The only club permitted to remain from the old system was Sydney University.

From *The Herald* and *The Referee,* a summary of each club's formation is provided.[13]

Sydney University

That the University Club has been included as a competitor with the new district clubs for the Sydney premiership is a matter upon which the Rugby Union is to be heartily commended. By a few who reflect little there was some bellow for the exclusion of the club on the ground that it possesses not the qualification of the district clubs, and that it must accordingly be unfavourable to football to allow it to remain a competitor. Happily the few holding such narrow views were unable to carry them into effect. The 'Varsity has a more rigid qualification than of any other club, and I feel that should the day ever come for it to drop out of football, the game will thereby receive a serious blow. But that day should not come at all. The restriction placed by the rules of the Metropolitan Union has had little or no effect as the University Sports' Union had a similar resolution, the club losing only a few players as a result. Though one graduate has deserted his old club for a district club. The University continues to wear blue and gold colours.

Eastern Suburbs

The Eastern Suburbs, like most of the other new clubs, has but one story of enthusiasm and success to be told, dating from the inaugural meeting to the present time. The name 'Eastern Suburbs' was once well-known in athletic and cricket fields. About the most famous of the now defunct amateur athletic clubs was the old Eastern Suburbs club. Also in existence at that time was the Eastern Suburbs Cricket Club. But since those days, until a month or so back, the name Eastern Suburbs had dropped out of the world of sport, and indeed, out of all others. It is now revived in football, but strictly it is a misnomer, for the area embraces a substantial portion of the city. That is however a mere detail.

The prominence gained by the cricket club of Paddington, and the fact that the new football club's headquarters being in Paddington, have made it rather difficult for many residents to regard Eastern Suburbs as other than the Paddington F.C. The club has adopted the Paddington red, white and blue but will play in black for the first season until jerseys, similar to those worn by Mullineux's English team, arrive from England. The coach will be Thomas Pauling, the NZ representative forward and the Firsts team includes players from Pirates and Randwick.

North Sydney

North Sydney is to be a stronghold of rugby. There are more football notabilities, past and present, residing there than in most of the other districts. The new club has fairly boomed and there are 100 financial members on the roll. Mr Richard Arnold (Wallaroo) is the patron, and Mr F. Waley (Pirates) the president. The team will play the first season in cardinal, black and gold jerseys, the Wallaroo colours, with blue stockings. Owing to there being no suitable hall available in the district, the teams train each Wednesday evening at Seale's Gymnasium, C. Hill being in charge.

For the North Sydney First XV there is no lack of good material available. The Shoremen possess a first class team on paper including many of the forwards from Wallaroo. A challenge match in aid of the North Shore Cottage Hospital was played between North Sydney and University last Saturday with a large gathering of 4,000 at North Sydney Oval.

Glebe

A stronghold of sport is the Glebe. It is not quite a far-extending district, but is thickly populated. The area allotted to the football club is not one to be measured by mere acres. It comprises all sorts and conditions of tenements — from palatial downwards — and of men, a considerable portion of whom possess the sporting instinct. The district has its clubs in cricket, rowing, bowling, cycling, lacrosse, baseball and tennis. The Glebe sporting colour is maroon, it has become practically universal in the district. The new district football club will take up the maroon, and will not follow the old Glebe club colours of blue, black and yellow.

The honorary secretary of the club is Lewis Abrams, who is strongly supported by the Glebe sports, as he has rendered them very good service in the past. The patron of the club is Sir Matthew Harris, the Mayor of Sydney, and the president is Mr James Hogue, M.P., a journalist who has always been allied with sport. The club will play its home matches mostly on the Wentworth Park Cricket Oval, which prior to this year had never been graced by a rugby football match. Training is at that same venue on Thursday evenings at 8 p.m.

There are at present 85 paid-up and 23 partially paid-up members on the Glebe roll. It shows that there are hosts of young men in the district who are too pleased to pay their way and play the game as sportsmen. The first team of the Glebe is particularly promising. Hardcastle though, the former Sydney club captain, is a Glebe resident, but has not yet joined the club.

Newtown

Newtown has had its rugby football team for many years. In the First Junior competition of recent years it has been one of the most prominent aspirants for the premiership, winning in 1896. A very thickly populated district, Newtown turns out hosts of young cricketers and footballers, who disport themselves on the various parks in the vicinity. At the initial gathering of the new district club over 200 residents attended at the Newtown Town Hall. The club has met with strong financial aid from men of good position, and also has a paid-up members list of 50.

The University Oval has been allotted as the chief home ground of Newtown. This arrangement meets with much public favour, for football patrons of that district have in the past often felt aggrieved with the football authorities for not oftener giving them good matches on the Oval. The colours are royal blue, with white knickers and blue hose. The teams train at Gumpett's Hall, Marrickville. The majority of last year's Buccaneer team has joined the Newtown Seconds side.

Western Suburbs

The Western Suburbs club covers a large area. It embraces the extensive Parramatta and Burwood districts. Such a far-spreading territory, the whole of which is noted for producing footballers and supporters in no small numbers, will require very careful and excellent management in the club. There are at present 75 financial members enrolled, and more to come. The club has three distinct training quarters. On Tuesday evenings the members meet at the Parramatta Cricket Oval, on Wednesdays at the Federal Hall in Burwood, and on Thursdays at the Assembly Hall in Parramatta.

The club has its headquarters at Parramatta, which is as the MRU originally envisaged. An attempt to base the club at Burwood was rejected by the MRU. What is the objection to a club in Parramatta and a Burwood club? A very capable fifteen will be moulded from the list of members. The Second and Third Grade teams will be drawn from players of the following clubs from last year: Burwood, Mercantile (Homebush), Summer Hill Orlando, Royal Oaks (Granville), Parramatta and other Junior clubs.

South Sydney

The South Sydney club has an immense area for selection. In places the population is not great, in others it is dense. It embraces a much wider area than the South Sydney and Redfern cricket clubs combined, and extends as far as Botany. The prospects of the club are very good, but the secretary, Mr Dent, is a trifle disappointed with the measure of support that has been accorded by wealthy and prominent residents. This may, perhaps, in some degree be due to the scattered nature of the locality — the residents of Botany and such remote suburbs are unlikely to feel a deep interest in a club whose boundaries extend in the city's heart.

To-night a start at training will be made at the Agricultural Ground, which has been obtained for Tuesday and Thursday evenings. The club will not play any matches on the Redfern Oval — it is too small. The MRU has decided to alter the name of the club from Redfern District Club to South Sydney.

There are at present 65 financial members and the club colours are cardinal and green.[14]

Balmain

Balmain: the expansion of the British Association (soccer) game in this district over recent years has seriously retarded the progress of rugby in Balmain. The residents there appreciate the 11-a-side game, in which it is an art to propel the ball with one's cranium and it is a crime to pick it up and try a drop kick. The new Balmain rugby club has the advantage of one of the finest football grounds in the colony in Birchgrove Park, and lacks no end of financial and public support. The only serious drawback the club has to contend with is that a few prominent footballers who are eligible to represent the district have so far seemed disinclined to second the effort of the Junior players. The Firsts team will include many Juniors, and with the assistance of some of the older hands it should make a commendable display. Not all the clubs can have a first-class team, and when the season is over some club or clubs must occupy low positions on the list. The club decided on registering a black jersey colour with a six inch gold bar.[15]

A LEAGUE SYSTEM

The MRU's move to a district scheme was meant to increase the popularity of Senior rugby in Sydney. It was intended to build on community preference for suburban clubs (as evidenced by their abundance in the Juniors). They recognised that a district scheme was the only means by which the Senior competition could grow — in both players and supporters. The suburban clubs wanted the new scheme so they could share in the gate-takings from all matches held accross the city.

This is clear from the premiership draw and competition structure implemented at the same time. The MRU adopted a home and away premiership (originally called 'home and home') with a trophy prize given to the winners. If the MRU's objective had been to enhance the appeal of Sydney rugby to middle and upper class young men, it could have simply introduced strict enforcement and auditing of the existing player and club subscription rules, but the new system appealed to the wider populace.

The working classes numerically dominated the suburbs of Sydney. Each suburb, or even borough, had its own identity and 'turf.' By fostering local rivalries into a systematic competition with a prize and glory at its conclusion, the district scheme was always going to rouse a desire to win at all costs, resulting in increased crowds.

The MRU had not done enough to suppress professionalism. While it wanted to reform the club competition and stop hidden payments to players, it also wanted to increase the popularity of the game with the general population. The result would be bigger crowds and more money coming into the sport.

The premiership system was modelled upon that used in England by the professional Football Association (soccer) and the Northern

Union. It was called a 'League' system, and was not encouraged by the RFU as it worked directly against the principles of amateurism.[16]

An English rugby writer discussed the league system and its implications.

> Still, it exists in some districts, especially where clubs are anxious to draw big gates. In the league system a certain number of clubs form a league to play one another twice each season; two points are counted for a win and one for a draw. At the end of the season the club that comes out with most points wins the competition. The advantage of this system over a cup competition is that interest is kept up during the whole season, and one defeat does not debar a club from eventually coming out first.

> When the clubs may be taken as representatives of two neighbouring rival towns, they arouse much excitement in their district. But when to this rivalry there is added the inducement to play for a cup, or prize, the excitement is much more intense. By 'drawing big gates' the temptation arises to reimburse the player for any out-of-pocket expenses he might be put to for playing the game. But in the case of working men, it often meant that they lost part of their weekly wage when they had to go a distance to play a match, or to go on tour. Consequently the claim was made on their behalf to recoup them for their loss of wage; while at the same time rich clubs began to be willing to offer inducements to good players to join their club, and these inducements were generally most acceptable in the form of money.[17]

The MRU sought to control this issue by keeping all the gate-takings from the club matches and enforcing a strong residential qualification upon players. In effect, the district clubs were not really clubs at all — they were local organisers of their district's representative team while the MRU had control of all other matters. Their only autonomy was in choosing who they elected from their district on the management committee. The MRU's income would be didived equitably amongst the districts.

The MRU also continued the use of an insurance scheme to cover medical expenses for injured players (though it did not cover loss of income or long-term care). Premium costs were paid from gate-takings.[18]

A DEMOCRATIC AND CLASSLESS COMPETITION

Even as they were being formed, the new clubs looked for additional funding sources. As with the old clubs, each office-bearer was expected to make a personal financial donation and then enlist wealthy benefactors to contribute further funds. The local club scheme actually made it easier.

'Community pride' would prompt wealthy residents, businessmen, and elected officials alike to prominently give their support. The clubs also held popular smoke concerts to raise funds.[19]

The adoption of the district scheme was a victory for the working class. Their overwhelming support for open suburban clubs in the Junior competitions effectively made the Senior grade irrelevant. What the suburban clubs lacked was funding. The MRU committee, led by Monty Arnold, had for better or worse seen that they had to accommodate the needs and aspirations of the community. The changes brought down the old gentlemen's clubs, with their cliques and covert payments and favours. Of course, the district system was equally suitable to the networking and social needs of local politicians and businessmen too — far more than under the old club scheme.

The scheme the MRU implemented was the definitive classless club competition. It had effectively handed over club rugby to the community. Its structure was as democratic and open as any public institution could be. Any club member could be nominated for a committee position and stand for election. From there, each club would have equal representation on the MRU committee, who would then choose a delegate to the NSWRU committee. The MRU's income would be divided equally amongst the districts.

'The MRU is one of the most democratic of sporting bodies,' wrote *The Sunday Sun*. 'Annually the MRU is formed by the elect of the players, and the MRU officials have to render an account of their stewardship, retaining or forfeiting office according to the sovereign will of the players.'[20]

If the clubs or players were ever unhappy with the actions of the MRU, they merely had to wait until the new year and elect new club representatives to serve on the MRU committee.

Being asked to pay a 5s subscription fee for a season of football (and the opportunity and honour to represent their community) was not ideal to the working man, but it was a small price to pay given the progress they had made.

THE OPENING OF THE 1900 SEASON

'The rugby football season of 1900 in NSW will be officially opened next Saturday,' wrote *The Referee*.

> As all our rugby world knows, the new local, or district, clubs will battle for the premiership. Although there are still to be found one or two who are not thoroughly satisfied that it will revolutionise the game, there cannot be any possible doubt that the success of the movement so far has astonished many of those who had been so long opposed to it.

One of the features of greatest surprise to anti-localists is the readiness with which players have paid their 5s subscription. All it required was the introduction of a hard and implacable rule and the non-believers would be silenced. It was announced at all meetings that only financial members of the club would be eligible to play, and that men would be chosen upon the form they displayed in the preliminary matches, and not on their past reputations. The prompt payment by members of their subscriptions at the meetings astonished those Rugby Unionists present who for years managed Sydney clubs.

There is every reason to hope that football will benefit immeasurably in many other ways, and in not the least important by the introduction of a greater array of new blood into the game, in the shape of young footballers of a good class, both as players and men. The new clubs have all elected their officials with many positions taken up by members of the NSW parliament, local mayors and aldermen — all of whom must meet the residential requirements, save the members of parliament, who must represent a division within the club's area. The club meetings were held in the various town halls, hotels, and council chambers in the boroughs and suburbs within each district.

The district matches, as usual at the start of each season, will be for the benefit of the hospitals, and the Union will give its share of the gate to that purpose.[21]

From the early matches it was apparent the district scheme would achieve its first objective of increased interest and participation in the first grade (formerly Seniors) competition. 'It is safe to say,' reported *The Herald* after the opening round, 'that never in the history of the game has the public sentiment been more deeply in favour of our winter pastime than at present. The various grade competitions commenced on Saturday afternoon, and in all cases in the first grade contests the attendances were good.'[22]

However, it was also clear that the new teams lacked combination and, initially, NSW rugby would suffer as a result. The question was how long would it be before the benefits of the new scheme were to be realised and the standard of football and players exceeded that of the old clubs.

BRISBANE AND NEWCASTLE RUGBY ON THE WANE

Brisbane and Newcastle soon followed the push for adoption of the district scheme. The club competitions in both cities were on the wane, and interest in rugby was falling away.

In early May of 1900 *The Referee* reported that in Newcastle, 'all efforts to run a Senior competition have failed and only Junior teams would play the season. If a move is not shortly made the game will have to go to the wall for a year at least, so far as the Senior players are concerned. The secretary of the Union has endeavoured on two occasions to have the annual meeting held, but without success. Out of four club meetings called recently, only one was held, the attendance at the other not sufficient. There is talk of one particular club entering the Maitland competition. Considering last season their players would not pay a twopenny tram fare to Newcastle, it does not appear likely that they will pay twelve times that amount every Saturday to play at the northern town.'[23]

In comparison, the soccer code had no problems in raising teams for the coming season at 'large and enthusiastic meetings.'

Brisbane rugby fared little better than Newcastle. 'Club football in Brisbane appears to be of a disappointing character in a community of football-lovers,' reported *The Referee*. 'There are practically but three Senior club in the city, where once there were three times as many. Brisbane needs more clubs and more players in Senior football.' A former NSW player, W.A. Baird, performing in Brisbane at the time as a stage actor with a drama and comedy company, wrote in the same newspaper, 'there are only two clubs here of any strength; the City F.C. and the Grammars - the public is getting very sick of going to see them play so often.'[24]

With demands in both Newcastle and Brisbane to follow Sydney and open up the club competitions, the decision was made to introduce district football.

Scott Laing, president of the Northern (Newcastle) Branch, announced that they would adopt the district scheme '…to preserve the interests of the game. I hope that under the new system to be introduced that the popularity of the game will increase and that all patrons of football would be satisfied with the arrangements.'

The players in Newcastle also benefited from an insurance scheme, funded from gate receipts, to cover the medical costs of injuries. However, in Brisbane, support at QRU meetings for similar conditions was insufficient and the 'question of insuring players was discussed, but, as usual with no good result.'[25]

DISTRICT CLUB FOOTBALL HAS COME TO STAY

'Has local football in Sydney proved a success?' asked *The Referee* at the end of the 1900 competition. 'It is a seasonable question and there can be but one answer — an emphatic success. A wider, general public

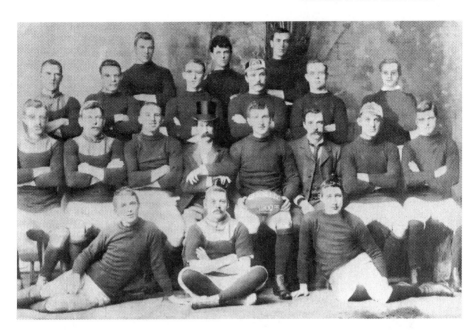

The Glebe District R.F.C. – Premiers of the M.R.U.'s 1900 First Grade Competition.

interest has been shown, and it has proved to be that the public will still pay in thousands to see good matches. District football was also the means of bringing to the front a large number of young players of merit, who otherwise would have been content to keep amongst the Juniors. The advantage of this will be felt to a greater degree as they mature. The opponents of the new system were prepared to try it for a season — success has been so strongly stamped that district club football would appear to have come to stay.'[26]

The Glebe club had carried off the 'Premiership of the Metropolis' in all three grades, winning first grade by six competition points. In the final match of the season the University Oval held over 7,000 spectators, who witnessed 'a brilliant game won by Glebe 20 points to 10 over the home side.' With experienced international Bill Hardcastle in their side, 'Glebe were too strong in the forwards, their weight and pace telling toward the close of each spell.' For Lewis Abrams, the Glebe club's secretary and the man who pushed so much for district football, it was an enjoyable afternoon to reflect upon the positive changes that come over the club game in Sydney.[27]

The MRU publicly presented the trophies and gold medals at the Glebe Town Hall to the district's three winning grade teams. This generated such fervour that 'local enthusiasm was not bridled.' The previous custom, was to hand them out during the MRU's annual general meeting in view of the RFU's edict that such awards should be a trifling matter, something 'quite minor, indeed.'[28]

THE LOCALS AFFECTIONATELY TROD ON YOU

Away from the success of Glebe, there were some matters of concern with the new district scheme — some habits from the old club system were flourishing. 'As was only to be expected, the organisation of some of the clubs was not perfect,' wrote *The Referee*.

> It has been said openly enough that the rule as to subscription fees has not been carried out by at least one club. The importance of insisting upon the fee being paid is not to be underestimated. Allied to a strict observance of the residential qualification, it is the only means of preserving football as a pure sport, free from the disintegrating and lowering influences of professionalism. This is a matter for the Union's careful investigation. The books must be thoroughly inspected by men who can rise above all club influences, and where the rules have been ignored the penalty should be of such a character as to deeply impress upon club officials that their displaced clemency to players is only damaging the status and success of the club.

> The subscription at present is 5s, it might well be increased to 7s/6p, as expenses one way and another for the clubs have so far shown to be too heavy for so small a subscription fee. It is not difficult for a club's secretary to be firm in this matter, yet diplomatic, and not at all offensive to anyone save those whose absence from a club is not to be regretted.[29]

It was tough going for the district clubs — they had no income other than the 5s subscription payment from players along with donations from supporters. All gate-receipts from local matches went to the MRU. The clubs lobbied the MRU for additional funds and at the final meeting of 1900 the Union gave each club £50 'for the purpose of meeting club expenses.'

One Sydney rugby writer issued a warning to the MRU that 'a proposal of this character is diametrically antagonistic to the principle of amateurism in football. If this money were to pay for the use of grounds it would be allowable, and quite a different thing. But the Union has already paid for ground fees. One of the main objects in bringing in the new order of football is to scotch semi-professionalism. Any club which cannot pay its way out of members' subscribers must either be badly managed, or must transgress the law as to football professionalism.'[30]

Local supporters also brought 'benefits' to the clubs. These were businessmen 'who were ever ready to put their hands in their pockets and show in a practical way their support.' The local publican would provide teas for the teams on match day, including the visitors, and after the match all the players and barrackers would return to his establishment 'bringing revenue to his tills.' The storekeeper who provided the best deal on jerseys, socks, and boots for the players enjoyed a similar return in business.[31]

Clubs, players, and their supporters all circumvented the Union's residential qualification rules. The most frequently used tactic was to find a 'billet' for the player, (a room or bed in a boarding house or work quarters within the district), paid for by a club supporter, often an employer. It meant the player would be residentially qualified and have an employer who would accommodate the flexible needs of a footballer when it came to time off work for injuries or trips away. In return the footballer would mention the business favourably at any opportunity.[32] Most of the clubs also utilised their networks and brought in fresh players from regional NSW, Queensland and New Zealand — such players had a one month residential qualification instead of the usual six-month waiting period.[33]

The change had effectively ended the social and business networks that dominated the gentlemen clubs of the 1890s, replacing them with an open club membership structure of instant appeal to local businessmen and elected officials who took the opportunity to set themselves up as leaders of the new clubs. The need for their local team to win was as strong for them as it had been for the networks that controlled the old clubs. Encouragement was given, in its various semi-professional forms, to the best players in the district to take up the game 'with full heartiness.'[34]

Billy Howe decided to end his self-imposed retirement and made himself available for Glebe in 1901. Many others though, having tried the district scheme for one season, walked away from rugby altogether. 'It appears that several of the retirements are attributable to the dislike of the new system and also to the roughness of the game as played last season,' reported *The Herald*. 'That there were many instances of even brutal play no one who followed the competition last year will deny, but that cannot be attributed to the system but rather the disposition of the players, and probably the want of severity in dealing with offenders.'[35]

The district scheme had failed to end the roughness of Sydney rugby. If anything it became a form of organised local warfare. 'Gone now was the cheery irresponsibility of play,' wrote a University footballer, 'this grade football was a serious business. We must win the premiership! There was now something in the games entirely new to me, and for which such terms as "vigour" or "robustness" was a euphemism. When you sank on the ball to stop a dribbling rush, half-a-dozen feet rattled on you like heavy knocks at a door which would not open. Sometimes in a distant suburb when you fell out of bounds the local partisans affectionately trod on you. This, of course, was not the sport for a purist.'[36]

The MRU was providing operational funds to clubs and doing little to temper the 'tone' of club rugby. The Union committee members, however, were content with the situation. They were delegates drawn from those same clubs they were meant to control.

A RIVAL RUGBY COMPETITION

The 1901 season also saw the birth of a rival rugby competition in Sydney, operating outside the three grades of the MRU. Called 'The Rugby Union City and Suburban Association,' it had no residential qualifications and was in effect a return of the Sydney club system that operated in the 1870s. These one-team social clubs were content to play outside of any formal premiership system, playing each other on invitation and strictly following the amateur principles. This appealed to former Great Public Schools footballers much more than the district clubs.

Away from the hustle and bustle of the district competitions, players could participate for the enjoyment of the game without the regimented enforcement of rules or the rough play and win-at-all-costs environment of the Grade scene. The clubs of 1901 included Petersham, Manly Federals, Double Bay Warrigals, and Wentworth.

This became the preferred entry point to football for many young men before moving on to the Grade competitions when they were ready. The first few seasons of the City and Suburban brought together some names that would rise to greater prominence including Billy Cann, Johnny Rosewell and Billy Spence (all Cleveland Street); Reginald 'Snowy' Baker (Womerah), Charles 'Boxer' Russell (St Peters Shamrocks), Sid 'Sandy' Pearce, Albert Rosenfeld and Herbert 'Dally' Messenger (all Warrigals).[37]

So threatened did the MRU feel from the growing popularity of the City and Suburban Association, and to accommodate internal rivalries inside some of the larger districts, the Union replaced its Third Grade competition in 1902 with a Borough competition. It adopted a less regimented residential rule and allowed each district club to divide itself into smaller clubs. Western Suburbs were unable to field a Third Grade team in 1901, but under the Borough arrangement the next season had enough willing players at Burwood and Parramatta for each to field teams.[38]

The emergence of the City and Suburban clubs was a response to the failure of the district scheme to quell rough play and semi-professionalism. Supporters of pure amateurism found much to dislike in football under MRU. The Union claimed it was an upholder of amateurism, but its competition was patently operating otherwise.

WHAT THE DEVIL IS THAT FOR?

A FASCINATING CONCEPT

NSW and Queensland played their first rugby matches as states under the newly federated Commonwealth of Australia in 1901. The season also marked the restoration of visits across the Tasman Sea with a NSWRU team visiting New Zealand.

The Arrow in Sydney, embracing the spirit of the new Federation, suggested that the team be sent as an 'Australian team, and include the best men in Queensland as well as in this state.' *The Referee* took up the idea, saying, 'this is a timely suggestion. From a Federal point of view it is appropriate, and from a football point of view it is eminently desirable. Far wider interest would be taken in the tour, both in this country and in New Zealand if an Australian team was sent across to play three Test matches, and no other engagements.'

The Referee also called for three Test matches to be played consecutively in the space of a week to reduce the length of the tour. 'There would, in an agreement of this kind, be a much better chance of getting a really strong side together. Many players who could make provision for an absence of a little more than a fortnight could not dream of taking a month. There is something fascinating in Australia v New Zealand at rugby football on New Zealand grounds.'[1]

The NSWRU wasn't taken with the concept of styling its representative team as 'Australia' and no Queenslanders were invited. However, the NSW players still thought of themselves as Australia's first touring team, claiming to be 'Australian representatives' and 'internationals'[2] — they were, after all, a team comprising Australians.

The NSW team left immediately after the final round of the Sydney competition, which concluded with Glebe and University as joint premiers. The Final was not played as several of Glebe's players had sailed to New Zealand with the Blues team. Under the guidance of captain Tom Costello, some of the younger players were Harold Judd, Dinny Lutge, Arthur Hennessy and Alec Burdon. For Burdon, it was a meteoric rise, having only secured a permanent first grade position in the Glebe front-row (alongside the experienced Billy Howe) earlier in the season.

The seven-match tour included contests against provincial teams, the most prestigious match being NSW v New Zealand. At Athletic Park in

Wellington, on a fine and breezy afternoon, a crowd of 8,000 watched the New Zealand backs have little trouble out-footing the NSW players on the soft ground. With the experienced George Smith showing the way, the New Zealanders ran over for six tries to nil in the 20–3 win.

The NZRU agreed to a return tour of NSW in 1903. The NSWRU also commenced negotiations with the RFU in England to bring a British representative team to NSW in 1904. Having restored its relationship with the New Zealanders after 'getting over a difficulty,' the NSWRU was confident that the British would be able to also visit Queensland and New Zealand.

CROWDS FLOCK TO SEE THE NEW ZEALANDERS

The New Zealanders' 1903 tour featured three major matches in Sydney — two against NSW and one, for the first time, against Australia. The opening match (v NSW) drew a record 32,000 spectators and gate-takings of £1,400. The aggregate crowd from the three headline fixtures was a remarkable 71,000. It would have been 20,000 more had the second NSW match not been badly affected by rain.[3] As on previous

Australian Team v. New Zealand (Sydney, 1903)

*Back Row: Alec Burdon, Dinny Lutge, Harrie Wood, Fred Lea, James Henderson,
James Joyce, Frank Nicholson.
Middle Row: Ted Larkin, Bill Hardcastle, Charles Redwood, Charles White,
Stanley Wickham (c), Harold Judd, John Maund, Sine Boland.
Front Row: Sidney Riley, Llewellyn Evans, Austin Gralton.*

tours, the visitors dominated — defeating NSW by 12–0 and 3–0, and Australia 22–3.

In the Test match loss, the Australian forwards, including Hardcastle, Lutge, Judd, Burdon and Ted Larkin, had played better than the New Zealanders in the first half, but the home team's backs failed to build upon the work upfront.

The Referee, who occasionally referred to the New Zealand team as 'the Blacks,' said of their victory: 'Two small words sum it up — too good. Great as the New Zealand forwards have shown themselves to be, they could not master the Australian pack in the first 45 minutes. It was flattering to Australia but the Maorilanders are like our cricketers — they rise to the occasion. After the interval, their superior combination and adhesion in the pack, and their stamina, power and pace made itself felt, and their backs began to get the ball and gambol about.'[4]

The New Zealanders ended their tour with a mid-week match against NSW Country at the SCG. The countrymen were able to hold the visitors early, but were eventually overrun 32–0. Despite the result, *The Arrow* was impressed by the play of the Country forwards: 'Notwithstanding that he had his head injured, Pat Walsh the Newcastle forward, played a solid game against the New Zealanders on Wednesday. Only seven men were packed in the scrummage in the second half, Walsh being accorded the post of wing-forward opposite Dave Gallaher. In that position he also shaped well. Country forwards this year possess more pace than the Metropolitan pack. With a bit of combination they would make a rather good division.'[5]

SYDNEY CLUBS WANT TO RUN THE GAME

Moves were again made, led by Lewis Abrams, to restructure the MRU in 1903. The first initiative was the scheduling of an annual match between a Metropolitan side and visiting Queensland teams. This offered the MRU further income and prestige, but Abrams' main objective was to provide a means for more Sydney players to stake their claims for NSW selection. 'You had to be one of seven or eight of the best in the Metropolis to get in a NSW side, for the country generally supplied a big percentage of the team,' said one Sydney footballer.[6]

The second proposal sought to reduce the number of vice-presidents on the MRU committee. These men were elected directly to the MRU committee and did not represent a club. This effectively 'watered-down' the say of the Sydney clubs and players. Abrams' proposal, fully endorsed by Glebe (including club captain Billy Howe), was for the number of vice-presidents to be reduced from seven to three, and that each club have two representatives on the controlling committee.[7]

Richard Arnold, speaking at a North Sydney club meeting, repeated the words contained in the club's annual report that 'efforts are being made by a certain section of clubs to amend the present efficient constitution of its Union and would urge upon the representatives of this and other districts to use every endeavour to oppose the proposed alterations. This is for the reason that the proposal will be detrimental to the cause of rugby as a game in this state.'[8]

Such a change would erode the power of the Arnold brothers and the men who had controlled NSW rugby since the 1870s. A revealing and forthright letter written by Robert Shute was published in *The Herald*, setting out the concerns of the Sydney clubs and players about the organisation of rugby in NSW.

A strange anomaly presents itself in the management of local football, which has long been a source of serious dissatisfaction amongst the players. It is that the Senior clubs who provide the sport and play the game have practically no voice whatever in the management of the larger affairs connected with it. This is owing to the existence of a somewhat ridiculous dual institution by means of which the control of the more important matters, such as inter-state or international matches is taken altogether out of the hands of the clubs in the city and in the suburbs — in reality the only ones vitally interested, and given over to a collection of gentlemen who represent no one.

These gentlemen form the council of the NSW Rugby Union, and the indifferent control of football here is to be found in the fact that the men who have secured seats on this council are utterly irresponsible. They represent for the most part no one who has any interest in the sport. Without any responsibility they have control of one of our most important sports.

Of course the members of the Rugby Union Council ostensibly represent someone. They are delegates from country branches or else they are vice-presidents of whom there are no fewer than seven. But those who know anything of sports organisations will appreciate at its full worth the representative capacity of a country branch delegate. The truth is that the country branches have no interest in common with the city, and they don't care who represents them.

As a rule the men nominated by the secretary in most similar institutions secure the seats. Thus the management of the more important matches (Tests, tours and inter-state), which should of course be directly in the hands of the clubs playing the game in the city and suburbs, is controlled by persons who may be entirely outside the sport.

As a matter of fact, the Metropolitan branch of the Union, into which ignominious position the clubs have been cleverly engineered, has only three delegates on the NSWRU council. By this means the clubs of the metropolis are practically disfranchised in the management of football in its more important phases without rhyme or reason.

It is surely time that the MRU determined to see that its members are properly represented by men carrying full responsibility on the body controlling the game. Why not wipe out the NSWRU altogether? It is only an excrescence on sport. It is not wanted to perform any one function that could not be done a great deal better by the MRU. The country clubs can be very well trusted to look after their own affairs, and no interference is wanted on one side or the other.[9]

Though defeated, the Abrams proposal highlighted the growing concern that Sydney's rugby community had no real say at the NSWRU level — which Abrams predicted when the MRU formed in 1897. No doubt the dissatisfaction was fuelled by the NSWRU's announcement at its 1903 annual meeting that it now had a credit balance of over £2,200. All these earnings were from NSW matches held in Sydney. The New Zealanders' recent tour had bolstered the Union's balances even further.

OYSTERS AND WHISKY

Aware now that their efforts were producing far more money for the NSWRU than it needed, the Sydney players quickly became dissatisfied. This was exacerbated by the behaviour of the Union's officials during the 1903 inter-state series. When Easts' John Maund boarded the train for Brisbane with fellow NSW players (including Burdon, Larkin, Lutge and Peter Moir), they all noticed the tour party included numerous NSWRU officials. 'There seemed to be as many officials as players on the trip,' said Maund. The situation was made worse when 'the officials ate oysters and drank whisky on the train, but the players didn't get any.'[10]

In comparison, the NSW players were provided with the standard 3s day allowance. Their first expense came before that had even left Sydney, being 'told to go to Farmers and buy a straw (boater) hat' to which a 'complimentary' light blue band would be added.

In Brisbane the daily allowance proved so inadequate that 'many players who had gone to Queensland paid away the 3s in one "shout" — a man could not take a drink if they were worthy of the name of "men" without reciprocating.' The players also had to pay their own washing bill, where 'a couple of shirts and collars cost you about 3s

— one day's pay!' The only way a footballer could comfortably enjoy a tour was to 'carry a bank' from their own savings. However, for a working-class player this was impossible.

'Fancy 3s a day,' said a friend of the players, 'away from home, staying in a hotel, and in a big city, where there is every inducement to spend money. They lose their wages and receive 3s a day to spend. No man upholding the credit of the state should be out-of-pocket. A truly magnificent return for their services — which are too frequently accompanied by broken limbs.'[11]

Players soon put to the NSWRU that, in view of the money now in the Union's bank account, the allowance be increased. *The Referee's* 1897 warnings about treating players fairly had been forgotten, as had the use of a 'manager's expense account.' The Queensland trip focused attention on the treatment of the players. It was the first sign of significant dissatisfaction from the players against the NSWRU.

An on-field incident during the series caused further antagonism between the players and the NSWRU. In a mid-week match between NSW and Brisbane, Blues forward Harold Judd punched opposition forward Rupert Cooke. The local referee, Bill Beattie, sent Cooke from the field after he retaliated. The fighting was far from over, Judd then 'pummelled' into Brisbane's halfback Mickey Dore. Beattie opted not to send Judd off, telling him to curb his unsatisfactory behaviour.

As was the custom, the NSW managers were given a list of referees to select who would referee the inter-state match on the following Saturday. NSW chose Beattie. However, he immediately announced that he would only referee the match if Judd was excluded. Beattie claimed Judd exhibited 'disgraceful conduct' and it was only because the NSW team were guests of the QRU (of which Beattie was on the committee) that he hadn't ordered him from the field.

The NSW management agreed to leave Judd out of the team. The NSW players, though, took exception, and many of them vowed not to play unless he was reinstated. The players eventually got their way, and Beattie refused to referee the match.[12]

RUGBY AND VICTORIAN RULES FORM A PACT

At the first MRU meeting of 1904, Abrams took up the issue of the 3s allowance given to state players. The matter was really outside the responsibility of the MRU as it involved players representing the NSWRU's team. However, no doubt through frustration at not having access to present issues at NSWRU meetings, Abrams proposed: 'That 7s/6d be allowed to representatives of the Metropolitan Union when playing outside of the state.' The motion was rejected. Abrams warned that the issue would come to a head — sooner or later the players' needs would have to be addressed.[13]

In a remarkable move shortly afterwards, the MRU, the NSWRU and the NSW Australian Football League (Victorian rules) held a number of meetings. The Victorian game gained a resurgence in Sydney and Newcastle after a number of VFL club competition matches were brought to NSW in 1903. An eleven-team district competition formed in Sydney in early 1903, with Victor Trumper (of the Paddington Australian F.C.) elected as treasurer, and NSW Minister for Lands, Edward O'Sullivan, as a vice-president. A staunch republican, O'Sullivan was recognised as having played a significant role in the push for federation of the Australian colonies. He also felt football should suit the needs of the new country, calling on the people of NSW to 'support a game that was invented by Australians for Australia.'[14]

The three footballing bodies agreed 'to complete reciprocity in regard to disqualifications.'[15] Disqualification of footballers was rare, it could only occur by a player carrying out an act of professionalism, serious rough on-field play, or some evil-doing against an official. In normal circumstances the governing bodies of rugby and Victorian rules did not work together. The NSWRU saw the Victorian clubs as money-making enterprises and the VFL as only following the amateur principles in words, not action. The NSW Victorian rules body, struggling for recognition, had little opportunity to stray from its amateur stance given its limited resources.

Why the three football authorities operating in Sydney suddenly felt a need to adopt this reciprocal recognition of disqualification, particularly given such an action against a footballer was rare, can only suggest they foresaw the possible need for a mass banning of players arising.

With no chance of banned players finding refuge in another code, the officials of rugby union and Victorian rules were in a much stronger position when it came to keeping players under control and quietening any discontent. Any disqualification would mean the footballer could not join a club or play for a state in either of the nation's two biggest football codes. With soccer a long way behind, there was no alternative. The players were now effectively 'under lock and key.'

THE NEW ZEALANDERS ARE DUDDED AGAIN

Confirmation of the tour by a British team was received by the NSWRU at the commencement of the 1904 season. The Union showed their entrepreneurial and presumptuous streaks when they announced that it was their intention to have the New Zealanders send a team to

Sydney to play against the visitors (again called by most as 'England'). The Union was clearly showing where it saw the current ranking of its own representative teams and players.

The NSWRU, as organisers and promoters of the tour, extended to the New Zealanders a repeat of the treatment meted out in 1899 — the Union wanted to ensure that it was compensated for the income that would be missed out on by the British being away in New Zealand instead of playing matches in Sydney. 'It could not be expected to make those sacrifices and accept terms that would not be to its financial advantage, more especially as it undertook the monetary risk of the tour.'[16]

The New Zealanders had endured enough. They immediately commenced negotiations directly with the RFU. *The New Zealand Times* summed up the feelings across the Tasman, as the colony faced up to missing out on seeing a visit from the British yet again. 'It is improbable that the English team will play in New Zealand under the terms proposed by the New South Wales Union. The overseas body wants £1,500, but the New Zealand Union refuses to pay this, and intends to try to make arrangements with the Englishmen without the help of any outside Union.' At the time the NZRU had just over £200 credit in the bank. 'In view of the demand for such a sum for the privilege of playing against a team from a Union with which we are affiliated, one casually wonders where do the benefits of imperialism (being part of the RFU's family) in rugby football come in.'[17]

The NSWRU and NZRU finally reached an agreement. The NZRU agreed to pay for transporting the British team from Sydney and back again. They also had to give half the net profits from gate-takings to the NSWRU. The proposed Sydney match between New Zealand and Great Britain never eventuated.

Meanwhile, the NZRU decided to proceed with serious planning for a tour of Great Britain, the first such tour from Australasia since the New Zealand Natives team of 1888. They would need £5,000 for the

Australia v. Great Britain 1904 Test match in Sydney – the home team wearing N.S.Wales blue jerseys.

tour, and would raise the funds with the assistance of all the provincial and smaller Unions across the colony.[18]

While it may have been a cheaper path to take, at no point did they ever consider seeking the assistance or a partnership with the NSWRU and sending a combined team to Britain. No doubt recent dealing had made them wary.

Still, why it made sense for the RFU to combine England, Scotland, Ireland and Wales as the 'British Isles' and send them to play against Australia, New Zealand or South Africa, yet the reverse of sending an 'Australasian' combined team was never contemplated. The New Zealand game had the better players and combination. Arguably they didn't need to be bolstered by 'Cornstalks' and 'Bananalanders.' As with the Federation debate, New Zealand chose to go its own way.

A NEW BRITISH TEAM, A NEW ATTITUDE

'The great event of the rugby season will, of course, be the visit of an English team, which leaves England for Australia in the *Ormus* on Monday.' So trumpeted *The Herald* in its 'prospects for the 1904 season' feature. 'It has been generally difficult to pick the winner of the first grade competition until it has almost reached its completion, and this year the rivalry between the clubs promises to be as keen as ever. An inclusion in the Australian team in the international contests ought to be and probably is the aspiration of all leading players, and it is safe to anticipate a higher standard of form in the clubs as a consequence.'[19]

The British team arrived in Sydney in mid-June, with Scotland's David Bedell-Sivright as captain. While this side was slightly more representative of the four Home Unions than Mullineux's 1899 team, it again was not the top echelon of players, only a handful having played international matches. The players were given the standard 3s a day 'wine money' allowance, which for the working-class men of Britain was not enough to convince them to make themselves available for the tour. *The Town and Country Journal* reported allegations that the British players had each received £500 before leaving England.[20]

Of the forwards, just the captain and Dobson (England), Edwards (Ireland) and Bevan (Wales) had appeared in 'the highest class of engagements.' The forwards also included the much-travelled Blair Swannell, a member of the 1899 team.

This British team, unlike most of their predecessors, were no gentlemen on the field of play. Bedell-Sivright and Mullineux could not have been more different. Bedell-Sivright, a doctor, was the heavyweight boxing champion of Scotland. His nickname of 'Darkie' had nothing to do with his skin complexion, and everything to do with his devious playing tactics.

The change in captaincy (and perhaps his own experiences from serving in the Boer War) released a different side to Swannell's play. 'His conception of football was one of trained violence,' wrote one leading rugby player of the time. 'He kept himself in perfect physical condition and this alone enabled him to conceal his slowness on the field. In appearance he was extremely ugly, but he could talk his face away in half an hour.'[21]

A crowd of 34,000 were present at the SCG on a bitterly cold day for the first Test. The 'Australian' team wore the NSW sky blue jersey emblazoned with a waratah. The side included debutants Pat 'Nimmo' Walsh, Mickey Dore, Bill Richards, and Snowy Baker, alongside Burdon, Lutge, and Judd. Australia surprised most of the judges by holding the score to nil-all at half-time. But reduced to fourteen players for the second half, they were overrun by the British 17–0 in the end.

The Test match won, the British began their trek north to Brisbane for the second Test a few weeks later. They were scheduled to meet a number of country teams in the major centres along the way. The first was in Newcastle, the 'coaly city' just up the coast from Sydney. There the visitors would play the local representative side 'Northern Districts,' who boasted NSW and Australian forward Pat Walsh amongst their numbers.

THE DOBSON INCIDENT

Played at Newcastle's Rugby Union Ground, the British defeated combined Northern Districts by 17-3. The match though was almost abandoned in the second-half, following a dispute between Bedell-Sivright and the referee, Harry Dolan.

The Sydney Mail reported that 'the Newcastle men with Walsh in the forefront were playing up [well], and were holding more than their own' against the British. Walsh collided with British winger Jowett, and the visitor landed heavily on his head, suffering concussion. Unable to continue, Jowett was forced to leave the field, meaning the British had to play the remainder of the contest with 14 men.

'After the (half-time) spell,' wrote *The Sydney Sportsman*, 'occurred the unfortunate incident that is now violently agitating football circles pretty well everywhere. The Britishers did not by any means like being penalised for their frequent recourse to a game at which they appear to be very apt, namely, funny business in the scrums, by not putting the ball in properly and not keeping their feet on the ground (until the ball is fed). It was after something queer on their part in a scrum that referee Dolan penalised them.'

It was then the British forward, Dobson, said, 'What the devil was that for?' The referee promptly challenged Dobson for his remark, who apparently replied using indecent language. Dolan gave Dobson numerous opportunities to apologise, but he refused. The referee then ordered him to leave the field. Bedell-Sivright signalled to his men and the whole of the British team walked off the ground to the dressing room. He claimed the referee's assertions cast a 'reflection on the personal character of the team' and could not be allowed to pass without protest. After twenty minutes Bedell-Sivright 'placed himself in a somewhat wobbly position by returning' with his team to the field and played on without Dobson.

*Newcastle's Pat 'Nimmo' Walsh
– played three Tests for Australia
in 1904.*

The Sydney Sportsman reporter commented that, 'after the incident or accident, or whatever it was, the play was very willing, and some of the scrums were very good places to be out of.' He also noted that, 'Pat Walsh performed brilliantly, but the visitors made a marked man of him, and tormented him all they knew.'[22]

In the aftermath, the NSWRU removed the investigation into the incident from the local Union and held its own inquiry. The NSWRU found that Dobson had used a hasty and improper expression in saying, 'What the devil is that for?'

Five of the Northern District players, including Walsh, supported the referee's allegation, and the reason for which Dobson was sent-off, that the player had also used an 'indecent expression.' Swannell and Bush of the British team, together with Dobson, denied that anything of the kind had been said at all.

The NSWRU believed the three visitors, and inferentially found that the referee and the five Northern Districts players had made a mistake as the 'indecent expression reported by the referee was not used by Mr Dobson.' As to the British team leaving the field mid-match, and any penalty against Dobson for his improper expression, the Union came to the conclusion that the incidents were so trivial as to not merit consideration. Nothing further was to be done.

The Newcastle players and the referee were outraged that the NSWRU had sided with the Britishers instead of standing behind their own. They were dismayed that they hadn't been believed, and worse, the NSWRU had ignored their evidence. Dolan vowed to have no further involvement with first class rugby announcing that 'he disqualified himself from holding any position under the Union.' The players, publicly, bit their tongues and remained silent.[23]

The rugby community was becoming roused by the 'tone' of the British team's play. First grade rugby fields were no place for the weak-hearted, so for the level of rough play dished out by the visitors to be so complained about, it must have caused many to question just what had come over British rugby. Admonished by the Reverend Mullineux in 1899, the current 'representatives of the Rugby Football Union' had sent out a completely different message to rugby followers and players in Australia.

THE FOOTBALL WAS FAIRLY ROUGH AT TIMES

The second Test was held in Brisbane, where the QRU invited eight NSW players to travel north and represent Australia. The NSW members of the national team came up in dribs and drabs, depending upon when they could obtain leave from work. Normally they would all travel together, and anyone 'unable to get away' would be replaced, but there was much confusion about travel arrangements and two players didn't arrive until the evening before the Test.

It was no way for the team to prepare for a Test match, particularly with six new players. 'Combination' was the key to success on the rugby field, and the QRU and NSWRU had given their team no training time whatsoever. 'Did we use our best endeavours to put the Australian team into the field under such conditions as made for victory, or, in other words, did we not ride for a fall? There is nothing like combination; nothing like training together,' wrote a frustrated reporter from *The Sydney Mail* after Australia were defeated.[24]

The Test match, held at Brisbane's Exhibition Ground, was marred by further on-field violence, with Swannell again amongst the main antagonists. He was an articulate man and had defended his so called 'dirty play,' and that of his team, in *The Referee* after the Newcastle match. The 15,000 strong crowd booed and jeered him when he entered the field.

The Australians, wearing the maroon of Queensland, scored an early try to lead 3–nil after Burdon chased down a kick the British had failed to gather in their in-goal area. Despite the efforts of Judd, Lutge, Walsh, and Burdon, the visitors got the upper hand, took control in the second half, and scored three tries to gain a commanding 17–3 lead.

The Brisbane newspaper, *The Courier*, reported that 'there were little bits of rough play every now and then, Swannell being the worst offender. But, overall, until the last two minutes the game was played in quite the proper spirit.' In those last two minutes of the match, Swannell went on a personal mission of mayhem. First he singled out Pat Walsh, flattening the Newcastle forward. He then took out Australia's fullback John Verge and, in the aftermath, the 'Maroons' pack retaliated. After feisty halfback Snowy Baker, a champion boxer, led the way with a few choice swings, the Australian forwards pounced upon the Britisher. The referee moved in and stopped Swannell suffering any further punishment, though he was the only player given a caution for foul play.[25]

The third Test again produced a new-look Australian side. Burdon stood down after suffering a serious shoulder injury in the Brisbane loss. He was 'on ice' for months afterwards — unable to work. 'What he used for money in that idle period is known only to himself.'[26]

Australia lost the third Test 16–0 (24,000 crowd) at the SCG. The match was again particularly rough, with the referee finding some difficulty in preventing a few 'ardent belligerents' fighting a personal war.

Even after the British had returned to Sydney from their visit to New Zealand the ill-feeling had not simmered. The New Zealanders had managed to do in one Test what the combined efforts of NSW and Queensland had failed to achieve — tame the British forwards. Before a great 20,000 strong crowd at Athletic Park in Wellington, New Zealand [still a colony] played their first-ever home Test match. The local team were able to defeat the British in an impressive 9–3 win, with winger Duncan McGregor crossing for two tries. *The Town and Country Journal* reported that the NSWRU made £1,200 from the New Zealand matches.[27]

The final date of the British programme pitted NSW against the visitors in a mid-week match, again at the SCG. Dobson didn't play while Swannell, perhaps somewhat wisely, preferred the role of touch judge. The Blues side was captained by Newcastle's Charlie Ellis and included fellow 'northern men' Walsh and Charlie Hedley at fullback. Newtown gained most of the forward places with Harry Hammill, J. Comber and Judd packing alongside Lutge and J. O'Donnell from North Sydney.

The Referee reported the match 'was hard and keen, and fairly rough at times. The home team played quite ably, excepting perhaps that they were not quite so cool. The weather was cold and the ground hard, but

Australian Team v. Great Britain (First Test Sydney, 1904)

*Back Row: J Beattie, James Henderson, Llewellyn Evans, Alec Burdon, Dinny Lutge, Thomas
Pauling (referee), Harold Judd, Paddy Lane, James McManamey.
Middle Row: Charles Redwood, Charles White, Fred Nicholson (c),
Bill Richards, Stanley Wickham.
Front Row: R 'Snowy' Baker, A 'John' Verge, Ed Dore, Thomas Colton,
John Hindmarsh, Pat Walsh.*

coated with thick clover, which made it difficult to obtain a firm footing
when moving with the speed.' As a result the match was played at 'close
quarters,' with the British team scoring the only points of the match,
a converted try. 'The tackling of both sides was strong and resilient.
Some little time before the finish Ellis, Walsh, and one of the British
forwards were temporarily disabled. The referee at one time cautioned
both teams about rough play after Harding and Walsh having come
into contact.'[28]

'WHAT BECOMES OF THESE BIG GATES?'

The visit of the British team, and their particular taste for a willing
form of rugby, had ruffled the game in NSW and Queensland. The
local players did not fear the tactics of players such as Swannell, they
just didn't expect it from a team purported to represent the RFU. The
support given to the British players by the NSWRU in the aftermath of
the 'Dobson incident' — and practically accusing their own players and
referee of lying — was of great concern.

It sent a confused message to the rugby community, that rough
and violent play was acceptable if you were part of the British team,

but not by anyone else. Haphazard Test selections and the poorly organised arrangements for the Brisbane match only added to the players frustration.

The NSWRU's inconsistent attitude also extended to the treatment of players. Some of the men worked out that the Union would secretly pay more than the 3s a-day allowance — but only if they asked for it and if the Union selectors felt the player could not be replaced without lowering the prowess of the team.

Upon being selected for the NSW v Britain match, Newtown's Harry Hammill was alerted by a club-mate 'who knew the ropes about rep. football on how to put the acid on the Union. I was earning good sugar,' said Hammill, 'and I put it to the heads of the Union about lost time for the match against England. After a bit of an argument they agreed to pay me 15s, but I had to render an account of my "expenses" to balance the budget. I often think that I would give a couple of bob to peek at that account, for you could get the best steak and oyster in the city then for a bob. What other items were on that account to make up the 15s I'd like to know. Training at four o'clock a couple of afternoons each week also produced 7s/6p each for lost time. But, I was always told

Glebe District R.F.C. First Grade Team (1902)

*Back Row: Lewis Abrams, J 'Puddin' Woods, H R Baird, Alec Burdon, Jim Abercrombie,
C Rundle, W Munn, Bill Hardcastle, W Johnson (trainer), W Booth, W Nesbit,
J Harrington (referee).
Middle Row: F Roberts, V Harris, W 'Billy' Howe (c), James Joyce, R Harris, John Conlon.
Front Row: D Parbury, James Clarken, Albert Conlon, G Roberts.*

when receiving that I must not tell any of the others, for they might all want it.'[29]

With the NSWRU enjoying far greater income as a result of the increasingly popular visits from British, New Zealand and Queensland teams, the players began to ask 'what becomes of these big gates?' The Union's answer was to quietly meet the demands of the few players that were asking for an increased allowance.

At the same time, it found other ways to spend the money, including employing a fulltime secretary to run the day-to-day operations of the Union, and leasing permanent offices in the Australian Jockey Club building (in Bligh Street in the city).

As one speaker enthused at the NSWRU annual meeting after the 1904 season, 'It would be unwise to spend money at the rate followed last season, still there would never be any fear that a visit by a British team would not be successful in every way.' In other words, as long as the tours by the British continued they would never run out of money. Still, that wasn't enough. The minutes also recorded that the committee was particularly disappointed at the NZRU's refusal to send a team to Sydney to play the British.[30]

The NZRU hadn't forgotten about its problems reaching agreement with the NSWRU over the past two British team visits either. In early 1905 the NZRU announced it had secured agreement with the RFU to send a New Zealand team to tour Great Britain (leaving August 1905). The decision's immediate effect was that a previously agreed visit of 'Australia' (a joint NSWRU and QRU organised tour) to New Zealand would see the locals field a second or even third rate team in the Test. The NZRU also found a few weeks later that it 'cannot accept the terms offered by the NSWRU to send the New Zealand team to Sydney on the way to England.'[31]

While the NSWRU was still seething over the news, it was hit with further rejection. An invitation to the South African Rugby Council to visit Australia was declined (they secretly held hopes that the New Zealanders would stop over on the way to or from England). With the NSWRU still wondering what was happening, the NZRU let the news slip out that the next British team (proposed for 1907) would only be visiting New Zealand and it would be a much stronger contingent than Bedell-Sivright's recent tourists.

'This information will be received by the public with a good deal of regret,' reported *The Herald*.[32]

CHAPTER SIX

MESSENGER & CO.

BILLY HOWE, MRU SECRETARY

The MRU opened the 1905 season by announcing that its secretary would now be a paid fulltime position as 'the work in each Union had become too extensive to expect gentlemen to carry it out in an honorary capacity.'[1]

In a move that initially might have given hope for more liberal treatment of clubs and players, the MRU also announced its new secretary would be former Glebe, Wentworth, and NSW player Billy Howe.

It was remarkable that a player who admitted receiving money and refused to initially take part under the new district club scheme, was now respected enough to be placed in charge of the MRU's operations. Since retiring, Howe had become a first grade referee and seems to have sufficiently reformed his reputation to become part of the game's administration. He had abandoned his old ways so convincingly that he became a director of the NSW Amateur Sports Club.[2]

The NSWRU was still blithely spending money. It found it appropriate to give retiring honorary secretary Mr Rand the sum of £100 as a testimonial for his services. Such payments to retiring officials were not uncommon, but this demonstrated the different treatment given to players and officials.

The NSWRU was also pleased to announce that the NZRU had decided that a New Zealand team could come to Sydney before the trip to Britain after-all. What they didn't know was that the NZRU's change-of-heart was based purely upon 'milking' money from the big SCG crowds to help fund its tour to Britain.[3] The New Zealanders asked for (and gained) three matches at the SCG to be held in the space of a week, with matches against NSW on consecutive Saturdays. With the New Zealand team set to leave for England on July 30 (sailing east across the Pacific), the visit to Sydney was set for July 5 to 13.

AN ENGLISHMAN IN THE NSW TEAM

In the Sydney competition, the city portion of the Eastern Suburbs district was removed and formed into a new club, Sydney (playing in the black jersey of the old Pirates club), which increased the number of clubs to nine, creating a bye. This allowed the MRU and the NSWRU to forge a combined plan which would see each club visit a NSW country area on their bye weekend.

The first surprise of the season was the appearance of a familiar face in the North Sydney forwards, Blair Swannell, who had taken up residence in Sydney. He had, it seems, as many friends as enemies in Sydney football. By the middle of the season he was in the NSW side, and it appears to have been at the expense of one his adversaries from 1904, Newcastle's Pat Walsh.

Walsh had earlier been selected in the NSW team that played two matches in Brisbane against Queensland. In the first game Walsh was one of 'three conspicuous men among the light-blue forwards' although the local team caused a surprise result by winning. Poor finishing by Teague, who was a 'first-nighter,' making his initial NSW appearance, saw three tries fall from his grasp in the first half and the 'win was a slightly lucky one' for Queensland.[4]

In the second match the next Saturday the 'Welshmen were clearly Queensland's masters at every point of the game' according to *The Courier*. 'The NSW footballers, though beaten the previous week, showed themselves in this game one of the best combinations that has come to Brisbane. In the Welsh pack, Judd and Walsh played grandly. Roe and "Boxer" Russell were a fine pair of halves (and there is mournful satisfaction in the fact the former is a Queenslander).'[5]

Blair Swannell – toured with the British teams of 1899 and 1904, before moving to Sydney in 1905.

In *The Newcastle Morning Herald* a report on Walsh's play was included. 'Walsh played a particularly brilliant game, and one writer went so far as to say that the Newcastle representative was one of the best forwards in Australia to-day, an opinion that will be shared by all those who have seen Walsh at his best.'[6]

Remarkably, when the players returned to Sydney and the NSW team to meet New Zealand was announced, Walsh's name was missing. It caused quite a shock, particularly as Walsh had played in all three Tests against Britain in 1904 and most thought he had improved. *The Referee* said, 'Walsh's exclusion is simply a Chinese puzzle.'

Immediately upon his omission, the NSW selectors claimed that Walsh had lost form in the Brisbane matches. *The Arrow* provided a timely 'independent' opinion that was completely the reverse of accounts made at the match: 'Walsh is a first-class forward, though his form at Brisbane in one respect was a trifle disappointing, inasmuch as he was too much inclined to play "on his own" when going for the goal line. A good judge of the game, who saw the first match, informs us that were it not for this defect in Walsh's play, NSW would have won the double.'[7]

Adding to the controversy was the choosing of Swannell, seemingly in place of Walsh. Despite having never played for NSW before, the Englishman was given the honour of appearing against New Zealand for his debut. It must have irked Walsh and his supporters greatly that Swannell, of all people, was in the team.

After having a few second thoughts on the matter, *The Arrow* joined the criticism being directed at the NSWRU: 'It is simply impossible to follow the line of reasoning or the critical judgement of the Selection Committee in respect of his omission.'[8]

Still, aberrations in NSW selections were not uncommon and the players had come to expect it. Walsh could yet regain his position in the Australian team to travel to New Zealand for the end-of-season Test.

THE THREE-BOB-A-DAYERS ON IRON RATIONS

The treatment of the NSW players in Brisbane was also the centre of much discussion when the team arrived home. After the loss in the first match the men were all placed on 'iron-rations' by the team's manager Charlie Hill.

The team's hooker, Harry Hammill, described the events that took place at the team's hotel. 'On lining up for tucker on Monday, we found that the "heads" had been chewing the matter over on Sunday, and decided that we were being too well fed. Anyhow, the players who pulled the crowds and earned the money to provide holiday trips for certain Union officials, such as Monty Arnold, Billy Howe, and one or two others, found that we were reduced to a regular "iron ration" diet of about three items, while the menu card for the manager and his fellow-selectors and visitors was loaded up with a long list of good eats, just the same as ours had been for the first three days! At the table there was no complaint, but there was plenty of growling when none of the "heads" were around. So I trots off to James McMahon (selector) and asks him what was the reason for the "iron rations" on the "three-bob-a-dayers," and he told me that some of the players were eating too much and becoming too fat for speedy action.'

Hammill was eventually told that the manager was targeting the country players who 'do nothing but ride round on horse-back all the week' and were now over-eating. Hammill continued, 'I came back with,

"Well, if these country blokes are eating their heads off, why not put them on a diet of peanuts and porridge, but we city fellows demanded something different to what we could get at home!" The "iron ration" continued until Thursday, with me always winjing, but the effect was opposite to that desired, for those country blokes were all up in the money, and they went and gorged themselves to repletion up town. The ordinary "three-pers" had to make the best of it. I'm not squealing — I, like everyone else, knew fully what we were taking on when we were selected for the trip, and, after all, there is great honour in representing your state.'

Four days before the tour was over, Hammill, like a number of others, had run out of money. 'In Sydney I was earning 15s a day,' said Hammill, 'but being married and starting a family, I could not afford to cut too deeply into the home accounts to help build up the Union's "three per," hence the weak state of the bank after being on tour about nine days.'

That day the selectors asked Hammill if he would be available for the New Zealand tour if chosen. He replied, 'Yes, but only on conditions that I get 10s a day — I've been here almost a fortnight on this three-bob-a-day racket, and, after a couple of rum-and-milks in the morning I've been broke all day!' The selectors told him they would have to consider it, 'but I knew from their dials that all the other hookers would have to get German measles or something before I'd have got my rise — fancy another six weeks trip on that "three-per"?'[9]

THE NEW ZEALAND TEAM FOR ENGLAND

The New Zealand team for the British tour was largely settled by May 1905. This gave the players time to seek leave from their employers and organise their private affairs. The decision by the NZRU to send the team on a three-week visit to Sydney (with almost two weeks of the time spent on the sea) did not find great appeal amongst the men. Some couldn't gain further leave from work and stayed in New Zealand, while others voiced concerns that 'there was a danger of incapacitating some of the best men in the team, for no particular purpose.'[10]

With captain Dave Gallaher one of those that remained in New Zealand, Taranaki's Jimmy Hunter led a nineteen-man tour party to Sydney. With very tight scheduling, the team arrived the afternoon before their opening match against NSW.

'The latter part of their voyage was rough, many suffering from sea sickness,' and the team were not expected to be 'in their best form' when they faced the Blues. The New Zealanders still posted an imposing team including George Smith, Duncan McGregor and George Gillett in the backs, with Charlie 'Bronco' Seeling, William 'Massa' Johnston and George Nicholson in the forwards.

Billed by the NSW press as 'The New Zealand Team For England,' everyone in Sydney rugby seemed to believe they were hosting a great send-off party for the tourists. Making use of the 'excellent vantage point' now offered by the 'recently increased mound' [The Hill] at the Randwick end of the SCG, a crowd of 30,000 cheered and applauded their way through a five-try thrashing (19–0) at hands of the New Zealanders. *The Herald* said, 'The visitors had no reason to complain about the warmth of their reception, which was intended to convey an enthusiastic expression of the hope that their tour through England would meet with every success.'[11]

The prospects for success in Britain by a representative team 'from the colonies,' had turned the New Zealanders into local heroes. On the following Saturday, even though there was clearly little hope of a NSW win, the attendance increased to a record 35,000. Over 10,000 also watched the visitors play a mid-week game against the combined Metropolitan team.

John Calvert, as NSWRU president, hosted an official function for the New Zealanders. The usual array of public figures was present, making their customary speeches, including the city's Lord Mayor and state government members. Also there were 'members of the NSWRU and MRU, footballers, cricketers, and representatives of aquatic and other sports.' Galbraith, the New Zealand team's manager, told the gathering, 'The undertaking to send a team Home is unique. A team has previously gone from the New Zealand colony to the old country, and while it had a good record, it had been in the hands of one individual'[12]

The possibility of a tour from one colony (or combined) had been speculated upon since the late 1890s. The question was whether enough money could be made during the tour to cover the costs and could working-class players afford to take part financially. Similar tours by Australian cricket teams had reaped vast profits, however they were undertaken as private speculations amongst the cricketers involved and others.

Speaking of the feeling at the time, one New Zealand player later revealed to *The Yorkshire Post* that, from the moment of the team's visit to Sydney (where 75,000 paid to see them), the tour was being treated by some men in Australasia as an 'experiment.'[13]

MUCH INDIGNATION AT NEWCASTLE

Immediately after the final NSW match against New Zealand, the Australian team to visit that colony was announced. Nine players of the 23-man squad were from Queensland, including Mickey Dore, Billy Richards and Doug McLean. The NSW contingent included Burdon,

Bede Smith, 'Boxer' Russell, Peter Burge, Ernest 'George' Anlezark, Stanley Wickham (captain), Judd (vice-captain), and Swannell.

For the second time in a fortnight Walsh had been snubbed by the selectors. His only hope of being able to press for a late call-up to the Australian side would hinge on his selection in the NSW team for visit of the Queenslanders to Sydney. His current and previous form seemed to warrant his return to the NSW team, a local report stated, 'On the Newcastle Rugby Ground the local representatives defeated the Hunter River team by 30-0. Walsh captained the Newcastle team and played a splendid game, scoring three tries.'[14]

It still wasn't enough, Walsh was not chosen by the NSW selectors for the Sydney match against Queensland. Everyone 'noticed that P. Walsh, the Newcastle crack, has again been overlooked, for some reason best known to the selectors.'[15]

This third exclusion set mouths talking and pens writing across the rugby community.

The Arrow, now well and truly onside, said, 'If the Australian team to visit New Zealand included Walsh, one would have no fear as to the forwards holding their own against anything in New Zealand. There is no better forward in Australia than Walsh, probably no one quite as good. In the Newcastle district the "Dobson incident" inquiry [at which Walsh gave evidence against the British tourists] is thought to have in some way prejudiced Walsh's chances of being selected. It is clear that the Newcastle forward has not been omitted on the ground of his ability not being good enough. If there is another reason the Union should be the judge, and not the selectors.'[16]

The Sydney Sportsman added, 'There seems to be a lot of gossip amongst footballers as to why Walsh was not selected to go to New Zealand. It cannot be said he is not good enough, as his form in the match at Queensland earlier in the season was tip-top. The large number of enthusiasts who are asking why, would like to know the true reason.'[17]

'Footballers in Newcastle and Sydney,' offered The Town and Country Journal, 'cannot understand why Walsh was omitted, especially as what are considered inferior players have been selected for the trip. At Newcastle there is much indignation, and the Northern Branch Union has written to the NSWRU asking for an explanation regarding the omission of Walsh. In some quarters the opinion is held that it is not want of form that has kept him out of the team.'[18]

The suspicion was that Swannell not only had been given Walsh's position, but he had enough influence upon the selectors or other Union officials that Walsh couldn't play in the same team.

The only positive for Walsh in missing selection in the NSW and Australian teams was that he could make an appearance for his club side (Carlton) in the Final of the local competition against Newcastle. *The Referee* reported, 'The teams met in the presence of a very large attendance. They had already played each other on three occasions this season, with Newcastle winning all three. Carlton had the services of P. Walsh for the first time this season and the big forward played a splendid game. Neither side scored in the first half, but ten minutes before time Walsh picked up the ball, and after running about twenty yards, scored between the posts. Gibb converted the try and dropped a goal from the field. Carlton won the match by nine points to nil. It was the "red and whites" eighth premiership success.'[19]

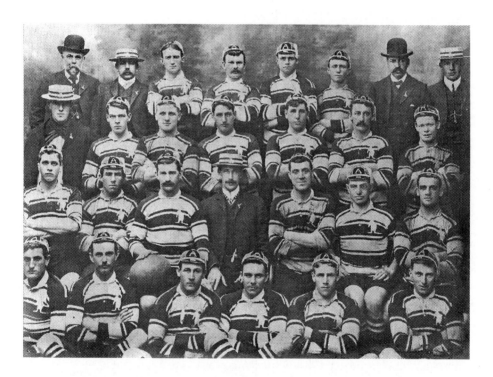

Australian Representative Team that toured New Zealand in 1905

Back Row: W G Judd, N Harris, Mickey Dore, Tom Colton, C 'Boxer' Russell, James Clarken,
C Hill, Edward Mandible.
Third Row: Charles Murnin, Arthur Penman, William Hirschberg, E 'Ned' O'Brien,
Bede Smith, Bill Richards, Alec Burdon.
Second Row: Peter Burge, Basil Lucas, Stanley Wickham (c), James Henderson, Harold Judd,
Blair Swannell, Allen Oxlade.
Front Row: Fred Nicholson, Doug McLean, Fred Wood, Philip Carmichael,
Ernest 'George' Anlezark, Lancelot Smith.

For Walsh, the end of a frustrating season had come to an end. Utterly dismayed at what had transpired he left Australia. Seemingly with no particular plan in mind, he jumped aboard a ship for South Africa. No one could blame him for wanting to leave.

Walsh's plight was not only discussed amongst footballers. James Giltinan, a forty year old commercial salesman, was keenly interested in sports. He had been involved in professional athletics and was a cricket umpire and tour manager. Giltinan attended many of the city's rugby and sporting functions in 1905 [perhaps earlier] and had become friendly with Walsh and other footballers. Given his cricket involvement, their discussions would have presumably covered the different conditions and opportunities afforded to players in each sport.[20]

As the newspapers clearly suggest, many of the senior players in Newcastle and Sydney were disgruntled at the treatment of Walsh and others. Their supporters, men such as Giltinan, would have been as equally incensed at the actions of the NSWRU.

Giltinan also had another matter on his mind. He and Test cricketer Victor Trumper were seeking out financial opportunities in international cricket. They were facing difficulties though, as the cricket associations of NSW, Victoria and South Australia had just commenced taking steps to form an 'Australian Board of Control.' If it succeeded, the Board would be in charge of all tours to and from England, ending the ability for players and private speculators to organise their own ventures. The financial plight (and voice) of the representative cricketer would then be little better-off than that of their contemporaries in rugby.

AUSTRALIA'S FIRST OVERSEAS RUGBY TOUR

The Australian rugby tour to New Zealand, the first ever to leave overseas, was a joint undertaking of the NSWRU and the QRU. The touring team wore the colours of both Unions: Cambridge (sky) blue of NSW and maroon of Queensland. The jersey also featured a white badge, cut in the shape of a kangaroo.[21]

The tour agreement with the NZRU included a requirement that a New Zealand team be sent to Sydney and Brisbane for Tests in 1907. No dividend from gate-receipts would be forthcoming to the NZRU until the debt owed to the NSWRU and QRU from the costs of the 1905 tour were paid off.[22]

The team was selected by Paddy Lane (ex Wallaroo and North Sydney), James McMahon (ex Randwick and South Sydney), and a Queensland official. The two NSW selectors, along with team manager James Henderson, were all vice-presidents on the NSWRU, the positions which Abrams and Shute pointed out represented no one and were a cause of frustration to the club players in Sydney. McMahon and Henderson were also vice-presidents on the MRU, as had been Lane until recently relinquishing the position.

As Shute said in his letter of 1903, these vice-presidents were dependent upon the support and nomination of the Union's secretary at the annual election. MRU secretary Billy Howe had a close association with Swannell. The Englishman had written numerous letters to Howe throughout the time the Australian team was in New Zealand. The letters found their way into *The Referee* and included Swannell's account of various incidents and observations on and off the field. However, they also included his thoughts on the performances of some of his fellow players.

Dally Messenger - guided Easts II to the 1905 premiership title.

Swannell wrote of Anlezark's performance at five-eighth in the Test match against the weakened New Zealand team, 'He is good in defence, but rather slow in getting his kick in, and doesn't seem to make very good openings for his three-quarters. The worst feature of his play is his passing. Time and again in this and other matches I have seen him pass the ball clean behind his man, and at the best of times, his passing is wild.'[23]

Yet, by way of comparison, *The Canterbury Times* reporter described Anlezark in that Test match 'as possibly the best of the Australian backs.'

After the scores were level at half-time, the New Zealanders won the Test 14–3 thanks to individual flashes of brilliance. 'The Australians have a great deal to congratulate themselves upon, for they proved on to-day's play a much better combination than they were credited with being.'[24] Anlezark, like Walsh, never played representative rugby union for Australia again.

Swannell did not come out of the tour without suffering though. Everyone suspected prior to the team's departure from Sydney that he 'was likely to receive some knocks because there were old scores to pay.'

The Referee, commenting upon reports of the match against Taranaki-Wanganui near the end of the tour said, 'Well, Swannell has not had his facial beauty enhanced by the application of a New Zealand boot. Reading between the lines it would appear that Swannell was not treated with loving tenderness by the New Zealanders on the field during the tour. They say, however, that Swannell on re-appearing on the field at Hawera, after having been injured, played more like a lion than a lamb.' It was also claimed that no Australian players went to his assistance. Swannell did not appear in the final match against Auckland, the injury over his eye apparently being too serious.[25]

MESSENGER WINS THE SECOND GRADE FINAL

The Sydney club competition of 1905 was decided after a 'double-bill' of matches played at the Agricultural Ground. In the early match, which commenced at 2 p.m., the struggling Balmain club defeated University for the first time since the district scheme had been introduced. The second game was a close win to South Sydney over North Sydney 5–3. It was enough to give Souths the premiership, one point ahead of Glebe at the conclusion of the club rounds. Some of the other clubs had already lost interest, including Newtown who failed to turn out with fifteen players in its final game.

Glebe were criticised in the press for utilising 'an influx of country players' at the expense of the residentially-qualified second grade players. With players moving from club to club in Sydney required to meet a six month residential rule, clubs could look to country areas for talent to immediately bolster their ranks.

Having 'kept back prominent second grade players,' the Glebe II side was a strong team, reaching the Final were they were defeated by Eastern Suburbs II thanks to a rising player, 23-year old Dally Messenger. *The Referee* stated that if Messenger had played for Glebe they would have won. In reference to a converted try scored by Messenger, the paper described it as 'the sort of try one has often expected Senior players to get, but they rarely think of anything unorthodox.'[26]

After receiving a penalty near the sideline, Messenger loudly told his team mates he would take the kick for goal and to 'Go on, get over, I'll never miss this. If I do you will have a chance at scoring.' They moved across, and most of the Glebe players went with them. Messenger then short-punted a kick over the head of the defender standing on the mark, collected the ball and dived over for the try.[27]

The season wasn't over for Messenger. The win by Easts in the second grade Final merely gained them two more points on the competition table tally. This drew them level with the first-placed Glebe, forcing a tie-off Final to determine the premiers. Messenger duly won the game for his team, scoring the only points of the match from a penalty goal from near the half-way line. *The Referee* described Messenger as 'quite the finest player' and 'he is good enough for the position of centre three-quarter for any team in Sydney.'[28]

Frustrated by his non-selection in the 1905 Australian team, Pat Walsh left for South Africa where he joined a Victorian rules club. Walsh is sitting in second row, third from right.

NSW REP PLAYS VICTORIAN RULES — IN AFRICA

The Australasian, a broadsheet newspaper with large reproductions of pictorials and photographs, was not a likely candidate to reveal some interesting news about rugby. In late 1905, *The Australasian* inadvertently revealed the whereabouts of Pat Walsh - he was in a photograph of a Victorian rules team in South Africa. Someone clipped the photograph from the newspaper and gave it to Walsh's family, but for the most part his travels remained a secret.

In Johannesburg, Walsh found a fledgling Victorian rules competition being played amongst ex-pats. As with many footballers in Newcastle, Walsh had dabbled in all the football codes and was no stranger to 'the Australian game.' He joined the 'Commonwealth Football Team,' quickly becoming popular enough to be elected vice-captain.

Commonwealth won the 'Australian Football League' premiership and duly sat for a team photograph with the trophy. The image was sent to Australia, where it appeared in *The Australasian*. All the players were named, including 'P. Walsh (vice-captain)' sitting alongside the club president.[29]

However, there was no news of Walsh's plans for the future.

THE TRIUMPHANT 'ALL BLACKS' TOUR

'The New Zealanders are still marching along the unbeaten path, thirteen victories against the Counties and crack clubs of England attesting to their quality,' reported *The Referee* in November of 1905.

The tourists were creating quite a stir in the British Isles, with the rapidity of the New Zealanders' passing and running disconcerting their opponents. 'The matches of the New Zealand team are now attracting very large attendances, and by this time the minds of the NZRU officials should be at ease respecting the financial side of the undertaking.'

The newspaper also printed a cablegram from London which stated: 'The match against England has been transferred to the Crystal Palace Ground owing to the enormous number of applications for seats. This is evidence of the remarkable impression the New Zealanders have already made on English sportsmen. They are giving rugby union football in England a lift that it badly needed. So far the team has not played in Scotland, Ireland or Wales.'[30]

Within a month of the tour commencing, in fact just the sixth game, the professional Northern Union (NU) clubs began making approaches to the New Zealand players. The team hadn't even yet been seen in the Northern counties.

'The doings of the New Zealanders are, as might be expected, arousing considerable interest in Northern Union circles,' reported *The Athletic News* in England (reproduced in *The Referee* in Sydney). 'When the Colonists played Gloucester last week a deputation from at least one Northern Union club was sent down to spy out the land with the object, of course, of seeing if it was possible to make a deal, and bring some of the New Zealand talent into the professional Union. From what we know and hear of the New Zealanders' aims and feelings, there is not the slightest prospect of any enterprise of this sort being successful.'[31]

The team, who soon came to be known as the 'All Blacks,' were only beaten once by the end of the thirty-two matches they played. For the first three months of the tour they were unbeaten. In that time they defeated the best of Scotland (11–7), Ireland (15–0) and England (15–0).

They then travelled to the North of England, and played the Yorkshire county side that was a shadow of what it had been a decade earlier, before the formation of the professional NU.

'In view of the great interest taken in the fixture,' the Yorkshire rugby union officials rented Headingley, home ground of the Leeds NU club. The All Blacks put on a spectacular display of rugby, winning by 40–0. Many of the 24,000 who witnessed the mid-week encounter were undoubtedly supporters, players and officials of the NU, and the All Blacks visit had a lasting-effect upon the locals.[32]

The Daily Chronicle said of the All Blacks during the tour, 'these New Zealanders do not stop short at stifling a rush. They turn defence into attack with such bewildering rapidity as to prove that the scrummage itself is a mere detail, the outcome of which is of the slightest consequence.'[33]

Three days after the Yorkshire match, the New Zealanders met Wales, suffering their only defeat of the tour. E.H.D. Sewell wrote of the Welsh match in his publication *The Book of Football*. 'I have often been asked whether they were stale when they reached Wales, and have no hesitation, in spite of their win over Yorkshire, in stating that Welshmen never saw the real New Zealand team. Several of the side were more or less crocked, including George Smith (broken collar-bone), who would certainly have played against Wales. Many people will long remember the terrific struggle at Cardiff Arms Park when Wales and New Zealand scored a try each, but that of the latter wasn't counted good. It was more a struggle than a game of football, and for the first time the New Zealanders showed they were human and possessed nerves.'[34]

The try that 'wasn't counted good' was the greatest controversy of the tour. According to the New Zealanders their backs broke out from near the half-way, which led to their winger, Bob Deans, reaching across the goal line in a tackle and placing the ball for a try. With the referee too far back to see, the Welsh defenders dragged Deans and the ball back into the field of play. The referee (who was from Scotland) called a scrum and the All Blacks hope of an undefeated tour was gone.[35]

NOT THE TRUE SPIRIT OF RUGBY FOOTBALL

The All Blacks weren't universally praised in the British Isles, many charged that their on-field play was against the spirit of amateurism. The timing and precision of their passing and running from hours of training, their eagerness to give away a penalty instead of a try, and the use of the maligned wing-forward position, were all the source of complaint and condemnation.

The most disapproved aspect of their play was their use of specialised forwards in scrum formations. The All Blacks didn't see it that way, nor would those back in New Zealand and Australia. They saw it as making the most within the rules, as they stood, and improving upon the skill and combination built within the game.

Sewell, like many others in England, disagreed. 'The best pack is that in which any man can take any place in it. The objection to the New

Zealand plan of "places" for each man cannot be argued against. Their plan, as played in this country, constituted unfair football, in that their pack never put their heads down to form a scrum, no matter whether their opponents were ready or not, until each man was in his allotted place. That is not the true spirit of rugby football. It is, in fact, a sacrifice of that precious spirit to the demands of an advance in the science of the game which would otherwise be admirable. Yet no referee ever penalised them for this unfair aspect of their splendid game. The best pack is the pack that has schooled itself to pack anyhow.'[36]

Each New Zealand forward had a pre-defined role at which he was 'skilled.' This was the problem. To practice and train to acquire expertise in a position or role was thought to demean the game into something akin to work or labour. The New Zealanders openly admitted that is exactly what they were doing. 'We have simply adopted the well-known industrial principle of specialisation,' said George Dixon, the team's manager. 'It stands to reason that a man continually practised in one position will perform the work of that position better than another who plays here one moment and there the next.'

Dixon also fired back some criticisms of his own claiming, 'rugby in England has, to put it mildly, stood still for a number of years.' He reasoned that English rugby was being held back from advancement as referees were prone to order scrums for infringements instead of free-kicks. Dixon also argued that a 'weakness of English rugby is the lack of direct tangible competition between clubs' as it is 'only under the stress and stimulus of competition that he (the footballer) is able to produce the best results.'

Dixon pointed out that most large cities in England had only one first-class rugby club, yet in much smaller New Zealand cities there were seven or eight Senior clubs. 'It is, without doubt,' he said, 'the rivalry which exists between these groups of local teams, and the ambition of the individual member to see his team secure the championship, that has been responsible for the advancement of football methods in New Zealand.'[37]

TALKING TO THE NORTHERN UNION

The financial and popular success of the All Blacks visit created a development totally at odds with the intentions of their organisers, the NZRU and the RFU.

'What many old players like myself would like to see would be a match between a picked Northern Union team and the Colonials,' wrote Fred Cooper to a London daily paper after the All Blacks thrashed Yorkshire. 'I have no hesitation in saying that I would pick fifteen players who would willingly give their services to play such a match, the proceeds of which could be devoted to charity, and I have little doubt that my side would achieve victory. The wearers of the silver fern have not been defeated, but they have not played the cream of English football. Such men play under the banner of the Northern Union.'

Cooper, a Welshman who played for the Bradford club in the 1890s, earning representative honours for Yorkshire under rugby union and then NU rules, was in a position to assess the

New Zealanders' opposition. 'The men who opposed New Zealand at Headingley are the weakest lot who ever donned Yorkshire jerseys,' said Cooper, 'and the visitors did not achieve anything out of the common when they beat them. I may add that Jack Toothill, the famous international, and Albert Goldthorpe, prince of goal droppers, are in accord with my views.'[38]

The NU was quite prepared and able to hold out a substantial gate guarantee for a match against the All Blacks. Since the divide of 1895, the NU had been isolated from international competition, apart from matches between England and a composite 'Other Nationalities' team comprised of Welsh and Scottish players scattered amongst the professional clubs. They knew any formal offer to an amateur All Black would be rejected outright in the midst of a tour. J.H. 'Jack' Smith, from the Widnes club and NU president at the time, made no official moves, but discussions with some of the All Blacks took place away from the public glare.

New Zealand's George Smith, during the 1905 All Blacks tour of Great Britain.

George Smith was the player believed to have had the most significant conversations with NU officials. Smith, who was also a successful hurdler and track runner, had been to England in 1902 to participate in the Amateur Athletic Association's British championships (winning the 120 yards hurdles from a strong field).[39]

Smith also knew George Stephenson, a New Zealand footballer and NU player. In the early 1890s, Stephenson was a junior auctioneer with his father's business in Dunedin. Sent to Bradford (in Yorkshire) to learn about the woollen industry, he took up rugby for Manningham, but was back home when the club joined the NU in 1895. Stephenson gained representative honours for Otago, and he and Smith (for Auckland) were star three-quarter backs of the late 1890s. Stephenson went back to the North of England in the early 1900s, were he joined the NU club Hunslet, thus becoming the first professional rugby player from the colonies. While there, he organised a professional theatrical company and toured it successfully across England.[40]

How much support Stephenson provided to Smith remains unknown. During the All Blacks tour Smith was encouraged by what he seen and learnt of the NU and the conditions enjoyed by their professional rugby players. It was enough for him to speculate on the possibilities of returning to England on his own, or with a team, to play professional rugby.[41]

NZRU PROFITS £10,000 FROM ALL BLACKS

After a short sojourn in France, most of the New Zealanders finally left for home. They sailed across the Atlantic to New York, took a train to San Francisco and shipped back across the Pacific Ocean to New Zealand.[42] With 'Massa' Johnston too sick to travel, Charlie Seeling stayed behind to keep him company and look after his needs. Harper and Glenn decided to see some more of the world, and travelled home via the Middle East and Indian Ocean. They also stopped over in Sydney in March 1906 where they were entertained by NSWRU officials, before finally reaching New Zealand.[43]

On the team's long journey home, discussion amongst some of the men eventually came around to the challenges made to them by the NU. It was perhaps true that they hadn't beaten the best rugby footballers in England, over half the clubs in England belonged to the NU. Welsh players, some they had played against, even some of the clubs, were now 'going North' to join the professionals.[44]

Would the New Zealanders ever be invited back to Great Britain? Scotland and Ireland made a lot of noise to the RFU about the 3s daily allowance given to the All Black players, claiming it was a form of professionalism. Even if the rate was maintained at 3s, the likelihood of any New Zealanders ever making such a tour appeared remote. The way they played on the field was criticised by the English for not following the amateur ideals. Australian rugby 'played to the whistle' as well, and tried to emulate the New Zealanders.

Where did the future of Australasian rugby lie? For that matter, where did the future of rugby in Great Britain lie?

The team was bringing home a profit to the NZRU of £8,908, in addition to the £1,000 earned from the matches in Sydney and New Zealand before the team sailed for England. This represented £370 a man, roughly equal to three times a working man's annual wages. After the team arrived back in New Zealand, the news of the tour's profit was printed in the Sydney newspapers. *The Referee* also quoted the difficulties some of the players were immediately faced with. 'One member of the team landed home with less than a shilling in his pocket, while another could only boast 3s/9p in addition to which both men had to look round for fresh employment. Other members of the team were in pretty low financial waters on reaching the colony, and three of them lost their old jobs.'

One club official asked, 'Was it reasonable to ask those young men to absent themselves from their homes for months, perhaps lose their positions, and then expect them, after enriching the NZRU to the extent of thousands of pounds, to rest satisfied with an allowance of 3s a day?'[45]

That is not to suggest any of the All Blacks had regrets at their decision to tour. None of them would forgo the experiences and memories they gained from the tour. But they had shown that such a tour could be organised and it could make a marvellous profit. Would working-class players be prepared to give their services freely, knowing the profits that would be made? It was only natural that men (within and out of rugby) in New Zealand, NSW, and Queensland would ask these questions — and examine alternatives.

The matter of how the tour's profit would be spent was considered by the NZRU at its first meeting of 1906. *The Referee* reported that, 'General speakers thought that no question of grab should enter into the disposal of the money. The surplus was held in trust for the footballers of New Zealand. It should be invested on business lines, giving preference to footballers. Ultimately, £5,000 was invested on fixed deposit, and the balance was loaned to the local Unions for improvement or purchase of grounds.'

The All Blacks and their manager had to content themselves with the accolades of the NZRU committee. 'This meeting desires to express its high appreciation of the services rendered by Mr Dixon as manager of the New Zealand team, and also of the spirit displayed by the team.' The players' position was made all the clearer to them after the NZRU voted its secretary and treasurer bonuses, of 75 and 35 guineas respectively, 'in view of the large amount of work which fell on the Union last year.'[46]

JAMES GILTINAN AND VICTOR TRUMPER

When James Giltinan, as tour manager, led a 'Sydney' cricket team, that included Victor Trumper, on a visit to Goulburn in mid-April 1906, the future of tours to England in both cricket and rugby was a hot-topic.[47] While rugby administrators were facing criticism for raking-in large tour profits from the unpaid labour of their footballers, the state cricket associations were trying to implement the same controls, ending the days of Australian cricketers organising and profiting from tours to England.

Cricket's newly formed 'Australian Board of Control' (ABC) issued an invitation to London's Marylebone Cricket Club to send an England team to Australia for the 1906/07 summer. On the advice of prominent Australian cricketers and the Melbourne Cricket Club, the Marylebone club chose to ignore the ABC, instead opening their own negotiations for the tour. The Melbourne club and its contacts in Sydney secretly signed the best cricketers, including Trumper and M.A. 'Monty' Noble, to form an Australian team to play England.[48]

Trumper had toured with Australian teams to England in 1899, 1902, and 1905, sharing in the generous profits. He and other senior Australian cricketers were not keen to simply let the ABC put an end to player-controlled tours. *The Bulletin* claimed that Trumper and Giltinan were two of a 'number of gentlemen (who) thought they saw a chance of placing cricket on a money basis. They and the Melbourne Cricket Club made a determined effort to grab control of the summer game with a view to running it on commercial lines.'[49]

But the Melbourne Cricket Club's challenge failed. The ABC took over international tours, and the players, instead of being cricket's chief organisers and beneficiaries, became servants of the sport. The lot of the Australian cricketer was now no better than that of the rugby footballers. Unlike in cricket, however, two organisations controlled rugby in England, the RFU and the professional NU. Giltinan and Trumper, inspired by the financial success of the All Blacks tour, turned their attention to rugby.

'While cricket was being attacked,' continued *The Bulletin* [somewhat facetiously], 'some of the brilliant gentlemen mixed up in that venture discovered that there was considerable dissatisfaction among footballers over the allowances for loss of time and the absence of any proper fund from which injured players could draw assistance while laid up. The NSWRU's affiliation with the degenerate and antiquated English Rugby Union (RFU) made reform impossible.'[50]

VICTORIAN RULES ON THE RISE

In Brisbane and Newcastle, the district rugby competitions collapsed and returned to the old social club system. In Sydney, Richard Arnold of the NSWRU spoke out against the district club system, claiming it hadn't been a success. 'Most of the players on leaving school are preferring to join whatever club they please (under the 'City and Suburban' competitions), and not be forced into any particular club.'[51] Other players, were satisfied to stay in the second grade or Borough competitions.

Meanwhile, interest in Victorian rules football was growing in Sydney, with a credible club competition now on offer. Soccer too was gaining popularity in some of the suburbs, particularly around Balmain and Granville. While neither Victorian rules nor soccer in Sydney was encumbered by the rules of amateurism, they ostensibly followed them anyway, primarily as they were not financially strong.

The Victorian Football League in Melbourne was not a professional game either, even with its large crowds and gate-takings. But it could be flexible when required and could financially compensate players. The NSWRU's rules, (particularly against professionalism), could always be enforced if there was no competitor. As long as it remained the preferred football game of Sydney, players had no choice. L. Deer of the NSWRU issued a warning, though, 'There is no doubt that the Victorian game has got a good hold in schools.'[52]

If Victorian rules continued to grow, so would the prospect of hugely popular NSW v Victoria inter-state matches. The NSWRU would then find itself in danger. With international competition difficult to arrange, it could not afford to lose its grip on NSW football. This was a concern not only for the NSWRU, but for all rugby enthusiasts.

Rugby had beaten off the southern foe before, but by 1905 many freely stated that rugby football had deteriorated and was again on the wane. With young men avoiding the district clubs, and increasing numbers of school boys taking up Victorian rules, rugby in NSW needed to be enlivened.

MESSENGER GIVES RUGBY A MUCH-NEEDED BOOST

'Messrs Messenger and Co. are now Senior players, with the limelight of public attention and the stimulus of public interest and admiration upon them. The past is gone. Let us congratulate them on their skill, for its exhibition last week (for Eastern Suburbs) surpassed the nimble young men of South Sydney,' wrote *The Referee*.

Eastern Suburbs started the 1906 Sydney season in a blaze. From a team barely able to win only twelve months earlier, they had given the club competition 'an impulse that had been badly wanting.'[53] In the opening two rounds, 'the Easterners' had defeated their neighbours Sydney and the 1905 premiers South Sydney. The latter match was held at the Sydney Sports Ground before a bumper crowd near 15,000. The crush of spectators trying to enter the ground was so great that the gates fronting Moore Park were pushed open and hundreds streamed in for free.

'They defeated South Sydney in a fair, and square contest, hot, fast, and at times fierce,' offered *The Referee* in its account of the match. 'The Eastern Suburbs backs to a man played well. All were fast, all determined and plucky. J. D'Alpuget, as fullback was reliable and cool, and his judgement in line kicking was never at fault. All four three-quarters individually were good. Collectively they have yet to perfect their game. Messenger played a very fine game, he has great ability, is very reliable, and very resourceful. His individuality is so strong that his supports find it difficult to follow him. But he will probably develop into a high-class centre three-quarter. Rosenfeld, the five-eighth, is a really good, solid and clever player. He will probably cultivate trickiness in a greater degree as he gains experience in Senior football. In defence he was admirable.'[54]

The premiership was also given additional interest by the inclusion of two new clubs, St George and Manly. The St George club was bolstered by the capture of Harold Judd, under the residential rule, who became their first captain.

After only a few weeks of the 1906 season, it was already 'tolerably sure to be the biggest on record in the matter of attendances at Sydney club football.'

The MRU formed a close alignment with the trustees of the Sports Ground, often scheduling two first grade matches on the same afternoon at the ground: 'a big bill of fare for sixpence, the ground should scarcely hold all who are likely to put in an appearance.'[55] The SCG management were inclined to only allow representative matches.

When the NSWRU's representative season started with a visit from country teams, they too used the Sports Ground for a 'double-bill,' scheduling South Sydney to play New England at 2 p.m., with Eastern Suburbs v Central Western to follow.

Souths claimed that, as premiers for 1905, they should have had 'pride of position on the programme' and not be relegated to the under-card. At the time, Easts were 'heading the table' and had been responsible for drawing much larger crowds to the 1906 competition. The NSWRU refused to change the matches around and South Sydney, true to their word, did not play. Their place was taken by the Sydney club side who had not been given a match at all.[56]

Selection controversy was again the centre of discussion a week later when the Metropolis Firsts and Seconds teams were chosen to play the combined Country at the SCG. The first placed Eastern Suburbs team had no players in the Firsts, and Messenger was placed in the Seconds, on the wing. The Easts fullback, D'Alpuget was not listed at all.

'The non-selection of Messenger as centre three-quarter is puzzling. He is clearly an abler all-round player than any of those chosen,' wrote *The Referee*. 'A match of this character would afford him experience valuable for the inter-state matches. The form shown by Messenger and D'Alpuget merely confirms the impression that the Metropolitan selectors are indecipherable in passing them over.' No one could work out who would be chosen from match to match, or in which position. Swannell was chosen in the forwards for the Firsts along with Burdon, Judd and Peter Burge, while the Glebe halfback Chris McKivat, was chosen at five-eighth.[57]

NEWCASTLE'S WALSH JOINS AN AUCKLAND CLUB

Pat Walsh returned to Newcastle from South Africa. He learned that the Newcastle Branch Union had put a protest to the NSWRU and demanded an explanation for his exclusion from the Australian team, but there had been 'no good result.' The Branch Union also continued to call for the NSWRU's inquiry of the 'Dobson incident' to be re-opened, eventually giving up after two years of trying.[58]

Walsh's stay in Australia was short. In April 1906 he suddenly left for New Zealand. *The Newcastle Morning Herald* reported that Walsh 'has taken his departure for Auckland where he expects to receive permanent employment in the railway workshops.' His Carlton club team mates 'were anxious to accord Walsh a fitting send-off but owing to his being called away suddenly there was not time to do anything in that direction. Last season Walsh was badly treated by the NSW selectors, and he cannot be blamed for the step he has taken. How he came to be left out of the team that toured New Zealand has not yet been satisfactorily been explained. His Newcastle admirers will all join in the hope that he will prosper in the Land of the Moa, where his capabilities are not likely to be overlooked as they were here.'[59]

Upon arriving in Auckland, Walsh joined the Parnell club. His first game was a fund-raiser between the 'Cricketers' (cricketers who play football) and the 'Non-cricketers,' the proceeds of the match going to the Auckland Cricket Association.

The New Zealand Herald reported that Walsh played with the Cricketers alongside Dave Gallaher, 'captain of the late All Blacks,' and George Smith who 'some of the Home critics singled out as the greatest rugby three-quarter back it had ever been their lot to see. The ball to be used is that employed in the great match in which the New Zealand team played against Wales.' Some of New Zealand's most notable footballers were scattered amongst the two sides.[60]

Smith played for the Auckland City club, who were premiers in 1905. In a season free of any international fixtures, the NSWRU invited Auckland City to come to Sydney for a series of matches against local club teams in July 1906.

One of their matches was scheduled to be played on a double-bill with the NSW v Queensland contest.

CHAPTER SEVEN

THE GREAT REUNION

AUCKLAND AND QUEENSLAND TEAMS IN SYDNEY

With the Brisbane stage of the 1906 inter-state series over, the NSW and Queensland teams made their way to Sydney for the return matches. The Blues travelled by train, stopping over at West Maitland where they defeated the Northern Districts team 19–3. Queensland decided to send its team via sea. 'They are a steady lot,' reported *The Referee* 'and under the genial QRU secretary they should have a good time, though the prospects of the sea voyage are not relished by some of the party, including the manager.'[1] Amongst the Queensland team were Mickey Dore (captain), Peter Flanagan, Allen 'Butcher' Oxlade, Phil Carmichael, George Watson, Jack Fihelly and Esmond Parkinson.

The gathering of footballers in Sydney swelled further when the Auckland City team arrived as well. Docking into Sydney at 3 a.m. on the Saturday morning, the New Zealanders had been delayed by a heavy crossing. 'However nimble they are on land, they have far to travel before they become accustomed to the sea,' wrote *The Referee*.[2] Auckland's first match was that afternoon, against Newtown.

The Auckland team, in red and black, played four matches against Sydney clubs in just under two weeks in mid-July. They were a very formidable team, having not been defeated in many seasons. Auckland easily beat Newtown and Glebe, but seemed lethargic in a lucky win over South Sydney and in a loss to University. Interest in the visit of the Auckland team was high. The side included four of the 1905 All Blacks: George Nicholson, George Tyler, Charlie Seeling and George Smith. Also in the team were talented footballers Lance Todd and William Tyler.

The tour was meant to provide a comparison between the standard of club football in Sydney and Auckland. However, the performance of the New Zealanders, and some of their opponents, was affected by the amount of off-field entertainment surrounding the visit. 'Auckland City on Saturday evening dined with the Metropolitan and other Rugby Union officials, and the Newtown club, at the A.B.C. Café rooms,' began *The Referee* in reviewing the first four days of the New Zealanders' stay. 'On Monday they took part in a tram outing. Yesterday they inspected

Tooth's Brewery. On Sunday they had an excursion on the harbour. On Monday night they attended Newtown smoke concert. Last night they witnessed boxing at the North Sydney Club. To-night they will be the guests of the South Sydney Club at "the smoker," to-morrow a motor-car outing will be followed by a theatre night. And there are other diversions to follow during the rest of their stay in Sydney.'[3]

It was traditional at such functions for sports to invite officials and notables from the wider sporting community. The opportunity to meet with members of the famous All Blacks was high on the priorities of most.

The papers aired some grievances after the Newtown match. While over a hundred people were invited by the MRU to the after-match dinner, there was no offer to the Newtown players. 'Will the MRU explain why so many non-entities were invited?' asked *The Sunday Sun*. 'Surely the players, who have to put up with all the knocks of the game, should be given preference over those who evince less interest in the sport.'[4]

Indeed before the match, the Newtown players, aware they were not going to be invited, staged a strike in the dressing-room and threatened 'not to go on and give the packed audience a run for its money.' Harry Hammill convinced his team mates not 'to let our friends down just for the sake of a feed,' and the game went ahead. He admitted though, 'it was very paltry of the Union.' While the Newtown players remained disgruntled, for subsequent after-match functions the MRU made sure Auckland's opponents were invited. As far as the players were concerned though, it was another event 'surely sowing seeds of discord.'[5]

PLAYERS PAY THEIR WAY — BUT NOT OFFICIALS

Entertainment provided for the Queenslanders by the NSWRU was also much discussed. Surprisingly, it was Blair Swannell who alerted the NSW players to what was happening.

Swannell had been up to his usual tricks in the inter-state matches in Brisbane. During a line-out, one of the Queensland players was punched 'a crashing blow.' The crowd 'roared for vengeance,' and the referee duly sent Swannell from the field. On this occasion though, it was another NSW player who had landed the punch. 'The guilty man himself hated Swannell' and no one came forward to save the Englishman from suspension. Most thought Swannell had got away with so much in other matches that he deserved the penalty anyway.[6]

'To show there was no animosity I rolled up to the NSWRU rooms to attend the official reception to the Queensland team,' explained

Swannell to *The Australian Star* some time afterwards.[7] 'Half-way up the stairs I was stopped by a burly policeman.' Swannell was refused entry as he didn't have a 'ticket of admission.' The Englishman told the officer he was a current representative player and should be allowed to pass, but the policeman could not be swayed.

'Of course he was just obeying instructions, but it got my back up,' said Swannell. As a club delegate to the MRU, Swannell had an alternative course of action. 'Producing my card I stated that I was an official of the MRU and intended going up to the MRU rooms. The policeman was compelled to let me pass. I entered the Union rooms to find them nicely filled with Union officials and the tables covered with sandwiches, biscuits, beer, whisky etc., which as a "rep" player I had helped to provide, though such was not for me, only for officials. Once within the room I was invited to stop, but incensed at such treatment, I naturally refused.'

'Going downstairs I met another "rep" who had also been stopped by the policeman. He had however graciously been allowed to pass on the nod of an official.' Just outside the building Swannell met three more 'reps' en route to the reception. 'I explained matters,' continued Swannell, 'but said if they kow-towed to some official they would be passed. They said they'd be ---! Well, they intimated they would not attend the reception.'

'Is that fair treatment for "reps"?' asked Swannell. 'In England, once an International, always an International — any England "rep" can get a pass to one of the best seats from whence to view the match. That ought to obtain in NSW, but does not; old NSW "reps" must "pay their way — not so officials.'

If the players were arriving at the Unions' rooms with full expectations of being entertained, then presumably in previous seasons they had no such difficulties. The NSWRU's decision to suddenly deny entry to NSW players was particularly ill-timed. They also introduced a requirement that NSW players must obtain, at their own expense, a medical clearance certificate from a doctor confirming they had no injuries. *The Referee* argued that 'surely it is going too far to expect players to pay the doctor's fee in such a case.'[8] With George Smith in town ready to talk of the possibilities of NU rugby, the NSW and Queensland players were in the mood to listen.

THE LITTLE AND RIDDELL ACCIDENT

The NSWRU placed the Auckland v Glebe match on the under-card to the inter-state clash. With the opportunity to see some of the best players from 'the three colonies,' over 32,000 spectators flocked to the SCG. It was the largest crowd ever on hand at a NSW v Queensland match.

The Aucklanders faced a tough challenge from a Glebe team that included Chris McKivat, Charlie Hedley, Albert Conlon and Peter Moir.

The 'Reds' took a commanding 8–0 lead early in the second half, but the visitors fought back to edge in front 11–8. With a great finish looming the crowd became quite excited.

Ten minutes before full-time, G. Riddell (Glebe) and C. Little (Auckland) ran towards the ball in open play and they both tried to kick it forward. They collided and both collapsed to the ground in agony — each with a broken leg. According to those present the collision was one of the heaviest ever witnessed on a football field. By the time Riddell and Little were carried off the field, their team mates had no desire to continue the game. Despite the large crowd, the referee declared full-time and the match ended early.

Mickey Dore – Queensland's star halfback from 1903 to 1907.

Both players were immediately taken to hospital. Their ordeal was a long way from over, as they faced a lengthy rehabilitation period, which for Little was particularly distressing as it meant he would not be able to travel back to Auckland for two months.

Smith, Nicholson, George Tyler, and many of the Auckland and Glebe players stayed at the ground to watch NSW v Queensland.

MESSENGER SHREDS THE CRITICS

The Blues team included Dally Messenger, however, his selection as a centre was heavily criticised — his propensity for roving about the field looking for opportunities worked against established rugby union principles of combination, staying in position and team work. Messenger said the 'critics went berserk' over his selection and that 'with some of them everything was hide-bound convention — anyone who broke the conventions was useless.'[9]

Messenger was fast becoming the most popular footballer with the Sydney public, but with the press and the rugby community itself he was causing a divide. Lauded for his individual brilliance, he was loathed by many for not being a team player. Messenger felt the barbs, but decided 'to play my own game, to rove as I liked.'

In a performance many rated as the most exhilarating seen in an inter-state contest, NSW overran the visitors 25–3. Quite apart from his exceptional goal and line kicking, Messenger provided some of the day's best play. *The Referee* recalling two efforts that resulted in tries for the Blues. 'Suddenly from a scrummage at half-way, Matthews (NSW) came away on the open side of the field. He gave the ball to Mandible, to Russell, to Messenger, who cut through. He sent it to Wickham, back to Messenger, who gave it back to Wickham, who scored in the corner. It was a very brilliant piece of play — the ball travelling at great speed.'

George Smith visited Sydney in 1906 with the Auckland City R.F.C. team.

In a later move, NSW punted down field where 'the Queensland backs went for the ball leisurely, and before the fullback was able to reach it the nippy Messenger flew along, gathered it in and was across the line in a shot.'[10]

The Sunday Sun interviewed George Smith after the match: 'When asked his opinion of the game, he said he never saw the Blues play better.' About the impressive display by the home team's backs, Smith said, 'Their passing was sure, and their line-kicking splendid. It was a good game to watch, and a great improvement has taken place in the style of game you play during the last couple of years.'[11]

Players and officials alike looked forward to that evening, when the NSWRU would host a function where all four teams (NSW, Queensland, Auckland and Glebe) and many others would be in attendance. It was the largest ever gathering of the best footballers in Australasian rugby and provided an unexpected opportunity for them all to meet and talk.

THE GREAT REUNION OF FOOTBALLERS

'There was a great reunion of footballers at the A.B.C. Café last night, when the NSWRU entertained the visiting rugby teams at dinner,' told

The Sunday Sun. 'The Queensland representative team and the Auckland City team were the honoured guests.'[12]

Also amongst the large numbers present (in excess of 100) were the NSW team, players from Glebe and University, as well as many of the prominent Union officials and men connected with the game, including Billy Howe (who refereed the game) and James McMahon.

The room was 'tastefully decorated with evergreens, and the tables were adorned with the colours' of the four teams that had played that day. *The Herald* reported that the 'gathering was an enthusiastic one.'[13] As Paddy Lane pointed out, 'It is a unique thing that the teams from three great colonies should meet. If the Queenslanders are our brothers, then the New Zealanders were first cousins.' After a meal and the obligatory speeches, toasts and singing, 'a very pleasant function was brought to an early conclusion.' However, the evening did not end there.

'Subsequently the company visited the Lyceum Theatre,' reported *The Herald*, 'and witnessed a reproduction on canvas [a movie] of the match between the New Zealand team and Glamorganshire, and also the return of the All Blacks. The audience included some of the players, whose "counterfeit presentment" were thrown on the screen, viz., Tyler, Nicholson, Seeling and Smith.'

On the following two evenings the Auckland team continued to be entertained, with the Glebe and Sydney clubs their hosts.

THE GENIE IS OUT OF THE BOTTLE

The festivities afforded George Smith an opportunity to meet, talk and make contacts within NSW and Queensland rugby about the implications of the All Blacks tour and his future plans (which included retiring from rugby union football). The NZRU organised tour to Great Britain had produced a lot of money, none of which went to the All Blacks. This had a lasting effect on rugby players in New Zealand and Australia.[14]

Smith confided with a chosen group of men about the possibilities a professional rugby team visiting England to play NU clubs. One footballer Smith formed a close association with was Glebe's Peter Moir. There are strong suggestions Smith met with Jack Fihelly (Queensland) and Giltinan in 1906 — this could only have occurred during the Auckland team's visit to Sydney.[15] Smith's initiative probably convinced Giltinan that the formation of a professional rugby team amongst the footballers of Sydney and Brisbane was worth pursuing. It is interesting to note that George Stephenson, the New Zealander who had played for NU club Hunslet, and who was a contemporary of Smith's, also passed through Sydney that week.[16]

Smith and the Aucklanders witnessed for themselves Messenger's prodigious talent, and had the opportunity to talk with him — after his star performance for NSW he was already well on the way to being one of *The Referee's* five 'most outstanding' players of the season. One of the other players named by *The Referee* was University's Herbert 'Paddy' Moran.[17]

A forward in the NSW team, Moran provided an insight into the state of his team mates. 'Cocksure yet shy, hyper-critical yet childlike in their belief in what a newspaper says,' said Moran. 'Humorous, but quick to resent anything unfair, hating the shirker terribly. Their one test is virility. These men in a war will never follow an officer merely because he is an aristocrat by birth. They do not easily forgive a wrong. They expect and demand a fair deal.'[18]

The players talked of how inadequate and embarrassingly meagre the 3s expense allowance for representative players was. They spoke of how players were tossed aside and ignored by selectors. How some All Blacks arrived home with no money, no job, and how others had seen their families go without while they were away in Britain. How they made £10,000 for the NZRU. How 'rep' players, current and old, were ignored while the Unions entertained, dined and rewarded themselves on the money earned from the matches.

They discussed the ill-treatment handed out to Pat Walsh; how he had moved to Auckland to start again. How Swannell had waltzed into a Test jersey; the 'spirit' with which he played the game. How the NSWRU favoured their links with the RFU in England; how they even sided with Bedell-Sivright's tourists instead of taking the word of their own players.

Sydney University's Herbert 'Paddy' Moran – rated alongside Messenger as one of the most outstanding footballers of 1906.

They lamented the structure of NSW football that denied the Sydney clubs a say at the NSWRU level. How everyone was making money from football — yet representative footballers couldn't get a decent allowance, let alone recompense for time they were away from work. New Zealand was coming to Sydney in twelve months time to play

NSW and Australia in four matches. There were 32,000 people at the inter-state game — the crowds for the 1907 All Blacks visit would be a financial goldmine. They talked about the huge crowds in England; the gates these games generated and the benefits NU players enjoyed.

They remembered their injuries and those of their team mates; of Auckland's Little and Glebe's Riddell, and the long lay-up they faced as a result of the injuries from the accident. It would be up to their team mates to look after them while they couldn't work, yet look how many paid to see the game!

Why should it be this way?

Their desire was 'to make the lot of the player a better one. We want no high-priced officials, nor any unnecessary incidental expenditure. We do not want to go cap in hand to any autocratic, conservative, hundred-years-behind-the-time body, to ask favours for any distressed player. We want our own funds, so we can grant relief to players ourselves.'[19]

AUCKLANDERS ACCUSED OF PROFESSIONALISM

'The Aucklanders left for home after their match against South Sydney, an early contest before the Metropolitan team played Queensland at the SCG,' reported *The Referee*. 'The Queensland and Metropolitan teams ceased playing as the visitors were leaving the ground's pavilion for the boat. The teams on the field came across to the edge of the track in front of the pavilion. They gave three cheers for the Aucklanders who then bunched and, taking the lead from their jolly-looking manager Mr Endean, gave their war-cry. Afterwards the band struck up "Old Lang Syne" and other tunes, and the parting was quite an event.'[20]

After such a hectic week-and-a-half of football, entertainment and socialising, *The Herald* thought 'they will undoubtedly be glad of a rest in the berths of the steamer today.' *The Referee* wrote, 'The Aucklanders were entertained with much hospitality during their stay and one fears that it did not help them to show their very best form.'[21]

At their homecoming they 'were welcomed by a good number of local enthusiasts, who gathered at the wharf.' Also present were the usual throng of reporters. Smith and Tyler had returned to New Zealand more impressed with NSW rugby than in the past, particularly their backs. They told *The Auckland Herald* that 'club football in Sydney is of a much better class than has been seen in Auckland for the past few seasons. NSW would no doubt have a very fine representative team. One notable feature in the improved play of the Australians was the splendid fielding of the ball by the backs.'[22]

The Auckland team were also confronted with accusations that their tour had the sniff of professionalism, with calls for the NZRU to investigate. How was it possible for a club side to travel overseas without its players having been paid for their three weeks away from work?

According to *The Auckland Star*, the calls for an investigation of the Auckland Rugby Union (ARU) and the tour were dismissed. 'Do they suppose that the NZRU would have sanctioned the tour if there was any possibility of professionalism creeping in, or that the ARU, even if lacking common honesty, would have connived at an action which would disqualify half a dozen of its representative team?'[23]

There was also growing opinion in New Zealand that play was becoming more aggressive and competitive — all signs that winning-at-any-cost was driving the motives of clubs and players.

The Referee reported that, 'Mr F. T. Evans, the well-known New Zealand referee, when seen on the subject, said he did not think there was any time in the history of rugby football in New Zealand that demanded more stringent measures on the part of the committees and the various Unions throughout the colony to keep the game pure than at present.'[24]

Evans added that if action was not taken 'the better class of people would shortly take little interest in rugby. If the youth of the colony are stopped from playing on account of these things, what is to become of the game?'

LITTLE AND RIDDELL GET HELP — EVENTUALLY

'Little and Riddell are getting along as well as possible at St Vincent's Hospital,' noted *The Referee*. The players injured in the Auckland v Glebe match faced an extensive hospital bill. Severe injuries, such as a broken leg, were uncommon but not unheard of. The existing insurance cover was adequate for initial treatment, although payments were 'capped,' and when injuries were severe enough to necessitate a long stay in hospital they fell short. The MRU, the NSWRU, or the player's club would sometimes make an additional contribution to assist with medical costs, however the involvement of any, or all, of the three was arbitrary.[25]

Time away from work recuperating was another matter. Players understood the risks in playing football and acknowledged the outcome of a debilitating injury. It was 'their look-out.' Even after severe injury, and extensive time off work, many footballers chose to restart their playing careers. Some kept playing with chronic or recurring injuries.[26]

While friendly societies [insurers] provided personal medical insurance and sick benefits to working men, they generally wouldn't cover injuries sustained on the football field. A player could expect some time away from work as a result of injury, but no more perhaps than might be asked for to attend a country or inter-state football tour.

For the most part, in working class communities, if someone fell on hard times everyone rallied around to help him. The players would never ask for assistance, never admit they were suffering, always understate how bad an injury was — they were too proud for that. Calls for compensation were not heard loudly until 1906, when the MRU and NSWRU, enjoying strong earnings from matches, failed to spend on improving conditions for players — the men who provided the entertainment.

In the case of Little and Riddell, it was Glebe who came to the aid of the players. They held a benefit concert for the footballers when they were released from hospital a few weeks later. The 'NSWRU were written to for their patronage and support' for the evening, but they declined, advising 'that the Union could not lend their patronage or support to anything that would tend to make any player a professional.'[27] The NSWRU viewed the benefits paid from fundraisers as professionalism.

As it was, Glebe proceeded with the event, and raised about £45 each for Little and Riddell, roughly three months wages each.[28] Glebe did not normally do this. Alec Burdon had received no assistance in 1904 from Glebe or the NSWRU to help with his long lay-off caused by injury in the Brisbane Test match. Glebe's decision to become involved in the Little and Riddell case, and NSWRU's failure to contribute support, exposed both bodies to criticism for their treatment of injured players.

Joe McGraw, former Glebe member, spoke out against the poor treatment of J. Woods. A Glebe wing three-quarter in first grade, Woods was a club mate of Burdon and Peter Moir. 'The Glebe club has decided to give a benefit to Riddell and Little,' said McGraw in a letter published in The Referee.[29] 'It is time the committee of the Glebe club did something to benefit members who get injured while playing for the club. There is one case in particular I would like to draw attention to — 'Puddin' Woods. He has been injured times out of a number whilst playing for the club.' McGraw noted that Woods has 'had his leg broken, his collar-bone broken, and has had concussion of the brain. He has had to undergo an operation for appendicitis — no doubt brought on by a bump whilst playing football — which has incapacitated him from work for some time.'

McGraw took exception to Glebe helping Little, the Auckland player. 'It is better to be a "stranger in a strange land" in order to receive sympathy from your club mates. The proper body to arrange for a benefit to Riddell and Little is the NSWRU seeing that they were injured in a match under their control at which 32,000 paid for entrance.

The Union ought to donate £100 to each player. The Union hoards up thousands of pounds every year and all the players get is the hard knocks and bumps.'

Soon after McGraw's comments the NSWRU stepped in with financial assistance to Little and Riddell. 'It may be stated that the New South Wales Union is defraying all the hospital and other expenses of these injured players.' This action didn't quell the criticism. Having made it clear that the fundraiser amounted to professionalism, the NSWRU was ridiculed for not stopping Riddell and Little from taking the payments. It was seen as further evidence of the Union's inconsistent methods. 'Is that not winking at professionalism when it suits?' asked one supporter of the players.[30]

Although some players were assisted when it was expedient for the Unions to make exceptions, the bulk of the men, such as 'Puddin' Woods, had to get by with nothing.

HOW SHOULD THE MRU SPEND THE MONEY?

While calls to compensate injured footballers forced to miss work were growing, the question of club footballers generally receiving travelling allowances or payment for lost working time was rarely raised. Club football was played on the non-working Saturday afternoon, with kick-off after 3 p.m. and most grounds within easy reach.

The only players who had a case for payment of lost time were those who owned or managed a business, such as a grocer or butcher that remained open on Saturday afternoons. If they wanted to play football, they had to pay for someone to work in their place. Most could not afford it and didn't play. In any event, it was still a breach of the RFU's rules. However, if clubs were desperate enough for the player, they or a supporter would pay for his replacement.[31]

It was only at the state representative level that players needed leave from work. Agitation for increased allowances continued to grow amongst the players at this level — since first being raised in 1897 the issue had never been adequately addressed. On occasions the needs of some were met with a 'nudge and a wink' from a state official — particularly the more important members of the team. However, this was seen as favouritism and deceitful. Many felt that it was demeaning to have to ask and receive secret payments.[32]

While a club player didn't need compensation for loss of time, he did incur other expenses. As well as having to pay the annual 5s subscription, '...he had to buy his own playing outfit. If he lived at North Sydney, and his team was playing at the Cricket Ground, he had to pay his own fare to reach the place — the same as the thousands who paid their shillings to see him and his club mates play. If he got hurt during the match and was unable to work, that was his lookout. He would (perhaps) get a couple of guineas from the Union, while any other support would have to come from his club mates, who would organise concerts to raise funds. At the start of the season each club received £30 for training expenses which, with three grades, hardly covered basic needs.'

In the days when the MRU spent all its earnings back into the game, it was difficult to present any argument that players should be compensated. Through 1906 the crowd interest in club rugby dramatically increased and consequently, so did the bank account of the MRU. Their preference to horde their income instead of spending it on the needs of clubs and players gave the dissatisfied something to squabble over.

This was mirrored in the players' working lives as well. With Australia in the midst of an economic boom, the working class were struggling to get a share of the profits (in the form of improved wages). It also coincided with an increase in the cost of living, which exacerbated the problem. The result was wide discontent, manifesting itself in the rapid growth of trade unions, labour disputes, militancy, and strikes during 1906 and '07.[33] The control of rugby was one area where the working classes could rise up against the 'employer' and take control of the business and its profits themselves.

THE MRU EARNS MORE, CLUBS AND PLAYERS LESS

'Young players who have been brought to the front by the local system of club football in Sydney are numerous. The value of the system in this particular direction is now being very clearly proved.' *The Referee* trumpeted the success that Sydney rugby had achieved by the end of 1906.

The game had taken a significant risk when it tossed away Wallaroo and the old clubs of the 1890s, with their combinations and training routines. The game was now on a rapid rise in popularity with the Sydney public. The newspaper rattled off a list of fresh-faced backs who had come into first grade during the season: Dally Messenger, Jack D'Alpuget, John Stuntz, Albert Rosenfeld, Edward Mandible, Dave Brown, the Prentice brothers, Arthur McCabe, Billy Cann, W. Ogaard, Charles 'Boxer' Russell, and Claude Corbett, together with at least another half dozen names.[34]

Club matches began to attract crowds of up to 20,000 and the MRU took in much more income than ever before. While it had previously given back nearly all its earnings each season as payments to the clubs for training expenses, and ground hire and improvements, from the latter stages of the 1906 season, despite its increased income, the MRU began to tighten its belt in regard to funding the clubs and players. The MRU was also moving away from the fundamentals of the district club scheme, to the criticism of players and supporters.

Why the change in approach remains uncertain. The growing dissatisfaction was readily apparent. Conceivably, the Union's reaction was to forcibly quell the unrest by taking a harder line. There is no evidence it was trying to drive working-class players out of the game, as the RFU had done in 1895 in the North of England.

What made it more bewildering to many was that Billy Howe, once one of their own, was MRU secretary during this period of increased financial restraint. Even if no one knew that he was the NSW player brought before the NSWRU in 1898 for telling 'all-and-sundry' that he was paid to play, there was no doubt that he and his contemporaries were catered for by Union officials in their playing days for NSW.

Was it fair that the MRU and Howe treat the current players so poorly? Limited by its amateur principles, in many ways the MRU could not spend every penny it earned on clubs and players. With the increased popularity of club football, its financial growth was inevitable. However, it cannot be argued there was nothing left within the bounds of amateurism that it could spend its money on.

Whatever its driving force, the changes were ill-timed. They began almost immediately after the Aucklanders' visit that brought George Smith to Sydney with his news about plans to form a professional team. At any other time the actions of the MRU and NSWRU may have passed without too much turmoil. Players and supporters may have been disgruntled, but they would have gotten on with the job and it would have passed, but now there was a group of men tired of being used as free labour and who knew of Smith's plans. There was now an alternative if the MRU and NSWRU did not satisfy their needs. Anything negative was another reason to look at the other option, follow the lead of Smith and align with the NU.

In such circumstances, small things can take on much larger significance — especially if someone rouses them into action.

THE UNIONS PROTECT THEIR FINANCES

Less than a fortnight after the Auckland team had left, the NSWRU attempted to draw on the financial reserves of the MRU. The 1906 season had been hugely profitable to the MRU. *The Referee* reported the Union 'had at least £1,500 solid profit over working expenses so far this year' and that 'the Sydney Union has had a record season from the financial standpoint, the gross gates have been comparatively enormous.' The concept of the MRU loaning money to the NSWRU went against the primary reasoning behind the formation of the metropolitan branch a decade earlier.

The Referee reasoned that the NSWRU had no entitlement, or indeed, any need for the money.

'A proposal has been placed before the MRU to grant a loan of £750 to the NSWRU for the purpose of paying off an overdraft, or of reducing the rate of interest thereon.' The newspaper then examined the request in light of the NSWRU's last publicly published balance-sheet. It pointed out that the NSWRU had issued mortgages of £2,250, had investments of £400, and '£1,150 was taken at the gates for the first of the two 1906 NSW v Queensland matches.'

'The proposal has very little to recommend it from the point of view of metropolitan football,' wrote *The Referee*. That money, or a good deal of it, can be spent more judiciously in fostering football within the metropolitan area by establishing headquarters for training, business and social meetings, in the different districts for rugby footballers. One has no doubt that a scheme of this nature is practicable, especially now that the

Dally Messenger made his debut appearance for the N.S.Wales 'Blues' in 1906.

MRU has a paid secretary. If it is carried out, its influence on football and its value to the men who play will be highly beneficial.'[35]

The criticism extracted a response — at the next annual general meetings of the MRU and the NSWRU both bodies, for the first time, withheld their balance sheets from publication.[36] But what was the motive behind the request? Lending the money would effectively shift half the MRU's financial reserves to the NSWRU. Future MRU committees would not be able to call on that money, preventing it from being spent. Had one or both of the Unions become aware of some disturbing news or rumours arising from the Sydney visit of George Smith and the Aucklanders?

The attempt to transfer the assets of the MRU to the NSWRU could have unsettled the clubs and players sufficiently for them to take Smith's plans far more seriously than they perhaps would have.

AN UNEXPECTED ARRIVAL FROM LANCASHIRE

At the end of October 1906, Tom McCabe was an established NU player with the Wigan club in the North of England. For some still unknown reason, McCabe suddenly left and sailed for Sydney.

McCabe had notched up more than 110 first-class games. He made his debut in the 1901/02 season with his home club Widnes, as a 20 year-old. He took some time to hold a permanent place in the First team, but by late 1905 his club form was good enough that he won a place in a Lancashire County team trial. After playing against Leigh on January 20, 1906, McCabe left Widnes and played the remaining 13 games of the season with Wigan. When the following season commenced he appeared a further ten times for Wigan and then abruptly left for Australia.[37]

While Widnes was also the club of the then NU President, Jack Smith, there is no inference that McCabe's move to Australia had any connection to the plans of George Smith. McCabe, a single man who apparently earned his income as a general labourer, was quite articulate, as his later writings in Sydney newspapers show.[38] While it seems certain he migrated to Sydney for personal reasons, his presence would prove to be a great benefit to the city's disaffected footballers. In particular, McCabe had experience of the radical rule changes introduced by the NU for the 1906/07 season.

THIRTEEN-A-SIDE

Influenced by the popular appeal of the attacking and entertaining play of the All Blacks the previous winter, the NU sought to effectively ensure its rugby became faster, more open, and move further away from the scrummaging focus of rugby union.[39] The All Blacks had proven that, even under the RFU rules, fast and open rugby (accompanied by a reduction in scrummaging) could be played. But the New Zealanders were an exception, and rules needed to be put in place if such play was to be more common place.

Over the decade or so since it had left the RFU, the NU management had changed the rules of rugby (including removal of the line-out option) to make it more appealing for money-paying crowds and safer to play.[40] The RFU had considered reduced player numbers in the early 1890s but this was seen as aiding those concerned with the professional and 'gate-chasing' aspects of the game. Under the NU, where a two-thirds majority amongst member clubs was needed to make rule changes, the idea of reducing player numbers still failed to gain the necessary support.[41]

Another ongoing concern was the vexed question of how to continue play once a player was tackled to ground or held with the ball. The RFU itself struggled with this issue, dabbling in changes and interpretations of the 'down' rule. In English rugby union referees tended to order a scrum immediately a player was tackled or held.

In Sydney, players were increasingly allowed to ruck and maul for the ball on the ground. The 'down' rule itself required the tackled or held player to place the ball on the ground whereupon it would be scrummaged.[42]

The All Blacks visit gave the NU clubs the impetus to finally adopt some radical changes. They reduced the number of players per side from fifteen to thirteen, removing two of the three forwards from the back row of the standard eight-man pack, and required half-backs (and wing-forwards) to remain behind the scrum once the ball was fed. The NU also replaced the 'down' with a new 'play-the-ball' rule — effectively a mandatory two-man scrum — to speedily restart play once a ball-carrier was tackled to the ground or held.[43]

The effect of the rule changes was dramatic. While designed to produce more passing and running movements, at the expense of scrummaging, the most significant effect was to make the ball, and what was happening to it, far more visible to spectators. These changes combined to greatly increase the pace of the NU game and its crowd appeal. The distinction between the RFU and the NU was now not just a matter of amateurism and professionalism, but one of different forms of rugby.

THE MRU WINS EVERYTIME

In Sydney, an increasing concern was the issue of ground allocations. The MRU scheduled big drawing matches at one of the city grounds, where the crowds were a certainty to attend, and the committee members would be in comfort. They would also schedule lesser matches on the bigger suburban grounds, irrespective of the clubs involved. At some of these matches crowds were only just into the hundreds — the local supporters were uninterested and the supporters of the two 'away' clubs would not travel.

'The Union committee is, to a large degree, ignoring one of the cardinal points in the district system, that is, playing on local grounds,' reported *The Referee*. 'Next Saturday Balmain will meet Manly at Wentworth Park (Glebe district), a ground widely foreign to both clubs. Newtown will meet St George at Rushcutters Bay Oval (Eastern Suburbs district), a ground widely foreign to both clubs. Glebe are booked to meet South Sydney at the Sports Ground, which is certainly local to South Sydney. But the fact of the first round match having been played on that ground should have been sufficient to have given this match to the Glebe district. Including next Saturday, South Sydney will have played eight out of their twelve matches at the Sports Ground, their home ground. That is certainly not in keeping with the spirit of district football, nor is it fair to the other clubs — not to mention the morale and other support which a club receives by reason of having half of its matches on a home ground.'[44]

Balmain was particularly frustrated at their allocation of matches against South Sydney. They had played against Souths fourteen times since the inception of the district scheme in 1900. However, only twice had South Sydney been forced to travel to Balmain's home ground Birchgrove Park — the last time being in 1901. Balmain footballers were so aggrieved that over recent seasons they had to be coaxed by officials of the MRU into forming a club to enter the competition. Interest was so low on one occasion that the MRU was forced to conduct its own Balmain district meeting and resolve to form a club for the coming season.

In late 1906 at a MRU meeting the Balmain representative, Pat McQuade, '...tendered his resignation over the allotment of grounds, but has withdrawn it.' At the same meeting the committee discussed entering into a long term agreement for the use of the Sports Ground. They held off making a decision in the hope the SCG Trustees were about to put forward a more financially attractive offer. The MRU also took the opportunity to vote Howe a bonus of £50, though no explanation was given of the reasoning.[45]

The MRU went so far as to use the University club, the greatest upholders of the amateur principles, in its efforts to make more money. Because the MRU enjoyed better terms from matches at the Sports Ground than at the University Oval, the well-performing University team rarely gained a home game. Instead the MRU scheduled lesser matches at the University Oval which, as a result of both teams being out of their area, attracted crowds that barely covered costs. The University itself (as the owner of the ground) was being denied income that could have been used to improve its facilities, while its amateur team was being used to fill the MRU bank account.[46]

In the end, the University made a mockery of the whole premiership by withdrawing from its semi-final match so it could undertake a tour of New Zealand. The tour was sanctioned without argument by the MRU and NSWRU.[47]

ALEC BURDON AND THE NOMADIC SYDNEY CLUB

Across town, the Sydney district club was living a nomadic existence, rarely given top billing at the major city grounds. Its club captain, Alec Burdon (who had left Glebe), was frustrated not only by the ground allocations, but by a rising injury toll and loss of training facilities.

Burdon '…is a great worker for his club' and was highly regarded by other footballers and officials in NSW and Queensland. Burdon was in '…1904–05–06, a grand forward — never saying a word, he was always in the thick of it, good in the tight scrums, smart in the open, a clever and popular forward.'[48] Playing in the front row, Burdon was a permanent member of the NSW and Australian sides since making his club and representative debut in 1901.

Owing to a lack of finances, Burdon's Sydney team was forced out of their training headquarters, the Royal Navy House Gymnasium. It also meant the club was 'not able to make further use of the services of their popular instructor, Mr J. Ryan.' The club's only option was to train in the late of day (or under moonlight) on the open fields of Rushcutters Bay Oval. Meanwhile, South Sydney, were enjoying the convenience of training in the evening under lights at the Sports Ground and using the grandstand's change rooms.[49]

The Sydney club also suffered a long injury toll from playing on the hard suburban grounds, made worse by an extended dry period throughout 1906. 'Owing to accidents and other causes, the Sydney club has had to change the first grade team more than any other club in the competition,' reported *The Referee*. The club had used thirty-four players with still a few rounds of the 1906 season remaining.[50]

Burdon and his club were seeing far more than usual just how much football injuries could cost a man. In the middle of the 1906 season, the club organised its own medical fund to supplement the minimal support provided under the MRU's scheme. *The Referee* lauded the work of the club's committee to bring about the extra benefits, saying 'it will accomplish a good deal more than the average footballer expects of any club.' Of course, the players still had to find another 5s contribution fee to participate.

NO MORE MEDICAL INSURANCE

At the first MRU meeting of 1907, the Sydney club secretary proposed 'that an accident insurance fund be instituted with the MRU.' Such a scheme had always been provided by the MRU since its inception. Given that the MRU was enjoying a rapid growth in gate-receipts from club matches (£1,336 in 1902, to £3,724 in 1906) there was no financial reason against continuing to insure players.[51] Indeed, a strong argument existed for the benefit to be raised — since 1895 the rules of the RFU had allowed for payment of up to 6s per day (except weekends) to injured players.[52] A lengthy debate ensued where some MRU members objected to players receiving the benefit at all. A final vote was taken which decided by ten votes to nine to end the insurance scheme. There would be no cover for players' medical expenses in 1907.[53]

Each club would now have to implement their own medical fund, relying on a contribution from each player. This effectively doubled a player's club membership fee from 5s to 10s. One footballer calculated that the 10s equated to a cost of 7.5 pence per match 'for the privilege' of playing, while spectators were seeing two or four teams play each Saturday afternoon for a mere 6 pence. 'The idea is farcical,' he told *The Referee*. 'It only shows that the greater the balance the MRU can put to its credit, the more they expect from the clubs, their supporters, and above all, from the playing members.'[54]

In a remarkably insensitive move, the MRU committee then voted to again increase the salary of Howe, its secretary, to £250 (to match that of the NSWRU secretary).[55] It was more than twice the average earnings of a working man.

Burdon and Howe were team mates (both in the front row) in the Glebe first grade team in 1902 and 1903. They were also the team's joint selectors. As someone who knew Howe closely, Burdon would have been particularly disheartened by Howe's change in attitude. Knowing how financially hard it was for injured players from his own lay-off in 1904, Burdon's frustration with Howe and the MRU grew as he saw more and more of his Sydney club team mates struggling through the same ordeal.

A TOUR TO BRITAIN — BUT WHO CAN AFFORD IT?

The NSWRU announced, unexpectedly, that it 'had received an invitation to send a team to England in 1908, the necessary arrangements for this tour were now being made.' The news was met with immense enthusiasm by the committee. One vice-president hypothesised that 'before long he hoped the various nations would meet for the supremacy of the world at rugby football,' to which the meeting erupted in wild applause.[56]

For the working-class players, who were well familiar with the experiences of the All Blacks from their British tour, they knew that such a trip would come at a great personal cost. Would it be worth it? Many would not be able to take the opportunity and would be left at home. Plus, they personally would not see any of the profits from their labour.

There were suggestions from the NSWRU that the tour profit would not be returned to Australian rugby union, but be put into an 'Imperial Fund' to develop the game throughout the British Empire. One member suggested: 'It would help to make the visit more memorable and more acceptable than it would be if we simply follow in the steps of New Zealand and South Africa [in 1906] and make as much money out of it as we can.'[57]

Barely six years had passed since federation of the colonies. Many of the NSWRU members still thought of themselves as colonial Britishers first, Australian second. The dogmatic desire of the NSWRU to maintain its attachment to the RFU in England at the expense of making changes to suit local Australian conditions frustrated many, particularly amongst the working class and younger men.

MORE SCOPE FOR THE AGITATOR

From August 1906 to mid-1907, the conditions enjoyed by the players deteriorated rapidly as a result of the two Unions' actions. It seems that George Smith's visit had left behind something that changed the attitude of the Unions. Their actions appear particularly heavy-handed — as if they were punishing the players and the clubs. It suggests the Unions suspected an uprising, or even the formation of a rival organisation, was on the horizon.

Strong support for an equitable alternative to the MRU and NSWRU now existed amongst the rugby players of Sydney, particularly the working class.

Glebe's Chris McKivat – shrewd halfback or five-eighth with an exceptional kicking ability.

A Sydney reporter, in *The Insurance and Banking Record*, wrote in July 1906 of the mood the city's working class were in. 'The Labor cauldron appears to be constantly seething. At the present time there is trouble at some of the collieries with the boy drivers and wheelers; tobacco workers to the number of over one hundred employees are out on strike; and the Government tramway employees have held largely attended meetings denunciatory of the management under which they work. The Arbitration Court apparently is all but useless in connection with these matters, and it would seem that legislation so far has only had the effect of giving more scope for the work of the agitator.'[58]

The Bulletin was prepared to name the men fuelling the discontent in rugby, saying, 'Messrs. Giltinan and Trumper raised the standard of the revolt — they prated of a reign of beneficence.'[59] They were soon joined by Henry 'Harry' Hoyle, a 54 year-old former Labor politician. Hoyle had spent much of his working life in the trade union movement — his fiery speeches often invoking workers to rise up and challenge their employers through strikes and other activities.[60]

With Hoyle providing the necessary 'call to arms' speeches, Giltinan organising the finances, and Trumper encouraging the players, they were ready to rouse the dissatisfied elements of NSW and Queensland rugby into action.

Their connection to the footballers would come through Glebe's Peter Moir 'who was in the habit of visiting Victor Trumper's sports depot.' Dally Messenger had also been a childhood friend of Trumper.

Messenger revealed later, 'I knew Victor Trumper and Peter Moir were discussing something.'[61]

CHAPTER EIGHT

THE MIRAGE OF PROFESSIONALISM

ALBERT BASKERVILLE

Albert Baskerville[1] was a 'rattling good player — fast and dashy.' He played mostly in the 'back division' for the Oriental Club in Wellington, New Zealand. Baskerville was not only a player, but a keen student of the finer points of the game. He was strongly influenced by the success of the All Blacks and, like many New Zealanders, called for the rules of rugby to be modified to encourage more spectacular and crowd-appealing play.

Baskerville claims that upon reading of the impetus the All Blacks were giving to English rugby, he conceived the idea of 'compiling a work [book] describing the methods in vogue in New Zealand' rugby. During the tour the All Blacks chose not to share their rugby philosophy and tactics. With clubs and players in England wanting to adopt the All Blacks style, Baskerville wrote *Modern Rugby Football: New Zealand Methods* and had it published in England in 1907.[2] In the meantime (mid-1906) All Blacks Dave Gallaher (captain) and Billy Stead (vice-captain) released *The Complete Rugby Footballer On The New Zealand System.*

While Baskerville may have been disappointed that Gallaher and Stead released their book before him, its contents appear to have ignited his interest in starting a new project. The two All Blacks wrote, 'During our tour many letters appeared in the sporting papers, written by prominent Northern Union people, which amounted to challenges to us to play them, and it was stated that we should then, and only then, meet the flower of English Rugby football, while at the same time it was very plainly insinuated that we should meet our doom. Of course we could do nothing of the kind, as it would have involved our becoming professionals ourselves, and it would have taken much more than a challenge from the Northern Union to have induced us to abandon our status.'[3]

Baskerville became consumed with the idea of linking with the NU. After making inquiries, he apparently met with George Smith in the late winter of 1906. Baskerville also came into possession of the letter from Fred Cooper published in England during the All Blacks tour. [This appears to be the same letter Gallaher and Stead were referring to].

'I gleaned that the Northern Union authorities had held out a substantial gate guarantee for a match with the New Zealanders,' revealed Baskerville. 'But, of course, this proposal could not be entertained then. This set me thinking why shouldn't a New Zealand team play the Northern Unionists? Strict amateur supporters will answer, "Because some of their players are professionals." This argument seems weak if we keep in view the fact that in the sister Association (soccer) code amateurs and professionals often play on the same side and frequently against each other. A representative fixture, Amateurs v Professionals, is sometimes played in England.' Baskerville pointed out that no one would object to a New Zealand soccer team touring England and playing professional clubs. 'Therefore,' he asked, 'why should an outcry be raised if a rugby team did likewise?'[4]

If only it were that simple! Rugby had different values and principles to soccer, cricket and other sports. Rugby's amateur ethos was part of the fabric of the sport. Even a New Zealand team of amateurs would be declared to be 'professionals,' the moment they travelled without the sanction of the NZRU and RFU, let alone take the field against teams under the NU banner. Baskerville speculated among his circle of rugby contacts, gauging their reactions to such a venture. He studied the 1888 New Zealand Natives tour to learn from their experiences. Other 1905 All Blacks offered their own thoughts on the NU game, and the prospects for success. They also warned of the NZRU's reactions, and the threat of life-long disqualification from rugby union.

'It was thought that perhaps friends would consider a player mercenary, and regard him in an unfavourable light, if he formed one of a team to go Home and share in the pleasures and profits, if any, of a British Northern Union tour,' said Baskerville. His doubts were overcome when many men he sounded out told him 'it would be a shrewd and rather sensible idea — in fact, they all seemed to like the scheme. Guarded conversations with prominent New Zealand players elicited the information that, with few exceptions, they would be willing to join a team if one was formed.'

Baskerville and Smith decided to work together. As the colony's leading sportsman, Smith had the network to bring everyone together. Baskerville had the organisational and entrepreneurial skills to handle the business and practical side of forming the team and negotiating with the NU. With Smith in Auckland and Baskerville in Wellington, they could cover both major rugby centres at the same time.

Armed with the support and hopes of New Zealand's senior players, Baskerville initiated the next move. In January 1907 he sent letters to the NU and its major clubs seeking an invitation and terms for a

New Zealand team to tour. Baskerville's proposal sought an agreement where the team would take 70% of the gate-receipts, with a minimum guarantee of £3,000.[5] It took more than a month for his letter to arrive in England. Baskerville, a postal clerk, continued his daily responsibilities and hoped for good news.

N.U. APPROVES A NEW ZEALAND TEAM

At the end of March (1907) the NU committee accepted Baskerville's proposal, provided they 'received an assurance as to the strength of the team.' The news was communicated to Baskerville in a cablegram, who received it in Wellington.

'It's come, it's come,' Baskerville told one of his colleagues, Dick Callam. His hands trembled as he showed him the paper.[6] In the space of just over four months he had to be ready to leave New Zealand with his team. Many players would have readily joined were they to be paid outright for the tour, but Baskerville maintained that the team would travel as amateurs,

'Our idea is to get players to travel Home as amateurs — that is, to pay their own expenses,' explained Baskerville. Unlike the 1905 All Blacks who were given no earnings from their tour, Baskerville's team would 'divide the gate proceeds equally, as Australian cricketers do.'

'We hold that we will still be amateur footballers because we will not, nor do we intend to, gain a living by playing football. We are making a trip to England at our own expense. The mere fact of our playing against teams which play a few professionals does not alter our status one jot.'[7]

Albert Baskerville set out in 1907 to organize and lead a 'professional All Blacks' rugby tour to England.

Baskerville was arguing that the 'amateur/professional' issue in rugby should be brought into line with the tour arrangements that had existed with Australian cricketers and their visits to England. The people of Australia and New Zealand were not necessarily against such a venture, only that it was in conflict with the rules of the RFU and the premise of the rugby union game.

Baskerville was also concerned with the 'new rugby' of the NU. While the 1905 All Blacks, and New Zealand footballers generally, played the attacking rugby that the NU was seeking, none of them had personally seen the effect of the 1906 rule changes. Baskerville studied match reports of NU contests in Northern English newspapers to understand the type of footballer he would need for the tour.

Baskerville noted, 'A number of conditions had to be taken into consideration which a majority of people, although well acquainted with amateur rugby points, knew very little of. The abolishment of the line-out makes a great difference. Some New Zealand players are noted for their cleverness in the line-out and are included in representative teams because of their skills in this direction, apart from other qualifications. These would not be ideal men for our purpose. It is easily seen that the NU rule changes should result in the play being faster and more open, so that a speedy man, providing he is a good scrummager, should be our ideal. A slow, heavy-weight would be a great disadvantage at once, so good all-round forwards are to be preferred.'[8]

Alec Burdon – since 1901 he had been a permanent member of N.S.Wales and Australian teams. Injuries he received in 1904 and 1907 focused attention on the poor treatment of footballers by the Rugby Union authorities.

Baskerville now had his task at hand. He had to form a small group of trusted and qualified players to act as selectors for his team, armed with their limited understanding of the NU game. They also had to sound out players who could be relied upon not to let the secret out, and who could come up with the £50 outlay needed to buy their share in the scheme. The amount equated to about half a year's wages to a working man, so Baskerville allowed players who couldn't find the necessary money to borrow the £50 against the tour's future earnings. However, interest would be charged on the loan and they wouldn't get a penny until it was paid off.[9]

News of Baskerville's plans moved quickly through New Zealand rugby. While full details were kept out of the newspapers, it was no secret to the footballers — more than three-quarters of the 200 first-class players in New Zealand applied to Baskerville for inclusion in the tour.[10]

BURDON INJURED IN CLUB MATCH

On May 4 the Sydney and Souths teams played at the SCG, with about 5,000 spectators on hand. *The Herald* reported that the weather was a 'shade on the bleak side, with threatening clouds hanging about and in some places light showers fell, but not sufficient to interfere with the play.' The opposing captains were Alec Burdon (Sydney) and Arthur Hennessy (South Sydney). Souths won 6–4, scoring two tries to their opponents 'goal from the field.'[11] Late in the match Burdon injured his arm.

Presumably the injury was not too serious, as no immediate reports of his condition appeared in the newspapers. By the end of May *The Sunday Sun* reported that 'Burdon is stepping down owing to a sinew in his right arm snapping — he will not be able to play for a fortnight.'[12] This ruled Burdon out of the upcoming inter-state matches.

However, of more concern would have been his inability to work. The only treatment for such an injury was to rest the arm in a sling as much as possible. Burdon was employed on the wharves, although he was also known to work as a barber — either way, with one arm in a sling, he was of no use.

With no insurance scheme in place, Burdon could not be given any money by the MRU to help him through this period. Having Burdon, one of the most popular rugby players in Sydney, get about with his arm in a sling did not hurt the cause of those seeking to improve the conditions for players.

AT TRUMPER'S SPORTS STORE

Two weeks after Burdon suffered his injury, the news of Baskerville's venture reached the Sydney newspapers. *The Herald* reported that the 'New Zealand Rugby Union expresses strong disapproval of the proposal to send an All Blacks professional football team to tour England.'[13]

It was a only a small mention, hidden away under the football matches (of all the codes) set down for play that Saturday. It didn't seem to have any direct relevance to rugby in Sydney or Brisbane, but there is no doubt it quickly attracted everyone's attention. Wherever rugby players met the discussion was about the moves across the Tasman. 'Why shouldn't there be professionalism in rugby football here in Sydney?' was the call from many.

'Professionalism' though could take many forms. There was the 'out and out' professional who earned his livelihood from sport, while there were others who simply wanted more reimbursement for out-of-pocket expenses than the amateur rules allowed. There was a big gulf between the two, but many just saw it, all the same, as 'the evil of professionalism.'

The NSWRU had also recently made it clear that the rules against professionalism applied only to players. All other roles (referees,

Victor Trumper's sports store (108 Market St, Sydney) – venue for lunchtime meetings of rugby footballers and their supporters that led to the formation of the NSWRL in 1907.

committee members, coaches), they argued, were not participants in the game itself and their status was irrelevant. They could be provided with compensation or income from the Unions where considered appropriate. On the other hand, every player must be an amateur — no matter how inadequate the allowances or bountiful the gate-takings were.[14]

These issues were being discussed on the city footpaths and elsewhere at lunch time. Most shops, factories and offices closed for a two-hour break and everyone was locked-out of their workplace for the duration. Some went home, while others had regular gathering points. A group that included many of the city's top footballers, and other sports-minded men, often met at Victor Trumper's sports store.[15]

Trumper owned the store in partnership with Yorkshire-born cricketer Hanson Carter ('The Best House in Town for Sports Material and Men's Mercery' — 108 Market Street). Both had played for Australia on the 1902 tour of England. By the time the news of Baskerville's tour reached Sydney, Giltinan, Trumper and Hoyle were regularly joined by Peter Moir, Jack Feneley and the injured Alec Burdon. On occasion the group also included Jim Moir, Arthur Hennessy, Bob Graves (from Balmain) and others.[16]

These meetings became serious after Peter Moir received a cable from George Smith asking if Sydney footballers were prepared to play against the professional New Zealand team. It was the final confirmation that Smith had followed through on the suggestions he had made during the Auckland team's visit in July 1906. Moir took the news to a meeting at Trumper's store.[17]

One of the group suggested, 'Why should we not play the New Zealanders, have our own business manager, and insist on a fair share of the gate money for ourselves?' They decided to form a team to play the New Zealanders. The clincher, for many, was Burdon's situation.

'Burdon by this time,' said one of the men involved, 'had dislocated his shoulder bone and dozens of players were indignant because he could not receive what they considered reasonable compensation, even though he was captain of Sydney and had given long, valuable and faithful service in the state and Australian teams.'[18]

'One thing led to another,' he added.

Engendered by Giltinan, Hoyle and Trumper, the footballers' contempt for the MRU and, in particular the NSWRU, inspired them to pursue the matter further — to take it to the ultimate conclusion.[19]

The two Unions were accumulating vast financial reserves. Yet here they had Alec Burdon, a regular of the national team, unable to work because of an injury suffered in earning that money for the MRU and they wouldn't help him. Burdon was the most high-profile of the working-class footballers — if he couldn't gain any assistance, what hope did the rest have?[20]

Then there were all the other problems: the NSWRU selectors preferring their favourites and ignoring better qualified players, the MRU paying little regard to the district scheme, and the MRU/NSWRU structure that prevented Sydney clubs and players from having a say.

The casual lunch time discussions gave way to evening meetings in the room above Trumper's store.[21] Most of them had met George Smith the previous winter or were at least aware of his plans. They contacted the New Zealanders and put a proposal to them.

TO FORM PROFESSIONAL CLUBS?

Trumper seems to have been the main conduit to the players — initially many thought he was the 'prime mover.' However, it was Giltinan, as the man providing the finances and taking the risk, who became the movement's leader and public face. Giltinan confirmed this in an interview with *The Referee* a few months later: 'When the movement to send a New Zealand team to England was made, I saw the opportunity, and communications were opened up with Mr G. Smith of Auckland.'[22]

But such matches alone would only be a short-term answer for the plight of the players. If the public didn't support the match, the participating players would get no return and be permanently banned by the NSWRU. The conclusion: a club competition should be formed — a permanent solution.

The New Zealanders were simply going on a tour. There appeared to be no intention to form a local competition. Crowds at club matches in Auckland and Wellington rarely exceeded 600.[23] There was not sufficient money, nor probably enough willing players, to sustain a professional competition. Even in a city of the size of Sydney, most doubted it could be brought into reality. Players nearing the end of their career could be attracted to a money-grabbing venture from a one-off tour, but any young player would be banned from rugby union for life. Many of the New Zealanders would look to the offer of a contract from a NU club and stay in England.[24]

The footballers in Sydney thinking of joining the new movement were given more confidence when they read in local newspapers about clubs and players in Wales moving to the NU game. They already knew that the strength of English rugby now lay with the NU. Scotland and Ireland were convinced that any tour 'from the colonies' had to be tainted with professionalism. New Zealanders were making their move, and now the Welsh, the only team capable of defeating the All Blacks, were attracted by the NU.[25]

With no footballers, the MRU and NSWRU would have nothing. All of the district clubs had senior players and supporters on the management and selection committees. Their experience could greatly aid the formation of a rival Union. Both Trumper (Victorian rules and cricket tours) and Hoyle (workplace unions and the Labor party) had been involved in creating organisations and agreements. All that was needed were the initial finances, and Giltinan had guaranteed to cover the upfront costs. Was it really a risk if NSW or Australian rugby joined the NU too?

THE PLAYERS MUST FIND THE REMEDY

A few months later Blair Swannell summarised in *The Australian Star* the situation the players were in at the time. Swannell was a staunch supporter of amateurism, but, unlike many he recognised the practices of the MRU and NSWRU as dangerous in a city with such a vast working-class population.

'It is of course admitted that there are many honestly hard-working officials on the NSWRU,' wrote Swannell, 'but how many are there who care not one jot for the game, but are simply on the NSWRU in order that they may drink beer and sing "For He's a Jolly Good Fellow" at the reception of visiting teams they neither know nor care about. They certainly attend some matches, and they may also be found at shivoos and dinners tendered to inter-state teams. It is after all the player who pays for officials' enjoyment, and it is the player to say if funds he provided are being spent legitimately, if not to find the remedy.'[26]

James J Giltinan – was involved in organizing cricket tours before turning his attention to professional rugby.

In the days immediately after the news of the New Zealanders' professional tour broke, it was announced that 'a special meeting of MRU will be held to consider the advisability of the Union purchasing its own ground.'[27] The MRU had for some time been endeavouring to negotiate favourable arrangements with one of the three major grounds at Moore Park.

On the surface, this announcement that they were looking for their own ground was a natural extension of sound business acumen, particularly if no satisfactory hiring arrangements could be found. However, it went completely against the grain of district football.

The clubs and the players thought that if the MRU had the money to invest in ground purchases, it should occur in the suburbs so as to build up the district aspect of the competition and lessen the need to bring matches (players and supporters) into the city. The sudden rush, via a 'special meeting,' to look at purchasing a ground hinted that the MRU had something urgent on its mind.

By sinking all its reserve funds into a ground purchase, there would be no money left to argue about how it should be spent. It also meant that if any future MRU committee wished to spend money on club grounds and player benefits, they would not have the funds to achieve their objectives.

Publicly, the members of the NSWRU and MRU appeared to be indifferent to the news from New Zealand concerning Baskerville. Their only stated concern was pondering the effect of the doings across the Tasman on the representative character of the NZRU team due to come to Australia in a few weeks. 'If the professional team for England is to be strong — and it is not much use for them to go as a speculation if it is not — then they will need to include a number of the leading All Black players,' observed a Sydney newspaper.[28]

The haste with which the MRU was acting to find and purchase a ground suggests they knew of moves being made to take control of the Union. Rather than quell the disquiet, their action added to the rapidly building wave of discontent amongst the clubs and players.

SOME NOTABLE ABSENTEES

News about who would be taking places in the 'professional New Zealand team' continued to fill paragraphs in Sydney newspapers. 'The developments in New Zealand are being followed with great interest in Australia, particularly as some of their more prominent players are quite familiar to many of us here,' wrote *The Herald*. 'It might be significant, though of course not conclusive, to observe that in the North Island team to meet the South Island team there are no Auckland players selected, including George Smith.' Fourteen of Auckland's best players had refused to sign a declaration that they were amateur and had no knowledge of a proposed tour to the Northern English counties.[29]

Baskerville himself was singled out for attack from the NZRU and its supporters in the press. The NZRU also wrote to the RFU in England declaring it had nothing to do with the venture and was doing all it could to put it down.[30]

The NZRU's representative team for the Australian tour was announced shortly afterwards, and there were a few missing 1905 All Blacks. 'Examination of the team shows it to be undoubtedly a very strong one, and Australia will have to play good football to beat it.' said *The Herald*. 'The most notable absentees are George Smith and George Nicholson. Smith, the Auckland three-quarter has been playing right to the top of his form this season. Smith's non-inclusion is as a big surprise to followers of the game. Probably their work did not come under the eye of the selectors in the inter-island match.'[31]

NOT EVEN A BAG OF PEANUTS

The first big Sydney club match of the 1907 season came in the sixth round of the premiership (June 1) with Eastern Suburbs and University meeting at the SCG. Both teams entered the match sharing honours at the head of the competition list. *The Herald* reported:

> East are fast establishing a reputation for open and sparkling play, with always the expectation of a brilliant incident, a condition due to the sensational things Messenger has done. There were anticipations of a great struggle and fully 20,000 people attended. There was never a slack moment in the game, nor one in which some section of the crowd was not cheering itself hoarse.
>
> Messenger was again the bright particular star of the contest, he was always doing something extraordinary. He kicked two goals to give the Tricolours a 6–3 lead late in the game, one was the best seen at the ground for years.
>
> Nearing the final quarter of the game, a 'Varsity player kicked into the East 25 yards where Messenger caught the ball, shook off a tackler and started the most brilliant item of the match. Messenger got clean away, and ran to within 10 yards of the University goal line where he was pulled down from behind. However, he got rid of the ball whereupon it was handled by two East men before it was passed back to Messenger who ran for the line and secured a try amidst an extraordinary scene of jubilation. Brackenreg failed at goal and the Eastern Suburbanites held a 9–3 lead, eventually winning 9–6 in a cracking football contest.[32]

It was the start of a demanding week for the city's top footballers. Teams representing each of the NSW country regions played each other in Sydney on the same day. Just two days later (Monday), each of the country teams took on a Sydney club. After these games, teams were selected for the City v Country contest on the Wednesday, with NSW v Queensland to take place the next Saturday.

'Many of the players were far from happy over the Country Week arrangements. First grade players, who had been battling hard for club

points on Saturday, were expected to chuck up work on Monday afternoon and play in matches in which they took little interest,' one player told *The Australian Star.* 'The city men were compelled to sacrifice their afternoon's work, pay their own travelling and other expenses etc., — all for what? The Country team went to dinner at the expense of the NSWRU, whilst the metropolitan players, who at all events had provided half the gate, were not even given a bag of peanuts.'[33]

Representative team selections were also again causing public debate. Arthur Hennessy, the South Sydney club captain, told *The Sydney Sportsman* that despite his team being leaders of the premiership with University, they could only get two players in either City Firsts or Seconds side.

Hennessy aimed most of his criticism at N. Johnson, captain of the University club and also one of the MRU selectors. 'He helps to select eight of his own team. He has not taken the trouble to go to any of our matches to see them played. So how can a selector honestly select a team, not having seen them play?'[34]

Sydney District R.F.C.'s Edward Mandible – one of the many talented young rugby footballers that came to the fore in the 1905-1907 period.

The Country team included 'George' Anlezark, making his first return to representative football since the 1905 Australian tour. His team mate and critic from that tour, Blair Swannell, was in the City team. The mid-week City v Country match was held at the SCG, before a crowd of about 5,000. The home side won 'a hard and exciting game' 9–6. Anlezark was reported to have played 'a splendid game, and was frequently cheered.'[35]

When the NSW team was announced after the match, Anlezark was given the five-eighth position ahead of Chris McKivat, Messenger was in the centres and Swannell was left out.

In an innovation, the NSWRU decided to house the Blues players together to prepare for the inter-state series and the matches against New Zealand. The decision shows the NSWRU was determined to use every endeavour to bring success its way (notwithstanding the complaints about the team that was selected). Some followers of rugby quietly objected, suggesting that such an arrangement was 'sharp practice' and not within the ideals of amateurism.

The Herald reported that the team stayed at the Adelaide Hotel, 'separated only by the old rifle range' from the SCG. 'In this way the players will be in the hands and under the eye of the selectors at all times. They are to receive proper dieting and regular and systematic work, starting before breakfast each day, with long walks. It will allow them to practice scrum formation and tactics, and indulge in other training operations.'[36]

The players did not take the honour of appearing for NSW lightly, but having to seek leave for weeks from their employers was again very hard — especially as they could not be compensated for lost work earnings.

25TH ANNIVERSARY OF NSW V QUEENSLAND

The Queenslanders arrived by train on the Friday morning and were taken to NSWRU's rooms in Bligh Street for a formal welcome at noon. It was a 'big do' for the rugby game, as the match marked the 'silver wedding anniversary of inter-state contests.' *The Herald* noted, 'It is the twenty-fifth year of matches between New South Wales and the Queensland — the two states that have remained true to the rugby game.'[37] In that period Queensland had only defeated NSW in a series three times (1895, '97 and '98), with nine series drawn.[38]

At the reception, NSWRU president, John Calvert, formally welcomed the Queenslanders and there was the usual collection of dignitaries and officials.

'I am quite sure the match on the morrow will be honestly and fairly contested, and the better team will win,' Calvert said. 'Speaking of the professional movement in New Zealand, we must fear the taint of professionalism entering our game. I trust the two states represented here will set their foot against it. One great advantage rugby has over the Association game in England is the absence of professionalism. Whenever it is introduced there will come the danger of gambling.'

Charles G. Wade, NSW Attorney-General, was pleased to be present as well, as the official representative of the state. A former Wallaroo player, Wade studied law at Oxford University in the 1880s and during his stay represented England in eight internationals. 'One of the banes of football in the old country is the encroachment of professionalism,' Wade stated. 'In the North of England, where professional rugby holds sway, the higher aspects of the game are completely lost. With a large amount of money in one pocket there is probably a larger amount of blue metal in the other!' This comment produced much laughter amongst the gathering. The 'blue metal' was in reference to the alleged habit of NU and Association supporters throwing stones at visiting teams or even their own if they didn't receive value for their admission fee.

Wade continued, 'I hope here the amateur status will always be maintained. I am sure the better side will win to-morrow and the match will be played in a fine spirit. The old cry of win, tie, or wrangle should be confined to the school grounds. It is the men who can play a combined game of football, of working towards a common end, who can go on to build up a young country like ours. In doing so they are increasing the good name of Australia and England wherever they go.'

Member of NSW parliament, Charles Oakes added: 'There is the mirage of professionalism on the horizon of football, but I am pleased to see that, from the men selected for New Zealand, it was only a mirage, for the cream of New Zealand football is coming over to Australia.'

Mickey Dore, the Queensland captain, responded on behalf of his team. He simply stated they had come down to win.

AN ALMIGHTY 'CRACK!'

At 3.15p.m., NSW captain Harold Judd led his team from the Members' pavilion onto the SCG. A cold southerly wind was blowing under leaden clouds, but it wasn't enough to put off a crowd of over 25,000. Queensland won the match 11–6, though the contest was marred by a serious injury to a player.

Early in the second half Judd followed up a kick with team mate Bede Smith. As Smith made a dart to tackle a Queenslander his legs got entangled with one of Judd's. There was an almighty 'crack!' that could be heard around the ground and everyone immediately gasped. Judd's leg had completely snapped at the shin.

The match was stopped while Judd received attention from the Civil Ambulance men. They called for assistance from a doctor, who came onto the field and he bandaged Judd's leg. There was no stretcher at the SCG nor any leg-splints, and Judd was forced to 'walk' his way off under assistance. He was immediately conveyed to St Vincent's Hospital. Judd was in hospital from his ordeal for 'some considerable duration.' He was visited regularly by team mates and officials, especially from his St George club.[39]

LITTLE BETTER THAN A FOWL-YARD

After the inter-state match the MRU held a meeting where it made two decisions that suggested panic and fear had gripped them.

The first was to pay £12,500 to James Joynton-Smith, a Sydney entrepreneur, for the Epping Racecourse Ground [Harold Park].[40] There were many who saw the purchase as an incredibly poor choice, including one club official who offered his opinion of the facility. 'I think it is a bad business transaction, for the place is little better than a fowl-yard. Where do you think people will prefer to go when having the choice of other places such as Wentworth Park, University Oval, or the SCG? Besides, people can see better from outside without paying than those can inside. It will cost thousands of pounds to put in a proper condition to accommodate spectators. Even when that is done I doubt if the place will ever find favour with those who may patronise it.'[41]

It was obvious to all that the merits of the ground were secondary to the MRU's objective of quickly sinking all their money into a long term commitment and thereby ensuring the clubs could not get their hands on it.

The second decision saw the MRU do what it had previously refused to — it arranged to pay injured players for time off work. 'The MRU has established an insurance fund, which provides for the payment of medical fees up to £10, and assures a gratuity of £1 per week for 21 weeks to injured players. The players of the three grades — First, Second and Borough — are eligible to participate in the benefits, which are no doubt liberal.'[42]

The announcement didn't come in time for Alec Burdon who had now recovered from his injury. However, it was revealed a few weeks later that the MRU was 'under extreme pressure' from the players to provide them with injury compensation.[43] Burdon's quandary over the past month had brought a solid resolve to the players to act in their own interests.

Adding to the criticism of the two Unions were the favours given to the injured Harold Judd. He was provided 'first-class treatment' while in hospital at the NSWRU's expense. Players complained that some were being favoured while others, like Burdon, were left on their own. No one saw the benefits given to Judd as the beginning of a new trend in the support of injured players.

As it was, the MRU's offer to provide players £1 per week gratuity was not enough to address the needs of the workers — most earned near £3 per week. 'That's a fine lot anyhow to risk your limbs for,' said one of the club secretaries who sided with the players.[44]

Discontent grew. The players viewed the policy as an inadequate and were cynical, believing the MRU had only introduced it under pressure. The MRU's ground-purchase decision only made its predicament worse.

'GIVE IT TO MESSENGER!'

Twenty-four hours of rain preceded the final inter-state match in Sydney, which kept the crowd down to only 6,000. NSW won 11–3 in a game that provided little spectacular play, understandably given the conditions. Anlezark was dumped in favour of McKivat, while Messenger was selected as a winger.[45]

Ernest 'George' Anlezark – one of the many N.S.Wales players who felt aggrieved at their treatment by the state selectors.

Messenger still wasn't universally applauded. A writer in *The Sydney Sportsman* said, 'At times this player has shown he is capable of some brilliant pieces of play, on the whole he is sadly lacking in the essentials of a good representative player. A player of Messenger's calibre shows to advantage in a team that is easily over-running its opponents, but where any solid defensive work or concerted action is necessary, this player is useless. The fulsome adulation meted out each week to this player by *The Referee* must be nauseous even to himself [Messenger].'[46]

A supporter's letter in *The Herald* offered an opposing view. 'My opinion of Messenger is that he is the best all-round player that has been unearthed for some considerable time. It would be very foolish of the selectors to leave him out of the Australian team to meet the All Blacks. Messenger can hold his position with any player on the Australian soil and, in my opinion, is a champion in every department of the game.'[47]

No doubt Messenger, now shunted-out to the wing position, recognised that he did not have universal support within the NSWRU. He also felt that the Union was treating (financially) some NSW players unfairly, including himself. Messenger was a quiet man, and only those who voiced their demands gained better allowances. He said that he 'hadn't received the hansom cab expenses which other members of the inter-state teams invariably expected and boasted they received.'

'I don't think the Union treated me very well,' said Messenger, 'I always had to walk to the Showground (Agricultural Ground) from

Double Bay while others got hansom cab expenses.'[48] Messenger felt that he shouldn't have had to ask for financial assistance. He believed that the Union should have recognised his situation and looked after him.

A DUMPED NSW PLAYER PROTESTS

Anlezark took his omission from the NSW team particularly hard. He boarded the steamship from Sydney and returned home to the northern NSW town of Lismore. Meanwhile, the Blues travelled to Brisbane for the return inter-state matches.

At about the same time that NSW were playing Queensland, Anlezark was leading his Federals team against South Lismore. Called 'the Messenger of local football' by *The Northern Star* newspaper, Anlezark created two tries for his team on a rain-soaked ground that was 'in a wretched condition' for football. The Federals won 8–3.

Anlezark, though, had made a protest against his exclusion from the NSW team — he played the entire club match wearing his NSW jersey! 'Anlezark sets a bad example by not wearing his club colours. He donned the inter-colonial blue with red waratah and no.6 on his back.' The reporter wondered why Anlezark allowed the jersey 'to get spoilt in the dirt.'[49]

SYDNEY PLAYERS TO JOIN BASKERVILLE'S TEAM

On June 27 a news cable from New Zealand arrived in Sydney. Its contents 'created quite a scare in local football circles' according to *The Herald*.

> It was stated that the New Zealand amateur team soon to tour Australia will include some of the All Black professional combination to visit England. It means that the team to whose visit Australians have anxiously looked forward to, will have the taint of professionalism. This will cause an uncomfortable feeling, to say the least of it, amongst the public and the governing body.

> A more important statement cabled is that the professional New Zealanders hope to strengthen their [three-quarter] backs by the inclusion of some Sydney players.

> A prominent member of the NSWRU is of the opinion there is nothing at all in the statement. In the first place he thinks it is hardly likely that an All Blacks party to visit England will do anything that could question their right to be All Blacks. They are going to England on the reputation of the 1905 All Blacks team.

As far as he knows, no advances have been made to any of the local players. Probably the statement has been made over there with an object in mind. Anyhow, it is a high compliment to the NSW players to say that their inclusion will strengthen the New Zealand team. He is emphatic in his opinion that the New Zealanders would be the last people to attempt it.

Perhaps the object of sending forth a rumour that some Sydney players would join the team is to cast a stigma amongst the sport-loving public upon the games to be shortly player here. However, it comes with a good deal of surprise that such a report should get about at all.

Another well-known authority remarked that he was told by one of the All Blacks team on their return from England that within twelve months he would be back there playing for one of the Northern clubs.

As to the question of professionalism a great deal has been written and said. There have been statements that players have received money, but they have not been substantiated. The majority of the members of the two rugby governing bodies are determined to use every effort to stamp out any sign of professionalism in Sydney, and the same feeling exists in Queensland.

Perhaps in a few years we shall find amateurs and professionals playing side by side in football teams, just as they do at cricket and golf. There are some games in which the professional has raised the standard of the game, notably in the two branches of sport mentioned, and there are some who take a prominent part in local football who see the professional is bound to come.[50]

Peter Moir (from the Glebe club) was one of the key men involved in bringing Baskerville's professional New Zealand team to Sydney in 1907.

Like other Sydney newspapers and officials before them, *The Herald* writer spoke in terms of the move to professionalism as a natural progression of the rugby game in Australia. They disagreed about when it would happen, and when would be the right time, but it would eventually come.

CHAPTER NINE

PROFESSIONAL LEAGUE NOW A CERTAINTY

CAN THE NSW BLUES DEFEAT THE ALL BLACKS?

With the final inter-state matches of 1907 out of the way, everyone looked forward to the arrival of the New Zealanders in just over a week. Harold Judd, still lying in hospital with his leg mending well, said he would somehow find a way to get to the SCG to see at least one All Blacks game.[1]

The New Zealand team arrived in Sydney at dawn on July 11 (Thursday), after sailing across the Tasman Sea on the SS *Warrimoo*. They had a bad crossing, so dreadful the team did not see sun for four days. The team was conveyed by carriage to the Oxford Hotel where they were to stay. The team manager, Edgar Wylie, was forced to attend to the multitude of reporters waiting with questions about the opening match against NSW to be played on the Saturday and, of course, professionalism.[2]

'We had a rough trip over,' said Wylie, 'and encountered a head wind all the way, right from Wellington.'

The reporters got straight to the point, 'Is the team fully representative?'

'Yes,' observed Wylie, 'it is as representative a New Zealand team as is possible to get on tour.'

'Would the inclusion of George Tyler have strengthened it?'

'Well,' replied Wylie, 'Tyler is a fine player, and no doubt he would have been of much assistance to the team, but he could not come. The team, I repeat, is as representative as can be got together for an Australian tour.'

'How many of the famous All Blacks does the team include?'

'Of the twenty-two we have brought over, twelve were in that famous combination. This is every bit as good a team as that which went to England,' Wylie stated.

'How is it that George Smith did not come?'

'Oh,' said Wylie, 'because the selectors didn't ask him.'

'It has been cabled to Australia that the New Zealand team includes some ten players who will accompany the New Zealand professional team to England,' stated a reporter. 'Is that a fact?'

'My opinion with regard to the professional team for England,' replied the manager, 'is that it will not go. I also believe that not one member of this team will go. I kept my eyes and ears open during the voyage, but nothing whatever was dropped to lead one to believe that any of the members of the team will accompany the professional team to England.'

'How do you regard your chances in the opening match against New South Wales?'

'I don't like to feel confident,' replied Wylie, 'but looking at the past form of our team, I think we ought to win unless New South Wales has very much improved.'

Wylie would never make such an admission to the newspapers, but the NZRU's 'team was chosen with care to leave out all suspected

New South Wales Team v. New Zealand (Sydney, 1907)

Back Row: John Hughes, James Hughes, C Hill (trainer), Peter Burge,
Bede Smith, 'Paddy' McCue.
Third Row: J L Groundwater, Edward Mandible, W Dibble, Norman Row,
John Stuntz, H G Waddell.
Second Row: Bob Graves, Chris McKivat, Charles Murnin (c), James McMahon (Mgr),
H B Oxenham, Dally Messenger, John Barnett.
Front Row: William Dix, 'Boxer' Russell, Fred Wood, Tom Griffin, John Rosewell.

applicants' for the professional tour. As it was, four 'applicants' had in fact avoided detection and were in the amateur All Blacks team.

The New Zealanders were officially welcomed at a mid-day function conducted by the NSWRU, followed by a public reception at the Sydney Town Hall that evening with over 3,500 present. Great enthusiasm prevailed, the hall was decked out in sky blue New South Wales and black New Zealand colours, and the function opened with musical entertainment from a band.

After a while the gathering was invited to sing 'For They are Jolly Good Fellows,' Wylie made a short speech of thanks in which he took the opportunity to point out there were no professional players in his team.

The New Zealand captain, Jimmy Hunter, after initially declining to speak, rose to his feet and said forthrightly, 'We will do our best to give you the biggest licking you have ever had in your life!' which produced roars of laughter across the hall. The visitors then gave their war-cry before the band resumed for the remainder of the evening.[3]

The anticipation for the big match continued to build across the city on the Friday. The New Zealanders 'walked' the SCG, while the ground's officials pondered how to cater for the expected 40,000 crowd. For a few days everyone forgot about words like 'professionalism' and talked about nothing but football. Could the NSW Blues defeat the mighty All Blacks?

52,000 AT A RUGBY MATCH

The next day produced a perfectly clear blue sky with a slight nip in the air, a pristine mid-winter Sydney day. It was a good day for fast and open football, and it turned out that most of Sydney wanted to be there. 52,000 people walked, rode or caught a tram to the SCG. The gathered crowd was the largest ever at a football match, of any code, anywhere in Australasia. *The Herald's* report noted it was a case of 'Hats off!' in front, 'which was unique at a football match and made for a remarkable appearance.'[4]

The cinematograph operators began turning the handles of their cameras as the Blues took the field in Indian file. The crowd arose and cheered. Then came the New Zealanders, 'ominous spots of black against the green carpet.' The two teams 'hurried their defiance' against each other, the 'hip-ray' war-cry of the Blues being followed by 'the All Blacks performing a kind of modified haka.' The match began at 3 p.m., the first time a major game had been started that early — too many recent matches had not closely adhered to the 3.15 start, consequently they finished in the dark.

'Bolla' Francis kicked off for New Zealand and the crowd let out an almighty roar. Messenger had an early attempt at a goal from a penalty but missed. Immediately afterwards, play stopped as His Excellency the Governor-General arrived, he was then cheered by the two teams. Play resumed and the crowd brought their long repetitive chant of 'Blues! Blues! Blues!' to a crescendo. The Blues came to the All Blacks goal line with a great forward rush, headed by Murnin and Burge, that included short passes and clever footwork. The ball was handed to Blues centre three-quarter Bede Smith, who made a final short burst and scored a try. The crowd erupted with excited cheering and applause.

Nearing half-time 'Massa' Johnston, one of the All Black forwards showed his dribbling skills, toeing the ball over the NSW line. But Messenger came with a great sprint, and saved by kicking the pigskin dead to the fence.

The crush in the front rows of the crowd forced people to stand. When they did, roars of 'Down, down!' were thrown at them, along with orange-peel, grass and earth. The yell soon turned to 'Up, up!' and everyone stood for the rest of the match, including many in the stands. A sifting blue [tobacco] smoke cloud steadily rose from the crowd all afternoon. In the bright sun it produced a thick haze that reduced the ability of many to be able to recognise the players.

Any hope of a Blues win over the invincible All Blacks was lost in the second half. The New Zealanders' superior weight in the forwards told the longer the match went on, breaking the Blues defence open for three tries and an 11–3 win. The full-time whistle sounded, and as the teams left the field and the public streamed from the gates, 'a large futile policeman chased invasive and evasive small boys from the sacred oval.'

The gate-receipts were £2,583 — an enormous sum for one afternoon's football. The consensus at the after-match function, held at the A.B.C. Café in the city, was that the game was a magnificent contest before an extraordinary crowd. It didn't pass by some of the footballers that the gate-money taken, all on the sweat and toil of the thirty players, amounted to over £86 a man.

The return match, to be played on the work-day Wednesday, was transferred from the smaller Sports Ground to the SCG 'to cater for a larger crowd and ensure no one is turned away from the gate.' The move proved to be needed as 23,000 attended the match. In a surprise to all, NSW defeated the All Blacks by 14–0. The match was remembered as the first time NSW ever kept New Zealand scoreless, and also for Messenger's 'sensational leap.'

The 1907 New Zealand rugby union team in Australia. Edgar Wylie (manager) is seated in the centre wearing a boater hat. Jimmy Hunter (captain) is behind the football.

Bede Smith secured the ball for NSW, and passed to Messenger. He dodged a tackle and made a dash for the line. Two All Blacks went at him, both making a low tackle. As they did so Messenger took a flying leap over them, and landing in the visitors' in-goal, scored one of the most sensational tries ever seen on the SCG. 'The crowd recognised the feat with a special cheer for the man who had performed it, and to clinch matters the same man with a remarkably fine effort found the way over the bar.'[5]

Reports of the professional movement had disappeared from the newspapers in the wake of the two NSW v New Zealand matches. The only news released was that the 'professional rugby team will leave New Zealand for London direct about the third week of August,' sailing eastward across the Pacific.[6]

WAITING FOR THE AUSTRALIAN TEAM SELECTIONS

In the weeks leading up to the first Test match between Australia and New Zealand (to be played on July 20) the talk was all about which players should be selected. With so many good players on show in

Sydney football, there was always going to be some disappointed footballers and their supporters.

Most pundits had Burdon, a Test regular since 1903, down as one of the forwards. Even Swannell, who had been passed over by the NSW selectors, had letter-writers to the newspapers urging his inclusion. Messenger continued to have his critics, and for the NSW team he was still posted out on the wing.[7]

Many of the views in the newspapers lauded Chris McKivat, who played five-eighth. In many ways he was the most important player to NSW and Australian teams of the time. 'McKivat is an absolute champion, the very man required,' wrote one supporter in *The Herald*. 'He can screw-kick with either foot, punt either foot, and finds the line every time. He is really the most valuable player we have. He gets his men going every time he handles the ball, and the pleasing feature of his play is that he is the most unselfish player we have, and plays brilliantly every match. He is the bright particular star of any team, a player who can extricate his side out of great difficulties with one of those lovely screw-kicks with either foot, and is a treasure to his side. His headwork is a treat, and he is one of the deadliest of tacklers — he gets his man every time.'[8]

The selectors sat down at lunchtime the day before the first Test to choose the team. Six hours later they had still not emerged. *The Herald* reported, 'Every few minutes after 6 o'clock the reply to the ring on the phone was "in a few minutes." Those few minutes did not reach the end of their tether until about 9 o'clock. Just when visitors to the rooms were looking forward to an all-night sitting, the names were announced. The team chosen is undoubtedly a very strong one.'[9]

Two of the players expected to be chosen were absent. Messenger, who had yet to play for Australia, was unavailable due to an injured ankle. The omission of Burdon though was considered to be somewhat of a surprise given that he was a permanent member of the NSW and Test teams in previous seasons. He had also been back from injury for four matches before the team was chosen. It could be readily argued that the selectors kept faith with the state players, but the suspicion remains he was overlooked for other reasons.

BURDON DISLOCATES HIS SHOULDER

An immediate consequence of Burdon's omission was that he was able to join his Sydney club mates on a two-match tour of northern NSW. The NSWRU dispersed the club teams throughout the state while the Test match was on. Players weren't compelled to go, but most did — it was an opportunity to travel, play some football and be entertained by the towns they visited. Their country hosts usually provided them with a filling banquet, drinks and entertainment.

The second match of the Sydney club's tour was against Manning on July 22 at Central Park in Wingham. The ball was 'passed to Burdon, who ran to the line, but was thrown heavily, and his shoulder put out.' Disappointed that his troublesome shoulder had again been dislocated, Burdon was still well enough to attend that evening's entertainment, where he made a speech thanking the opposing team and his hosts.[10]

By the time Burdon, his arm again in a sling, and his club mates returned to Sydney, news of NSW players' involvement in the professional movement had broken.

COMBINING BLUES AND MAROONS

On the morning of the first Test match (July 20) *The Herald* published startling news from Wellington. 'Proposals have been made to the New Zealand professional team from Australia, which may lead to a series of matches in the Commonwealth. Private advice has been received in Wellington to the effect that a professional Rugby Union, destined to affiliate with the English Northern Rugby Union, is being formed in Sydney. Mr Baskerville declines to say more than that he had been cognisant of the fact for some time past. A few Australian enthusiasts have made a proposal to him regarding the New Zealand professional team playing in Sydney on the way to England. Negotiations are still proceeding, and if the guarantees and assurances were satisfactory no doubt the Australian public would be afforded an opportunity of seeing the All Black professionals play.'[11]

No doubt the revelations were widely discussed by the great crowd of 48,000 at the Test match. The game itself, won by New Zealand 26–6, was described as 'absolutely rotten.' *The Sunday Sun* called it 'deadly dull' and those who argued that the local Unions should change the playing rules to make the game more attractive had more ammunition.[12]

For the first time in Sydney, the Australian team didn't wear the blue NSW jersey. *The Herald* noted, 'The home team's jersey being of light blue with maroon bars, with a kangaroo on the breast.' The design was the same as that used on the 1905 tour to New Zealand. 'Australia's colours, the blue of hope barred with the deep red of defiance. The New Zealand war-cry was pretty well drowned by the noise of the crowd admiring the new colours.'[13]

In the aftermath, the Queensland contingent of the team were blamed for Australia's poor performance. The argument was that the NSW side, who had already defeated the All Blacks in one of their two contests, were the strongest side in Australia — the inclusion of Queenslanders in a Test team only served to weaken NSW.[14]

Some of the SCG spectators also exhibited the sort of partisan behaviour that the amateur idealists abhorred. 'I always notice in Sydney,' said W.M. Allen, 'the very biased mind the crowd holds at any inter-state or inter-colonial match. An extremely brilliant exhibition of play by the visitors will be very feebly applauded, if at all. But when a member of the home team does anything a little better than usual, there is a roar of applause from all parts of the ground. I need scarcely say how babyish that sort of thing is, and to a certain extent discouraging to the visitors. I hope all who are loyal patrons of the game will understand what I mean.'[15]

Charles 'Bronco' Seeling – a member of the NZRU teams of 1905 and 1907. It is claimed that he acted as a selector for the New Zealand professional team in 1907.

Even before the Australian team arrived in Queensland for the second Test, a proposal was put to the NSWRU by James Henderson that 'in the event of Australia not being successful in Brisbane, the concluding match of the tour, at present arranged as against Australia at Sydney, be cancelled and that one against NSW be substituted.'[16]

With Australia a young nation, there was still far more appeal and glory in an 'inter-colonial' NSW v New Zealand match to many people. The two matches between these teams already played on the tour had seen one victory to each — but no third match had been provided for in the schedule. Thus Henderson, with the full support of the vast majority of rugby followers in Sydney, saw a deciding match having far more interest than a 'dead-rubber' contest between Australia and New Zealand.

Henderson hoped a 2–1 win by NSW over the All Blacks would generate publicity for the NSWRU tour to Great Britain in 1908. It was never intended by the NSWRU that it would join with the QRU to send a combined representative team 'Home.' The proposal to change the Test match was adopted by the NSWRU, but rejected by the QRU.[17]

THE ALL BLACKS BOARD THE 'BRISBANE EXPRESS'

The All Blacks left Sydney by the 'Brisbane express' train for matches against Queensland and Australia. At Newcastle the players stepped onto the railway platform for a break and were confronted by a throng of newspaper reporters. A ship in the Tasman Sea had sent through to Sydney a telegram from New Zealand that identified 'the names of twenty-one players as certainties for the professional football team to visit England.' The names included six of the current amateur All Blacks.[18]

Wylie, the team manager, 'denied any knowledge of such an arrangement, and was not disposed to discuss the matter in any way' reported *The Herald*. 'Several of the players whose names were mentioned, when questioned on the subject, displayed a calmness which seemed quite remarkable. The one thing that struck the inquirer was that the names, and the fact that professional band of footballers had been gathered together, did not provoke any surprise or denial of the project. It is clear that they were perfectly well aware that negotiations in which their names figured were going on.'

Charlie Seeling, a member of the New Zealand team and one of the 1905 All Blacks, commented: 'I was approached in the matter, and that is all — it is a gross libel. You can take my word for it that the list cabled from New Zealand is almost entirely wrong. There may perhaps be one, but no more. The whole of the team have booked their passage home again. I do not think professional football would succeed in New Zealand. It might in Sydney. In New Zealand the attendances at club matches are very small — 500 or 600 is a good crowd at a club match in Auckland.'[19]

A NOD AND A WINK FOR MESSENGER

Dally Messenger had been selected to make his debut for Australia in the second Test team in Brisbane. However, he advised the team manager, James McMahon, that he could not make the trip.[20] Disappointed by the news, McMahon left for Brisbane to watch the Queensland v New Zealand match and prepare for the Test to be held a week later.

Messenger managed his family's boat building business at Double Bay. 'It was a fairly big business,' said Messenger, 'and took all my time. I said I would have to put a man in my position while I was away. I said that if they were willing to pay a man £2/10s a week to do my work I would be able to go. The NSWRU wouldn't even consider the offer and so the team left without me. But when they arrived in Brisbane apparently there was dickens to pay from a gate point of view. I got a wire from McMahon in effect to say: "Money's all right. Leave straight away." That was OK by me. I knew he meant the money for the man who took my job, and off I got as fast as the train could take me.'

'I wasn't looking for veiled professionalism,' explained Messenger, 'I simply put the proposition to the Union and was prepared to abide by the decision. I didn't want nor did I ask for any laws to be broken. I had never received a penny for playing.'[21]

Despite the reasoning Messenger offered, it is an admission he knew the payment was a clear breach of the amateurism rules under the RFU and the NSWRU.[22] Dally Messenger was paid by the NSWRU to make his international rugby union debut for Australia. He had committed an act of professionalism which, if exposed, would have seen him expelled from rugby union.

Two weeks later the *St George Call* wrote about 'those who know of some recent proceedings — it is an open secret that these very "amateur" bodies were accessories to, if not the actual offerers of, a handsome sum to a NSW player to go up and play in a Test match in Brisbane.'[23]

Messenger took his place in the Australian team (August 3), in front of 17,000 eager Brisbane spectators. The All Blacks were again too strong for the home team, winning 14–5. Messenger was embroiled in controversy once the match was over, having to answer questions about the professional All Blacks tour.

'There was a widely circulated rumour in Brisbane on Saturday,' a local reporter wired to Sydney 'that Messenger, the brilliant NSW three-quarter, had been invited and had accepted an invitation to join the professional rugby team. Messenger was interviewed to-night, and the rumour brought under his notice.'

'There is nothing in it as far as I am concerned,' said Messenger. 'I have had no communication with or from the organisers of the team. The rumour that I have joined the team is untrue, and you may contradict it flatly.' Messenger added that none of the NSW players in Brisbane had been approached to take part.[24]

In Sydney *The Arrow* placed a large photograph of Messenger on its front page declaring him the 'Man of the Moment.' The newspaper commented that 'Professional football cannot live here unless a miracle happens. And miracles do not enter into the football world. If any Sydney player be so foolish to join this team he will merely commit football suicide, so far as Australia is concerned.'[25]

The professionalism issue seemed to be spreading, with *The Newcastle Morning Herald* reporting, 'The Rugby Union of Australia and

The 1907 Australian rugby union team that played in Brisbane. Dally Messenger is sitting in the front row, third from right. The team was: William Dix, Esmond Parkinson, 'Boxer' Russell, Bede Smith, Dally Messenger, Edward Mandible, Fred Wood, Bill Richards, Peter Flanagan, Jack Fihelly, Peter Burge, Bill Canniffe, John Barnett, H B Oxenham, Allen Oxlade (c).

New Zealand are not alone in their struggles to preserve the amateur game. The success of the Springboks in Great Britain has also been followed by a proposal that a South African professional team should visit England.'[26]

Amidst a seemingly never-ending stream of news and rumours during that weekend, *The Australian Star* published a report from Wellington that 'it has been announced that the professional rugby team will play three matches in Sydney.'[27]

IT WILL SPLIT RUGBY INTO TWO FEEBLE HALVES

On August 5 *The Herald* broke the news that confirmed professional rugby had arrived in Sydney. 'The fact that the Agricultural Ground has been engaged for three matches against the New Zealand professional team was on Saturday discussed in those places where rugby contests were played. Everyone was asking everyone what sort of a team would be got together to meet the professional team.'

The air is full of rumours, and though some of them are bound to be correct, there is not much likelihood of anything tangible being known until after the final Test match. On the strength of remarks dropped by officials in high authority, there is a feeling amongst a number of our players strongly in favour professionalism, and it is only necessary for some guiding spirit to take up the matter for quite a large number of our present players to follow the lead.

Another whose advice has been for long respected in the counsels of the game fails to see why any harm must necessarily following the wake of such a movement. It is a big question, and is one that will cause a great deal of heart-burning before it is settled. As to what shape that settlement will take is at present a matter of speculation.

Supporters of professionalism ask why should we not have the amateur and professional appearing together in the one side (as in cricket). The local Unions will, of course, work tooth and nail against the introduction of the professional. If he ever did become an established fact, under the control of the NSWRU, it would mean, of course, the cutting of the thread which binds the NSW daughter to the English parent. Indeed, there is no knowing what it would mean in the world's rugby.[28]

For the first time a name arose in connection with the movement. *The Herald* announced, 'James J. Giltinan, a gentleman well known in another branch of sport is, it is understood, taking an active part in making the arrangements for the matches, and, if the rumour speak truly, some success has been met with in regard to one or two captains of first grade teams.'[29] *The Herald's* editor added,

Any change that strikes at the roots of our national sports touches most of us in a vital point, and it is clear from the comment on the mere rumour of a coming professionalism in football that this subject will arouse much more heated controversy than would the fall of a Federal Ministry or a state election. As yet professionalism in football is any empty threat that may very well fail to realise itself, but the talk of its possibility has brought to the surface an undercurrent of feeling, familiar enough to those who follow the game closely, and which is all the better out in the open and faced fairly.

We are told that we shall be making no real change; that we shall only at last be calling things by their right names, and that in fact many clubs pay directly or indirectly for the services of their players. Of course there is some truth in this charge, but such insidious happenings at their worst fall far short of outright professionalism, and they do not affect the amateur status and self-sacrifice of the immense bulk of players. Again, it is easy to accuse the MRU of not offering a 'fair deal,' and there will no doubt be malcontents to catch as this argument, and the only reply is that the Union is human and does its best.

To divide the players (professional and amateur) would be to split rugby into two feeble halves. This is folly in itself, and exceptional folly in the circumstances. Rugby, with all its tenacity, cohesion and prestige, has as much as it can do to hold its own against the Australian game — a game well enough, but not rugby — and the enthusiastic Rugbyite who listens to the pleadings of the would-be professional will rub his eyes a little later, it may be, to find his sport extinct.[30]

The Herald also interviewed a secretary of one of the more powerful clubs in the competition, and asked if his men would join a professional movement.

Turn professional? Why the boys would turn anything so long as they got a bit better deal than they are getting from the MRU. Why shouldn't they get something out of the game besides kicks? You take it from me, if the right men start this professional movement in Sydney, they will get nearly every man playing in the Union competitions.

Of course, it doesn't do to mention names at present, but I can tell you that every member of my club will go over. Not that the boys want to be paid for Saturday afternoon fun; but they think — and rightly so, too — that as they draw the crowd they should get something out of the gate-money.

Thank goodness the players are taking a tumble to it now. Next season you will see something different. The Union officials see the change coming too. That's why they bought Epping. They saw that the men who made the sport were going to try and get some of the returns, and perhaps some of the thousands the Union had tied up, so they straight away purchase Epping. In so doing sink all their reserve, and leave a tidy lot to be paid off in future years.

They have been very clever, but before the matter has been fixed up they will find they have bitten off more than they can chew.[31]

IT IS SPOKEN OF AS THE RUGBY LEAGUE

'A Wave Of Discontent — MRU Administration — Irruption Of Professionalism — New League Forming' were the headlines in *The Herald* on August 6. All of the city's papers were full of articles and opinion pieces on the professional movement. It was clear the day of decision had come.

It would seem that the formation of a New Zealand professional football team was all that was needed to fan into flame a smouldering discontent in our own rugby world. There is decidedly trouble abroad to-day, and already a struggle between amateur and professional football may be said to have been entered upon. Interviews in various quarters yesterday elicited the fact that there have been murmurings against the administration of the MRU for some time, the players objecting to that body amassing huge balances while they themselves, the instruments of the amassing, were allowed to be out-of-pocket in regard to various matches.

When the news was passed round that the New Zealand professional team wanted matches here the state of local feeling was clearly demonstrated in the fact that, at the risk of disqualification from the amateur Unions, a large number of first-class players volunteered to represent this state. This gave the secessionists something tangible to work on, and a professional Union or League — it is already spoken of as the Rugby League of New South Wales — is now regarded as a certainty.

One prominent figure in the new movement declares unequivocally that six first-class teams will be playing under the League next year. On the other hand, the MRU officials, while admitting an undercurrent of discontent, do not view the advent of professionalism with alarm, believing that the public will not support it, and that it will speedily work itself out.[32]

The newspaper also printed the views of many officials. The Eastern Suburbs club secretary, J.A. Paton, talked with a reporter of *The Herald*. 'He said that he was afraid there was at present among the players a very strong undercurrent of feeling in favour of professionalism. The big gate-money appeared to be responsible for it.'

Paton though was not a supporter of the new movement. 'I really do not think that professional football could last here, we do not have the population to support it even if the public did throw over the amateurs. The scheme will eventually break down for want of players, and every man for himself.'

However, he said that 'he could see a good deal in the matter from a professional point of view. If a man were a champion footballer, and he thought that he could make more money at it than at anything else, should he not be entitled to earn it if the professional game could be properly organised?'[33]

The 'champion player' which Paton was sharing the 'thoughts' of, could only have been Easts' Dally Messenger. He was the one player in Australia with (seemingly) enough crowd-drawing power to secure a fee large enough to earn a living from rugby if professionalism got up and running. Put with the rumours that Messenger had already agreed to join the New Zealanders, it seems he was much more closely involved in the movement than he would publicly admit to.

Giltinan immediately became the public face of the new Rugby League. 'You can take it for certain that next year will see six teams playing under the Rugby League of NSW,' he declared emphatically in *The Herald*.

> To suggest that the thing can't last is absurd. The very best rugby in England is being played professionally and when we link up with New Zealand and England there will be far more interesting games to be witnessed than at present. There can be no doubt that professional football will be the better game, for the simple reason that the players will have to take it very seriously, and see to it that they are in absolutely the very best condition to do any good at it at all.
>
> Of course, what will be called professionalism here will not be anything like what is so-termed in England. In the old country the professional footballer can absolutely live on the game, but he won't be able to do that here. As a matter of fact, it will be no more strictly professional than our international 'amateur' cricket of to-day. We will simply see to it that a man's expenses shall be paid in connection with each match — and not let him be seriously out-of-pocket, as is often the case with players from the ranks of working men under the niggardly policy of the MRU — and at the end of each season the players will probably be given bonuses, according to the results achieved in the matter of gate-money.
>
> There will be no piling up of great balances and the buying of racecourses, while the men who earn the gates are allowed to be at a loss. That is the crux of the whole position, and the MRU has only itself to blame for the turn events are taking. At the same time, it is going to be all the better, from a point of view of the public, as the new 'professionalism' must make for a decidedly higher standard of play.[34]

In an interview with *The Referee*, Giltinan also revealed that, 'All the new clubs to be formed will play under the Northern Union rules with 13 men-a-side.' Then asked as to why he had not encouraged the players to seek improvements in conditions through the NSWRU, Giltinan replied: 'It is an impossibility under the constitution of the NSWRU to get those concessions without seceding from the English Rugby Union.' The reporter also noted 'though he (Giltinan) has had no connection with the Rugby Union, the only time he ever communicated with that body he received a letter in reply which he considered an insult.'[35]

CLUBS TO DIVIDE THE LEAGUE'S INCOME

Lewis Abrams, by then recognised as 'the father of electoral football,' and a man who persistently fought for improved conditions for the players, talked to *The Herald*.[36]

Abrams was one of the delegates from the Glebe club on the MRU committee. His comments displayed a strong knowledge of what was being brought about, suggesting he may have been closely involved with Giltinan and the others, particularly in regard to organisational matters.

Abrams said, independently of Giltinan, that there should be a NSW Rugby League formed, and in 1908 there would be a club competition of professional teams. He also referred to the co-existence between amateurs and professionals in cricket, a game in which he, as well as Giltinan and Trumper, were all involved. Abrams also said, 'In the metropolis they could form about eight district clubs. Membership should be confined to bona-fide residents of districts, the same as at present, and before long there would be a strong competition going. The League should govern the sport and manage the matches, and the proceeds, after deducting certain expenses, should be divided amongst the competing clubs pro rata.'

As a member of the MRU committee, Abrams' comments were revealing. He added, 'The Union was responsible for the strong support the professional movement was receiving. If they had treated the players a little more liberally, the players would have shown loyalty. Under the present state of affairs the players, by joining the movement, were losing little, with a chance of gaining much.'

Abrams then confirmed that the MRU was aware since at least the middle of May (when it held a special meeting and resolved to find and purchase a ground) that professional rugby was being organised in Sydney. 'The professional movement had been anticipated by the Union. For fear the clubs next year would vote themselves some of the accumulated funds, they decided to remove the temptation by sinking the money in purchasing the Epping racecourse.'

Abrams' fate appeared to be sealed — asked by *The Herald* if he would be connected with the managing of the new movement he replied: 'My services are not required by the amateurs, and if I am requested I may do something for the professionals.' Despite this statement, he remained within the rugby union ranks, hoping that he could push reforms from within.

After talking to some players, *The Herald* pronounced that the failure of the MRU to follow the principles of the district scheme was at the root of the problem. 'These players are connected with various clubs, and the spirit of rivalry for local distinction and supremacy has been the key-note of their energy and enthusiasm. There is friendly rivalry on all sides, but the Union, it is claimed, has killed that rivalry by dragging the leading clubs out of their own districts Saturday after Saturday in order to provide gate-money.'[37]

The purchase of the Epping Ground proved to the players and clubs that the MRU was more interested in large profits than improving suburban grounds to foster local support and rivalry. Working-class people defined themselves by their town or suburbs; it was important to them to play home and away matches — not to be used by the MRU to make money by dragging them to the SCG or a ground outside the areas of both teams.

BURDON'S INJURY NOT THE CATALYST

Claims that the Rugby League was formed in response to an injury suffered by Alec Burdon cannot be supported. The implication of Lewis Abrams' admission is that the final decision to form a professional Rugby League was made in early May 1907 — immediately after George Smith confirmed the New Zealanders were proceeding with their NU tour.

Clearly, Burdon's injury in Wingham on July 22 occurred more than two months later. His earlier injury (on May 4) was also not a catalyst. It was initially not thought to be a serious injury. By the time the MRU held its special meeting in mid-May, it was only just becoming apparent that Burdon was facing another three weeks off work. Burdon's predicament strengthened the resolve of the players, and was used in arguments against the Unions to improve conditions, but it did not cause the professional League to be formed.

The movement began as far back as 1903 when serious discontent over the 3s-a-day allowance emerged with NSW players on tour in Brisbane. When the plight of the players was compared to the profits being made by the NSW and New Zealand Unions (especially the 1905 All Blacks tour) the dissatisfaction grew. The move to form professional teams in New Zealand and Australia began with the visit of George Smith and the Auckland City team to Sydney in July 1906.

DIGGING THEIR OWN GRAVES

'A gentlemen prominently connected with one of the Unions' was also interviewed by *The Herald*, and provided an additional insight into why the rugby rebellion had ignited.

It must not be forgotten that the young men who take part in football must be of the strong, burly kind, and necessarily a large proportion of these men must come from the working class. The game is a hard one, and there are plenty of hazards and hard knocks connected with it. A man may get badly injured, and be laid up for weeks or months.

Then, too, is the manner in which our representatives are treated when away on tour has aroused a feeling amongst them that they are not being anything like fairly dealt with. Is 3s a day a fair remuneration for men, many of whom have nothing but their hard-earned wages to depend on? It is said that if they cannot afford the time or loss of money they should not make the trip, but that principle would eventually be a serious blow to our great winter game. Besides that, it would be very humiliating if a man's position prevented him from representing his state when called upon to do so.

I think it would be a very good thing for the clubs if a certain percentage of the takings were handed over to them. There is no doubt it is a very sore point with many that the MRU has thousands of pounds sunk in investments, and they want to know why the clubs at least should not receive some portion of the proceeds which the public pay to see the different matches.

The adoption of the professional movement would mean that there would be no connection in any way between the English and NSW Unions — well, so what if it does? It would be a pity in one way, but if we are going to have rugby at all let us have it under Australian conditions. We must think of those of our boys who have not been born with silver spoons in their mouths.

The Unions here and in New Zealand, by their same mean, niggardly policy, must be held responsible for the new movement. This team of professional All Blacks which is going to England may be the beginning, but I am certain that it will not be the end of professionalism in New Zealand. If there are Unions in Australia and New Zealand where the professional element is admitted, what would it matter if they were not recognised by the amateur organisations in Great Britain? The professional Union in England is far stronger and has better players than its rival Unions. It would be possible to have an interchange of visits between professional teams from New Zealand and England just as we have now of amateur combinations.

Another thing, it would be all very well if we had pure amateurism; but have we got it here at present? How often do we hear of men playing with a team simply because it is made worth their while in the shape of a situation or some other consideration. Again, when some of our teams are touring, how much in the way of compensation or additional pocket money is charged to 'managerial expenses'?

Amateur sport is one of the best things in the world, and I thoroughly believe in it. But if we are to have it, let it be without any subterfuge.[38]

Harrie Wood, the president of the MRU, talked to *The Australian Star.* 'There is absolutely no necessity for the introduction of professionalism in rugby in this state. Have the public, the supporters of the great winter pastime, asked for professionalism? No. And did we not, only a few weeks ago, see 52,000 people on the SCG to witness a match between NSW and New Zealand? Does not the enormous dimensions of that crowd convince the most sceptical that the NSW rugby football public is thoroughly satisfied with the game as purely an amateur sport? If the players were to take such an injudicious step (by adopting professionalism) it would be found eventually they had been the instruments of destroying a sport which is now at its zenith in NSW.'[39]

The Sydney Sportsman offered its view and, like many others it criticised the current move toward professionalism, but also reinforced the feeling that it was eventually going to come to Australian rugby. 'Sydney players, with an idea of professionalism in their heads, should get rid of such as soon as possible, as we are not nearly ready for that class of football yet, and may not be for years. Should any of the backs of this state join the New Zealand professional team they practically dig their own graves as far as football is concerned in Australia.'[40]

'The mind immediately flies to Dally Messenger, the bright star of to-day's rugby' wrote *The Northern Star* on behalf of just about everyone else.[41] Messenger continued to deny his involvement telling 'one of the NSW selectors that he had no idea of playing against the New Zealand professional team, nor of accompanying it to England.'[42]

The professional version of the New Zealand All Blacks were now being referred to as the 'All Golds.' The name was a derogatory reference to the players' arrangement where they would each share in the financial rewards of the tour. *The Herald* on August 7 being the first to bring the name to wider public awareness by using it in a headline. *The Newcastle Morning Herald* also issued the surprising news the following day that 'arrangements will probably be made for a tour of a NSW professional team to Yorkshire in 1908 and for a visit to Australia and New Zealand in 1909 of a Northern Union team.'[43]

The Daily Telegraph carried an advertisement on August 7 for three matches between the 'Professional All Blacks' and the 'NSW All Blues' on August 17, 21 and 24. It was the first official confirmation of the matches — but under whose authority were they being held?

NO QUEENSLANDERS FOR AUSTRALIA'S TEST TEAM

Gaining far fewer headlines during those hectic few days was another remarkable occurrence in the history of Australian rugby: the team chosen to play the third Test against New Zealand comprised entirely NSW players. The three-man selection panel consisted of one from Queensland and two from NSW. The deciding vote was given to James McMahon, from the NSWRU, if the other two selectors failed to reach agreement. In every case he sided with his fellow NSW selector and thus ruled out every Queenslander.[44] Henderson had gotten his wish and most New South Welshmen would now view the match as a NSW v New Zealand contest to settle the 'series' which stood at 1–1.

In reality, the selected Australian team was the same fifteen NSW players who defeated New Zealand in the final clash in Sydney. On form, both Oxlade and Richards from Queensland who played for Australia in the second Test, should have been in the team — Oxlade was the Australian captain in Brisbane. The QRU called the whole affair, 'extremely detrimental to the interests of Australian rugby and calculated to endanger the pleasant relations existing between our two Unions.'[45]

One sports editor called it the 'most unfair and unsportsmanlike tactics ever known adopted by a responsible body of men.' However, the condemnation was far from universal, particularly in Sydney, where '99 out of every 100 followers are so over-excited with the match' that they hadn't paused in the slightest to consider what had been done to bring the contest about.[46]

Given the dramas that were occurring in rugby at the time, the actions of the NSWRU in offending the only other state where rugby was played was particularly short-sighted and may well have contributed to subsequent events in Queensland.[47]

The NSWRU also proclaimed that after an investigation into every player selected for the third Test, it found none had been approached to take up professionalism, nor had any ever been paid money for their services. Apparently all was well, and there was 'no suspicion of professionalism' at all to do with the team.[48]

BATEMAN'S CRYSTAL HOTEL (AUGUST 8, 1907)

On the evening of Thursday August 8 'a meeting of players and others interested in the professional movement was held at Bateman's Crystal Hotel,' reported *The Herald*. Located at 432/434 George Street in the city, it was advertised as 'Bateman's Hotel: The Sportsman's Rendezvous.'

> There were about fifty present, including a number of first-grade players; no fewer than five captains being amongst those in attendance. Eight

clubs were represented, the remaining three being University, Manly and Western Suburbs. Before business was entered upon, all present had to sign a document agreeing to play against the New Zealand professional team shortly to visit Sydney. It was resolved to form a body called the NSW [Rugby] Football League. Matters in connection with the project were discussed at length, the general tone being that members were not to go in for out and out professionalism, but simply to make good out-of-pocket expenses. A selection committee was appointed, consisting of three, who are captains of first grade clubs.

It is stated on good authority that some leading players and supporters have received intimation from their employers that they must either forego their positions or professionalism. The question of grounds occupied some attention. There are three grounds mentioned as available for the new League next season, viz., Wentworth Park, Agricultural Ground and Hampden Oval. The organisers of the movement are Mr J. Giltinan and a prominent cricketer.[49]

The meeting was chaired by Henry Hoyle, who became the first president of the NSWRL.

So secretive had the planning of the meeting been, that very little mention of it appeared in the newspapers for days. *The Sun* allegedly broke most of the details, including names, after the supposedly trusted doorman, Charlie Wilson, divulged the details.[50] *The Australian Star* also claimed to have sourced its information from an amateur rugby player who gained admittance under the guise of being a professional.[51]

The Sunday Sun reported that the formation of the NSWRL was due to 'pique' [resentment] on the part of 'certain players at their non-inclusion in representative matches' and the 'large amount of money handled by the NSWRU and MRU.'[52] In its view, the financial concerns of the players could have been remedied by the election of sympathetic MRU officials. The

An advertisement for Bateman's Hotel in Sydney – where the NSWRL was formed on August 8, 1907.

events that led to the formation of the NU in 1895 were not present in the colonies. 'There can scarcely be doubt the somewhat dunderheaded policy of the RFU actually formed the NU against the original wishes of what afterwards became the NU. No such reason existed in Sydney. The players' grievances against the MRU could have been dealt with when MRU officials were elected.'

Cajoled by Giltinan, Trumper and Hoyle, many of the players and officials turned their backs on the Unions, ignoring the path of reform from within. It suggests the primary reasons for the formation of the NSWRL were not simply to obtain better conditions for players (which reforms under the MRU could have achieved), but to gain control of NSW rugby and the rich income it could generate.

PLAYERS DON'T DRAW THE CROWDS

The third Test match between Australia (all-NSW) and New Zealand was played on August 10 at the SCG. Messenger was continuing to deny any involvement with the NSWRL, and the stands and grassed areas were 'full of tension for many reasons.'[53]

The Sydney Mail noted there was a good deal of anxiety in the Members' pavilion for fully an hour before the match, with 'sinister rumours of professionalism' abounding.[54] While there were no late changes to the team, *The Herald* reported events on the opposite side of the field on the hill. 'Much was anticipated and feeling ran high in spots.

There were two hot arguments which ended in bouts with fists. There was bad language, rough humour and betting talk.' It was hardly a fine example of how one should behave at a rugby union international match, and told much about the character of the typical Sydney sporting spectator. 'The few women present had either to pretend they did not hear it or keep moving.'[55]

'The game itself proved such a sparkling one,' reported *The Herald*. 'Several times the occupants of the shilling reserve rose like one man when the game became too exciting.' Australia scored a try in the 'Paddington corner' amidst an 'extraordinary scene of excitement.' It left Messenger with a difficult conversion from the touchline, but he put in 'a capital effort' which went through the posts to give the locals a 5–0 lead. The All Blacks, though, secured a late converted try of their own after two

Australian players collided attempting to catch the ball, leaving the final score a 5–5 draw.[56]

It is also interesting to note that, under favourable weather conditions, the crowd of 29,000 was 19,000 less than had attended the first Test, and only 6,000 more than the mid-week NSW v Zealand match a few weeks earlier. This was despite the match being billed as a 'NSW v New Zealand' tie-off and Dally Messenger making his first Sydney appearance for Australia.

It is wrong to say that Messenger's presence in the NSW or Australian team was a sure way to attract extra spectators. The first Test match attendance of 48,000 — in which Messenger did not play — was only 4,000 less than had been present at the first NSW v New Zealand game. The third Test match saw the crowd drop 40%, even though in his previous Sydney outing against the New Zealanders, Messenger had performed his sensational leaping try.

Crowds at state and international matches in Sydney and Brisbane had been on a steady rise throughout the decade. Messenger had only played his first state game in 1906. Although he was a draw-card to some spectators, Messenger alone was not the reason rugby crowds were growing.

In summing up the 1907 season, the NSWRU's Monty Arnold offered the observation that none of the players were responsible for attendances. 'There is an idea that players draw the crowd,' said Arnold. 'They do not. When Messenger did not play there was a bigger crowd than when he did.'[57]

The final gate-receipts for the four matches against New Zealand in Sydney amounted to a staggering £7,238.[58] Many, unsure whether to transfer their allegiances to the new League, were simply persuaded by the colossal sum of money, particularly when it was compared to the plight of the players. It was a difficult argument for the MRU and NSWRU to counter in a city where the bulk of the populace was working class.

MESSENGER JOINS THE PROFESSIONALS

With the final representative match over, Messenger confirmed he was joining the professional movement. On Monday August 12, he visited James McMahon to personally give him the news of his decision before it hit the newspapers. 'Messenger came and saw me yesterday afternoon,' McMahon informed *The Australian Star* newspaper. Messenger explained to McMahon he was going to give football away altogether after the season to take up professional rowing. 'He told me that this season would be his last in football, and that he was going to join the ranks of the professionals, as he thought he might as well do the best thing he could for himself out of it. I certainly got the impression from his conversation that he was going boat-racing.'[59]

By saying he was retiring from football, Messenger was providing a reason for his actions that many people would accept. He was also implying that he really had nothing to lose by taking part in the professional matches. Unfortunately, by saying that he might as well do the best he could for himself, he added to the rumours.

The newspapers were full of allegations that Messenger had been paid to appear in the upcoming matches, unlike all the other players who had agreed to join the NSWRL. McMahon was asked what he knew of the payment. 'I'll not say,' replied McMahon, 'but ask Mr Giltinan this: will he make a statutory declaration that Messenger is not getting £50?' Giltinan and Messenger duly issued statements asserting that no payment had been made.

Exactly when Messenger agreed to join the professional movement and how much, if anything, he was paid has always been open to conjecture. All reports at the time allege Messenger was paid a total of £50 to appear in all three All Blues matches.[60] Later accounts increased the amount three or four times.[61] Messenger's visit to McMahon was just two days after the third Test — if his earlier denials were honest, then he must have met with Giltinan and finally agreed to join on Sunday August 11.

This appears to be confirmed by comments attributed to Messenger in *The Truth* newspaper over three decades later.[62] He said that after the agreement with Giltinan was made, 'Mother came to see me the following Saturday when we played Baskerville's team.'

However, other aspects of Messenger's version in *The Truth* of how he committed to rugby league seem inconsistent. Messenger stated he was aware of what had appeared in the papers (how could he not) and he knew Trumper and Moir were involved. He said he was working under a boat in his family's boatshed at Double Bay and three men walked in who he didn't know 'from a bar of soap — they were Hoyle, Giltinan and someone else.'

Why Messenger, so long after the event, chose not to identify the third person remains unknown. His family claims it was Trumper. The two men had been friends since their younger days and, while Messenger had no problem mentioning Trumper's involvement in the formation of the NSWRL elsewhere in the article, he may have been trying to protect Trumper. It is also unlikely that Giltinan, who was a regular at the city's numerous official sporting functions, particular after NSW matches, could have been unknown to someone such as Messenger.

'They asked me if I would turn "pro",' claimed Messenger. 'They said "we'll pay you so much for three matches" — I didn't say anything to that. I said I wouldn't decide anything and to go over and see my mother. I'm busy.'

Messenger recalled that he then handed over all responsibility for his momentous decision to his mother: 'Get her answer it will be all right.'

'They went over and saw mother. The answer came back, "You can play." So I took mother's advice, as the old saying is, and I played. They offered me sport cash. I said I didn't want the money. "Give it to mother, give it to her in notes." They did.'

His mother was apparently swayed by the NSWRL's offer to provide payment and support for injured players — something she feared would befall Dally.[63]

It could be suggested Messenger's version of events were merely a smokescreen to hide his deep connection with the establishment of the new League. If he really left the decision to the day after the third Test, and to his mother, it is remarkable that all the rumours from July concerning Messenger were eventually proven to be true.

It is also significant to note that as soon as he went public with the news, Messenger immediately became a member of both the organising and selection groups of the NSWRL.[64] It is apparent Giltinan did not first set up the new League and then, in early August, set about trying to obtain Messenger's allegiance to ensure its success.

Though Messenger was now part of the professionals, it could hardly be said that the fight for Australian rugby was over — far from it. Baskerville's team was due to arrive in the following days, with the first match on Saturday (August 17), and no one knew how the public would react.

For its part, the officials of the MRU felt 'sanguine that the professional movement will be, in a month after the departure of the professional New Zealand team for England, absolutely dead.'

'You take my word,' said one of the MRU officials to *The Australian Star*, 'any player who identifies himself with the professional rugby in this state will be disqualified, and that for life.'[65]

CHAPTER TEN

LILY WHITES *v* ALL GOLDS

GILTINAN TAKES ON HIS CRITICS

As he awaited the arrival of Baskerville's team, Giltinan attempted to respond via the press to criticism of the League and professionalism. 'It seems to have been taken for granted by certain people that because a number of players here are willing to meet and play the New Zealand professional team for England, the sport is threatened with dire consequences,' Giltinan told *The Herald*,[1]

> One would be led to believe by what has appeared in the press that professional rugby was first heard of when a team was formed in New Zealand. The fact that the game flourishes in England under professionalism and that this All Black combination will meet the most famous players in the old country is completely ignored.

> England is the home of rugby, and there is a larger number of the public support for the game under the system by which the players draw expenses, than the section which supports the pure amateur element.

Giltinan continued to refer to Australian cricket as proof that the payment of players was necessary to ensure competitiveness against other countries.

> If paying the players ruined the game, where would our chance of playing England at cricket be? Every player worth picking has had his share of the gate abroad, and a fat fee for 'expenses' at home. Supposing the worst comes to the worst, and a new Union is formed, which will pay proper expenses to the men and treat a player liberally when he is required, is it not likely that the game will be strengthened here?

> It would be a fine thing, no doubt, if every player could afford to neglect his work and travel on 2s/4d per day, but who is to keep the pot boiling while the worker is away playing the noble game, and drawing thousands of pounds to a central exchequer? It is an open secret that while the All Blacks were making Great Britain ring with their exploits some of the families dependent on players were almost starving in New Zealand.

I am confident that the public will take a fair view of the case for the players, and that they will attend to see a good game with an All Black combination, that is setting out to take on the best team in England.

THE LEAGUE REVEALS THEIR ALL BLUES TEAM

After the second meeting of the newly formed NSWRL, held on August 12 at Bateman's Hotel, the press reported the names of players in attendance, including Messenger and the captains of four clubs: Bob Graves (Balmain), Arthur Hennessy (South Sydney), Harry Hammill (Newtown) and Alec Burdon (Sydney). Also present were Jim Abercrombie (vice-captain of North Sydney), Fred Henlen (ex-NSW rep) and twenty-five other players. Victor Trumper also revealed his involvement to the public for the first time. *The Herald* reported that during the meeting it was noted that 'so far 138 first grade players have declared themselves in favour of the League.'[2]

During the meeting Giltinan reiterated much of what he had already told the newspapers. He urged 'the men to stick to their guns and hoped to be able to hand over a bumper cheque to the new clubs after the forthcoming matches' against Baskerville's team. 'Mr Trumper, who was acting with him in this matter, was one of their straightest men. He said they did not look to make anything out of the venture. They spent their money as sports, and if they lost, that was their lookout. However, they wanted the men to back them up, and he was sure that when the time came they would not object to the promoters taking out the little dividend they had in the venture.'

Giltinan confirmed to the meeting he had written to the NU 'trying to arrange for a team to leave Australia in 1908, so they could also hold out the inducement of a trip to the old world, though not on a 3s a day basis. (Cheers). The men would get a certain percentage of the gate, and if they came back with £200 in their pockets, well and good. (Cheers). They were going to select the men for Saturday's match, but they would not publish the names of the other players who had signed so that they might be able to play for their clubs on Saturday.' The only clubs not represented at the meeting were University and Western Suburbs.

Giltinan also announced that he had engaged the Town Hall for Thursday night, for a public reception for Baskerville's team. Giltinan undertook to fund legal action against any employer who dismissed a man or took away his billet because he had joined the NSWRL.

The selectors for the NSW team (named the 'All Blues' by the NSWRL) were Dick Burdon, Hennessy and Graves, with assistance provided by Messenger. Dick Burdon (Alec's brother) also took on the role of coach, with the team training at the Agricultural Ground. The selected players were

Backs: Charlie Hedley (Glebe), John Stuntz (Easts), Messenger (Easts), 'Son' Fry (Souths), Frank Cheadle (Newtown), Albert Rosenfeld (Easts), Lou D'Alpuget (Easts), Bill Farnsworth (Newtown) and John Hickey (Glebe).

Forwards: Bob Mable (Easts), Hennessy (Souths), Hammill (Newtown), Sid 'Sandy.' Pearce (Easts), Peter Moir (Glebe), Billy Cann (Souths), Graves (Balmain), Herb Brackenreg (Easts), Harry Glanville (Norths), Alf Dobbs (Balmain) and 'Tedda' Courtney (St George).

FROM MUDGEE TO SYDNEY IS A LONG WALK

The MRU and NSWRU relied upon their many supporters in the daily and weekly newspapers to put fear into any wavering footballers. The city's editors and columnists were not hesitant in attacking the NSWRL. *The Sydney Mail* was one of the more outspoken — and colourful.

> One of the minor sensations of the week was the floating to the surface of the inflated carcass of discontent which is going to try to make the name of rugby odious. Splendid in its past, splendid now, and splendid in its promise for the future, the grand old game stands king of winter sports, and its loyal subjects will rally round the flag and put to rout the rabble revolutionists whose weight in the scrum is to be let out for hire at so much the pound.

> What fools to kill the game, because the Union is not archangels! The organisation of sport is even more democratic than that of politics. It has its representative government and its majority rule. All this muttering is better out and done with; it will leave the sport sweeter. Professionalism is a curse, and an unsportsmanlike curse at that.[3]

In effect *The Sydney Mail* writer was advocating the approach taken by the RFU in England in 1895. The formation of a professional rugby body that could cater for the needs of the working class would see these men all leave the game. The remaining players would all play in the true spirit of amateurism, thus the rugby game under the MRU and NSWRU would be cleansed of the 'bad element.'

But were there enough men willing to remain amateur in Sydney? In talking to *The Australian Star* about 'Messenger's fee,' Victor Trumper discussed the ability of Australian rugby players to follow amateurism.

> It is not the intention of the NSWRL to encourage the professional spirit in connection with the rugby game. The intention was to bring

rugby to Australian conditions. Players should receive expenses for out-of-pocket costs and other calls made upon them in connection with playing the game.

It is not the intention of the League to pay a man to play simply because he was a 'star' player, but rather to bring the game within reach of all who desired to play it. Under Australian conditions players cannot afford to pay all fees out of their own pockets. In England there are more moneyed men who can afford to pay their own expenses, and can thus play as strict amateurs. In Australia the players cannot afford to do this, and therefore we really have few players who are entitled to the name of amateurs.

The objects of the League are, in a nutshell, not to foster professionalism, but to make it possible for the players to play the game under fair conditions, and not to be out-of-pocket to provide money for the upkeep of expensive governing organisations.[4]

The Sydney Sportsman suggested there was no likelihood of the players remaining true to the amateur bodies. 'It is reckoned that professional football will be in full blast in Sydney within a few seasons. The Union has been scooping the great pots of boodle, and the players, who get all the bumps and bruises, are beginning to ask where do they come in.' The paper also repeated a reason being offered as to why improved player allowances were not forthcoming: 'Possibly the Union is afraid to pay the jerseyed gladiators a few quid expenses for each match, thinking they might go on the bust with it, and injure their constitutions.'[5]

Alf Dobbs read of his inclusion in the NSWRL team in the newspaper while on tour with the Balmain club at Mudgee. With his allegiance now exposed and training for the All Blues match to commence, Dobbs asked the team manager for his train ticket so he could immediately return to Sydney.

Howe, the MRU secretary was contacted, and he advised the manager that if Dobbs' only excuse was to play for the professionals, he would have to pay his own way back. The Balmain club secretary, Pat McQuade, incensed at Dobbs' treatment, wired an instruction to the team to come home and not play the following match in Lithgow in protest. After he made the necessary arrangements to get Dobbs back to Sydney, McQuade raised the matter at the next MRU meeting — whereupon he was accused of involvement with the League.[6]

Dobbs was back in Sydney in time to join the other All Blues players in signing a further undertaking to join the League and having a team photograph taken. Wearing their full playing kit, the players

**The NSWRL All Blues team selected to play against the Professional All Blacks
(Sydney, 1907)**

*Back Row: Charlie Hedley, G Brackenreg, Arthur Hennessy, Bill Farnsworth, 'Tedda' Courtney,
George Boss, Alf Dobbs.*
*Third Row: Henry Hoyle, Bob Graves, Peter Moir, Harry Hammill, Harry Glanville,
Sid 'Sandy' Pearce, Alec Burdon, H Cleeve.*
*Second Row: John Stuntz, Billy Cann, 'Son' Fry, James Giltinan, Dally Messenger,
Herb Brackenreg, Bob Mable.*
Front Row: Lou D'Alpuget, Frank Cheadle, Albert Rosenfeld, John 'Darb' Hickey.

appeared confident. Most seemed completely untroubled by the step
they were taking.[7]

However, shortly afterwards 'influences at work' got to John 'Darb'
Hickey and Bill Farnsworth. They both withdrew their services from the
NSWRL.[8] Despite signing agreements to play for the League, the MRU
felt that that Hickey and Farnsworth had not damaged their amateur
status (despite the RFUs *Rules As To Professionalism*), and were free to
return to their clubs.

THE PROFESSIONAL ALL BLACKS ARE NAMED

'The much discussed New Zealand professional rugby football team
(or, at any rate, the majority of players) has now left the colony for
England, via Sydney,' reported the Auckland based *New Zealand Herald*.

The southern members of the team, numbering 15, have already left Wellington, and seven members of the Northern contingent left here by the *Victoria*, for Sydney, last evening.

Their names are: Jim Gleeson, playing manager, from Hawke's Bay; Bill Mackrell, William Trevarthen, William Tyler, Lance Todd, Dick Wynyard, and Harold Rowe. Messrs Gleeson (brother of the playing manager), Heath, and Nesbitt, of Hawke's Bay, were also passengers by the *Victoria*, but they are not going with the team. George Smith, Billy Wynyard, and Charlie Dunning, will leave for Sydney next Monday, to join the team, which will probably be further strengthened by the inclusion of some of the All Blacks who were playing in Australia. The Southern members of the combination are: C. J. Pearce, H. S. 'Jum' Turtill, Joe Lavery, Duncan

New Zealand Professional All Blacks (Sydney, 1907)

Back Row: Bill Mackrell, Edgar Wrigley, William Tyler, Dick Wynyard.
Third Row: Tom Cross, Charles Pearce, Con Byrne, Richard 'Bumper' Wright,
Dan Gilchrist, Eric Watkins.
Second Row: Albert Baskerville, Edward Tyne, Duncan McGregor, Harry Palmer, Lance Todd,
H S 'Jum' Turtill, William 'Massa' Johnston.
Front Row: Harold Rowe, Jim Gleeson, Arthur Kelly.
Remaining members had not yet arrived in Sydney.

McGregor (Canterbury), Edgar Wrigley (Masterton), Albert Baskerville, Arthur Callum, Adam Lile, Dan Gilchrist, Eric Watkins (Wellington), and Tom Cross, Con Byrne, Richard 'Bumper' Wright, Edward Tyne, and Arthur Kelly (Petone).

It is understood that four of the Auckland members of the All Black team in Australia were prepared to go some time back, but that they had asked for certain guarantees, which were not granted, and it is believed that they declined to go. However, some of the All Blacks now in Australia, will certainly go, although the full strength of the team will not be known until all the players have gathered in Sydney, and a consultation is held. In any case, it is stated on the best authority that there are several men remaining in New Zealand who are prepared to depart as soon as they are notified.

The team already selected, includes three members of the famous 1905 All Blacks, viz McGregor (Canterbury), and Smith and Mackrell (Auckland). The others, however, with very few exceptions, have represented their respective provinces and are all fine players. If the team proves successful, the theory advanced by the NU clubs, that they were superior to the All Blacks will be dispelled.[9]

'Massa' Johnston was the only amateur All Black who remained in Sydney to join Baskerville's team — thus the team included four of the original All Blacks from the 1905 tour. Baskerville revealed that another thirteen had made applications but for various reasons they were not part of the team.

Before leaving for New Zealand with the amateur team, Johnston's fellow 1905 All Black Bill Cunningham provided an extensive interview with *The Referee*. In answering questions about the prospect for success in England of Baskerville's team, Cunningham confirmed that 'he knew some of the NU players,' though 'he had not been greatly impressed with their play.' Cunningham added that 'he did not consider the men going Home were professionals in the strict sense of the word.'[10]

A RUMOUR ABOUT TOWN

When the first of Baskerville's team arrived in Sydney they were met at the Margaret Street wharf by Giltinan, Trumper, Rosenfeld, Alec Burdon, Henlen, Johnston, and numerous other players and officials of the League.

Under its 'Union v League' headline *The Herald* commented that, 'The "All Golds" seemed to recognise the contest they had entered into was going to be a hard fought one, while on the other hand their (amateur) opponents, who have been dubbed the "Lily Whites," think that the affair is hardly worthy of notice, calling the League a nine days wonder. The public, who are being appealed to for a decision, appear to be pretty well divided on the matter, although the general feeling amongst the followers of the game is that the crowd will go where the best football is to be seen.'

Baskerville made a few comments to the waiting reporters. He said 'the movement to send professionals to England was started by him nearly twelve months ago. The team consisted of the cream of New Zealand footballers, and he claims it is equal to any that has ever left New Zealand.'

'Every one of the men going,' Baskerville said, 'are good. There are no "has-beens" amongst us. The New Zealand public regarded the team as thoroughly representative, and looked on it to emulate the great performance of the 1905 team in England.'[11]

The following night the team were welcomed at a NSWRL function at the Town Hall. 'The visiting team entered shortly after eight o'clock and were accorded a great ovation by the 400 persons present. The cheering was persisted in till it reached almost a deafening roar. The All Blacks were clearly delighted at the reception, and took their seats along the front rows blushing like schoolboys. The NSW team filed into the room next and the cheering was renewed. Messenger was specially singled out for a demonstration, but that player was shy at taking compliments and found a seat as quickly as possible. The outbursts of enthusiasm having subsided, a good time was had by all. Henry Hoyle tendered the New Zealanders a hearty welcome.'

After the function Baskerville was confronted by newspaper men '...concerning a rumour about town that Messenger was going with the New Zealanders' to England. 'How could he go as a New Zealander?' was Baskerville's only reply.[12]

Later in the evening Baskerville waited at the wharf for the remainder of his team to arrive from Auckland. There was some anxiety as hour after hour passed with no sign of the overdue ship. 'The visitors were fretting, owing to the absence of information as to who were coming — there was always the chance that some of the players had been persuaded against making the trip.' Relief finally came when the boat arrived in the early hours of the Friday morning, with seven of the expected ten players.

Baskerville was quickly informed the remaining three were travelling on the steamer that left Auckland on Monday, George Smith among them. Smith had to tidy up his dealings before sailing, one of which was relinquishing his position of 'steward to the Auckland Sports Club.' His replacement was Australian Pat Walsh.[13]

179

Messenger scoops the ball off the ground in the first NSW All Blues v. New Zealand Professional All Blacks match at the Agricultural Gound (Sydney, 1907).

PROFESSIONALS PLAY RUGBY UNION

There was no mention in the newspapers of the first professional match being played under anything but rugby union rules. Even if a copy of the NU rules was on hand, there was no time for players to gain a grasp of the game. It was a big enough risk in simply offering the concept of professional rugby to players and spectators, without adding to the uncertainties by playing to a new set of rules.

The SCG and Sports Ground authorities were restricted by contracts with the Unions, so the NSWRL sought to hold the three matches at the nearby, but smaller, Agricultural Ground. The NSWRU and MRU fought particularly hard to ensure even that ground was denied to the League. Without one of the three grounds in the Moore Park area, Giltinan's plans would have been dealt a serious blow. The next best ground in the city area was the University Oval which was certainly unavailable, leaving only perhaps the suburban Birchgrove and Wentworth Parks to host the matches — with little hope of a sizeable gate.

To thwart the League, the Agricultural Society was offered an exclusive rental agreement by the Union bodies, and they seemed destined to close the deal until Frank Horan (a supporter of the League) pointed out to the Society's secretary, Monty Somer, that there was no way the Unions could be forced to use the facility. This would mean advertisers would shy away from paying for ground signage, cutting the Society's income. It was enough to convince the Society to gamble on siding with the League. It also placed them in a prime position if the professional movement proved to be a success.[14]

August 17 had 'perfect weather conditions' for the opening match between the professional NSW and New Zealand teams. Baskerville and Giltinan both wondered what number of spectators would turn up. The latter was particularly nervous as he had given the New Zealanders a minimum £500 guarantee for the matches.

The Sydney Mail reported,

On Saturday 20,000 people gave a splendid kick-off for the new professional
body, the NSWRL, and the New Zealand team and that 20,000 would have
reached perhaps 30,000 had the match been played on the SCG. The figures
are far beyond anticipations (£1,000 was taken at the gate). The feeling
in favour of professionalism has spread with extraordinary rapidity. Go
where you will, you will hear the subject discussed, and for every one who
will look upon the movement as a blow to clean football, you will find
perhaps a dozen to support it more or less enthusiastically. A hearty cheer,
which meant more than the actual reception of the two football teams, was
accorded the New Zealand and NSW representatives when they entered the
arena of the Agricultural Ground. It was cheer which meant a recognition to
those men who were playing under the new regime that they had right on
their side in the breakaway from the NSWRU.[15]

The Referee's reporter observed 'that the grass was very short, and
the turf dry and hard, and dustier than any other rugby ground I have
seen this year. The local men, led by Hennessy, came out in a darker
shade of light blue than the orthodox light blue of NSW. The jersey
was emblazoned with ['1907' and] a kangaroo which we have come to
regard as the federal and not state badge.'[16] The decision to replace the
NSWRU's waratah with a kangaroo appears to have been a statement
by the NSWRL that its first allegiance would be to Australia. Each of

*NSW All Blues and New Zealand 'All Golds' players and officials after the first
professional rugby match.*

the NSW players was also given a specially designed honour cap with the kangaroo on the front. This further indicates that planning and preparation for the breakaway had been underway long before news of the match became public.

The New Zealanders, led by McGregor, then came onto the field and 'with lusty, deep-chested voices, gave a war-cry in Maori.' Giltinan was given the honour of kicking-off the first professional football match, of any code, held in Australasia. The teams comprised

NSW: Hedley, Stuntz, Fry, Messenger, Cheadle, Rosenfeld, D'Alpuget, Hammill, Hennessy, Mable, Moir, Pearce, Cann, Graves, Brackenreg.

New Zealand: Turtill, Wrigley, Todd, Rowe, R. Wynyard, McGregor, Kelly, Tyne, Watkins, Mackrell, Cross, Wright, Byrne, Gilchrist, Pearce.

New Zealand won 12–8. 'The play created a good deal of enthusiasm from kick-off to full-time — it was always interesting,' reported *The Herald*. 'The forwards on both sides shone well in every department, the visitors having the advantage over the home team in cohesion, pace and skill in footwork. The men found the ground hard, as their knees and elbows gave evidence.'[17]

Messenger played in his preferred position of centre three-quarter, instead of on the wing where the NSWRU selectors had tended to select him. The All Blues backs did not play spectacular football, but most reports mentioned that Messenger was by far the best of them. *The Sydney Sportsman* called it 'the very best game I have ever seen him play — he was far better than in any of the matches against amateur All Blacks.'[18]

MESSENGER A PROFESSIONAL ALL BLACK

By the second match, a mid-week game (August 21), the reports concerning Messenger joining the New Zealand team had made headlines.[19] As with previous rumours concerning Messenger, it eventually turned out to be true.

Before the tour, the New Zealanders had read of the amateur All Blacks matches, and saw the plaudits Messenger was gaining. It has been suggested that 'Massa' Johnston sent a wire to George Smith during the amateur All Blacks tour, saying they should convince Messenger to join the professional New Zealand team.[20] Johnston may have sent a wire, but it also should be remembered that Messenger was already familiar to Smith following the visit of the Auckland team in 1906, and the rumour of a NSW back joining Baskerville's team appeared two weeks before the amateur New Zealanders had arrived in Australia.

'The reports from the amateur All Blacks concerning Messenger's ability are admitted by the present New Zealand team to be not in the least exaggerated,' reported *The Herald*. 'So strongly do some of the visitors appreciate the Eastern Suburbs man that they are anxious to make him an offer, and it is even asserted in some quarters that he is already in the team.'[21]

With a bitterly cold westerly blowing, the weekday crowd for the second match was just under 4,000. It was a poor result compared to the 23,000 at the mid-week NSW v New Zealand amateur contest held a month earlier. Given Messenger played in both those matches, it proves that spectators were not going to take up the new League simply because of his presence.

The All Blues selectors kept Messenger in the centres for the second match, while the team was reorganised around him with many positional changes and new players. Billy Cann went from the forwards to the wing, while the other new winger was Jimmy Devereux. Other fresh players were Dave Brown and Arthur 'Pony' Halloway in the halves, while Glanville, Dobbs and Courtney came into the forwards.

The home team was completely outplayed by the New Zealanders 19–5. NSW had their chances but failed at critical moments to make the right decisions, perhaps from a lack of combination.

After the match the unsurprising news reached Sydney that the rugby authorities in both Auckland and Wellington had disqualified their players who were participating in the tour — it mattered little.[22]

THE CONTRACT

The last three New Zealanders — George Smith, Charles Dunning, and Billy Wynyard — arrived late in the week. For the first time in the venture, Baskerville's team were together.

The voyage had been a bad one and Smith, in particular, was quite ill. On the Friday evening he was unable to attend 'a conference' held at the Gresham Hotel. The small gathering, which excluded the press, appears to have doubled as a celebration for the chief organisers of the new movement as the only men present were Giltinan, Trumper, Baskerville, Burdon, Messenger, Hennessy, Hoyle, Gleeson and Palmer.[23]

Over that evening and the next day the New Zealanders looked over the tour contract and signed. Messenger signed too and announced to the press that he was joining the team.[24]

The players who weren't required for the final match sailed to Melbourne to meet with the ship for England. The others would catch the overnight train from Sydney on the Sunday evening.

The contract, which included the names of the men involved, appears to have been prepared in early August (or before) and brought to Sydney by Smith. The fully typed document names Messenger as part of the team and includes numerous clauses referring to the involvement of players from 'the colony of New Zealand or the state of NSW.' The contract was not amended at the last moment to include Messenger.[25]

Though Messenger did not sign the contract until August 24, he must have given his commitment to Baskerville and Smith sometime in July or earlier for his name (and references to NSW) to be present in the typed contract. It was not possible for the contract document [as it is] to have been prepared at the last moment in Sydney.

This means that Messenger had decided to become a 'professional' before he made his rugby union Test debut for Australia — and that the opportunity to take part in the tour to England and share in its profits was a major reason for his defection. It also suggests Messenger, knowing he was leaving rugby union, was persuaded by Giltinan to ask the NSWRU to be paid for his Australian Test

A G R E E M E N T made this *Twenty Second* day of August in the year one thousand nine hundred and seven WHEREBY GEORGE WILLIAM SMITH CHARLES DUNNING WILLIAM THOMAS WYNYARD WILLIAM THOMAS TYLER JAMES GLEESON ALBERT HENRY BASKERVILLE CHARLES PEARCE HARRY JOHN PALMER JOHN RICHARD WYNYARD ARTHUR CALLUM ARTHUR FREDERICK KELLY DUNCAN MC GREGOR WILLIAM JOHNSTON EDGAR WRIGLEY ERIC LESLIE WATKINS HERCULES RICHARD WRIGHT HUBERT SYDNEY TURTILL CONRAD BYRNE JOSEPH ALOYSIUS LAVERY *Harold Francis Row* WILLIAM HENRY MACKRELL WILLIAM MACVAY TREVARTHEN THOMAS WILLIAM CROSS DANIEL GEORGE FRASER ADAM LILE EDWARD TYNE DANIEL GILCHRIST LANCELOT BEAUMONT TODD all of the Colony of New Zealand and HERBERT HENRY MESSENGER of the State of New South Wales MUTUALLY COVENANT AND AGREE with each other as follows. :-

1.   THE said parties hereto shall form themselves into be constituted an from the date hereof a combination known the "New Zealand All Black Rugby Football Team".

The first page of the New Zealand professional team's contract. The document, that includes Messenger, appears to have been prepared in New Zealand weeks before the team arrived in Sydney.

appearance in Brisbane (and therefore obtain documented proof of the Union's 'professional' practices).

While there was much speculation in the newspapers about whether Messenger was paid £50 to play for the All Blues, there was no examination at all of the terms of his inclusion in the New Zealand team. The contract, supported by newspaper reports, shows that Messenger was not a guest-player or that he had any special agreement. As with the other members of the team, he had to contribute £50 to take part. *The Herald* reported that Messenger 'will play as one of the team, share and share alike.'[26]

Messenger either paid the fee himself or Giltinan paid it for him. Perhaps it is more than a coincidence that £50 was exactly the same amount the newspapers alleged Giltinan paid Messenger for the All Blues matches. Giltinan and Trumper were particularly insistent that Messenger had not been paid — if the £50 was given by Giltinan directly to Baskerville, to pay Messenger's entry fee into the New Zealand team, then they were telling the truth. Equally, Messenger's claims in Brisbane, (that he had no communication with Baskerville and had not agreed to join the New Zealand team), were also true if Giltinan was acting on his behalf and no contract had yet been signed.

The depth of Giltinan and Trumper's involvement in the bringing forth of a professional New Zealand team were not revealed at the time. It is clear that they were in communication with the New Zealanders over Messenger's inclusion for almost two months (at least). It may also be conclusive to note that the team's contract followed that used by Australian cricketers for tours to England — the terms of which Baskerville repeatedly made mention of. No New Zealand sporting team had ever made a tour along similar lines. It is not inconceivable that Giltinan and Trumper provided Baskerville and Smith with a cricket contract and guidance in organising the arrangements for the tour to England.

A PURSE OF SOVEREIGNS

Jim Abercrombie from North Sydney was the only new player to appear in the NSW team for the final match, the big man taking his place in the forwards. Another poor crowd for an inter-Tasman match of 8,000 witnessed what was a largely an uninspiring game, won by the New Zealanders 5–3.

The encounter of Smith v Messenger was a major disappointment, both players being determined to ensure they did not sustain an injury. Nor did they play opposite each other, with Smith opting for the wing position. After his first tackle on the hard ground he seemed to lose interest in the contest. To be fair though, he still wasn't well and was 'quite sick at half-time' (his fellow late-arrivals, Dunning and Billy Wynyard didn't play at all).[27]

Despite news of his departure only breaking that morning, Messenger was the subject of a large farewell gathering at the Oddfellow's Hall in Woollahra in the evening. Undoubtedly, his friends knew of his intentions to join the New Zealand team long before it was announced in the newspapers. Organised farewells and gifts to players leaving overseas were not uncommon — though being able to arrange and hold one with less than 24-hours notice seems particularly unlikely.

At the function, Messenger was presented 'with a purse of sovereigns from his admirers in Double Bay and the Eastern Suburbs by Mr McLaughlin, a well-known resident.' Giltinan then spoke about the benefits to players the League would bring and a tour to England in 1908.

He again denied that Messenger had been paid — and promptly presented to Messenger, on behalf of the NSWRL, another purse of sovereigns. Messenger 'seemed rather taken aback by this second presentation and thanked the donors.'[28]

Giltinan would have benefited from Messenger's inclusion in the All Blacks for a number of reasons. Messenger's talent would be a measure of the standing of the NSWRL in the eyes of the NU — this would assist with Giltinan's desire to take a team to England in 1908. Messenger himself would gain experience in the NU rules which would ensure he would be the star player of the new League upon his return.

News of the All Blacks tour and Messenger would keep the fledgling professional movement in the eyes of Sydney's footballers and sports readers over the summer months.

Messenger promised to return to Sydney and play under the League in 1908, rejecting any offers from English clubs. In the space of two weeks, Messenger had gone from denying he had any knowledge or involvement with the professionals (including not knowing Giltinan), to playing three matches for the All Blues, becoming part of the management of the League, joining the New Zealanders for their trip to England, and farewelling friends and family at a local hall.

It seems unlikely the fortnight's events came as a surprise to Messenger.

A further clue to his earlier involvement with the professional movement, was his choice to room with George Smith for the trip to England.[29] Given that Smith was so unwell, and Messenger's time was consumed with meetings and farewells, they barely would have known each other. It hints that the two must have formed a friendship during the visit of the Auckland team to Sydney twelve months earlier.

Two hundred people farewelled the New Zealanders as the Melbourne train left Sydney. Attempts to stage a match between the All Blues and All Blacks in the southern capital had to be abandoned due to the limited time available before the New Zealanders were to sail for England.[30]

THE GREATEST CRISIS IN AUSTRALIAN RUGBY

The effect of the three professional matches on the MRU attendances was modest (to say the least). The 8,000 at the third match was less than the 9,000 at the University Oval to see the home team play South Sydney in a semi-final match. The only impact appears to have been upon Messenger's former club Eastern Suburbs. Easts lost more players to the professionals than any other, and only 3,000 were at the SCG to see their semi-final match against Glebe.[31]

The fight, though, was still taking a toll on the MRU members. A few days later a committee meeting erupted into a shouting contest as tempers reached boiling point. Much of the public sympathy was with the plight of the players, and the majority of the footballers would follow the benefits. Many held back from joining the professionals, hoping the Unions would adopt the necessary reforms and the need for the League would be over.

At the MRU meeting Lewis Abrams put forward a proposal to give the players the same benefits being offered by the NSWRL, particularly increased allowances and payment for time off work from injuries or tours.

His proposal was ruled out of order by the chairman, Harrie Wood, in an attempt to prevent any discussion on the scheme. Abrams contended that it was a matter of such vital importance that it had to be discussed. He then was forced to deny his 'trend was toward professionalism.'

'The public and the players need to see that the MRU wants to do what is right,' said Abrams. 'We are face to face with the greatest crisis in Australian rugby.'

A Mr Clayton, supported by other members, said that he thought the best course of action would be for a conference between the NSWRU, NZRU, and QRU to formulate a joint response to the RFU in England and ask them 'to recognise Australian conditions.' Clayton acknowledged, though, that if the RFU didn't agree (which was almost certain) there would be a major problem: 'I am convinced the Unions will have to make good the losses which players incur. Both the public and the players demand it.'

Abrams then decided it was time to bring up his previous attempts at improving the players' conditions. 'I told you four years ago that it would have to be done. Had anyone else brought the matter forward it would have been all right.' The meeting erupted with loud and forceful voices — above it all Wood was crying out 'Order! Order!' to regain control.

Wood took exception to Abrams' remarks, saying they could only have been directed at him. A vote of dissent against Wood's decision (as chairman) to not allow Abrams' proposal to be considered was then taken. The vote was lost and the matter ended.[32]

The chances of the players getting what they wanted from within the Unions now seemed minimal. If they wanted to achieve their goals, the League would now have to be brought into full reality.

At a NSWRL meeting across town at Bateman's Hotel, the All Blues players agreed to forgo any claims for a cut of the League's £180 share of the gate-money from the three matches. They accepted (perhaps unwillingly) that the money should go towards a fund to help establish the NSWRL club competition.[33]

Some of the players claimed later they were offered £10 by Giltinan to play in the matches.[34] Instead each player was given £3 and was bestowed life membership, which meant free entry to all subsequent NSWRL matches (if there were any). Also given life membership were Burdon, O'Farrell, Giltinan, Hoyle and Trumper — the last three were also elected as the first executive committee.

By mid-September the MRU had disqualified the players who had appeared for the All Blues. No duration was placed on the exclusion, they were simply disqualified. At the same time the MRU, in conjunction with the NSWRU, arranged a testimonial fundraiser for Harold Judd who was incapacitated for so long with his broken leg.[35] The favourable treatment of some over others was apparently continuing. To be fair though, if the Unions had ignored Judd the professional movement would have had further reason to be critical. The Unions would not admit it, but the League was forcing them to make changes.

MANY ARE SITTING ON THE FENCE

Giltinan initially intended the 'season to be closed with a series of League fixtures between the clubs joining the new League.'[36] However the idea was abandoned. His purpose may have been to have as many players as possible, caught up in the excitement of the new League, commit an act of professionalism from which they could not return. The League had signed many players who indicated a support for the professional movement, but were hesitant to actually play until matters were more certain.

Many hoped that the mere formation of the League would force the Unions over the summer to make the changes being sought by the players. Then, presumably, the League would be no more.

This is supported by comments Baskerville made to a reporter after leaving Sydney. 'All the leading players in Australia,' explained Baskerville, 'are amenable to the movement, and may turn professional at any moment. They are at present sitting on the fence. The players would like to see the degree of professionalism advocated by the NSW League. But they are loath to throw in their lot with that body, preferring rather to leave the management of the game in the hands of the NSWRU, who they are hopeful will see their way clear to take up the work commenced by the League.'[37]

NO JOY FOR LEAGUE IN QUEENSLAND

The Queenslanders were still smarting from the exclusion of their players from the Australian third Test team. In Brisbane, the local clubs sought £5 each from the QRU for training expenses but, as the Union had just got itself out of debt for the first time in many years, were refused.

The Queensland correspondent in *The Referee* (firmly on the side of rugby union) observed that the state's rugby community 'are watching with keen interest the attempts being made in NSW to get in the thin edge of what appears to be professionalism, or the spoon-feeding of players. One has reason to believe that the NSW Professional League will endeavour to start a Professional Rugby League in Brisbane, and for that purpose will send a representative up to this city. One wishes him joy, and predicts a big disappointment to anyone who attempts any such scheme on the clubs at present attached to the QRU.'[38]

THE PHANTOM TEAM ARRIVES IN YORKSHIRE

In September, 1907, *The Referee* reproduced an article from England's *Athletic News* explaining the differences between the NU game and RFU's playing rules. Written by Widnes' Jack Smith, who had recently relinquished the NU presidency (in an annual rotation of positions), the column was basically an official NU piece. Smith used the article to respond to critics of the professional All Blacks tour.

'It is perhaps too much to expect,' wrote Smith, 'that any NU project should be mooted without an attempt being made to throw cold water upon it, but the suggestion that it would take a rugby union team a full season to grasp the possibilities of the NU game is surely very wide of the mark.'[39] It is somewhat revealing that Smith would refer to the initiatives of Baskerville and the New Zealanders as a 'NU project.' Whether Smith was referring to NU as instigators of the tour, or only their actions once Baskerville put his proposal to them, is not clear.

When the professional All Blacks arrived in England they were met by NU officials who entertained them in London before bringing them to Yorkshire. The delegation included Jack Smith, even though he no longer held an official NU role.

Smith, who was also a first-class referee, took on the role of coaching the New Zealanders in the NU playing rules. Two practice matches were held at Headingley in Leeds, where Smith explained the rulings and interpretations to the players.[40]

The New Zealanders' arrival had been preceded by disparaging comments in *The London Times* from C. Wray Palliser, New Zealand's representative on the RFU committee in England. He also held the position of the colonial government's Agent-General, and used this position to remark that Baskerville's men constituted a 'phantom team' and they were 'hoodwinking the people' of the Northern counties.[41]

Evidently the NU supporters weren't persuaded by the comments as the professional All Blacks received a great reception upon their arrival in the North of England. Even though they arrived in Leeds in the dark of the evening, there were over 6,000 people in and around the railway station to meet them. Amongst the throng was a contingent of NU officials led by Joseph Houghton (of the St Helens club).

'A shout of welcome arose,' said Baskerville recalling the moment they stepped off the train. 'This swelled to a roar as we emerged from the station. It was with the utmost difficulty that we pushed our way through the cheering crowd.' The team performed their haka and the crowd went wild again.

Conveyed to their hotel in an open carriage through the centre of Leeds, they were cheered the whole way along streets crowded with so many well-wishers the trams and other traffic were brought to a standstill. The four members of the original All Blacks team described the welcome as far in excess of anything they had received in 1905.[42]

The NU held an official welcoming banquet at the team's hotel. During the evening Joe Platt, secretary of the NU, surprised the already fevered audience with the news that Baskerville had brought with him a letter from Australia. The letter was written by Giltinan, who wished to inform the NU that a Rugby League 'to be carried out on similar lines to your Union' had been formed in Sydney. Platt read out the contents of the letter, in which Giltinan boldly proposed to the NU that an Australian team be permitted to tour in twelve months time, and that in 1909 a NU team visit Australia and New Zealand.

For the NU the possibility of regular matches and tours against New Zealand and Australia was a tremendous boon. It also coincided with a number of Welsh clubs joining the NU and the formation of a Wales international team. A Scottish journalist described the NU situation prior to the arrival of the New Zealanders as 'moribund' [on its last legs]. 'Can it be denied that the NU have secured a new lease of life — more's the pity — through the visit of the New Zealanders and the Welsh revolt?'[43]

PROFESSIONAL ALL BLACKS MAKE A FORTUNE

According to Baskerville, the NU game was everything he had hoped for. After watching a Leeds v Hunslet match under NU rules he said, 'There was more crammed into the first half of it than one would see in three New Zealand club matches. It was a revelation to us.'

Taken during the New Zealand rugby league team's tour to England and Wales in 1907/08.
(Left to right) Jim Gleeson, Jack Smith (N.U. official), Dally Messenger,
H.R. 'Bumper' Wright, George Smith.

'Football played under NU rules would suit New Zealand spectators right down to the ground. It seems very much faster than the amateur game.' He added that there was quick passing and none of that 'tiresome monotonous kick into touch and the subsequent line-out. When tackled the player gets up quickly on their feet, with the ball in his possession. He then drops it to the ground between himself and the opponent's goal line, and then either side may play it with their feet. If other combatants arrived on the scene while this was being done they gathered around and practically formed an impromptu scrum.'

Baskerville added to his description of the play-the-ball, calling it 'far safer and more attractive' than the 'down' rule used in rugby union. When a player was tackled to the ground or held in rugby union 'it is a common sight to see his opponents gather around him and hustle or grab him along. Nothing like this occurs on NU fields. The NU amendments have made rugby a game of skill.'[44]

All fears of the tour being a financial failure soon dissipated, as the New Zealanders proved to be formidable opposition to the NU clubs. In the opening nine matches they were undefeated. In the first days of December *The Times* reported 'the attendances have ranged from about 5,000 to 15,000, and once or twice up to 20,000. As the charge is one shilling, and the New Zealanders receive 70% of the gates, they must be doing good financial business.'[45]

An article from another English paper, reproduced in *The Referee* in Sydney, said the gate must be considered satisfactory, 'for the horny-handed sons of the north do not take kindly to a minimum admission fee of one shilling.'[46]

The reports of the financial success of Baskerville's team must have made pleasant reading for Giltinan, the NSWRL and the prospective players of the new competition. On Christmas Eve, 1907, *The Referee* announced the news that the NU had officially invited the NSWRL 'to send a team to England next year, under a guarantee of £3,000 and 70% of the gate.'[47]

On New Year's Day, 1908, the first international match held under NU rules was played, when the New Zealanders, including Messenger, met Wales at Aberdare. Before a crowd estimated at between 15–20,000 the visitors held an 8–3 lead at half-time. They ought to have been further in front but fine defensive work by fullback 'Chick' Jenkins (of the Welsh NU club Ebbw Vale) kept the scores close. A last-minute try by the Welsh saw them win 9–8, the local *Western Mail* calling it a 'red letter day for Wales.'[48]

The decision to include Messenger in the New Zealand team proved a success. Most judges in England singled out Messenger and Lance

Todd as the best players, comparing them both favourably to the 1905 All Blacks. 'Both these men are really great players, and have amply confirmed their reputation.'[49]

During the tour there were many accounts lauding Messenger as a great player, primarily for his goal-kicking. Messenger kicked 56 goals on the tour. Along with the 8 tries he scored, his total of 146 points was a 101 more than the next best player. At the time, a great deal of prominence was placed on kicking goals in both forms of rugby — the majority of matches were won and lost on the success and failure of a team's goal-kicker. A goal-kicking contest or exhibition would frequently be held between the exponents of each team before the start of the game. Often a trophy, cash or other prize was on offer to the winner.[50]

The Yorkshire Post though offered a wider opinion of Messenger. 'He is something more than a goal-kicker. A trim-built athlete, 24 years of age, he has pace, and the faculty [knack] of always turning up at the right place. The critics describe him as "the greatest marvel of the age." Messenger does not suffer from a swelled head nor has he been spoilt by flattery. It was an education to see him pass the ball. He could do it smartly with his left arm as with his right, and a peculiarly effective movement of his was a pass from behind, delivered in much the same style as a pugilist gives a back-hander.'[51]

Messenger played for New Zealand in the three Test matches against England. The home side won the first match 14–6 at Leeds, before the New Zealanders took the second (in London) and third (in Cheltenham) to win the series.

Overall Baskerville's team played 35 matches in England and Wales, winning on 19 occasions, with two matches drawn. From those games the New Zealanders' share of the gate-takings amounted to £8,838 — only £70 less than the 1905 All Blacks who were able to play in Scotland and Ireland as well. Each player eventually received his share — £300 each.[52] It was enough to set themselves up in a business or buy a house.

As expected, some of the New Zealanders took up the offers of NU clubs. George Smith joined Oldham, where he received £150 for the remaining eleven matches of the season. Lance Todd accepted a £400 signing-on fee to join Wigan. Duncan McGregor and Joe Lavery also joined NU clubs, while Jim Gleeson stayed in England to undertake the final stages of a law degree.[53]

Messenger kept his promise to Giltinan and his mother, returning with the team to Sydney. Baskerville had considered staying on in

England himself 'to see more of it,' but decided he should see out the return-leg in Australia.[54]

What the New Zealand team would find when they got back to Sydney was still a mystery to them. Had the professional movement lost all momentum in their absence, or could they optimistically look forward to a new era of Australasian rugby?

The six-week sea voyage south via the Suez Canal and the Indian Ocean would give Baskerville, Messenger and the others plenty of time to consider their future, and reflect upon their already substantial profits and on-field achievements.

CHAPTER ELEVEN

1908: THE LEAGUE'S OPENING WHISTLE

THE LEAGUE COPIED ALMOST EVERYTHING

Apart from introducing payments to players and adopting NU playing rules, the NSWRL made only two other significant changes to the established practice and customs of rugby in NSW and Australia. The first was to ensure there was no equivalent of the MRU body, the 'middle-man Union' that prevented the Sydney clubs and players from having a say in the running and control of the game at state level. The second was the placement of the Federal symbol, the kangaroo, on all state and national team jerseys and honour caps, identifying that the new code held its allegiance to Australia first.

The difference between the NSWRL and NSWRU was minimal. They only removed the main items of dissatisfaction: the MRU and the slavish adherence to the RFU in England. The NSWRL's state team were still 'the Blues.' Club, state and national team colours remained the same, district boundaries and management structures followed those laid out in 1900, representative teams and routines were continued, even the scheduling and format of the Sydney club competition was the same as in 1907.

By continuing these traditions of the rugby game, the players, officials and supporters of the NSWRL were carrying their ownership (at least equally) of Australian rugby into the new code. In their minds, these things didn't belong to the NSWRU, they were owned by everyone. The uprising had been against the controlling power, and their refusal to introduce reforms that improved player conditions and the spectacle of rugby. The formation of the League was an attempt to takeover NSW rugby, not the introduction of a rival sport.

The response of the MRU and NSWRU to the crisis was to attempt to match or better the changes introduced by the League. What before was seen as illegal, was now being introduced by the Unions (for example, providing free jerseys to players). The NSWRL announced it would be playing three grades in club football — the MRU replaced the Borough competition with Third Grade. Where the League attempted to hire grounds, the Unions tied them up with liberal offers to the trustees and Councils for exclusive rights (even where there was no intention to use the ground). The most galling aspect of all this for the players was that the gate-money they provided to the Unions was now being used against them.

As a number of observers noted, every rugby union player in NSW should be praising the arrival of the NSWRL — it had improved their circumstances out-of-sight.[1]

THE FOUNDATION MEETINGS OF THE CLUBS

The opening days of 1908 were busy for the founders of the NSWRL, as they set about organising district meetings held to form their clubs. There was no likelihood of a current club joining the NSWRL — it was

simply impossible for one of these clubs to exist outside of the MRU structure, even if every member wanted to align with the NSWRL. Under the MRU system, the clubs were a committee voted by the members each season to select and organise a representative team from the district's footballers to play under the Union. They were local versions of the method used to put a state representative team into the field, not autonomous bodies who could decide their own futures.

The NSWRL adopted the same district club system used by the MRU. However, the one significant difference was that the League would give each district independence and self-sufficiency by guaranteeing them one-third of all profits from each match they participated in — over time, if they survived, they would become 'clubs' in the more conventional understanding of the word. It was therefore not surprising that (with one exception) their NSWRL colours were identical to those worn by their district under the MRU. In the same way each state or nation had its own sporting colours, so did the district.

Henry Hoyle – the fiery politician and labour official who rallied the footballers and supporters at the foundation meetings to form rugby league clubs.

The process of calling a public meeting to form a club was therefore not foreign to rugby followers in Sydney — since 1900 identical meetings had been held before the start of every season in each of the districts. Such meetings were normally called in March, but Giltinan wanted to be ahead of the MRU and began to organise official gatherings in the first weeks of 1908.

While some districts made tentative moves in the last months of 1907, the first to hold a founding meeting was Glebe on the evening of January 9 at the Glebe Town Hall.[2] It was typical of those to follow, with Hoyle and Giltinan at the forefront as they delivered rousing speeches (though sometimes lengthy) denouncing the Unions' administrators and their supporters, and setting out a rosy future under the NSWRL.

They repeated the message that players under the League would not be professionals — footballers would not be able to live off the money they earned from rugby, 'that would be absurd.' They would, however, be fairly recompensed for expenses, time off work for injuries and their playing equipment would be provided. All this would be paid for from the gate-money.

'The League was formed,' said Hoyle at the Glebe meeting, 'because it was believed that the set of conditions controlling the football Unions were not suitable to the democracy and social conditions of the Australian people. It is proposed to not only treat the players as men, but when they are away to another state they will be able to maintain their dignity by having money in their pockets for expenses.' He told the footballers if they were now shouted a beer, they would have enough expenses money to be able to reciprocate.

Giltinan would also produce the cablegram from the NU, confirming the tour to England at the end of the season. Giltinan, presumably through Baskerville upon his arrival in England, had put a persuasive argument to the NU that it was imperative the tour be given approval for 1908.

The NU had their reservations, but Giltinan knew that without the security of the tour he would have a far more difficult task in gaining followers to the new game. The amateur All Blacks tour to Britain had proven what returns could be made. The confirmation of the tour and its arrangements were used to encourage players to join and offered as evidence of the long-term financial security of the NSWRL. 'The sum of £3,000 is in the bank there (England) as a guarantee, and the NSWRL will receive 70% of the gate-money,' Giltinan would say.

On the stage would be various prominent players and rugby identities including Peter Moir, Tom Costello, Harry Hammill and Arthur Hennessy.

Following the Glebe meeting, clubs were formed at Newtown (Newtown Town Hall, January 14), South Sydney (Redfern Town Hall, January 17), Balmain (Balmain Town Hall, January 23), Eastern Suburbs (Paddington Town Hall, January 24), Western Suburbs (Ashfield Town Hall, February 4), North Sydney (North Sydney School of Arts, February 7) and St George (Rockdale Town Hall, February 28). A meeting was also held in Newcastle (Pike's Rooms, February 8), but the resolution to form a club failed.[3]

In most cases the League's clubs gained the support of about half the players and members of their old MRU district clubs. By far the strongest allegiance to the League came from Balmain, with very few in that district remaining loyal to the MRU. Meanwhile, Western Suburbs was formed almost entirely by players from the Ashfield rugby union club, who had grievances with the 'Burwood dominated' Wests rugby union club. Unlike the other new clubs, Wests refused to wear their district colours (bottle green) and adopted Ashfield's black and white instead.[4]

NEWCASTLE IS IN, ST GEORGE IS OUT

At the St George meeting a majority of those present voted in favour of forming a new club. However, when it came time for men (players and non-players alike) to come forward and sign-on as members of the St George rugby league club, only 'Tedda' Courtney and two others did — everyone else left the hall.[5]

Why so few came forward remains a mystery. St George, as with Manly, had only been in the MRU competition the two previous seasons. These clubs consisted primarily of younger and far less prominent players who may have felt more hesitant at defying the MRU and their own club officers. St George's Harold Judd was also reluctant to side with the NSWRL. Perhaps his subsequent favourable treatment by the NSWRU was an influencing factor amongst the footballers of St George. Whatever the reason, no second attempt to form a club was made.

There was a similar situation in Newcastle. Aware of the lingering dissatisfaction with the NSWRU over the 'Dobson affair' and the treatment of Pat Walsh, the League tried to establish their eighth club at Newcastle. Hoyle delivered his by now much versed speech to a large gathering at Pike's Rooms (in Bolton Street). However, when the motion to form a 'Northern District Rugby League Club' was put to those present, it was not carried. The belief is that the public meeting had been 'stacked' with men loyal to the NSWRU, ensuring those who wanted to support the League were out-voted. The fight for Newcastle appeared to be over.

This tactic wasn't lost upon the supporters of the League in the Balmain district. On March 17, the MRU held an annual meeting to form a Balmain rugby union club at the local Oddfellows Hall. Even though Balmain already had a League club, the MRU meeting was 'packed to overflowing' and the 'meeting became quite enthusiastic' with the numerous officials of the NSWRU and MRU present on the stage given a difficult time. Even though the majority of Balmain members had joined the League, many simply turned up to voice their dissatisfaction and vote against proposals put forward.[6]

Enough support was eventually found to vote to re-form the Balmain rugby union club for 1908, but it proved impossible to elect any vice-presidents or the treasurer. *The Herald* reported that 'the meeting, which was distinctly in favour of League football, adjourned until a future date.'

The Evening News was able to add that 'feelings ran very high in the hall, and at the close of the meeting two players got into an altercation, and a rough and tumble took place — when separated one man was found to be bleeding profusely from the head, and it was stated the wound was caused by a knife. The man was taken to the hospital and was seen by an *Evening News* reporter afterwards with his forehead bandaged up and abrasions on his cheeks, nose and chin.' The MRU scheduled the follow-up meeting for the same evening as the next Balmain rugby league club meeting (March 26) where it was able to quietly conclude its business.[7]

The NSWRL made a second attempt in Newcastle. This time it did not call a public meeting. On April 11 the press reported '...the eighth team in the competition will be Newcastle and district up to Tamworth. This team will come to Sydney each Saturday. Each week finds the Rugby League growing stronger, and the Union climbing down a bit.'[8]

Newcastle adopted the red and white hooped jersey of Pat Walsh's old club, Carlton.[9] The NSWRL agreed to pay the team's travel and hotel expenses, as well as compensate players for any time off work. With all NSWRL matches to be played on enclosed grounds in Sydney, the men would have to travel down by train from Newcastle each Saturday morning for the afternoon game and return overnight. This arrangement was not uncommon for sportsmen from the Hunter, but it was far from ideal. The ride home after the match was most often via the overnight ocean-going steamer. This got the players back to Newcastle quicker and was cheaper for the NSWRL than finding Saturday night hotel accommodation.

The NSWRL probably never contemplated a Sydney district club; there simply weren't enough first grade footballers residing in the area. In fact, a move was made by the rugby union players in the Sydney district to have the club absorbed into Glebe and Eastern Suburbs for the 1908 MRU season. However, at the subsequent election the non-playing members out-voted the footballers and the Sydney club continued.[10]

As for the University, Giltinan claimed there were sympathisers of the new movement within the club, but gaining its inclusion in the NSWRL competition would be a particularly unlikely proposition (unless the Unions collapsed). Giltinan stated that 'the League did not wish to exaggerate its success or the strength of its success or the strength of its footing. A number of players have joined and even some of the University sympathise with us; Balmain has come over in a body, but it would put the League, the players, and the public in a false position to give private names. With Hedley and Messenger the League has the best footballer and best back in Australia, and its members have no doubts of success.'[11]

UNION V LEAGUE: THE FIGHT IS ON

'The League's main difficulties will be players, grounds and finance,' wrote *The Sunday Sun*.

> So far as players are concerned I think that in all events at first they will experience no difficulty. Many good players have joined, more will follow, and, at first, so far as players are concerned the League will boom. Juniors will be their trouble. Unless they can get and keep them (which costs money) they are gone a million. The question of grounds will solve itself. At present the MRU have most of the available football grounds, but if financially successful the League will in the future be able to get all the grounds they require. It is merely a business transaction.
>
> I do not profess to have any inside knowledge respecting the Rugby League. I am as curious as the general public to see a Rugby League match, and can only be sure of this: If the Rugby League play fair and square, putting up good clean, interesting games, the Sydney public, by no means hide-bound [narrow-minded], will give them the measure of support they deserve.[12]

The Sydney Sportsman (now a strong supporter of the NSWRL) added that 'the League has beyond all question an up-hill fight, for it has arrayed against it the opposition of the press, and the purse they (the players) have filled for the Union. So far as can be seen, the fight is, so far as the Union is concerned, not one of principle, but one of interest, in which the broader interests of the game are lost sight of.'[13]

The NSWRL gained use of three major grounds for 1908: Birchgrove Park, Wentworth Park and the Agricultural Ground. The non-use of Birchgrove by the MRU had been the centre of the dissatisfaction shown in Balmain — it was no surprise that the League would want to use this ground, and would have no trouble gaining access to it. The linking of the NSWRL to Birchgrove was a particularly symbolic move.

Wentworth Park was the home of the Glebe club that won the 1907 MRU competition. It was with some surprise that the trustees of this ground opted to accept the offer from the NSWRL, even though financially it was far less than the MRU's 'liberal terms.' The Glebe rugby union club, no longer having access to the best ground in its district, was condemning of the trustees' decision. The main support for the League appears to have come from Sir Matthew Harris, the former patron of the Glebe rugby union club. His switch of allegiance to the League was pivotal.[14]

Harris was president of the Wentworth Park Trust and vice-president of the Royal Agricultural Society that operated the Agricultural Ground. Again in the face of a strong bid from the Unions, the Society continued to side with the NSWRL, staking that if League was successful they alone (instead of the SCG and Sports Ground) would reap the rewards. The Society donated a 'Challenge Shield' to be awarded to the winners of the inaugural Sydney first grade competition, while Harris became the NSWRL's first patron.[15] The support of the Agricultural Society was critical to survival of the League — there was no other major venue in Sydney that was accessible to all and large enough to cater for (and charge an entry fee from) the bigger crowds.

The use of Birchgrove and Wentworth Parks was a statement that the League was committed to the principles of local football. However, with four matches each Saturday on three grounds, they still needed other suburban grounds. Without one more, they would have to schedule a double-bill on one ground each week, starting with an early '2 o'clocker' match.

The League gained agreement in the early months of 1908 to use both Redfern Oval (South Sydney) and Hampden Oval (Eastern Suburbs), but Council issues frustrated these plans. Redfern Oval first had to be enclosed so a fee could be charged, and for some reason this plan, agreed to with the local Council, did not proceed. Meanwhile Paddington Council accepted an offer from the NSWRL for Hampden Oval, but rescinded the decision when a number of Councillors suddenly changed their minds, taking the lesser terms of the MRU. The League also seemed to have secured 'a ground in Newtown' before that too fell away.[16]

As for attracting the junior players of Sydney, a letter to The Sydney Sportsman indicated the League was making progress. The correspondence was in response to the MRU announcing it would be providing jerseys to first and second grade players (whereas the NSWRL provided gear for all three grades).

Surely the Union can go a little further and provide the third grade players with jerseys. But I suppose these players are looked upon as millionaires, and quite capable of buying their own jerseys. Now that the question 'Who are you playing with — League or Union?' is in everybody's mouth, I think the Union is making a false move in the above mean, grasping distinction between the younger players and the senior ones. The new League promises to provide their men with the whole rig-out, and if the Union want to keep their men why don't they treat their younger players in the same manner? In Borough football last year I think it cost me £2 for clothes and boots alone. If the Union does not alter its resolution the third grade players should join the League.[17]

W. Mackenzie, Secretary of the Balmain Juniors, wrote to the same newspaper offering the view that the MRU's overtures to junior players simply weren't being seen by anyone as genuine, given their past treatment. 'How the Union comes to take such a sudden interest in the Balmain Juniors, when, for the past three years, they have done practically nothing to foster junior football in our district. Is it not owing to the advent of the League that the Union has now come with their shandygaff [watered-down] proposals?' Both Balmain and South Sydney were able to form Junior club competitions under the League for 1908, with the premier club from each district playing-off for the 'Munn Cup' at the end of the season.[18]

POLITICIANS, PUBLICANS AND FOOTBALLERS

Another criticism the new League had to contend with was the question of who would be running the NSWRL. *The Referee* raised concern that 'the NU does not give professionals a voice in controlling the game. That is one of its safeguards. In a country like ours, where the democratic feeling permeates the people, it may be very difficult for a new body such as the League to carry out the NU rules.'[19]

The players involved in the initial moves of 1907 were content to allow Giltinan, Trumper and Hoyle to take control of the formative management — with the expectation that the 'rank-and-file' would decide the leadership once the League was on a sound footing. The fear with the players having control from the start, was they may only look at short-term gain, instead of re-investing for the future. The first NSWRL meeting after the 1907 All Blues professional matches provides a clear example, where the players wanted to divide up the initial gate-money rather than save it to fund the 1908 season.

Much confidence in the League was engendered by the large number of senior players and prominent members of the community who were involved with the club and the NSWRL committees; current and retired state politicians, including John Storey (Balmain), Edward Clark (North Sydney), Billy Hughes (Glebe), and Chris Watson (South Sydney) who, in 1904, was Labor's first Australian Prime Minister. Many local business owners were also involved — for example, at Glebe the local publican, Jack Shearer, became a vice-president. Senior players took management roles, most notably Peter Moir and Alec Burdon (Glebe), Arthur Hennessy (South Sydney), Harry Hammill (Newtown), Bob Graves (Balmain), Harry Glanville and Dinny Lutge (North Sydney) and Harry 'Jersey' Flegg (Eastern Suburbs).[20]

THE N.U. MAN IN SYDNEY

Tom McCabe, the English NU player who had migrated to Australia in late 1906, had become part of the professional movement by the end of 1907. This is confirmed by his presence amongst the group on stage, alongside Giltinan and Hoyle, at the first club meeting (Glebe) held on January 9. The full extent of his involvement in 1907 will perhaps remain a mystery. His subsequent contributions indicate he quickly became more than merely an advisor of the NU playing rules.

At Glebe, McCabe was voted onto the club management committee alongside Burdon, Moir and Hedley, and was also made club auditor. At Balmain he was elected as one of nine club vice-presidents. He was also involved with the NSWRL Referees' Association where, at that body's founding meeting (held at the Supreme Court Hotel, March 13), he was given a position on the management committee. The work of this committee was critical to the integrity of the new League, and is reflected in the names of the other men chosen. They were practically the men who formed the breakaway movement: Hoyle, Giltinan, Trumper, Burdon, and Messenger. The latter was elected even though he had not yet returned from England.

In preparation for the start of the competition, McCabe trained players in the NU rules. Having appeared in the first games of the 1906/07 season with Wigan, McCabe possessed the personal experience of the new 13–a-side and play-the-ball rules. The training runs were held at Latta's Picnic Ground at Lansvale in the city's outer reaches, as well as at Botany. Despite his coaching work and official positions, McCabe decided to play — Glebe gaining the benefit of his substantial experience.[21]

THE PROFESSIONALS CAN BE LEFT ALONE TO DIE

'Professionalism has killed every other sport it has touched,' offered *The Herald* in April 1908. 'As everyone knows, it killed sculling — a sport which in the days of Bill Beach drew bigger crowds than ever football or cricket has done since — and it killed running and cycling. Whether football will escape unscathed remains to be seen. When professionalism comes in at the door, the spirit of sport generally prepares to fly out of the window.'[22]

While the NSWRL was busy forming its clubs, the fight for allegiance of players and the public was on in earnest in the city's newspapers. Comments like *The Herald's* predicted dark days for football in NSW if the League survived. Yet this practically ignored what had been occurring under the MRU and NSWRU for a decade. Few accepted the Unions' self-portrait in 1908 as upholders of amateurism in light of the seasons before. The definition of an amateur appeared to many observers not how much expense money a footballer was paid, but under whose banner he took the field. *The Sydney Sportsman* wrote,

> As matters stand the whole case in a nutshell is, whether 3s or 7s/6d (personal expenses per day) brings a player within the present hybrid definition of a professional? Either this, or whether refusing to be any longer bound by the Union is in itself sufficient to warrant the Union in harrying those players who fail to see any specific virtue or advantage in the said Union. The Union barrackers affirm that only those that bear its brand are the aristocracy of amateurism. The posing and posturing of professional politicians on the Union platform, and all the jawing and jabbering of the Union forces, will not convince the public that the members of the League are one bit more professionals than the supporters and members of the Union.

> If payment of players creates professionalism, we have it on excellent authority the Union has repeatedly made professionals of its members. We should be pleased to have an official contradiction to the effect that the Union has never directly or indirectly paid players to compete in matches. Further, the Union might throw some light on the subject matter of its correspondence with Messenger, and the reason for its extraordinary anxiety to obtain its return from the player in question. Pure amateurism demands an answer.[23]

The correspondence *The Sydney Sportsman* was referring to was the cable sent to Messenger from Brisbane informing him 'money's all right' and that the NSWRU would pay his costs of employing a man to work in his place at the family's boatshed. Members of the NSWRU committee were terrified that on his return from England Messenger would make the document public, effectively proving their deception and use of 'professional' payments to ensure a player's appearance.

The NSWRU arranged a conference of leading amateur bodies in sport to put down a firm definition of what an amateur was. *The Referee* reported that 'the bodies represented included the Rowing and

Swimming Associations, NSWRU, Amateur Athletics Association, Lawn Tennis Association and Baseball. One of the results of this conference will be the welding together of all truly amateur bodies for the preservation of amateurism in sport.'

Given practically all sports in NSW relied upon gate-money for funding, the conference found it particularly difficult to form a definition that didn't make everyone a professional. 'The Rugby Union is still floundering and fussing in an attempt to frame an Amateur definition that will embrace its cheap and nasty professionalism' wrote *The Sydney Sportsman*. 'Up to date, neither English nor Australian amateur rulings on the subject can be twisted to suit the Union purposes, hence the delay in a pronouncement.'[24]

The problem for the Unions was that if the definition was too restrictive in terms of expenses and payments to players, it would ultimately drive the footballers into the arms of the NSWRL. To suggest the amateur/professionalism question was the sole reason players and supporters favoured League or Union is plainly wrong. It would be too simplistic to say that that the Union were strict followers of amateurism and the League were providing footballers with a professional living. The reality was they were both semi-professional bodies, with the League offering (openly) more generous compensation for expenses. The true position was in the middle of a murky cloud of debate.

Letter writers to newspapers raised many other issues that had swayed their allegiance. H. Skinner, in *The Herald*, blamed the poor showing of NSW and Australian teams against visiting international sides on the NSWRU's ill-management. Skinner saw League as more likely to select the best available players under a management that was determined to see their teams win.

> We, the Sydney paying public, who have followed the game for the past 25 years or more, have seen, I think, three English and about seven New Zealand teams playing on our grounds. In all, I suppose, we have seen between forty or fifty matches, of which number our men have won about six or seven. In nearly all others we have suffered ignominious defeat, a state of affairs which, when we come to consider our consistent success in all other branches of athletics, can only reflect discredit on our system of management.

> True, last year we tasted a little of the sweets of victory, but our past experience hardly inspires confidence, in a continuance of that form, and I think quite justifies both players and public in supporting a body which gives every reasonable promise of lifting the grand old game out of the thraldom of unprogressive mediocrity. What we, the paying public wish,

is not only to see a fair game, but also to see our men come off the field victorious, a little at least, oftener than they have been in the habit of doing, and under the altered conditions as promised by the League we have a fair prospect of realising that wish. Therefore, it is up to the Sydney public to support the League.[25]

The older NSWRU members, those who had brought rugby to Sydney, felt little need to take dramatic action. 'Too much importance had been attached to the professional movement,' Monty Arnold told *The Herald*. 'We have nothing to fear. The great heart of the public has always preferred clean sport. As soon as you could hire a man to win a game you could hire a man to lose it. There was no doubt that certain players would join the movement, and it was just as well they should be out of the amateur ranks.'

Arnold denied the Unions had lost significant players. 'The best players are from the country. Last year the most successful men in the representative team were Dix and Bede Smith, both country men.' Calvert (NSWRU president since its inception) simply stated: 'The professional element could be left alone to die.'[26]

What Arnold and Calvert were saying was that with the professionally-minded and working-class players out of the game, rugby union would return to the social and truly amateur days of the 1870s and '80s. They would welcome it.

LEAGUE IN QUEENSLAND AND NEW ZEALAND

While the major events in the formation of the League were occurring in Sydney and Newcastle, the movement was also initiating behind-the-scenes activities in Queensland and New Zealand. The first reference to a League in Brisbane was made after the All Blues matches in August 1907, and by the time the QRU committee held its initial meeting of 1908 (March 14) they intimated a rival organisation was on the horizon.

In New Zealand, now a country (dominion) in its own right, it was thought any progress towards forming professional rugby competitions would await the return of Baskerville and members of his team. However, it appears Baskerville left behind a network of followers to continue the work he had started — perhaps they were even following his plans.

The Referee revealed in mid-January the process being used in New Zealand (and a pointer to the methods used in Sydney in 1907 and later in Brisbane). 'A movement is being worked up in Auckland in a systematic manner, though the greatest secrecy is being observed with all that is being done — Northern Union literature is being disseminated in the city amongst players and others. From what can be learnt, an attempt will be made to get professional football going in Auckland and other parts of the Dominion, especially in Wellington, in time for next season, and an endeavour will be made to get a ground at Kingsland.'[27]

Whether 'next season' was 1908 or not is unclear — if it was they were unsuccessful. However, it is interesting to note that *The Sydney Sportsman*, claimed in April 1908 that 'applications are also in from clubs in New Zealand for matches here, but will not be granted.'[28]

There were significant factions seeking changes within the ranks of the New Zealand provincial Unions to quell the growing support for professional football. They demanded player allowances be increased, on-field rules be changed to make the game more open, and if necessary, the NZRU sever its association with the RFU. Calls were made for 'straight-out payments' instead of 'the practice followed by every club in Wellington of procuring employment for players.'

In Brisbane the news broke on March 28 that the Queensland Rugby Association (QRA) had been formed 'with a view to improving the game of football and bettering the existing conditions of footballers in the state of Queensland. The new association has affiliated with the NSWRL.' *The Referee*, announced that 'the executive officers of the Queensland Rugby League (the QRA) consist of the following well-known names in the football world: Sine Boland, Mickey Dore, George Watson, Jack Fihelly, Jack O'Connor and Buck Buchanan. With men of this stamp at the head of affairs up there, the success of the League seems assured, as lovers of the game must follow their best players.'

Cricketer Victor Trumper, 'that matchless magician of the willow', played a leading role in the founding of rugby league in Australia.

The management also included Alf Faulkner as chairman, the only one of the group not to have played rugby for Queensland. Watson, a state representative in 1907, commented that in its early stages the QRA was 'almost entirely in the hands of the players and I am sure that in the future those actively taking part in the game will be given full representation on the controlling body.' The first meetings were held in the homes of the men, with Fihelly given most credit for bringing the QRA into reality. He also had the assistance of Giltinan and Trumper who had been in Brisbane during the summer. Fihelly and Dore were appointed as Queensland's representatives in selections for the League's Australian teams.[29]

The involvement of Fihelly, Dore and Watson, all members of the Queensland team that visited Sydney in July 1906, provides further evidence of the significance of the 'great reunion' held after the final inter-state match. A meeting between Fihelly and George Smith is cited as the beginning of the League movement in Queensland.[30] Sine Boland was a Queensland and Australian forward between 1898 and 1903, and was well-known to Burdon, Hennessy and other senior players involved in the formation of the League in Sydney.

The QRA announcement also included a schedule of Queensland representative matches against NSW, New Zealand, and a team called the 'New Zealand Maoris.' It also noted that the tour to England would be of a 'combined Australian team, composed of NSW and Queensland players.'

No attempt was made to form any Brisbane clubs, with the focus fully on providing players for the Queensland and Australian teams. The smaller number of available players in Brisbane explains the reticence to form new clubs. The QRA would establish its credibility and enjoy better income from holding representative matches and being involved with an 'Australian' team — a club competition could wait.

MESSENGER AND THE NEW ZEALANDERS RETURN

The Queenslanders' path suggests that similar goals were probably held by the NSWRL. The priority for 1908 would be ensuring strong gate-takings from NSW and Australian matches to finance the immediate needs of the League and the future, as long as the Sydney club competition survived and maintained its credibility.

The NSWRL's fixture list for 1908 included twelve NSW or Australian matches in Sydney, including three Tests against the returning professional All Blacks. Club football would be suspended for up to three weeks a number of times during the season. The first club round would be on Easter Monday (April 20) instead of the Saturday to avoid a clash with the initial MRU games.[31] The New Zealanders would open the tour in Newcastle then return to Sydney for the first representative match against NSW on May 2.

While some clubs had played informal 'possibles v probables' games, the first rugby league inter-club matches were trials held at Rosebery Park Racecourse on March 28. Newtown defeated Glebe 3–0, while Souths and Easts ended their contest in a 6–all draw. The League's referees were each given a half game to get accustomed to the NU rules.[32]

New Zealand Rugby League 1907/08 Tourists to England and Wales

Back Row: William Trevarthen, 'Bumper' Wright, 'Massa' Johnston, Tom Cross, Adam Lile, Charles Pearce, D G Fraser.
Third Row: Harold Rowe, George Smith, Bill Mackrell, Edgar Wrigley, Joe Lavery, Con Byrne, Dan Gilchrist, Eric Watkins, William Tyler.
Second Row: Dick Wynyard, Charles Dunning, Lance Todd, Duncan McGregor, Harry Palmer, H S 'Jum' Turtill, Jim Gleeson, Billy Wynyard.
Front Row: Arthur Callum, Edward Tyne, Albert Baskerville, Dally Messenger, Arthur Kelly.

Albert Baskerville and the New Zealanders returned from England in time to assist at further trial matches held on April 11. 'Members of the All Blacks team visited the various trial games on Saturday last,' reported *The Herald*, 'and openly expressed their surprise at the grip the players and referees already have of the new rules. As one of the New Zealanders remarked, it is not learning the new rules that is hard, it is forgetting the old ones.'

Dick Wynyard told the Sydney footballers that the key difference from rugby union was to not kick the ball back to the other side, but to retain possession and use the ball through passing and having players back-up each other. Arthur Hennessy was one who quickly grasped the significance of Wynyard's insight, and immediately adopted this philosophy at South Sydney. Others took longer to learn and continued to kick for the sideline — as a result the first matches under NU rules in Australia were blighted by constant scrummaging.[33]

On the Monday evening (March 30) the New Zealanders, including Messenger, were given a public reception at the Town Hall. According to *The Referee* 'the hall was crowded' and the team was cheered upon their arrival on the stage. The captain, Richard 'Bumper' Wright, told the audience 'they had learned many lessons on the tour, and one of these was that the old amateur rugby game was not the only game in the world. He was sure the public would flock to see the new game.'

It was announced that Messenger would continue to be part of the New Zealand team for matches in Newcastle and Brisbane, presumably to add to the appeal of the games. He told *The Herald* of his impressions of the NU game: 'The thirteen team always means hard playing from start to finish. You never know the result until the whistle blows. A team might be 14 points ahead of you in the first half, and 14 points behind you in the second. You've got to play hard until the last moment.'[34]

THE LEAGUE COMPETITION MATCHES BEGIN TODAY

A few days before the opening of the season, *The Sydney Sportsman* provided a summary of the extent of the League's intrusion. 'It will be seen from the teams (the club sides selected for the opening games) that despite the reports from the Unions that the League have done them no harm, the latter have at least a good half of the best players that the metropolitan area can produce, so it is only fair to assume that the public, whose sympathy is already with the League, will get something decent for the their money when the competition starts.'[35]

One of the biggest fears the NSWRL held was poor weather — a run of wet Saturdays, particularly for the representative matches, could ruin the financial stability of the new body. The decision to move the opening round to the Easter Monday proved to be a winner for the NSWRL. The MRU began their season on the Saturday of the Easter weekend and were hit with blustery wind and constant rain. To the relief of the League officials, the Monday turned out to be a sunny, even slightly warm, day.

The Agricultural Ground was unavailable because of the Easter Show, leaving the NSWRL to play double-bills at Birchgrove and Wentworth Parks. The Show (80,000 visitors), as well as the Sydney Cup Day at Randwick Racecourse (30,000), meant the League had stiff competition. The entry fee to each of the League grounds was 6 pence, with the grandstand at Wentworth Park an additional 6 pence — approximately 3,000 people attended each venue.

The lower grade matches were held at Double Bay and on a second oval at Birchgrove Park. With Newcastle not entering teams in the lower grades, clubs were accepted from Enfield (Second Grade) and Sydney (Third Grade). Wests did not have enough players for a team in the Thirds, and Drummoyne was allowed entry in their place.

Eastern Suburbs v Newtown at Wentworth Park, 2 p.m.

Glebe v Newcastle at Wentworth Park, 3.15 p.m.

South Sydney v North Sydney at Birchgrove Park, 2 p.m.

Balmain v Western Suburbs at Birchgrove Park, 3.15 p.m.

Eastern Suburbs 32 d. Newtown 16: The game was described 'as fast as the wind' by *The Referee*. Quick early work along the wing by a Newtown three-quarter puzzled the defence of the Easterners. Jack Scott then secured at centre for Newtown and dodged fast through the pack, scoring behind the posts (at the city end of the ground). Scott converted and with it took the honours of the first try and goal scorer in first grade under the NSWRL. Easts held an 11–10 lead at the spell. In the second half Stuntz scored four tries for the 'Stripes' in a runaway win. Late in the game Stuntz and a Newtown player came to blows. 'Three onlookers jumped over the fence to come to the aid of the Newtown men, and play stopped until they retired. The game ended shortly afterwards.'

Glebe 8 d. Newcastle 5: 'The play, like the preceding one, became very fast from the kick-off — too fast to last on a hot day. Newcastle opened the scoring with a rattling piece of work' along their back-line that ended with Bill Bailey diving over in the corner. The match became an indifferent exhibition with the referee blowing a 'whistle fantasia' as the players often broke the rules. Glebe eventually won the match 8–5 with Burdon, Moir and McCabe their best. 'The northerners played up well, but the quality of play was below expectations.'

South Sydney 11 d. North Sydney 7: For the first part of the match the defences of both sides held firm. Souths were eventually penalised and Glanville kicked Norths to a 2–0 lead. Butler responded for South Sydney with a 'splendid goal' from well-over half-way to draw the scores level. 'The game continued fast and even' until Souths' winger Tommy Anderson crossed for a try. Dinny Lutge scored a try for Norths early in the second half making it 5–5. The last moments of the game were particularly exciting as South Sydney held a 8–7 lead.

Their halfback, Butler, scooted away from a scrum and scored a try, securing an 11–7 win.

Balmain 24 d. Western Suburbs 0: 'The game opened in very lively fashion, both sides showing great willingness, and the ball travelled up and down the ground with great rapidity.' From a Balmain scrum win the ball was passed to Latta, who 'got across after a clever dodging run.' Graves scored another try for Balmain and they enjoyed a 6–0 lead at the break. Western Suburbs were on the defensive throughout the second half and were beaten easily 24–0.[36]

AT THE HORSE AND JOCKEY HOTEL

Later that evening Giltinan convened a meeting at the Horse and Jockey Hotel in Homebush to form a ninth club, Cumberland. The call for the formation of the club came from Wests rugby union players. Most of these men chose to remain loyal to rugby union when the Ashfield members of the district gained control of the new Wests rugby league club. However, a further split occurred in the Wests rugby union club just days before the opening round of the season.

At the meeting, Giltinan encouraged the 27 players present to join the Wests rugby league club and bolster its strength, but they could not bring themselves to work with the former Ashfield footballers.

The Cumberland club formed, but unlike the other clubs did not truly represent an established district. To (presumably) prevent conflict with any other district, in either code, Cumberland adopted the blue and gold colours of the University of Sydney. The NSWRL insisted that final acceptance of Cumberland would not be made until they played a trial match to confirm their viability. A game against the top-flight Eastern Suburbs was arranged for the under-card of the first NSW v New Zealand match.[37]

THE NSWRL HAVE MADE A GRAVE ERROR

Messenger and the New Zealanders left for Newcastle on the Tuesday evening train (April 21) for their opening match the next day. On the Wednesday morning the visitors were officially welcomed by the Mayor of Newcastle, Alderman A. Cook, at the Council Chambers in Watt Street. Baskerville spoke on behalf of his team, while Newcastle captain Stan Carpenter was also present. The locals requested that the first match be played under rugby union rules, apparently to even up their chances. The New Zealanders agreed.

Unfortunately when kick-off came Newcastle could only muster 14 players from their limited resources. With the team quickly down 13–0 local representative player George Cox, who was amongst the crowd of only 400, decided to change codes on the spot and joined the team on the field. The 'Maorilanders' won 53–6, with Messenger kicking six goals from as many attempts with 'one being a magnificent effort from the touchline.' Harold Rowe, an outside back from Auckland, scored three tries for the visitors.

Attention then turned to the second match, which would be played under rugby league rules. The local newspapers, staunchly in the rugby union camp, gave the League practically no support. The NSWRL was forced to advertise the first game of rugby league in Newcastle in the public notices section of the newspaper alongside theatre events and other amusements. The Show Ground also wasn't the most suitable venue for a football match, but it had to do as the Union authorities had control of the city's best ground.

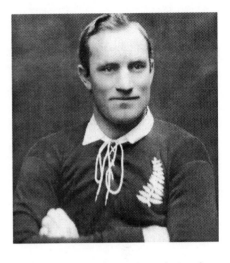

Messenger amassed 146 points during the New Zealand rugby league team's tour – 101 points more than the next best.

Ultimately, only 700 spectators were on hand to see the contest. However, it was described as 'a good attendance' and in comparison, the top rugby union games at the time drew no more than 2,000. Newcastle took the field in their red and white hooped jerseys and faced a New Zealand team ready to show off their newly acquired expertise in the NU game.

Newcastle had no answers to the visitors who performed in a 'magnificent style.' Rowe grabbed another four tries to follow up his work from the earlier match and the New Zealanders won 34–8. Some of the press gave the NU game a favourable write-up: the new rules 'made it a good deal more interesting than the previous match' and 'the differences between the Union and the League codes are in favour of the latter, for they all make for pace and attractiveness.'[38]

Not all matches in those first weeks were inspiring efforts. Back in Sydney on the same afternoon Glebe defeated Newtown 7–2 at Wentworth Park. *The Sunday Sun* reporter wrote: 'Taking the game as an exhibition it was not good. It is probable that the New Zealand team just returned could give a good exhibition under NU rules — probably the Glebe-Newtownites were book-perfect but on the field they were all astray. I was sitting alongside a Leagueite, one who was a great footballer in days gone by. He agreed with me that the game wasn't worth watching, and as we heard the roars coming from the University Oval we both wished ourselves there. I think the NSWRL have made a grave error in adopting NU rules en bloc. The NU had taken a dozen years to change over and so should have the NSWRL.'[39]

CHAPTER TWELVE

THE BROKEN TURNSTILE

FIRST BIG LEAGUE GAME: NSW V NEW ZEALAND

The New Zealand v NSW contest was the first big match under NU rules in Sydney, and there was some uncertainty as to how the public would view it. Many were likely to attend simply for a look at NU rugby, and the NSWRL recognised that poor weather could cruel their chances of a good gate and an entertaining exhibition of their game. Much to their relief, the day provided 'perfect weather for the spectator' and a crowd of 14,000 pushed through the turnstiles of the Agricultural Ground in anticipation of the match. While Baskerville and Giltinan sat in the stand expectantly looking on, the two teams delivered the contest they needed to convince the waverers and some opponents. *The Herald's* summation was simply, 'Many went out to the ground out of curiosity — they remained to applaud.'

In the early match, Cumberland were defeated 18–4 in their trial against Eastern Suburbs, but sufficiently impressed the NSWRL to be granted entry to the club competition.

The NSW side appeared to most judges to have been chosen on form (rather than as a reward for their work or loyalty to the League). The Blues were led by Arthur Hennessy. Messenger, still yet to play first grade for Eastern Suburbs, was in opposition to his former (New Zealand) team mates. *The Herald* noted that the early part of the match 'was very fast — the game was interesting, and the crowd were soon cheering. Messenger was applauded for some brilliant work. In the midst of some remarkably fast play at the home 25, Barber secured, and took a flying shot at goal, and scored. NZ 2–0.' Barber was a versatile back who joined the New Zealanders to cover the players left in England.

Soon after NSW levelled scores through a Messenger penalty goal, 'Lutge broke away, and another dash by NSW, in which Davis figured prominently— he played a splendid game all through — opened the way for Stuntz, who scored behind the posts.' Before half-time Cheadle scored another Blues try which Messenger converted from near the touchline amidst loud applause.

The New Zealanders struggled against the rule interpretations of the referee — which must have frustrated them given they had a greater experience under the NU rules. 'When Wynyard showed a bit of temper because he did not agree with the decision, the crowd hooted.' The game then became quite vigorous and 'was not child's play — the boot was used freely when there was a scramble.' Through penalty goals NSW stayed well clear of the New Zealanders eventually winning 18–10 despite both sides scoring two tries. Messenger's personal tally was 12 points from six goals.

The press did not diminish the standing of the game in comparison to the previous contests between the two former colonies: 'The game was in willingness quite up to the traditions of NSW v New Zealand, both sides being fully extended to play their hardest game,' wrote *The Herald*. The New Zealand team were not rated as easy-beats by anyone — they had proved in England they were a strong football side irrespective of the amateur/professional debate. The NSW win was widely applauded in Sydney and earned the League much more respect and credibility.

The NU rules also made a very positive impression. *The Herald* observed 'the differences between the Union and the League codes are in favour of the latter, for they all make for pace and attractiveness. There were many brilliant forward and passing rushes.'[1]

Lewis Abrams took himself out for a look at the match, feeling it was his duty to know the competition. He still supported Union, but continued to condemn the 3s player allowance ruling. 'I keenly watched the All Blacks game on Saturday,' said Abrams to *The Sunday Sun*. 'I am now bound to say that it is my humble and honest opinion that their game, certainly from a spectators point of view as well as a player's, is preferable, and outclasses the game of rugby under which our NSWRU and MRU have to play. In fact, I go even further, and predict that unless our Union breaks away from the Mother Union (RFU), and adopts the same rules in the immediate future our Union will be as dead as "Julius Caesar," as far as the public interest is concerned. As the NSWRU on the whole are a splendidly managed body, I ask them to earnestly set to work at once and have their rules altered, and brought into line with the NU rules, or if possible, improved upon. I urge this because I want to arouse our Union to what I consider is going to be the most formidable rival they have had to deal with.'[2]

JIMMY DEVEREUX — THE HERO OF THE DAY

Before the first Saturday Test, the mid-week NSW v New Zealand match saw the local side make eight changes. The three-quarter line remained intact, but elsewhere young players were given an opportunity. Most interest was in the new halves Sid Deane and 'Pony' Halloway. The Englishman Tom McCabe gained one of the forward positions. The New Zealanders chose 'practically the same side.' Another thirty local players were on show in a 'Possibles v Probables' match that kicked-off at 2 p.m.

The Blues' Jimmy Devereux was the 'hero of the day,' far outshining his centre partner Messenger. The fast and diminutive North Sydney back scored two tries in NSW's 13–10 win. According to *The Sydney Sportsman*, Devereux's tries were 'worth a day's walk to see — he is without doubt the most improved player in the game, his pace and headiness in this match surprising those who had been watching his general improvement this season.'

The New Zealanders were 'in far better condition, thus keeping the excitement boiling right to the finish.' If not for a last minute try being disallowed by the touch judge, they could have won. The NSW win ended speculation by the 'prigs' that the League would ensure the visitors won to get a bigger gate at the Test match.[3]

The mid-week attendance of 6,000 was described as 'a very good crowd for an off day.' With the 14,000 from the Saturday match, the League could be reasonably pleased with the 20,000 aggregate for the two matches. Still, it paled in comparison to the 75,000 that attended the two 1907 matches between NSW and the amateur New Zealanders (52,000 on the Saturday, 23,000 on the Wednesday). Messenger played in all four of these matches — clearly the fight between the codes was not to be resolved by simply securing the allegiance of Messenger.

THE KANGAROO IS ON HIS TAIL

The selection panel for the first Australian rugby league team showed how much say the senior players now had. These players, already assured of a place in the team, would choose the rest. This was a response to one of the major grievances the players held against the NSWRU selection system. Still, for a number of reasons the League system was not perfect.

Giltinan took one of the places on the selection panel, alongside Hennessy, Burdon, Lutge and, as Queensland selector, Mickey Dore. The NSWRL was determined to involve the Queenslanders in the Australian team, even though no League matches had yet been played in Brisbane. Along with Dore, two other Queensland players were named in the team: winger Doug McLean and front rower Bob Tubman. Burdon stood down due to a cut hand and missed the match, while Hennessy was elected captain.

Albert Baskerville agreed to make himself available in the New Zealand team as a winger. Harold Rowe, a fast and experienced three-quarter, was chosen as the reserve back, which suggests that Baskerville wanted to play, rather than there being a run of injuries forcing him to take the field. Jum Turtill, playing fullback, was the New Zealand captain.[4]

Australia: C. Hedley (Glebe), D. McLean (Qld), J. Devereux (N.S.), H. H. Messenger (E.S.), F. Cheadle (Newt.), A. Rosenfeld (E.S.), M. Dore (Qld), R. Graves (Balm.), A. Hennessy (S.S.), J. Rosewell (S.S.), T. McCabe (Glebe), D. Lutge (N.S.), R. Tubman (Qld).

New Zealand: Turtill, Baskerville, Wrigley, Kelly, Tyler, Barber, R. Wynyard, Mackrell, Pearce, Trevarthen, Cross, Johnston, Byrne.

Yet again the League had perfect weather for one of its most important days of the season. On Saturday May 9 over 20,000 patrons were at the Agricultural Ground to witness a 'stirring and strenuous game.' Just before 3.15p.m. Australia, wearing the light blue jerseys of NSW (emblazoned with a large 'A' and a kangaroo), 'filed onto the enclosure, the men were greeted with a roar of welcome.'

'Soon the redoubtable warriors in the black jersey came striding into the arena,' recorded *The Herald*, 'and were greeted with salvos of applause. The two previous splendid battles between the leather-kicking gladiators had stimulated public interest to a fever pitch.' After the New Zealanders performed their war-cry, 'Black and Blue rapidly raced into position for the start of play. A shrill pipe of the umpire's whistle, then Johnston, the colossal New Zealander kicked-off, and the fray began. Right from the start it could be seen that the piratical-looking New Zealanders were out for keeps in deadly earnest. Their forwards attacked like tigers, keeping the thin blue line battling for dear life, just on its own. It was only by superhuman battling and a fair share of luck that our boys prevented New Zealand from scoring in the first few minutes.'

Hennessy received a 'nasty stinker over the eye, the result of a blow, and had to be carried off the field.' The touch judge reported Johnston as the 'culprit' and he was asked to leave the field by the referee (the New Zealander was later exonerated). Jones took Hennessy's place while he received treatment, Messenger became captain. Hennessy did not know he had been replaced and returned to the play, for a time Australia had 14 players to the visitors' 12.

'The Blacks' then attacked the Australian line, using a dribbling rush with the ball at their feet. Byrne picked the ball up for the New Zealanders and he passed it to Wynyard who scored the first try of the match. Shortly afterwards, Baskerville got a pass from Wynyard, and 'with a splendid run, beat Hedley badly' to claim New Zealand's second try. Baskerville, 'who was sprinting in fine form,' nearly scored again a few minutes after, but was brought down by a try-saving tackle from Devereux. New Zealand were not to be denied though, as they spread the ball to Wynyard who raced across to score their third try (and lead 11–0). Messenger had three attempts at goal as the first-half neared its end, landing one from a Devereux 'fair catch.'

Australia came back hard in the second half, with Messenger featuring strongly in general play; at one point he shook off three tacklers before successfully punt kicking the ball downfield, even though he was facing his own goal line. *The Sydney Sportsman* reported on Australia's comeback, 'The Blues forwards rushed the leather down field, Graves securing, and had the mortification of being held up on the line. Dinny Lutge soon after made amends for this by scoring the first try for his side, after a bumping run.' Messenger missed the conversion attempt of Australia's first rugby league Test try. 'The Blues, playing with great heart, kept "knocking at the door," and another try was soon forthcoming — Rosenfeld following on a ball kicked over the line scored.' Messenger converted the try and the New Zealanders were now only ahead 11–10.

With time fast running out the crowd reached fever pitch. New Zealand were penalised for shepherding, but Messenger yet again failed with the kick (his eleventh goal attempt, with just two successes). Minutes later, Messenger took a fair catch on the half-way mark which gave him another shot. He missed. However, the referee ruled that one of the New Zealand forwards had baulked Messenger, (clapping his hands and yelling 'fearful exclamations in Maori'), and gave him another kick. Messenger missed again. The whistle then immediately sounded for full-time, giving New Zealand a one point victory.

Action from Australia's first rugby league Test – against New Zealand at the 'Agra (Sydney, 1908)

In the aftermath, Turtill was praised for his play, as was Baskerville. Although he was reported to 'have taken a gruelling' at the hands of the Australians, Baskerville's form 'was an eye-opener in the New Zealand three-quarter line, and took any amount of stopping.' Another account added that 'it was due, in a great way, to his efforts that the All Blacks won.'

The press almost unanimously condemned the inclusion of the Queenslanders. 'There is only one opinion,' wrote *The Sydney Sportsman*, 'and that is the best team on the day won. The Queensland reps in no way strengthening Australia's chances. Dore was not the Dore of old. He was to all appearances, clean out of condition. McLean was too much inclined to stand off, and Tubman was not noticed among the ruck. The combination among the Blue backs appeared to be thoroughly disorganised by the new blood introduced, while the week's training seemed to make a new team of New Zealand as compared with the previous Saturday.'[5]

The NSW press were not trying to demean Queensland, they were merely stating what they had observed — they did not condemn the notion or importance of an Australian team. Of course NSW would have a stronger combination — even Dore, McLean and Tubman knew that. For each of them it was their first game of the season and their first under NU rules (for McLean it was his first rugby game since 1906). Their presence is what was important for the League (and its hopes for expansion in Queensland), not their contribution to a victory.

The League game had proved attractive to a wide section of the Sydney patrons over the three matches (40,000). However, it wasn't simply that NU rules were gaining appeal, the League's popularity also stemmed from NSW and Australian success on the field. In 24 years, Australian rugby had hosted eight visits from the New Zealanders (including the professional All Blacks of 1907) and three from Great Britain. Never before had NSW, Queensland, or Australia sent any team back home defeated in a series.

The public demanded a winning team — but under the NSWRU other factors influenced selections. Some of the best players were overlooked for reasons that had nothing to do with their skill, while others were picked out of position. The players and the public were tired of losing. While they attended matches in their droves in 1907, they wanted to see their team win. Opposition players and news reporters both chastised the Sydney crowds for not applauding moments of good play from the amateur All Blacks. The League could see that if they gave the public what they wanted, their venture would be very well supported.

The defeat of the New Zealanders in the first two matches gained the League far more credibility than anything had (the Test match was regarded by all as the third contest of a NSW v New Zealand series). Under their own control, they had achieved what the NSWRU had been unable to do in a quarter of a century. The editor of *The Herald* praised the win as a triumph for NSW and Australian sport. 'Australians, more particularly New South Welshmen, have made an extraordinary advance in skill and form.'[6]

The Sydney Sportsman celebrated in poem:[7]

> *The kangaroo is on his tail, his leap is full of glee,*
> *He's been and downed the great All Blacks — by best two out of three.*
> *The games were fast and furious, the air oft times went blue;*
> *But as you know they ended in a triumph for the Roo-*
> *Thus comes this joyful jumping of our football kangaroo!*

A SAD GOODBYE TO A FRIEND

On the following Tuesday (May 12) the New Zealanders boarded the sea-going steamer for the trip north to Brisbane. Baskerville was said to be still not himself in the aftermath of the Test match — it was just the second match he had played in the past twelve months (perhaps longer). Messenger too was injured, and he did not rejoin the New Zealand party as originally planned. Though they had lost to NSW, the tourists were content to have defeated Australia and looked forward to receiving their share of the profits from the 40,000 crowd over the three matches.

Baskerville's priorities had been off the field, as he sought to make the remainder of the tour a success. 'Massa' Johnston recalled later that Baskerville told him he was already looking forward to taking a team to America if he could manage it. In his slightly weakened condition Baskerville caught the flu while on the ship — it was an accepted hazard of travelling via sea, but, all the same, he could have done without it.

The first match in Brisbane was against Queensland on Saturday May 16. Baskerville attended 'though not feeling too well, sat in the sun and watched the progress of the match.'

Dore and McLean coached the Queenslanders in preparation for match. The Maroons had 'only four or five rugby men of note, in the team — the old New Zealand and Australian rep Bill Hardcastle surprised the visitors with his appearance in the Queensland team.'

Queensland: R. Allingham, D. McLean, G. Watson (c), A. O'Brien, W. Evans, W. Abrahams, M. Dore, J. Horan, R. Tubman, W. Hardcastle, V. Anderson, J. Cartmill, J. Fihelly. Reserves: A. Baird, A. Moxley.

Queensland wore the conventional maroon jersey. As with all the League representative teams in Sydney, their jerseys had the Federal kangaroo and '1908' on the breast. A crowd of 3,000 welcomed the teams onto the Exhibition Ground. The Maroons scored the first try of the match, to wild applause, after O'Brien scooted away from the midfield to score next to the posts. As expected though, the locals were no contest for the New Zealanders, with the final score 34–12.[8]

The New Zealanders returned to the team hotel, but Baskerville's condition gave great concern to all. The next day he was taken to the Victoria Private Hospital where he was diagnosed with acute pneumonia. On the Wednesday afternoon (May 20), New Zealand played against a Brisbane 'Metropolitan' team (composed primarily of the Queensland team members in different positions) and won easily 43–10 in front of a 'meagre attendance.' Word that Baskerville's situation was now grim reached the players while they were in the change rooms after the game.

They hurried to the hospital, some still in their playing gear, and were stricken to find he was unconscious and failing fast. They 'bid a long goodbye to one of the truest comrades man ever had.'

Baskerville passed away at 6 p.m. He was 25 years old.

Understandably, they were devastated. 'The members of the team are much depressed, and tried very hard to abandon the tour (scheduled to go for over two more weeks). But owing to the liabilities incurred by the NSWRL, that body found it imperative that the tour must be completed,' reported *The Herald*. His remains were accompanied to Sydney by six members of the team (one representing each New Zealand province), including the manager Harry Palmer.

They sailed out of Sydney Harbour for Wellington mid-afternoon on Saturday May 23. Flags were flown at half-staff at all matches in Sydney club football, of both codes, while the League players wore black armbands as well.[9]

Back in Brisbane the rest of the New Zealand team was readying themselves for the return match against Queensland. Messenger had arrived from Sydney, but it was decided he should play with the Maroons to even up the contest. Again before a very poor crowd, the match produced few highlights in the first half with only goals being scored. New Zealand scored two tries early in the second half to lead 12–4 before Messenger sparked a fight-back from the Queenslanders. He scored a solo try in the corner late in the match to level scores at

12–12, but was unable to convert and the match ended soon after in a draw.

The New Zealanders' final engagement in Brisbane was the second Test against Australia (May 30). As the 'Australian' team was playing under the auspices of the QRA, the side wore maroon jerseys. Four Queenslanders (in addition to Messenger) were selected, including Dore and Hardcastle. A good attendance of 7,000 was present as the sides took the field. The New Zealanders declined to perform their war-cry. The 24–12 win to the visitors came as a bit of shock, given their ranks were depleted by the men who went home. The Australian side played as if the win would come easily, and were content to let Messenger do most of the work. The home team was greatly changed for the third Test, and the only Queenslander invited to travel back to Sydney was Hardcastle.[10]

A BLOOD-CURDLING WAR-CRY

In Sydney the 27–man New Zealand 'All-Maoris' team arrived at the harbour wharf on the SS *Moana*. The city put on 'a wet reception, both inside and out' for the visitors. From the deck of the ship the Maoris 'startled the occupants of Sussex Street with a blood-curdling war-cry.' The League organised for them to be carried by drags [horse-drawn coaches] to St James' Hall in Phillip Street, 'where the usual formalities were gone through.'

The Maoris were captained by Albert 'Opai' Asher, known for his spectacular leaps over tacklers and who was last seen in Sydney with the New Zealand team of 1903. The team practically followed the model of the New Zealand Maoris (Natives) tourists of 1888/89 — where football was only part of the attraction to the public. Asher's team included a number of Maoris chiefs, and evening concert performances and pre-match hakas directed at the crowd were featured as well.

Speaking at the welcome function, Asher told the audience, 'We have come over here to do our best, and you will have to play hard to beat us. I thank Mr Giltinan and the League very much for their promises to make our trip enjoyable. When we meet you on the field we will give you a bad time. We have come over here to beat the kangaroo!'

'After a parting glass they were driven to their hotel at Waverley. In their street clothes they do not look as heavy as their published weights, but seem a young lively lot,' observed *The Sydney Sportsman*.

Asher and his team are reputed to have been unaware they would not be playing rugby union until arriving in Sydney. *The Sydney Sportsman* reported the Maoris 'did not like the idea of taking on the 13–a-side game at first, but after seeing it played on Saturday last (club match) are delighted with it. Asher says his men will pick it up in a day's practice.' The League appointed referee George Boss to act as the team's coach and 'general instructor.'[11]

THE END OF THE 'ALL GOLDS'

The Maoris were part of a crowd of between 15,000 and 20,000 at the third Test at the Agricultural Ground. The early entertainment was a match between Balmain Juniors (blue jerseys) and South Sydney Juniors (green). The Test match was a tense struggle throughout. New Zealand led 6–0 at half-time, and then 9–3 before Australia began to rein in the gap. Tries to Graves and Anderson got the Blues to 11–9 behind. Lou Jones, the Eastern Suburbs forward, dived over for the match-winning try with only moments remaining, Australia winning its first ever rugby league Test 14–9.[12]

For the New Zealanders it was the end of ten long months. Early in the evening they sailed out of Sydney and across the Tasman. Their first priority at home would be a benefit match for Baskerville's family in Wellington, in what would be the first game of rugby league on New Zealand soil. Played on June 13 at Athletic Park, 'Wright's Blacks' beat 'Turtill's Reds' 55–20 — £300 was raised from a crowd of 8,000.[13]

It was hoped that Messenger and other NSW players would be allowed to participate in the benefit match, but with the Maori games impending, the NSWRL did not agree. However, they decided to donate half the gate-receipts of the first NSW v Maoris match (Monday June 8 at the Agricultural Ground). In a heartening move, the NSWRU and MRU called off all games scheduled for the day so that the match would have no competition for patrons. Whether the decision of the Unions or sentiment for Baskerville had any effect upon the crowd no one can know, however the League was stunned when 30,000 attended.

'It was a day absolutely made to order for football, just enough warmth in the air and scarcely any wind,' reported *The Sydney Sportsman*. The Maoris, 'with a string of beads and smile on,' went around the field before the match 'giving their hakas to the different sections of the vast audience to their evident amusement. Many inquiries were made by the fair sex as to whether the Maoris players were kept in at night, or the telephone number of their hotel.' The team then marched back into the stand to 'dress for sterner business.'

The Herald enthused about the match, describing it as 'a brilliant exhibition of the Northern Counties game, and the result was a win for NSW by 18–9. From the kick-off to the full-time whistle there was not an uninteresting moment. An extraordinary pace was maintained, and the ball travelled with ever-changing advantages and disadvantages, which kept the crowds in an effervescent condition. There was probably not a spectator who did not leave the ground satisfied that he had witnessed a game well worth seeing.'

'It must have brought an immense amount of satisfaction to the hearts of the men who have been labouring for months and months in their efforts to bring League football before the Australian public, when they saw thousands upon thousands streaming through the various gates till when the game started there was a full 30,000 present,' wrote *The Sydney Sportsman*.

The League seemed to be living a dream run since having kicked-off less then two months earlier. The weather was always perfect for spectators — as one newspaper put it, 'it would seem that the gentleman in charge of the weather, must like most others, have a leaning towards League football.' The decision to bring forth a Maoris team seemed to be a master-stroke.[14]

THE BROKEN GRANDSTAND TURNSTILE

The Maoris match was the NSWRL's greatest success to date — yet on that very day it all began to unravel, starting with a broken grand-stand turnstile.

It was normal practice for a touring team to ensure it was fully aware of the various ground entry gates so that it could keep an eye on them, making sure no one was given free access (apart from members of the ground).

The crowd was so unexpectedly large at the Agricultural Ground for the Maoris match, that it began bank up outside the turnstiles.

The League's president Henry Hoyle saw what was happening. 'I was at the gate at the time,' Hoyle recalled, 'and was approached by many acquaintances among the public, struggling for admittance, as to why the other turnstile was not opened. I at once, seeing the reasonableness of the request, had the door of that particular stile opened for about twenty-five minutes. This had the effect of getting rid of the temporary blockade. The money was taken by a gentleman in whom we have every confidence, and was banked separately the following day.'

Unfortunately, all the Maoris' management heard was that an additional turnstile had been opened without them being advised. On inspection they found the turnstile was 'minus the clock which registers takings' and became suspicious of the League. Perhaps not wanting to cause any trouble so early in the tour, they did not take it up with the NSWRL. Giltinan and Hoyle though had no trouble admonishing the Maoris for supposedly informing the press the full amount of the gate-takings for the day.[15]

The visit in 1908 of 'The New Zealand Maoris' rugby league team was a spectacular success in NSW and Queensland. This photograph was taken during a match against NSW in Sydney.

Asher also had problems of his own over the gate-money. It seems that in October, 1907, a Sydney man, Robert Jack, wrote to Asher 'with a view to organising a team of Maori footballers and conducting a tour through Australia.' Jack does not appear to have any link to the League movement, and presumably was inspired by the successful visit of Baskerville's team in August. Over the last months of 1907 Asher and Jack exchanged letters in which there was apparently an agreement reached, which involved Jack receiving five per cent of the team's net gate-receipts. Jack was then to give half of this money to Asher in return for his efforts in arranging the team.

In early 1908 'the team decided to conduct all future negotiations in regard to the tour with the NSWRL.' No contract was signed between the Maoris and Jack, and Asher believed the matter was over, though he did not write to Jack to confirm it. When the Maoris arrived in Sydney, the two men met and Jack insisted the agreement be honoured. Asher did not agree, instead offering Jack two and half percent of the team's share from the first NSW v Maoris match 'so that he should not be disappointed.' Jack refused, demanding Asher and the team honour the so-called agreement, and the matter remained unresolved.[16]

LEAGUE'S FIRST COURTROOM BATTLE

NSW and the Maoris met in a second match the following Saturday, with another 20,000 present. Messenger, captain for the day, took a personal tally of 18 points in a 30–16 win for the Blues. For the following Maoris v Metropolis [a Sydney representative team] match at Wentworth Park (held mid-week), the home selectors brought in to the side Miller, D'Alpuget, Conlon, Dobbs, Flegg, Courtney, Moir and Notting. The League was praised in the press for the state selectors 'giving all of the players who are showing good form a chance.' While most of the new men had played rugby union for NSW in previous seasons, one newcomer attracting interest was Horrie Miller (Eastern Suburbs), 'who has any amount of pace, and is fast learning how to use it.'[17]

The Maoris defeated Metropolis 23–20 in a magnificent game that, unfortunately for the spectators and dangerously for the players, continued in the dark for the last part of the match. There were a number of heated exchanges in the match, and at one point Giltinan came down from the grandstand to remonstrate with the referee over his failure to take action over some of the heavy-handed tactics of the Maoris players.[18]

Feelings between Giltinan and the Maoris seemed to be on a decline on a number of fronts. For the next match, to be played in Newcastle, Asher advised the Referees' Association of his choice of Aub Welch as referee (which was the touring team's prerogative).

However, Giltinan stepped in by giving Asher a list of just four referees, which excluded Welch, and demanding he make a further choice. Asher declined to change his mind and Welch travelled to Newcastle with the Maoris. Giltinan then refused to pay Welch's expenses, claiming the Maoris had to recompense him as they chose a referee outside the League's list.[19]

The Maoris defeated Newcastle 15–2 before another big crowd, estimated at nearing 4,000. Considering the match was held in competition with a Newcastle v Balmain rugby union game, it was another example how popular League (arguably through the Maoris) was becoming. The Maoris then continued on to Queensland where another five matches were scheduled.

'Maori Footballers: Dispute Over Gate Money,' barked *The Herald* news banner. Jack had taken legal action against Asher, the Maoris, and the NSWRL in the NSW Equity Court. Jack successfully argued that the League be prevented from paying the Maoris their share of the gate-takings until a full account was made and his share (as per the 'agreement') was paid to him. The Court issued an order upon the NSWRL directing them not to pay the Maoris. Believing the order also applied to the upcoming matches in Queensland, the League instructed the QRA to also withhold their payments. The NSWRL had already paid the Maoris £800, but before long the team would be unable to pay its bills if no more income was forthcoming.[20]

Meanwhile, no doubt with costs in mind, Asher left ten members of the team behind in Sydney. Amongst them were three of the Maori chiefs, who were very much part of the League's entertainment package for the tour. When Giltinan found out they were not in Brisbane, where they were supposed to be performing before the games and at concerts, he immediately sent them up. Giltinan's view was that the Maori team was in Australia having made an undertaking with the League — he could therefore send the Maoris wherever he wished, irrespective of Asher.[21]

WILD SCENES IN QUEENSLAND MATCHES

'George' Anlezark, still smarting from being dumped by the NSWRU selectors in 1907, decided it was time he joined the League movement. After playing in the Country Week trials in Sydney during June, he was again overlooked for the NSW side. Knowing he now had no chance of being picked in the NSWRU team to tour Great Britain, it appears he had discussions with NSWRL officials in Sydney. As soon as he got back to Lismore he packed his belongings and moved to Brisbane. He arrived in time to take a place in the Queensland team against the Maoris.[22]

Anlezark's move to Brisbane gave him a better chance of selection for the Australian rugby league team for England. It also meant the League would have another 'Queenslander' to add some state-equity to the Australian team. Had Anlezark joined a Sydney club, there would have been no guarantee he would even get into the NSW side.

A crowd of 8,000 (1,000 more than at the Brisbane Test match) was present for the first of three games against the Maoris. The Maroons lost that match (19–16), as well as the mid-week encounter (13–5) but had shown marked improvement since the visit of Baskerville's New Zealand team. Anlezark and Dore formed a successful halves combination which gave the Queenslanders far more organisation.

By the third match the Maoris were quite agitated about their share of the profits being withheld. The game was marked by the 'exceptional vigour with which it was played.' Towards the end of the first half, the Maoris 'suddenly made a move as to leave the ground, dissatisfied apparently with the management of the game.' The match continued and the spectators seemed to take pleasure in the physical nature of the contest. According to *The Courier,* 'the crowd enjoyed it thoroughly, but certain sections showed an undue disposition to act the partisans at the expense of the visitors.' The Maroons snared a last-minute try through Hardcastle to defeat the Maoris 6–5. It was Queensland's first ever victory under the League banner.[23]

Both teams then travelled to Toowoomba and Warwick to play two exhibition matches, with the Maroons winning each. The game at the Toowoomba Royal Agricultural Society Ground ended in bedlam with what can only be described as a riot. A push between two opposing players escalated when another Maori (F.Pakere) came in and dealt the Queenslander 'a couple of fierce blows.' Then the 'music began' as the fight drew in other players. The referee (who was Mickey Dore) sent-off Pakere.

'Meanwhile the spectators had rushed the ground from all directions and the field was a surging mass of humanity,' reported *The Toowoomba Chronicle.* 'A fighting spectator vigorously struck Pakere and a blow — or a shove — sent the spectator to earth. Pandemonium reigned. There were wild cries from the spectators.' Asher then decided to lead his team from the field. The Queenslanders followed a few minutes later and 'there were heated words exchanged in the dressing room afterwards.' Hardcastle later supported Asher's move, saying it was a matter of safety for his team. The local reporter was so dismayed at the events that he suggested the League game would never return to the town: 'the scene at the commencement was disgraceful and has just about rung the death knell of the NU game so far as Toowoomba is concerned.'[24]

The Maoris returned to Sydney, stopping off at West Maitland where they defeated Newcastle 30–16. The Queenslanders also travelled down for a series of inter-state matches against NSW that would double as selection trials for the team to visit England (set to depart in mid-August).

GILTINAN TACKLES A DIFFICULT TASK

The League's club competition had been badly arranged, and marred by the constant interruptions to allow the fixtures with the Maoris and New Zealanders. 'Of course,' offered *The Referee,* 'in its first season the League has done excellent work, and any shortcomings in this direction may be overlooked. Perhaps next season matters will go more smoothly.'[25]

The disjointed arrangements of the club rounds made it very difficult for the competition to generate interest and continuity. Souths, Glebe, Easts, Norths and Newcastle were the best performing teams, while the others struggled (Balmain were unlucky at times, but showed promise of better things). Attendances were generally small, at times in the few hundreds — to be fair such small crowds were far from unknown in the MRU club competition either, particularly between two lower ranked teams. A number of matches were also played on the under-card (kicking off at 2 p.m.) to the representative games.

The club competition was concluded using the same semi-finals system that had been used by the MRU. Teams would gradually be eliminated (starting with the bottom team missing the final 'qualifying round') though points to the premiership tally would continue to be added for wins and draws during the play-offs. Some argued that, as not all clubs were well organised at the start of the season, the competition points should be ignored once the semi-finals started. Others replied that the Australian team would have already sailed for England, taking away many of the top clubs' players.[26]

South Sydney Rugby League Club's Billy Cann – played for the Australian rugby league team in the Third Test against New Zealand in 1908. Cann was adept at playing most positions in a rugby team – anywhere from winger to the second-row.

The Maori tour money also caused much debate. July was a particularly difficult month for Giltinan. Already faced with numerous conflicts with the Maoris, and a Court order over the League, he had also been appointed by the NSWRL as the manager for the team to England. He had to organise all aspects of the tour and complete the team selection process. The initial months of the tour needed to be financed until, hopefully, gate-money started coming in. The NU's financial guarantee was only payable at the tour's end if gate receipts fell short. The League hadn't the resources for the venture, and plans to take the Australian team to New Zealand to generate some profits were abandoned as there was insufficient time.[27]

To keep the tour alive (and save much embarrassment and ridicule) Giltinan had to find the finances himself. The tour effectively became his 'speculation' — the NSWRL would not cover any shortfall if one occurred. As a consequence the League committee also gave up any say in the final selection of the team (though not all understood this).

The tour was to be conducted on the 'share-and-share alike' model used by Australian cricket teams and the professional New Zealanders the year before. However, unlike Baskerville's team, none of the players would be asked to buy a share in the tour. Giltinan therefore provided the money, but would have to share any profits with all the players (as well as pay the NSWRL two and half per cent). If it succeeded, he would gain little financially. If it failed, he alone would lose money and be answerable to his creditors. *The Referee* cautioned that 'Mr Giltinan is tackling a very difficult task, a much more difficult one, I fancy, than he, or those associated with him on the League are disposed to imagine.'[28] Still, given the NU guarantee and how much profit the New Zealanders made in 1907, most did not agree.

A FEW UGLY RUMOURS MAY BE HEARD

Questions were also starting to be raised at NSWRL meetings, and in the press, about the management of Giltinan, Hoyle and Trumper. It was clear that in forming the League, they were to control the management and organisation for the first season. A management committee was created (with members elected from each club and therefore the players) but it had a restrained role until the time was right to hand over power. Some committee members didn't see it that way, and the early financial success of the League from the Maori matches triggered internal arguments over where the money went. The three men were accused of secrecy and deliberately withholding financial accounts. In response, Hoyle pointed to the success of the representative matches as proof that their management of the League was beyond question.

The Sydney Sportsman wrote on July 8, 'In League football circles at present, murmurings of discontent and a few ugly rumours are to be heard. Many leading players and ardent supporters of the game have expressed bitter dissatisfaction with the methods and actions of the men at present at the helm of affairs.' At League meetings Hoyle (as chairman) ruled out of order all requests for a management and financial committee to be formed. The newspaper continued, 'A couple of gentlemen who had been League committee men, immediately left the room on the motion being sandbagged, and several others have decided to sever their connection unless this matter is rectified at once. These men, who hold important positions in business in this city want to know if everything is aboveboard, why the necessity for all the secrecy? Correspondence which should be read by the League secretary (Giltinan) at the meetings is misconstrued to suit the reader's own ideas, and other letters forwarded get mislaid or never arrive when the contents are not palatable to the secretary.'

A number of club delegates were also accused in the newspapers of having 'an eye to a trip Home' and therefore 'vote whichever way the wind blows. Outside the meeting they air their complaints, but they are like so many oysters [shut] when the meeting starts.' The matter of the referee (Welch) not being paid was also a sore point. Hoyle responded by pointing out, 'The success of this movement was not a question of footballers, but was one of good organisers, and we claim to be that, and nothing more. I may add that we are sports and not mischief-makers.'[29]

Whatever promises Giltinan, Hoyle and Trumper had made to the players and club officials during the formation of the movement in 1907 and early 1908, they were not about to hand control over just yet. They had told the players that, as investors, they would perhaps want a return one day. Giltinan's actions (running onto the field to confront a referee and refusing Asher's choice of official for the Newcastle game) exposed the limited understanding the three men had of the rugby game. The longer it took for Giltinan, Hoyle and Trumper to reach a point where they could walk away with their dignity intact, with or without a profit, the more they risked conflict.

The Referee reported that Hoyle told the League committee 'he would not continue to act (as chairman) very much longer.' 'The sooner he relinquishes the position the better,' said a member of the League. 'A man who has played the game and thoroughly understands footballers, and who will not be too rigid in his rulings, would suit better.'[30]

BLUES V MAROONS

'For the first time since the inception of the Rugby League in Sydney an inter-state match, as differentiated from one against New Zealand, has been played,' reported *The Referee*, 'and it cannot be said that it provoked much enthusiasm.' Played at the Agricultural Ground on Saturday July 11, before 'a large attendance,' the match was a distinctly one-sided affair as the Blues won 43–0.

Again, the NSW newspapers made no account of there being no club competition in Brisbane to improve the form of the team. *The Herald* wrote, 'There can be no doubt the NSW men are improving a good deal in their manner of playing under the new rules. They cannot be blamed for the farce, for it was nothing else. If the Australian team depends on Queenslanders to strengthen it, one is afraid it will be found wanting. They are quite the weakest lot of footballers I have ever seen come down from Queensland. The play needs no detailed description as it was simply a practice match for NSW, and certainly did not advantageously advertise the new game.'[31]

The following Wednesday the Maroons played against a 'Metropolitan' selection. Anlezark came into the Queensland team at five-eighth, but it made little difference. The local side, which included none of the NSW players, won 37–8. Eastern Suburbs' front rower Herb Brackenreg landed six goals.

The second NSW v Queensland match was the early game before the Australia v Maoris contest. With practically the whole NSW side called up to the Australian team (Anlezark and Hardcastle were the only Maroons), the Blues team featured most of the players from the Metropolitan team. Queensland put in a better effort in this match, losing by 12–3. *The Herald* rated the NSW win as lucky with the Maroons unable to convert sustained periods of attack in the second half into points.

Queensland were hampered early in the game when they could only muster 12 players. The surprise man who 'made a belated appearance' in the team was Pat Walsh, the discarded Newcastle forward who had moved to Auckland in 1906. Whether Walsh was coerced on the spot to take the field or not is unknown, though he was not named in the team.[32]

Walsh had been playing strongly for the Auckland City club. *The Newcastle Herald* reported that many of the 'Auckland public were of the opinion that he should have been the first forward in the New Zealand rugby union representative team (against a touring British side). The ex-Newcastle crack is said to be playing better than he ever did in his life.' Overlooked for international selection yet again, Walsh didn't hesitate to respond favourably to a timely offer he received from Giltinan.

According to *The New Zealand Herald*, 'Walsh received a cablegram from Sydney asking him if he would accept a position in the professional

The first inter-state contest between the NSW 'Blues' and Queensland 'Maroons' under rugby league rules (Sydney, 1908).

team about to leave for England.' Walsh sailed out of Auckland on the evening of Monday July 13, arriving in Sydney on the following Friday (or very early Saturday morning) in time to appear for Queensland. Of his overall game, *The Sydney Sportsman* said, 'Walsh, always a good forward, has developed into a player of the highest order.'[33]

In the late contest, Australia defeated the Maoris 20–10 in what *The Herald* described as 'a splendid match — the game was full of exciting surprises.' By all accounts the Maoris in the first half appeared likely to 'utterly annihilate the combination of the Australians' but luck was against them.

The Maoris played another 'Metropolitan' selection on the Wednesday at Birchgrove Park. The local team had only two players who had appeared for 'Metropolitan' the week before (H. Bloomfield from Cumberland, and Jim Abercrombie from Wests). Messenger was a late inclusion on the wing. The Maoris were in trouble by half-time, down 13–0 and Metropolitan looked to 'blow the visitors' light out.'

'The Maoris opened aggressively in the second half, and Tuki obtaining got across in great style less than a minute from starting,' reported *The Herald*. What followed was the Maoris' best performance of the tour 'as they completely overran the Metropolitan team' who failed to score another point, losing 34–13. 'The Maoris showed particularly fine combination, dodging, and pace, every man giving a good account of himself, and showed splendid lasting powers. They played a beautiful game and Metropolitan were badly beaten.'[34]

It boded well for the return match to be played against Australia the next Saturday. The public could look forward to an exciting game, while the League contemplated the prospects of yet another bumper gate.

Albert Asher and the Maoris team had other plans.

CHAPTER THIRTEEN

OUR COLONIAL FOOTBALLERS IN ENGLAND

THE MAORIS TAKE AIM AT GILTINAN

The ill-feeling between the Maoris and the NSWRL, or more particularly, Asher and Giltinan, boiled over on the morning of the Australia v Maoris match. Asher announced that his team would not be playing and the tour was over. The League was forced to abandon the match, along with the following contest against NSW and plans for a game in Melbourne (against the team for England).

Asher was convinced that the League was being untruthful as to the net receipts the Maoris were earning. He cited the 'broken turnstile' incident as one example, along with the League deducting ground hire fees even though it had a lease over the Agricultural Ground.

Giltinan argued that the Court order preventing the League from handing any money over to the Maoris was the real cause of the dispute. 'Had it not been for the injunction against the Maoris everything would have gone on splendidly,' suggested Giltinan. 'It was no advantage to me to be receiving injunctions of the Court notifying me that if I paid any monies to the Maori team I would incur a penalty. And on top of these, orders from the Maori team managers requesting me to pay for clothes etc., bought on accounts, which I could not do because of the Court order. I will not pay anything until authorised by the Court to do so.'

Asher's reply was to question Giltinan's financial management of the League, suggesting the tour to England might not eventuate. No doubt Asher, the Maoris and Giltinan were all frustrated by the injunction. In the end, the Maoris decided it was pointless playing on when it was obvious they were not going to see any of the profits from the tour. The immediate concern for the Maoris was how were they to get back home. Giltinan made it clear that the League would not pay the Maoris' return fare, no matter how dire their financial position.[1]

SELECTING THE UNION AND LEAGUE TEAMS

The League and Union teams to travel to England were both finally settled on August 4. The custom with touring teams was to select the bulk of the players, but leave extra places for late inclusions depending on acceptances. Both teams added players following complaints to the selection committees and in the newspapers. This method of finalising the team was more of a consultative process than the poorly managed confusion it may appear to have been.

The Balmain rugby union club were particularly condemning of the NSWRU when they had no players selected. They claimed that at the troubled meeting to form the club at the start of the season, the NSWRU officials had made it clear that their forward Bob Craig would be in the team. On that promise enough members stayed loyal to the Union to form the club when it appeared practically certain that everyone was set join the League. Craig was eventually added to the team at the expense of Queensland's Bill Canniffe.[2]

Suspicions that some of the players had been involved with the professionals delayed the timing of the NSWRU team selection. It was important that the team would 'bear the searchlight of investigation should there be any occasion for it when the team arrives in England.' There were whispers that some players did not intend remaining loyal to the NSWRU upon their return. The Union established an 'examining committee' to ensure the amateur status of the team.

The primary concern surrounded John Hickey, who had changed his mind at the last moment and decided not to play in the professional All Blues matches of 1907. Hickey had signed a document undertaking to play for the League and was photographed with the All Blues team wearing the 'League's uniform.' The Unions imposed no penalty, but were concerned that the RFU in England would view his actions differently — particularly his signing a League contract. The NSWRU feared the document's appearance in London during the tour, where they would be unable to repair the damage to the team and the Union's reputation. Ultimately, Hickey was included, but it was again seen by many as further evidence of the NSWRU's duplicity - there was no doubt Hickey had broken the RFU's laws against professionalism by signing with the League.[3]

Meanwhile the League initially announced the names of thirty players. In the days that followed, the merits of several omitted players were pointed out by their supporters in the newspapers. Concerns were also raised about the quality of the forwards, and their ability to carry the work load from what was clearly going to be an arduous 45 match tour. Over the following days three extra forwards (Courtney, Abercrombie and Dobbs) and a back (Albert Rosenfeld) were added.[4]

Both teams each included five Queensland representatives (until Canniffe was replaced in the Union team by Craig). The NSWRU agreed to style their team as 'Australia' but retained the light blue jersey and waratah badge of the NSW team. The League team wore the maroon and blue hooped jersey, identical to that used by the last Australian rugby union side (1907). The jersey also incorporated the kangaroo symbol within a badge shaped in the outline of the Australian continent.

The NSWRU selectors appointed Herbert 'Paddy' Moran (now a doctor in Newcastle) as captain. The League team would choose their leader after leaving Sydney. The team included four of the five senior players who selected the tour party: Hennessy, Lutge, Burdon and Fihelly (Dore was unable to tour due to business reasons). Some of the League committee criticised the selectors for choosing themselves over younger players, but news reports suggested each deserved his place. *The Herald* commented that Burdon 'should be one of the first chosen, and no doubt he has quite recovered from his accident.'

As with Baskerville's team, some of the players who had committed to the movement in its formative days were given preference over more recent 'converts.' The League team also included an element of making up for the past treatment of players under the NSWRU, with Anlezark chosen after only a handful of League matches for Queensland. At the last moment Giltinan revealed Pat Walsh's inclusion. Englishman Tom McCabe was an interesting choice. No doubt his NU experience warranted his inclusion. McCabe's involvement in the upper organisation of the League continued, with his appointment on the touring team's management committee and as a trustee of the finances.[5]

With over sixty talented footballers in the two tour parties, the entrepreneurial streak in Giltinan's character again came to the fore. He proposed 'that the Union and League teams should play a series of matches in the aid of charities' at the SCG or the Agricultural Ground before they left for England. The NSWRU declined the offer by saying that, as amateurs, they couldn't play against professionals, even if all the proceeds were for charity. Giltinan could only dream of having the players from both teams under the League.[6]

Rugby Union touring team: Herbert 'Paddy' Moran and Joshua Stevenson (both Newcastle); Tom Griffin, John Hickey, Chris McKivat, Syd Middleton, Fred Wood, (all Glebe); Herbert Daly, Edward McIntyre, Charles McMurtrie, Bede Smith, (all Central Western); Philip Carmichael, Peter Flanagan, Esmond Parkinson, Tom Richards, (all Queensland); John Barnett, Paddy McCue, Charles 'Boxer' Russell, (all Newtown); Charles Murnin, Malcolm McArthur, Norm Row (all Easts); Arthur McCabe and Edward Mandible (Sydney); Peter Burge (Souths); Danny Carroll (St George); Bob Craig (Balmain); William Dix (New England); Charles Hammand (University); Ward Prentice (Wests).

Rugby League touring team: Dan Frawley, Lou Jones, Larry O'Malley, Dally Messenger, Albert Rosenfeld, 'Sandy' Pearce, (all Easts); Alec Burdon, Albert Conlon, 'Pony' Halloway, Charlie Hedley, Tom McCabe, Peter Moir, (all Glebe); Tommy Anderson, Arthur Butler, Billy Cann, James Davis, Arthur Hennessy, Johnny Rosewell. (all Souths); Dinny Lutge, Sid Deane, Jimmy Devereux, Andy Morton, (all Norths); Frank Cheadle, 'Tedda' Courtney, Bill Noble, (all Newtown); Bill Bailey and Pat Walsh (both Newcastle); Alf Dobbs and Bob Graves (both Balmain); Jim Abercrombie (Wests); 'George' Anlezark, Mick Bolewski, Jack Fihelly, Bill Hardcastle, Bill Heidke, (all Queensland).

THE MAORIS BENEFIT MATCH

The Maoris meanwhile formed themselves into a new tour party, taking on the name used some twenty years earlier, the 'New Zealand Natives' team. They attempted to raise money by holding a concert and also a rugby union match against a NSW team comprised of 'sympathetic footballers' who wanted to help the Maoris out of their plight. The Maoris sought to earn enough money to clear their local debts and pay their passage home.

Though the game was a 'benefit match,' this didn't prevent the Unions and the League from warning their players off. The MRU claimed the Maoris and League players involved were professionals, so anyone playing against them would earn the same mark. Henry Hoyle, on behalf of the NSWRL, said that no League player was permitted to take part in an unsanctioned game, and any who did would 'go up' for life.

Alexander Knox, the North Sydney club delegate on the NSWRL committee, was on the organising group for the benefit match, along with Harold Judd from the St George rugby union club. Knox openly challenged Hoyle, Giltinan and Trumper's methods. Knox saw the League's treatment of the Maoris as further reason to attack the NSWRL leadership. He told the press that Hoyle's assertion players would be disqualified for taking part in the match was far in excess of the president's official capacity and authority.

The League was also criticised by footballers and the public. Many thought 'the Maoris had been treated shamefully, considering that they had been responsible for the largest gate the League had. The League benefited to the extent of about £1,200 (from the tour) — the League ought to have helped them.' The Maoris even went so far as to tell the League that they didn't want their share of the tour profits still withheld by the injunction. They decided to abandon the money, 'and allow the League and Mr Jack to cut it up as they wish.'[7]

While the benefit match and concert failed to attract much public support, the League was seeing its reputation as a well-managed sporting body rapidly evaporating. Even before Giltinan boarded the ship for England, it was clear that that he, along with Trumper and Hoyle, would struggle to retain their control of the NSWRL in the new year.

IRELAND AND SCOTLAND UNIONS DON'T WANT US

The final club round was the last set of League matches before the Australian team sailed. 'Some of the stars did not take a risk by playing, but they can hardly be blamed, as a man would be very stiff to "do a leg" or get some other injury that would end his trip.'[8]

Being the eight-team qualifying round for the semi-finals, the last-placed (using points for and against) Cumberland dropped out. The matches saw each of the top four teams randomly drawn to play one of the bottom four. The winners earned another two points to their tally on the competition table, with the top four remaining clubs progressing to the semi-finals. The final top four were Souths (18 points), Easts (18), Glebe (16) and Norths (14).

The semi-finals were drawn as 1v3 and 2v4, meaning Souths were to play Glebe, while Easts were pitted against Norths. With two points again to be given to the winners (or one point each in the case of a drawn result), and Souths and Easts enjoying strong points differentials, there was little chance of Glebe displacing either club for a place in the Final. With very little at stake, interest from the public in the semi-final matches was expectedly to be low.[9]

In contrast, the NSWRU was enjoying good crowds at NSW matches against Queensland and a visiting Great Britain team on its way home from an unsuccessful Test series in New Zealand. With the last NSW rugby union match scheduled for the same day as the NSWRL Final, the League decided to postpone the decider a week. It was a prudent move as, despite a thunderstorm breaking in the hour before kick-off, over 26,000 watched the British fall to NSW 6–3. While the visitors were not a particularly strong opponent, *The Herald's* headline was still keen to boast that the 'Kangaroo Defeats Lion.'[10]

More often referred to as 'the Anglo-Welsh' team, the British tourists did not include representatives from the Ireland and Scotland Unions. These two Unions believed that exchanging tours with southern hemisphere countries encouraged professionalism — starting with the 1905 All Blacks. The profit taken by these tours caused two serious concerns: money filling the coffers of the colonial Unions could aid the establishment of professionalism if any of these Unions transferred their allegiances to the NU, and the All Blacks and

Springboks tours had encouraged Baskerville and Giltinan to mount similar professional tours.

The Scotland and Ireland Unions took a much harder line than the RFU. They viewed the payment of player allowances on tours, even 3s a day, as unwarranted. They declined to schedule any matches against the Australian rugby union team about to visit Britain unless player allowances were eliminated and the tour was managed (and profits shared) jointly by the Home Unions. Scotland also opposed moves to give Australia, New Zealand and South Africa membership of the International Rugby Board.[11]

Scotland and Ireland's position was also supported in England. *The Morning Post* made the view plain enough. 'The rugby game required no "boom;" it was a great and flourishing sport before the New Zealand invasion. These recurring tours are merely a highway to exhibition and professional football. The football dictum laid down at the Exeter Church congress many years ago was that in football we want players not spectators. New Zealand and Australia easily acquired the arts of the game, but they forgot the foundation on which all games of recreation are built; the instincts of sport.'[12]

The Herald chastised the Ireland and Scotland Unions for their stance: 'It means the likely development of what the RFU was striving against — professionalism in the Commonwealth. The NSW and Queensland players had set their minds upon a trip Home with the rugby union team. They are practically told that Scotland and Ireland want nothing to do with them. What must be the consequence? Simply that the men will say, "All right, we cannot be appreciated as amateurs, we'll go Home as professionals." The team to visit the NU will be strengthened. There will be a further reduction in loyalty to the RFU, which will lose prestige in the colonies.'[13]

Tom Richards, a Queensland member of the Australian rugby union team said in *The Referee*, 'It is the one discordant note that will forever mar the harmony of the tour. It cannot very well be taken as other than a slur on Australia's good sporting character, and the slight will be keenly felt by the thousands of Irish and Scotch colonists whom we have always been pleased to welcome to our land of sunshine and content.'[14]

The Football Evening News claimed the actions of the two Home Unions effectively ruled out working-class men from playing rugby union — and predicted with confidence that a reaction to this would soon eventuate in Australian rugby. 'This craze for amateurism that is almost impossible — the amateurism that must include social position and a University or Public School education — is a serious hindrance to the spread of the imperial [British Empire] sporting spirit. There is no room for class distinctions in imperial sport and they must be swept away. The Irish and Scottish Unions did more harm than they were aware of when they refused to meet the Australians, and that fact will be brought home to both bodies before long.'[15]

LEAGUE TEAM SAILS ON ONE-WAY TICKETS

The players from both the Union and League teams were given individual farewell functions by their friends and supporters, similar to the send-off Messenger received in 1907. They were given gifts such as travel bags, pipe sets, mementos, and purses overflowing with gold sovereigns.[16]

The two teams sailed for England a week apart. With James McMahon as their manager, the Union team left on August 8. The League team were officially farewelled at a NSWRL function held on the evening of August 12. The 'banquet' was held at the A.B.C. Café, the same rooms

The Kangaroos (1908/09)

Back Row: Bill Hardcastle, Tom McCabe, Jim Devereaux, Andy Morton, Charlie Hedley, Sid Deane, Frank Cheadle, Lou 'Baby' Jones, Bob Graves, Arthur 'Pony' Halloway.
Middle Row: Billy Cann, Dan Frawley, Tommy Anderson, Bill Heidke, Sid 'Sandy' Pearce, Peter Moir, Alec Burdon, Larry 'Jersey' O'Malley, Jim Abercrombie, Billy Noble.
Seated: Bill Bailey, Jim 'Barrow' Davis, Johnny Rosewell, Dinny Lutge (c), James Giltinan, Herbert 'Dally' Messenger, Arthur Hennessy, Albert Conlon.
Front Row: Mick Bolewski, Alf 'Bullocky' Dobbs, Albert Rosenfeld, Jack Fihelly, Arthur Butler, Tedda Courtney, Ernest 'George' Anlezark.
Pat Walsh travelled to England separately.

where the 'great reunion of footballers' occurred back in July 1906. Giltinan and his team boarded the *RMS Macedonia* at the P. & O. Wharf. As with the Union team, a crowd of 3,000 saw them off. Even the New Zealand Maoris team were there 'in full force, and gave war-cries and hakas galore — they also presented the team with their flag, old Bill Hardcastle taking possession of the token.'[17]

The League team was travelling on one-way tickets, apparently at their own request so they could return to Australia at their leisure. Critics suggested it was a money-saving action by Giltinan (and may well have been) which didn't bode well for the tour — perhaps the players would be stuck in England by its end. More than a few players had designs on gaining a lucrative offer from a NU club and remaining behind (though the tour agreement with the NU did not allow the clubs to sign players until the end of the final tour match).

As emotional as it was for all the players to farewell their friends and family, for South Sydney's Johnny Rosewell finally stepping onto the ship was the end of a turbulent week. Rosewell had failed the doctor's test and was ruled out of the tour. Despite there practically being no chance of Rosewell contributing on the playing field in England, the rest of the team decided to take him along anyway, as 'he thoroughly deserves the trip.'

Pat Walsh, unable to get a berth on the team's ship, travelled separately on the *SS Suevic*. 'He is reported to have taken a kangaroo with him — he is going to teach the 'roo on the way Home so it will be able to lead the team on the field carrying the ball,' noted *The Sydney Sportsman*. The same newspaper reported that, after leaving Sydney, the team elected Norths' Dinny Lutge as 'skipper' with Messenger voted as vice-captain. 'The men will do more for "old Dinny" than for three of the others together.'[18]

The team's first stopover was in Melbourne. During the stay Giltinan met with officials of the Victorian rules game. In July he had put a proposal to them for the 'federation of football' — he was essentially seeking an agreement in principle for the merging of their game with the NU rules to create a national football code.

It is a demonstration of the NSWRL's desire to adopt changes to suit Australian conditions and act without regard to the RFU (and perhaps even the NU). Of course, it was also about Giltinan's personal desire to profit from inter-state matches. He offered to take any agreement reached to England, and endeavour to convince the NU officials to adopt the rules of the merged football code so that international tours could be held. Time, though, was against Giltinan. He did 'receive a very favourable reception' from the Victorian rules officials, but the task was simply too big to be able to make sufficient progress before he had to leave for England.[19]

Rule changes were also on the agenda of the Unions in Australia and New Zealand. The NU game was recognised as more attractive and safer than rugby union by a large portion of the rugby community. There is no doubt that the Unions were concerned that over time their game would be eroded — in player numbers and gate-receipts. They made a joint submission to the RFU in England. Others said the Unions, in the end, should not concern themselves with the issue: 'Public interest is desirable, if not indispensable, but, after all, the main thing is the game and the enjoyment, the exercise, the health it may give to the players themselves.'[20]

The reality was, despite the treatment given to the Maoris and signs of internal friction in the NSWRL itself, the League was still increasing the number of players under its banner. 'At a meeting of the MRU a spirited defence of amateur principles was fired off. But the League is gaining new recruits to its ranks every week,' reported *The Sydney Sportsman* in August of 1908. Aside from changing the playing rules of their game, the Unions could do little to stop the trend. The lure of inclusion in the team for England had initially kept many players in the rugby union ranks. Remarkably, the NSWRU declined an offer from the NZRU of a visit by the All Blacks in 1909.[21]

Eastern Suburbs' Horrie Miller was appointed Giltinan's replacement as League secretary for the duration of the tour. One of his first actions was to pay the fares home for the Maoris. It was a sign of goodwill that overcame the growing criticisms in New Zealand of the professional movement's management. Alexander Knox also made a personal donation to the team of half-a-guinea.[22]

SOUTHS V EASTS — THE FIRST LEAGUE FINAL

As expected, South Sydney and Eastern Suburbs progressed to the Final of the League's club competition at the Agricultural Ground. As both teams were even on points, the match (unless it was a draw) would decide the premiership winner. In accordance with the NSWRL's constitution, one-third of the profits from the day were to be devoted to hospital charities, with the remainder contributing to the League's insurance fund for injured players.

An additional attraction of the performance of a touring Queensland Aboriginal group was added to the bill. They gave various displays including spear and boomerang throwing at targets from the centre of the ground before and after the match. They also gave the war-cries of six different tribes, including one from the warriors of Stradbroke

Island 'to be used by the Australian League team during the tour through England, which was given to Jack Fihelly by Archie Meston, manager of the Aborigines. If sufficiently dark at the conclusion of the game they will give a display of fire boomerang and fire spear throwing,'[23] announced *The Herald*.

The League enjoyed their biggest club match crowd of the season, with 4,000 present on what was a sunny and overly warm Spring day. The early match was between the third grade winners (Sydney) and the runners-up (Drummoyne). Sydney had not been defeated all season and were again victorious, winning 11–3.

The Herald reported the first grade Final 'was brilliant, and at times rather rough.'

> South Sydney lost the toss, and kicked off from the southern end, an easterly wind blowing across the ground, and the sun shining strongly against them. Play hummed from the beginning. South Sydney having the better of matters, the forwards putting in splendid work. Getting the ball from the scrum repeatedly, South Sydney's backs executed several brilliant bursts, but the tackling of their opponents was very safe. However, they broke through once, Conlin making a beautiful feinting run, and then passing to Senior, on the wing, the latter scoring a pretty try.
>
> Immediately afterwards Brackenregg kicked a penalty goal for Eastern Suburbs. South Sydney now attacked strongly, and appeared likely to score, but Miller, intercepting a yard or so from his own line, raced the whole length of the ground and scored a beautiful try behind the posts.
>
> On resuming South Sydney obtained the upper hand, forwards and backs playing brilliantly. They made repeated dashes, but could not break through for a long time. Once Storie got across, but was tackled. Then the three-quarters made fine dashes on either wing. From the last of these, which ended on the line, Golden scored a try, which Green failed to convert. Just before half time, Fry marked at Eastern Suburb's 25, and Conlin kicked a fine goal, South Sydney leading by 8 points to 7.
>
> The second half proved exciting from start to finish. South Sydney's Leveson obtained the ball from a scrum and passed to Conlin, on the wing. The latter dashed for the line, and scored. South Sydney 11 points to 7.
>
> Eastern Suburbs put in fine work. Frawley and Brackenreg dribbling almost to the line. Then McNamara dropped a field goal from centre, which reduced South Sydney's lead to 2 points. McNamara almost repeated the performance a few minutes later, South Sydney rallied, and Leveson getting

from a scrum at the 25 passed in to Butler, who scored. The kick at goal failed. South Sydney ahead 14–7.

Play now became very rough, several players being knocked out temporarily, and the referee had to administer cautions. Near time, Eastern Suburbs came with a rush, and Miller scored a good try in the corner, which Brackenreg failed to convert. There was no further scoring, South Sydney winning by 14 points to 12.[24]

Conlin was carried from the field shoulder high by the South Sydney players. *The Sydney Sportsman* admonished the Easts' 'tortoises' who repeatedly made 'desperate efforts to cover themselves in glory' instead of passing to the fleet-footed winger Horrie Miller.[25]

With the season now over, *The Referee* reviewed the progress made by the NSWRL. It predicted that if the playing rules of rugby union were not improved, then the League would have the upper hand. 'There can be no question that the new game caused quite a stir in football circles generally. Of course, the new rules are responsible for this to a great extent, many people having been attracted out of curiosity. Next season will prove whether the League can survive against the formidable and long-standing Rugby Union. There are thousands whose allegiance to the Union game cannot be shaken, and if the proposed alteration in the playing rules takes place, one must admit there can only be one ending in the controversy — the side with the larger battalions [players and financial reserves] must win. Anyhow the fight has begun, and it will now be survival of the fittest.'[26]

In Melbourne, Giltinan is reported to have said that in two years there would be no rugby union, but only rugby league in NSW. The consensus of the press in Sydney was that 'Mr Giltinan, as a prophet, is unwittingly humorous.'[27]

As hard as the League were fighting with their limited resources, the battle was draining the finances of the Unions. The MRU posted a loss of £1,780 on the 1908 season's transactions. If this amount of spending was continued in the coming seasons it would result in the MRU's bankruptcy.

ON THE WALLABY

When the Australian rugby union tourists arrived in England the team management impressed upon their hosts at every opportunity their loyalty to the RFU and its principles. 'Paddy' Moran, as captain, 'was thankful to say that they themselves (despite professionalism in Sydney rugby) had remained strong adherents to amateurism, and although they might be beaten in forthcoming encounters they could never be robbed of their amateur status.' Moran then added a remark that the working-class members of his team, though used to it, must have found derogatory: 'We have more college and professionally trained men in our ranks than in the other Union' (the NSWRL).[28]

For the management and the players, the tour to Great Britain was a trip Home. A mere seven years had passed since the federation of the Australian colonies. The older members of the NSWRU, rather than the younger footballers, were strong upholders of the 1800s colonial view

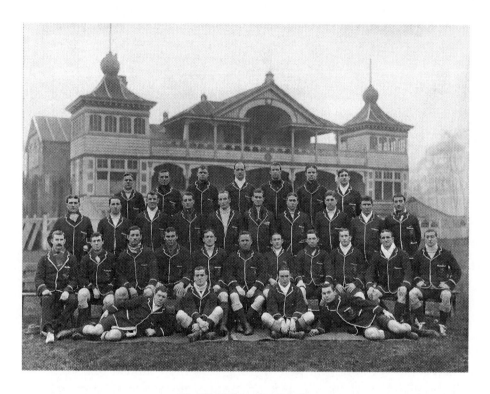

The Wallabies (1908/09)

Back Row: William Dix, Philip Carmichael, C 'Boxer' Russell, Norman Row, 'Paddy' McCue, Charles Hammand, Ward Prentice.
Third Row: John Barnett, Edward McIntyre, Charles McMurtrie, Tom Richards, Syd Middleton, Albert Burge, Peter Burge, Bede Smith, Kenneth Gavin, Peter Flanagan.
Second Row: Stanley Wickham, Chris McKivat, Bob Craig, Edward Mandible, H 'Paddy' Moran (c), James McMahon, Fred Wood, John 'Darb' Hickey, Joshua Stevenson, Tom Griffin, Esmond Parkinson.
Front Row: Herbert Daly, Arthur McCabe, Malcom McArthur, Danny Carroll.
Norm Row absent. Charles Murnin fell ill on board the ship to England and returned to Sydney.
Albert Burge and Kenneth Gavin joined the tour to replace Murnin, and the injured Peter Burge and Peter Flanagan.

that they were British first, Australian second. This position appears to have influenced the choice of nickname given to the team.

The New Zealanders in 1905 had been bestowed the 'All Blacks' name, while the 1906 South African team were given 'Springboks' (taken from the animal on their badge). *The Manchester Weekly Times* reported news from Sydney that the team had adopted 'The Rabbits' and a number of English postcard makers issued team photographs with that nickname on it. The 'rabbits' name had been suggested at the team's Sydney farewell.[29]

The team eventually adopted the 'The Wallabies,' and Moran provided an explanation to *The Sydney News*: 'We dropped considerable cold water on "Rabbits" — we could not labour under an appellation borrowed from an English imported pest. There was considerable discussion in the English papers. Letters flocked in from all sides, Wallabies, Kangaroos, Kookaburras and Wallaroos were suggested. The position demanded a conference. For a brief day we, who for six weeks had been "Rabbits", were "Waratahs", but that was emblematic of NSW. All were agreed that any name would be preferable to "Rabbits". "Wallabies" won by a few votes.'[30]

A question remains though as to why the team favoured 'Wallabies' over 'Kangaroos.' There is no support for the view that the League team had already taken the name 'Kangaroos,' or that they alone were entitled to it. The Australian rugby union team had worn a kangaroo badge since 1905, and the 1899 team wore the unofficial coat of arms that included a kangaroo (their British opponents wore a kangaroo symbol on their straw boater hats). In 1908, match reports referenced the kangaroo in describing both Union and League teams who played against visiting international teams. The New Zealanders merely distinguished their teams by adding 'professional' or 'amateur' to the common nickname of 'All Blacks.'

Arriving in England first gave the Union team the opportunity to adopt 'The Kangaroos' as their name. There is no doubt that by 1908 the kangaroo was the sporting symbol of Australia. So why was it rejected in favour of Wallabies?

Clearly, the team was conscious of ensuring their nickname had a meaning they were comfortable with — hence the rejection of rabbits and waratahs. However, the greatest influence on the team, and the man who would make the final decision (irrespective of any team vote), was the manager McMahon. Moran admitted that, as was traditional under the NSWRU, his role as captain began and ended on the field. 'The Manager is all-powerful,' said Moran, 'he is the Union's plenipotentiary' [agent invested with full power and obligation].[31]

McMahon was a captain in the NSW Lancers, giving him a strong military background.[32] He, and other members of the team, would have been well aware the term 'wallaby' was in general use as a nickname for native-born Australians who had joined the British navy. Its origins probably lie in the nineteenth century expression 'on the wallaby [track]' which was used to describe the act of travelling from place to place as an itinerant worker.[33]

'The Wallabies' had been used in newspaper headlines, including *The Herald* in Sydney, to describe two contingents of Australians who had travelled to London for enrolment and training with the navy. The second contingent had in fact arrived in England just twelve weeks before the Union team.[34]

The inference is that being a 'wallaby' was more preferable than a 'kangaroo.' A 'wallaby' can be seen, by its use in the navy, as a man who was both Australian and British. A 'kangaroo' was merely a reference solely to an Australian. 'The Wallabies' nickname sat better with the NSWRU, through McMahon, as it mirrored the way that the Union members saw themselves — they were both Australian and British. Since the late 1870s the NSWRU had staunchly refused to make decisions that favoured Australian conditions and sever its connection with the English RFU. The choice of 'The Wallabies' over 'The Kangaroos' was a direct expression of that position.

Announcing the news in Sydney on September 30, *The Referee* said that the 'Waratahs' name would have been a better choice for the Union team. Providing further evidence that the League team had not taken a nickname before it left Sydney, and that the Union could have picked whatever it liked, *The Referee* then added, '...the professional rugby team will, no doubt, take the name of The Kangaroos.'[35]

NO POT OF GOLD FOR THE PROFESSIONALS

The Kangaroos opened their tour in the South of Wales on Saturday October 3. The match was against the new NU club Mid-Rhondda at Tonypandy. The visitors won 20–6 in a solid performance watched by 7,000 spectators. The local press remarked that 'the Kangaroos were a dashing side, very fast and clever individually.' In the opening stages Messenger kicked a goal from inside his own half, which he almost immediately followed up with a marvellous individual try from the centre of the field. 'I could at the moment name no more than two or three men who might have performed such a wonderful feat.'[36]

Messenger was to be the main drawcard of the tour. His exploits with Baskerville's team the previous winter were known throughout the

Northern counties. It is reported that it was the English crowds who bestowed upon Messenger the name 'The Master.'[37]

Despite being unbeaten in their first seven matches, it was already apparent that the gate-takings were lower when compared to the New Zealanders' tour and far below expectations. There were many factors that were making it difficult for the Australians. The immediate problem was a major labour strike in the cotton mills had erupted just as the tour began. It saw a lot of men without work and with little spare money for football matches. This alone though was not the reason as many NU matches at the same time were very well attended.

The entry fee to a Kangaroos' match was one shilling, which was well above the usual asking price of sixpence. It seems in the view of some the Kangaroos weren't worth the extra money. Their performances were seen as 'too orthodox, lacking the imagination and brilliance of the New Zealanders.' They also didn't have the advantage enjoyed by Baskerville's team who followed in the wake of the 1905 amateur All Blacks.[38]

By the time of the first Test match the Kangaroos had played 19 matches, with only five defeats. With three Tests included in the remaining 27 fixtures, the prospects of a successful tour, both in results and financially, still appeared to be sound.

The NU had decided to take the three Tests against England and a match against the 'Northern League' to venues outside the stronghold areas, namely Park Royal (London), Newcastle, Aston Villa (Birmingham), and Everton. The NU was accused of using these matches as exhibitions to 'educate' new areas in the merit of their game, but, they strongly denied this. They said the idea of 'education' never entered into the minds of those responsible for the arranging of the matches. 'The motive is simply one of finance,' a NU official told *The Athletic News* at the start of the Kangaroos' tour. 'Hasty critics would do well to consider that the Colonials will appear no fewer than twenty-seven times in Lancashire and Yorkshire. The Australian sub-committee recognise that even their enthusiastic patrons may have too much of a good thing. Hence, in order to benefit the Australians, and incidentally the NU, an extended area is necessary.'[39]

Indeed, the game against the Northern League (match 14 of the tour) at Everton's Goodison Park produced a mid-week gate of £332 from a 6,000 strong crowd. This was comparable to the best spectator numbers that the Kangaroos attracted at the more traditional venues.

Given a crowd of 15,000 had paid to see Baskerville's New Zealanders play England in the second Test at Chelsea earlier in the year, Giltinan and the NU were confident that the first Test against the Kangaroos in London on December 12, would also prove lucrative.

Giltinan duly paid out £40 in fares to transport the Kangaroos from their base in the North of England down to London — where he got the shock of his life. A crowd of only 2,200 ventured into the ground, producing just £22 for the visitors. 'You can imagine how bucked our manager, Mr Giltinan, must have been,' one of the players recalled later. Instead of a much-needed fillip to the team's bank balance, the long day's efforts had delivered a loss. The reason was put down to counter-attractions (a 'Varsity rugby union match at Kensington and a crucial soccer contest between Chelsea and Newcastle United) and a poor transport service to the venue.[40]

Unfortunately, people only choose to be present at sporting contests if they anticipate it is worth their time and money. The Test itself produced a game rated as one of the best matches of NU football yet seen. The London news reports were a great advertisement for NU football, but it was of little use to the Kangaroos. 'No better sporting match could have been offered for the attraction of the Metropolitan public,' wrote one reporter. 'It was fast, open and interesting throughout, abounding in points of individual and collective excellence, and fought out on the whole in a good, healthy sporting spirit.'

Widnes' referee and former NU president Jack Smith was given the honour of taking the whistle in the first Test match. His final decision of the match would prove to be crucial.

The match provided end-to-end excitement throughout. England held a commanding 17-5 lead early in the second half, with winger Billy Batten scoring two of his team's five tries. The Australians fought back to 17-15 with Messenger converting tries to Devereux and O'Malley. The home side appeared to have the match in their keeping when they scored another try to hold a 20–15 advantage.

However, with five minutes remaining, Messenger snapped an intercept on his own quarter line. He mesmerised the English defenders as he swerved and cut his way to within sight of the goal line. The defending fullback moved to bring Messenger down, just as he delivered a long and low pass to Devereux. The three-quarter secured the ball and crashed over under the posts. Messenger converted and soon followed up with a penalty goal. It put the Kangaroos into the lead for the first time in the Test, 22–20.

A minute before full-time, with the Kangaroos running the ball, the referee ruled against the Australians for obstruction. It was a hotly debated penalty, but Smith stood his ground. Brooks made a successful attempt a goal and the game immediately ended with the scores level at 22–22. 'For this infringement all English referees are very strict,' said Giltinan. 'Such things in Australia are considered only trivial matters.'[41]

It was a bad day all round for Giltinan and his team. They would not have felt any better when they woke the next morning to hear that the Wallabies v Wales contest had drawn a gate of £1,999 from a 30,000 strong crowd.

SNOWBOUND KANGAROOS

'So long as weather conditions were favourable, up to the end of December, we did very well indeed,' said Giltinan. 'Afterwards the weather and the ground conditions were entirely different to what we had been used to. In many cases we had to play in snow or on frostbitten ground. At Everton, the snow was nine inches deep, which was something new for Australian footballers.'

The team's financial woes began to take on a serious concern, with the weather the primary cause. *The Yorkshire Post* observed that 'rain, frost and fog have all united in a conspiracy to make the financial success of the tour more questionable.' Giltinan slashed the player's weekly allowance from £1 down to 10s. Even the NU guarantee of £3,000 now appeared insufficient to cover the tour's costs.[42]

Giltinan would be personally liable to those he borrowed money from in Sydney if there was any shortfall. He was beginning to show the personal strain. Every penny he had went into the team's financial reserves. He had nothing left and began to have doubts how the team would get home.

Dissention amongst some of the players began to come to the surface. Some of the men outside the 'clique' of Easts, Souths and Norths were barely getting any matches. Meanwhile, despite an agreement to wait until the end of the tour, the NU clubs began to circle the star players of the team.

Huddersfield were accused by other NU clubs of having already signed Pat Walsh. Rather than condemn the activity of the Huddersfield officials, Giltinan seemed to have ensured Walsh wasn't going to miss out. He told the NU that, as Walsh wasn't officially a member of the Kangaroos, he wasn't off-limits to any NU club. For a so-called unofficial member Walsh played a major role for the Kangaroos, appearing in all three Test matches and being one of the team's standout players.[43]

The one bright moment (from a financial viewpoint) in the first months of 1909 was the second Test match, held at St James Park, Newcastle on Saturday, January 23. The NU had been vindicated as a crowd of 22,000 paid £568 to see the game. The home side had the better of the first half and led 8–0 at the spell. In the second half, Messenger scored one of his best ever tries. After taking a catch in the centre of the field from an England kick, Messenger 'dodged, swerved, and beat off man after man' eventually scoring under the posts. After kicking the conversion, the Australian captain received a 'great reception on returning to his place.'

For the Kangaroos there was little more good play. England scored another try and James Lomas potted over two more goals for a 15–5 win. The loss was the second in what would become a 15-match streak without victory for the Australians. It only ended in what turned out to be the last match of the tour. England won the third Test in a lacklustre game 6–5. Held at Villa Park in Birmingham, it attracted a modest crowd of 9,000. While it was roughly equivalent to the best attended Kangaroos' matches in Yorkshire and Lancashire it wasn't sufficient to give Giltinan any hopes of the tour returning a profit.[44]

The final scheduled match of the tour, against Wales, was abandoned due to the weather. By then Giltinan and some of the players had already left England for Sydney. The tour ended in a shortfall of £370 which Giltinan hoped the NU would meet. They declined to contribute any money other than the £3,000 guarantee. However, they did agree to fund the passage of the players back home.[45]

Throughout the tour Giltinan also lobbied for a NU team to accompany the Kangaroos back to Australia. However the NU were not convinced. They decided that it would not be appropriate until the NSWRL was in a more secure position, and 'New Zealand matters had developed.' The NU also announced that it would not entertain any further 'speculative' tours — they had to come from organised bodies affiliated to the NU. This put an immediate end to 'Massa' Johnston's plans to bring forth another New Zealand tour for later in 1909.[46]

Many of the Kangaroos agreed to terms with NU clubs, though a number were not to start until the following season and they returned home with the team. Those that were 'left behind' included Walsh (Huddersfield), Anlezark and Deane (Oldham), and Devereux and Morton (Hull). The Englishman Tom McCabe also stayed, taking up again with Wigan, the club he left in late 1906 to migrate to Australia.[47]

IT WASN'T ME — IT WAS MY BROTHER

The Wallabies' tour was one of mixed fortunes. The team was entered into the rugby competition of the 1908 Olympics, where they duly won the gold medal — though their opponents in the 'Final' were the only other team in the event (with the Cornwall club 'representing' England).

Still, you can only beat who is in front of you, and the players were particularly proud of their gold medals.

The tour included Test matches against Wales (lost 9–6) and England (won 9–3), with a game against France cancelled due to the same horrid winter weather that haunted the Kangaroos. The team played 38 matches, winning 32 of them. Each of the players still had to get by on the meagre 3s a day allowance that had been a sore point with representative rugby footballers since 1903. It was tough, but like the 1905 All Blacks they got by and enjoyed their trip of a lifetime.

The amateur and professional Australian teams came across each other on a number of occasions, including train journeys. The Wallabies' Tom Richards is known to have attended the Kangaroos match against Wigan, while Giltinan reportedly met with some of the Wallabies in Wales. He tried to tempt the Wallabies with another offer of a charity match between the two teams but, not unexpectedly, failed. NU club officials also put offers before some of the Wallabies during the tour.[48]

The Wallaby tour was not proving to be as profitable for the NSWRU as the visits of the All Blacks and Springboks. By the time the team was home the NSWRU posted a loss of almost £1,400. The main discrepancy was the absence of big drawing Test matches in Scotland and Ireland due to the stance taken by their Unions.[49]

While the Wallaby tour was an enjoyable experience for the players, there were troubling signs that must have given them cause to ponder their future and that of rugby union in NSW and Queensland.

The Scotland Rugby Union cancelled an upcoming match against England. They claimed that the RFU had sanctioned professional payments to the Wallabies by playing against the Australians knowing they were receiving a 3s per day allowance. Scotland argued that it could not therefore play against England or its footballers too would have to be classed as professionals.[50]

Without allowances, the bulk of Australian players could not afford to take part in a tour. To ensure the England v Scotland match went ahead, the RFU announced that it would follow the recent decision of the IRB that banned the payment of cash allowances to players — even at 3s. Still not content, Scotland unsuccessfully pushed the RFU to make its pronouncement retrospective to 1905 — and therefore make the tourists from New Zealand, South Africa and Australia banned as professionals.[51]

It was clear to the Wallaby players that it would be impossible for an amateur team to ever tour England again. Moran admitted that, '…the subject was therefore constantly before our minds.' When Moran criticised his team in a half-time talk against Abertillery for not tackling, McKivat completely undermined his captain's efforts by exclaiming, "Blimey, doctor, it don't work out a penny a rush!" The dressing room erupted in laughter, but McKivat had made his point — men can't be expected to constantly play tour matches and deliver their best without a reasonable allowance to keep them happy.[52]

Evidence of Hickey's signing with the League in 1907 also briefly came under examination during the tour — Giltinan showed documents to J.B. Cooke, a NU official. Speaking at a function at a NU Yorkshire v Lancashire match, Cooke told the audience and newspaper reporters that he had seen a photograph of a Wallaby in a team of professional players and his signed contract to play for the NSWRL. Pressed to give full details by the newspapers, Cooke revealed the player was Hickey.

The Wallabies' managers and Hickey successfully stopped the controversy from growing. McMahon told the press that it was a beat-up, while assistant manager Stanley Wickham said, "Had he [Hickey] done so he would have been sent back by the next boat." Interviewed by *The Yorkshire Evening Post*, Hickey said his brother had joined the League, hence the confusion.[53]

HOSTILE AND TREACHEROUS ALIENS

The Wallabies were vilified in the press and amongst the English rugby fraternity for the on-field play. It was much of a repeat of the opinions handed out by the Reverend Mullineux in Sydney in 1899 and the treatment given to the All Blacks in 1905. The Wallabies were prepared for criticism of their playing to the whistle, however, accusations about the men's character soon cut far deeper into the team.

A prime example were comments by E.H.D. Sewell in his publication *The Book Of Football*.

> After the first match one knew instinctively that the tour was not going to be a repetition of the athletic and scientific feast of 1905–06 (All Blacks), or of the social and sporting treat of 1906–07 (Springboks). I was never more disappointed in a side than this one, though I could not agree with those who maintained these men habitually played foul.

> They seemed to have saved up their real character for the two games against Cambridge and Oxford, after which exhibitions one could not help feeling cordially sorry for such fine sportsman as Dr Moran (the captain) and Captain McMahon (manager). Forthwith all interest in the tour vanished, and unless compelled to do so I never went near the team again.

> They defeated both Universities by the employment of deliberately unfair means. They held men who hadn't got the ball but were likely to get it; they

handed (the ball) out of the scrum; and they got between the would-be tackler and their own man with the ball, and in fact did most everything but play the game. After the match they drove away from the ground at Oxford singing loudly in the presence of a silent and disgusted crowd. When the next team comes from those regions [hopefully] all its members will play football under rugby union rules.[54]

Hamish Stuart, another English rugby writer, also attacked the Wallabies. Stuart maligned the character of the men themselves, asking his readers to look beyond the team's acts of unfair play and examine the 'spirit that prompts the act.' The unfair play of the 1905 All Blacks was forgivable to Stuart. Their motives were simply a difference of opinion about what 'playing to win' and 'playing to the referee' meant. But Stuart believed the Wallabies, and Australian rugby collectively, had no limit to the methods they would employ in the pursuit of victory and, worse still, had no recognition they were doing anything wrong.

Stuart wrote, 'The Australians seemed to be concerned by the same motive (as the All Blacks), though it is probable that custom and the national idea have so blunted their moral sense that they are sublimely unconscious of their delinquencies and are sincerely surprised when accused of unfair practice.' He called the Wallabies 'clumsy imitators' of the New Zealanders.[55]

The Wallabies were playing a different game to the one expected by men such as Sewell and Stuart. The only places they escaped criticism during the tour were in Wales and the North of England. Alf Joseph, a former Cardiff player, claimed that the play of the Wallabies was no better or worse than that employed in other first-class matches. 'To condemn,' said Joseph, 'in wholesale manner, the unsportsmanlike

John 'Darb' Hickey – despite joining the League in 1907, successfully escaped scrutiny by the English R.F.U. during the Wallabies tour of 1908/09.

practices and methods of the team, is unjust and savours much of the old adage "give a dog a bad name and you can hang it".'[56]

Mullineux had warned Sydney rugby union during the British team's tour of 1899 that they were failing to play the game in accord with the principles of amateurism and the RFU. Bedell-Sivright's 1904 team gave an entirely different message of how rugby union should be played. This reinforced the Australian methods. But it turned out that the 1904 British team, a long way from watchful eyes at home, was an aberration. Now the Wallabies were seeing for themselves what amateur rugby union was meant to be — and not only didn't Australian rugby fit it, but couldn't comprehend the criticism.

The team's manager, James McMahon, told Australian reporters that 'as visitors to the Mother Country, as representatives of part of the British nation, they could not understand and were certainly not prepared for such hostility as shown (against) them by the press.' Tom Richards also spoke out. 'If we were hostile and treacherous aliens, instead of colonial Britishers playing a national game, some of the criticisms poured upon us would not have been too hot.' Moran wrote of the tour, 'For a mixed lot of men they got on remarkably well together. But, under the carping criticism, and beneath the magnification of minor incidents, their British patriotism wilted. Most of them developed a dislike for everything English.'[57]

The events of the Wallaby tour brought into question the players' loyalty to rugby union and the impossibility of any further exchange of visits between Great Britain and Australia. The NSWRU would not be able to afford future tours unless it made a profit, particularly with the fight against the League already draining resources. The absence of matches against Scotland and Ireland meant the NSWRU could only give its players matches against New Zealand, Wales and England — the same as the NSWRL. With the England rugby union team in decline, and player allowances eliminated, the NSWRU was left with little to offer against the League. On top of that, there was the criticism about the way the Australians played their football. They felt unwanted by British rugby union.

As the team travelled home via North America and the Pacific, they discussed these issues, and the League back in Sydney. They had stayed loyal to the NSWRU and been rewarded with the tour — and that weighed heavily in their thinking. So did the pettiness of the cries against their meagre 3s a day allowance. Moran speculated on a 'heresy hunt' of sportsmen who had taken money, stating that the Australian rugby players would be a long way behind others. 'W. G. Grace was there to answer questions about appearance money, Australian cricketers pleaded guilty, the prosperous aces of the tennis world were trying to prevent their bank accounts from being searched for "assistance" from certain manufacturers, and a Welsh back explained that he had merely found the gold in his boots, by accident, after the match.'[58]

While Moran chose to remain behind in England to further his medical career, 'several of the Wallabies met in conclave and discussed the desirability' of following the suggestions made to them by Giltinan and perhaps some of their own. One who certainly spent the tour secretly contemplating a future move to rugby league was Chris McKivat.[59] He hid his feelings so well the tour management had no idea he was mulling over a change of loyalties. With Moran injured for the Test match against England, the popular McKivat was given the honour of being Australia's captain.

McKivat had a strong influence over the other working-class men in the team. If any offers were to be made to the Wallabies by the League, they would have to win over McKivat to succeed.

DEAD TO THE WORLD

GILTINAN, HOYLE AND TRUMPER OVERTHROWN

'James Giltinan is returning by the *India* this week. Will the fatted calf be killed? The goose that laid the golden egg has been.' This rather cryptic comment published in *The Sydney Sportsman* on April 21 was a summary of the predicament Giltinan was about to step into when he arrived back in Sydney from the Kangaroo tour.

At the annual meeting of the NSWRL, held on March 5, each of the club representatives took their position on the committee to elect the office-bearers for the coming season.

As was usual, Newcastle did not send any representatives to Sydney for the meeting, relying on two local men to act on their behalf — their names were Weymark and Fry, both were members of the South Sydney club.

The meeting was particularly fiery. The questions about the management of Hoyle, Giltinan and Trumper that had been raised in 1908 by Knox, the North Sydney delegate — namely the secrecy of their activities and the withholding of financial accounts — were again on the agenda. While a balance sheet of the League's activities up to July 31, 1908, had been produced just before the meeting, there was none forthcoming up to the current date.

Hoyle, the president, had expected the acting secretary, Horrie Miller, to produce the books and presumably all would appear well. However, Miller had been unable to provide an explanation for so many missing vouchers that he had decided not to make any entries at all. Despite this, when it came to a vote no one opposed Giltinan's re-election and Trumper also retained his position. Hoyle's re-election was much tighter, though he eventually held on by 11–10.[1]

Knox was not content with what had occurred at the meeting, particularly with Weymark and Fry who had voted for Hoyle. Before the meeting took place Knox had sent a telegram to the Newcastle secretary, A. Chambers, seeking confirmation of who would be acting for them, but there had been no reply. A few days after the meeting Chambers confirmed to *The Herald* that Weymark and Fry had indeed been authorised in writing by the club and a copy had been sent to the League and Hoyle before the meeting. However, the letter from the Newcastle club was unsigned.

A hastily arranged meeting of the Newcastle club was held on March 10 to confirm their position. Knox travelled to Newcastle to be present at the meeting. The club members 'unanimously repudiated and cancelled' the appointment of Weymark and Fry. This meant that the elections made at the NSWRL meeting were all invalid.[2]

A further NSWRL meeting was then convened on March 15 to hold fresh elections. Knox took the opportunity to attack Hoyle over the first balance sheet and why it had remained suppressed for so long. Knox claimed that it did not show the full amounts of gate-receipts and expenditures, and asked Hoyle where the missing the money was.

'By direction of the NSWRL committee,' explained Hoyle, 'an amount was retained out of the proceeds of last year's gate and kept as a separate amount for the next season.' While it was a plausible answer, it still did not explain why it wasn't shown on the balance sheet anywhere. Hoyle, Giltinan and Trumper used the account to fund payments to footballers and pay for other items without consulting the League committee (whose agitation grew during the 1908 season). Perhaps Giltinan also had in mind to use the funds to sign Wallaby players upon his return to Sydney.

The three men who had taken on the task of forming the NSWRL felt they could not trust some members of the committee. The democratic process had placed club representatives on the committee who either wanted to know what was going on, or weren't prepared to let Giltinan and the others continue to act autonomously. In a public body such as the League, a secret account was clearly a matter of concern. Did the three men have sufficient support on the League committee to continue?

Knox told the meeting 'that the delegates let the management drift into the hands of three men,' rather than keeping it open and supervised by the League committee. Hoyle could see what was coming: 'I have had enough. I mean to retire. Tomorrow I withdraw all my bonds. Now I tender my resignation.' Ernest Broughton (a director of Sydney Hospital) was elected unopposed in Hoyle's place.

No one nominated Giltinan, who was still on his way home from England, and Miller became secretary after a close battle with George Ball from South Sydney. T. Phelan took Trumper's place as treasurer. The three men who had done the most to bring about the formation of the NSWRL were no longer part of the body's management.[3]

Within weeks, Broughton was forced to resign as president due to ill-health. His replacement was Edward O'Sullivan who, like Trumper, was involved in the formation of the Sydney Victorian rules competition in 1903.

O'Sullivan was chairman of a meeting held on April 21, which considered a letter from the League's solicitor. The correspondence recommended that Hoyle, Giltinan and Trumper be asked to fully account for 'all monies received and expended by them' in regard to all the League's matches of 1908. If they didn't satisfy the request, the advice suggested that legal action in the Equity Court should be brought against the three men.

Knox moved that the solicitor's advice be immediately acted upon as 'it was the League's duty to find out what had been done with the money of last season.' O'Sullivan agreed, stating that 'he was averse to cloaking up anything. It was necessary to start clear, and unretarded by the past. He did not know the gentlemen named, but there appeared to be the want for a thorough overhaul, and he therefore considered that the solicitor's advice be acted upon.' A vote was taken and carried.[4]

Giltinan arrived back in Sydney the next morning and was immediately besieged by reporters asking questions of what he was going to do. *The Herald* reported that 'he was not prepared to say anything about local developments, he wanted time to go into matters.'[5]

THE LEAGUE IS GOING UNDER

Some observers suggested that the turmoil of the first months of 1909 was evidence that the League was losing its way. While Knox's efforts may have been zealous, it is difficult to argue that he was wrong. The sentimental view of some League supporters was that Hoyle, Giltinan and Trumper could do no wrong and were owed some sympathy. Yet, if unacceptable practices were occurring in the management of the NSWRL, it would be better for the League's longer term credibility if they were exposed. One of the major criticisms of the MRU and NSWRU was the lack of control the clubs and players had. The operation of secret accounts, no matter how well intended, was directly against the democratic principles upon which the League had been formed.

Meanwhile, the annual meeting of the MRU saw no change in the issues that were still at the core of the rugby divide. One delegate told the meeting that if the RFU could not see its way to increase the allowance to players then 'Australia must go her own way' and sever links with the other Rugby Unions. There were further calls to sell the Epping Ground and distribute the funds to improve the suburban grounds. Lewis Abrams rose to his feet and delivered his annual call for players to be treated more fairly.

The NSWRU were criticised in many quarters for allowing Snowy Baker, who was now a professional boxer, to play for the Sydney club.

They said that there was no barring of footballers just because they had been declared a professional by other amateur sporting bodies — as long as they weren't a professional rugby player.[6]

The first club matches of the season didn't bode well for the League as spectators turned up in the hundreds rather than thousands. With Cumberland now defunct the League was down to eight teams. It was still restricted to just three grounds, forcing a 'double-bill' at the Agricultural Ground each Saturday with one game starting at 2 p.m.

Faced with very little income, the clubs agreed to forgo their cut of the gate-takings (one-third each) and give all the income to the League. As it was, the only ground drawing reasonable numbers was Balmain's Birchgrove Park. The income from Balmain home matches was practically the only worthwhile money the League received in the opening months of the 1909 season — without it the NSWRL could well have been bankrupt. 'What a pity some of the other districts don't draw similar crowds,' remarked one newspaper.

Albert Burge (from South Sydney Rugby Union Club) was called into the Wallabies touring party after injuries.

Recognising the support it was getting through Balmain, the League gave the club a home match every round. Playing at home, a sound Balmain team now became practically unbeatable — ensuring further good crowds. It was an expedient decision based solely on survival.[7]

In late May the new regime at the NSWRL decided it was worth a try to give Newcastle their first home game, sending Easts to play them. It was held at suburban Broadmeadow before 'a fair crowd' — the consensus was that if the League could secure a ground in the city itself it would do well.[8]

Meanwhile, 10,000 attended the SCG to see a club rugby union match between Glebe and Newtown. The MRU drew crowds in excess of 20,000 during the 1909 season, rivalling the heyday of 1906 and '07. It seemed that the League's problem was the lack of star players in its club matches.

Besides the Kangaroos who stayed behind in England, others chose not to turn out for their clubs when they got back to Sydney. 'One would have thought,' wrote one columnist, 'that for the sake of the game and out consideration for their clubs, that players like Abercrombie, Hedley, Burdon, Conlon, Lutge, Jones and co. would have played this season, and given a hand to boost the game along. It looks suspiciously like a trip was all they were after.'[9] By mid-season others, such as Rosenfeld and Frawley were packing their bags for England and joining NU clubs.

Another absentee was Dally Messenger, who appeared to have given up all interest (though there were a few references to him being injured).[10] The fact he had toured to England and Wales twice in the space of eighteen months, plus played in almost every feature match of 1908 in Sydney and Brisbane, was probably sufficient to demand a break. Perhaps if Giltinan had been still involved, Messenger might have been cajoled into returning to the field and helping the League. As it was, they had to go on without him.

The true test of the League's survival would come with the representative matches. It sent Charlie Ford (from the North Sydney club) to New Zealand to help organise the formation of New Zealand and Maori teams. The NSWRU stuck to its decision to decline a visit of the New Zealand amateur team.[11]

Newtown Rugby Union Club's John Barnett – one of the Wallabies challenged by the League to play in a charity match against the Kangaroos in 1909.

Upon returning to Sydney the Kangaroos were trotted out by the League for matches so the local supporters could see them in action. The two Kangaroos v Rest of NSW matches (won 34–8 and 43–10 by the tourists) drew a total crowd of 3,000, a meagre £150 in gate-takings — Messenger and others declined to take part.[12]

The NSWRL's president decided it was time to re-ignite the public debate about what the League v Union fight had been all about. O'Sullivan asked *The Herald* to stop referring to League players as 'professionals' when it was clear they were not. O'Sullivan used the case of Snowy Baker to illustrate his point. He argued that as it was acceptable for a professional boxer to play rugby union, then surely it was reasonable for the League (and the Union if it chose) to compensate players for their actual expenses. 'The public will form their own opinion regarding the ethics of amateur and professional athletic sports,' O'Sullivan concluded.[13]

The League's president was also quoted in *The Sydney Sportsman* telling the League community that it was in a fight to maintain its survival. 'He warned the League that it would have to battle for its life this season. He hinted that, owing to the methods of the late executive, dissension was rife among the players, and public support and sympathy was on the wane. Confidence in the League must be restored, otherwise there was a mighty big chance of the League going under and being drowned in its infancy.'[14]

O'Sullivan, following on previous attempts by Giltinan in Sydney and in England, went so far as to again challenge the NSWRU to 'at least for once, bury the hatchet by agreeing to give a combined football display [Wallabies v Kangaroos] during the season' for charity. 'There is not a ground in Sydney sufficiently large enough to hold one-half the crowd that would turn-up to this match.' Once again the NSWRU rejected the offer, claiming it would be a breach of the RFU's rules of amateurism.[15]

THE QUEENSLAND AMATEUR RUGBY LEAGUE

In Brisbane the NU enthusiasts also struggled with claims from Union supporters, including the Lord Mayor, that the players under the banner of the Queensland Rugby Association (QRA) were all 'out and out' professionals. This was despite the fact that Brisbane obviously had neither the population nor economy to support even semi-professionalism, let alone players making a full-time living from football.

At the start of the 1909 season the QRA changed its name to the Queensland Amateur Rugby League in a further attempt to make their position plain. A four team district club competition was commenced in Brisbane on May 8. Both opening round matches were played on the same afternoon at the Brisbane Cricket Ground, in front of 'a fair attendance of spectators.' North Brisbane defeated Toombul 8–0 in the first match, with W. Evans scoring two tries for the winners. South Brisbane won the second game, with a 12–2 win over Valley.

As in Sydney, spectator and press interest in club matches was minimal. Representative matches would continue to be the only potential source of income for the QARL. The Queensland team would be bolstered by the inclusion of country players, but with rugby league not played outside Brisbane, all they could do was wait for the QARL to call on their services.

Herb Brackenreg, who played for NSW against Baskerville's team in 1907 and for Easts in the 1908 Sydney club Final, moved to Brisbane and joined the South Brisbane club. No doubt his presence helped the local players understand the NU game.[16]

A MOTOR CAR COMPARED TO THE BULLOCK WAGON

'Cripes! And just as we thought our old pals were dead to the world!' *The Sydney Sportsman* suggested this quote might have been uttered by NSWRU officials after the League's first two NSW v New Zealand matches.

Held over the June long-weekend, the NSWRL's fortunes practically turned around in the space of three days. 'The clerk of the weather must have looked with a kindly eye on the little band of enthusiasts who had taken it on themselves to try and lift the game from the position it was rapidly falling into through mismanagement, financially and otherwise. With 20,000 on Saturday and nearly double that number on Monday, the League will now be in a position to liquidate all outstanding accounts, and have a tidy bit to put away for a rainy day,' said *The Sydney Sportsman*.[17]

The 20,000 attendance must have come as a welcome surprise to the NSWRL, especially as next door at the SCG a similar number watched the Wallabies play a NSW select team. With no competition from the Union on the Monday the League enjoyed a bumper afternoon, and a new found confidence. O'Sullivan and Knox must have been reassured by the stunning turnaround in the League's position. Their objective was to make the League self-sufficient so that it could take a permanent place in the state's sports, irrespective of the NSWRU's and MRU's success. With further matches against New Zealand and the visit of a second Maoris team to come, League spirits lifted.

The NSW team adopted a 'three-two' pack formation for the match, utilising Billy Cann as a 'loose winger' similar to the rugby union wing-forward position. The New Zealand forwards packed in a 'three-three' formation, hoping to use their extra man in the pack to push NSW off the ball.

'Blues! Blues! Blues! was the cry from the crowd as the two teams of football gladiators entered the enclosure' at the Agricultural Ground reported *The Sydney Sportsman*. Each team gave their war-cry, with NSW employing the one adopted by the Kangaroo tourists (of whom only Woolley and Conlin weren't members).

NSW kicked an early penalty goal but it was the New Zealanders who set the pace. The visitors failed to convert their dominance into points, and 'Pony' Halloway began to bring the Blues into the ascendancy.

After some fast open play, Halloway gave the ball to Butler, who passed beyond his nearest three-quarters to Rosenfeld. He cut-back in-field so as to give Frawley more room. Frawley took the pass and ran round and scored nearly behind the posts. Conlin's kick was successful, NSW 7–0. The next score for the Blues was equally meritorious. Rosenfeld picked up a rolling ball at the centre of the field and made off. He dodged two three-quarters, outpaced another, and had only the fullback to pass. He side-stepped the usually reliable G. Spencer and left him grasping at the air while he ran on and scored behind the goal posts. Conlin kicked the goal, NSW 12, All Blacks 0.

It was clearly the Kangaroos' day out, for another score went up in their favour three minutes later, when a magnificent passing attack was managed by Halloway, Butler, Rosenfeld, and Conlin, the latter getting across.

At last the All Blacks got a look in. Houghton picked up from a rebound off Pearce, and running around the western wing passed to McDonald, to Byrne, to J. Spencer, who crossed the line.

After the spell New Zealand made every effort they could, and handled the ball more reliably than in the first half, and their three-quarters began to show what had made the names of the clubs they came from. Barber made a rush with the ball for the corner, and scored a try just inside. Houghton took the kick, which was from a most difficult angle, and brought off a beautiful goal. NSW 15 points, All Blacks 13.

With 2 points to equal the home team's score the excitement was intense. The All Blacks were not to be denied, and Rowe, taking a short pass, darted across the home line and scored a try. The kick was a failure. All Blacks 16, NSW 15. The keenness of the play from this stage was remarkable, and the men showed great physical fitness in maintaining the pace they did. Incident after incident crowded thick upon one another, each side doing great things.

Rosenfeld soon had another opportunity to show his ability, which was above the ordinary all afternoon. His next try was the result of a capital effort. Frawley did the early work, trip-stepping and dodging through the pack, with Cann near him. When tackled he attempted to pass to Cann but it went behind. That speedy player Rosenfeld gathered the ball, and scored a try, after a brilliant finishing run. A minute later he was again the star man in a passing attack, ending in a try, in which clean handling was performed by five men. Rosenfeld was in it twice, but Butler, Halloway, Conlin, and Frawley all did their share. Rosenfeld kicked a goal, NSW 26–16.

265

There was no let-up in the final stages of one of the most exciting games ever seen in Sydney. The crowd remained at fever-heat to the end, and the applause was long-sustained when the All Blacks scored their last try, and added the goal points. The final whistle blew with NSW in the lead by 26 points to 21. From every point of view it was a great game.[18]

The Sydney public found much to like in the NU game, but to attract the really big crowds required the NSWRL to ensure their star players were on the field. There were too few of them in the League's club ranks to generate strong interest in the premiership.

The appeal of the game itself was the biggest asset — at times the only asset — the League had. *The Referee* said 'what has so far saved the League from itself is that the game it controls is spectacular, and therefore popular when played properly.' *The Herald* added that 'the verdict of the 50,000 people who witnessed the matches on Saturday and Monday was that the difference between the new rugby and the old rugby is as a motor car compared to the bullock wagon.'[19]

SHAKY NEW ZEALANDERS

The New Zealanders completed their tour with matches in Newcastle and Brisbane, and a three-match Test series against Australia. The lack of interest in the two Sydney Test matches (6,000 attended each) illustrated the parochialism of the city's sporting public. Even though the Australian team for the first Test included just one Queenslander, Kangaroo tourist Mick Bolewski, the desire to witness another 'Blues' match against an under-performing New Zealand team just wasn't there. The adjacent SCG hosted a crowd of over 22,000 to view the MRU's top-of-the-table club contest between Newtown and Souths.

As it turned out, the New Zealanders surprised the pundits by winning the first Test 19–11 on a wet and slippery ground that better suited their team. Nine Queenslanders, including Mickey Dore, were brought into the Australian team for the Test in Brisbane at the Cricket Ground (Bolewski did not play). Brisbane Norths' Charlie Woodhead, playing in the centres for Australia, scored two tries as the New Zealanders were beaten 10–5. It was the first defeat suffered in Queensland by the professional All Blacks. However, rather than the victory being a recognition of any rapid rise in the standard of Brisbane rugby league players, the loss clearly demonstrated how quickly the New Zealand playing standard was slipping.

On returning to Sydney, the New Zealanders defeated a second-string NSW team 20–8 mid-week. The win squared the contest between NSW and New Zealand for the 'Black-and-White' Challenge Cup at 2–2, with the third Test left to settle the result ('Australia' playing in Sydney representing NSW). The New Zealand team decided to play with two five-eighths, reverting to the old rugby union system of just three three-quarters — one of whom was the English NU player T. Houghton making his Test debut. Held at Wentworth Park, the Test match produced a close contest but in the end the Australian team seemed to have more luck scoring tries. They eventually won 25–5 with Woodhead again securing two tries. The crowd rushed the field at full-time and surrounded the presentation of the Challenge Cup. The League's President, Edward O'Sullivan, handed the Cup onto Australia's captain Bob Graves (of Balmain). Graves and New Zealand captain Con Byrne made some suitable speeches as darkness began to fall upon the scene.[20]

The visitors left Sydney that evening for home on board the *Ulimaroa*. Their tour had significantly boosted the shaky finances of the NSWRL, but questions remained about whether New Zealand would continue to provide the necessary public appeal on future visits.

Upon the New Zealand team's return, a public meeting was organised in Auckland to form a New Zealand Rugby League (NZRL). It was held at the Auckland Chamber of Commerce, with the city's mayor, C.D. Grey elected as the League's first president. The first clubs, Devonport Albion and City Rovers, came into existence shortly afterwards. Their initial match was held at Takapuna Racecourse, with Devonport Albion winning 44–24. The NZRL found obtaining grounds very difficult; they had been tied up by local Unions across the country.[21]

MAGGIE PAPAKURA RUNS THE SHOW

The NSWRL continued to be attracted by the potential of taking matches to Melbourne. The League's Alexander Knox travelled to the southern capital in mid-July seeking to arrange some matches for the New Zealand Maoris team who were about to arrive in Australia. Knox 'found much opposition from the Victorian Football League, which tried to discountenance the visit in every way — the governing body is very jealous of the introduction of any game outside its own.' Knox could not even hire a suitable enclosed ground until after the Victorian rules season was completed in mid-September. By that time the Maoris would have ended their tour and be back across the Tasman.

What Knox also found during his Melbourne visit was that 'professionalism' (paying of footballers) was on the rise in the VFL. 'Players in their League,' told Knox, 'are ostensibly amateurs, but there is no secret made of the fact that some of them receive from £3 to £6 per week each.' Melbourne provided yet another example of where professionalism had entered a large city's football clubs (whatever the code). Anyone who believed that Sydney football could forever be contained under the rules of amateurism would have to be quite naïve.[22]

Knox was back in Sydney when the Maoris arrived. A reception was held at the Sydney Town Hall. The tourists were accompanied by two Maori chiefs and an interpreter, Makereti 'Maggie' Papakura, 'who made a pretty little speech acknowledging the great welcome given to them.' Papakura, 'renowned for her beauty, charm and ready wit,' was a popular tour guide (hostess and storyteller) in Rotorua. A strong-willed woman, who fully understood both the Maori and 'Pakeha' (white) worlds, Papakura's presence greatly aided the stability and well-being of the team.

Despite the difficulties they suffered during the Maoris' 1908 visit, nine of the players decided to again tour, including Albert 'Opai' Asher, Riki Papakura (Maggie's brother), Niko Ratete and H. Pakere. The team's black jersey included a badge on the breast that displayed a kiwi.[23]

The Sydney club competition continued while the Maoris spent a week in intensive training under Kangaroos captain Dinny Lutge. The Maoris visited the Newcastle v Wests / Easts v Balmain double bill at the Agricultural Ground where they were introduced to the crowd. Newcastle easily beat Wests 28–5 in the '2 o'clocker' before the 3,000 spectators witnessed the most contentious game yet seen under the

The 1909 'New Zealand Maoris' rugby league team and touring party. Maggie Papakura is seated in the centre.

NSWRL. In the Easts and Balmain game five players were sent-off 'and the official was not as severe as he might have been.'

An Easts player was sent-off late in the first half following a touch judge's report, with Balmain leading 6–5. *The Herald*, like other newspapers at the time, was reluctant to publish exact details of rough play in football matches. Suffice to say that if they were prepared to describe actions such as 'players were out to win anyhow, some of them to kick their opponents off the ground' then the game was definitely a brutal affair. Two players from each team were ordered off in the second half as Balmain turned a 16–15 lead into a 24–15 victory. As *The Herald* put it, 'had the match lasted much longer it would have expired by effluxion [running out] of players!' With just one round remaining before the semi-finals, the win lifted Balmain into a clear second place, four points behind the undefeated South Sydney team.[24]

THE AGRA' RIOT

'Twenty-four thousand people witnessed a match on Saturday, which, for sensationalism, more than rivalled any football contest played in Sydney,' opened *The Herald's* report of the first NSW v Maoris rugby league game. 'The Maori team beat NSW by 24–21, a result that was due not so much to the visitors' knowledge of the League or NU rules, as to their athleticism and remarkable condition. The Maoris are heavier than the home team, and, moreover, they play a more fearless game. They dreaded nothing in the way of injury to themselves or opponents, and they played that rushing, tearaway game which made the fame of the New Zealand (All Blacks) teams. As a display for the spectators it would be difficult to imagine anything more attractive. It was full of individual effort of most brilliant character, yet it was not wanting without teamwork.'

Some of the greatest thrills were provided by Asher and Ratete who would 'go clean over the shoulders' of the NSW defenders time and time again. Also impressing the crowd was seeing the Maoris fend off tacklers with their shoulders — described as 'a method of defence when attacking' which was rarely used by the local players.

The decision to bring forth a Maoris tour was an immediate success for NSWRL. NSW were depleted by the loss of O'Malley, Rosenfeld, and Frawley to English clubs just as the Maoris arrived in Sydney, and Messenger was still nowhere to be seen. It didn't matter to the public as the Maoris first match attracted over 24,000 spectators. The form of the visitors gave great hope that an even larger crowd would attend the 'Test match' against Australia the following Saturday.[25]

After the Maoris again disposed of NSW in a mid-week game, the excitement for the Australia v Maoris match reached fever pitch. By winning the first two games in Sydney, the Maoris had won the 'O.T. Cup' [sponsor's trophy] and would be presented with it after the Australia match. The League officials were overwhelmed when 30,000 spectators ventured into the Agricultural Ground — the ground was buzzing with excitement well before kick-off. Sensing the moment perhaps, Messenger made himself available and took his place on the wing, though there were serious doubts as to his fitness.

'Feeling ran high from the outset,' reported *The Herald*, 'and it gained in intensity as the game progressed. The crowd was completely carried away by the pace of the men on each side, by the evenness of the struggle, by the alternating ascendancy of one side or the other, and by all-round brilliancy.'

By half-time Australia was ahead by one point. However, 'there was a growing disposition by a section of the crowd to disapprove of the rulings of the referee, Mr Hutcheson, and there were also a few incidents of a belligerent character in the play which passed without anything more serious than a temporary loss of temper, and which the referee, with his eye necessarily on the ball, could not always see.' Meanwhile Messenger was practically a passenger and it was apparent to all that he shouldn't have been on the field.

'In the second half the struggle increased in determination and therewith came from the crowd an unceasing roar,' reported *The Herald*. 'There were many instances of unnecessary rough play. The feelings of the crowd were loudly expressed in hoots when the referee gave the Maoris a try. A few moments later some of the spectators on the other side of the ground thought Australia had scored, whereas the Maoris were awarded a force-down, and another demonstration ensued. Just before the end of the game there was still a greater outburst from the crowd.'

The Sunday Sun described what eventuated as a riot — and it is difficult to argue otherwise. With the Maoris ahead 16–14 and full-time nearing, Messenger kicked down field towards the touchline. Tuki, the Maoris' centre, came across field and stretched out his leg to stop the ball. Unfortunately, Australia's Bollard tripped over Tuki's leg and fell heavily to the ground. 'The crowd all round the ground hooted with vigour, and the referee ordered Tuki off' even though most of the newspaper reporters present thought it was clearly an accident.

The play then 'waxed hot' along the Maoris' goal line until the full-time whistle sounded a few moments later. The Maoris 'in the exuberance of blithe spirits rushed across the ground and grabbed the silver cup' rather then waiting for the official presentation. That was enough for the crowd.

> The riot, for a riot it was, came with startling suddenness. About 5,000 of the 30,000 people present climbed the fences, and tore across the arena to where the players and officials were making their exit for the dressing-rooms. In the pandemonium it was at first impossible to see what was happening.

> There were only about a dozen police present, and they, after striving hard to protect the referee from the fury of the crowd, drew their batons, and struck about right and left. Unfortunately they hit the referee's brother, who was assisting in his protection, and eventually three arrests were made before the ardor [intensity] of the mob began to cool. In his struggle to the stand the referee had his clothing torn, and he sustained a nasty cut over the eye. A dozen or so of the misbehaving ones were more or less injured, and it was close upon an hour after the game before the police officers were able to get the referee away from the ground.[26]

The debate over the decisions of the referee continued in the newspapers over the following days. Many claimed the referee erred in giving the Maoris a particular try, however there were just as many letters who pointed out 'referees are mortals too' and nothing justified the day 'descending to personal violence.'

For the referee's part he claimed: 'It was only a certain section of the crowd. A lot of hoodlums. There's a crowd that gets out there that doesn't absolutely understand one item of the game. They go there, and it's Australia must win by hook or by crook. It takes a lot of nerve, I can tell you, when you hear the crowd howling at you. But I want to show them that I'm not going to back out of it. No, I won't turn it up yet.' Commenting upon the resolve of the referee, one reporter added: 'Once a man embarks upon a course of refereeing, it would seem that he is unable to drop it.'[27]

LEAGUE AND UNION SET FOR LONG BATTLE

As the Maoris headed north for matches in Newcastle and Brisbane *The Referee* summed up their visit as 'a triumph for the visitors and a financial coup for themselves and the League.' The gate-takings for the Australia match alone were over £1,100. For Knox and the other officials of the League it was a moment to pat themselves on the back — the NSWRL now appeared likely to escape the season with a small financial deficit instead of the complete collapse that seemed certain back in April.[28]

Plans were announced for a 'Kangaroo' team to visit New Zealand in September to play in 'Auckland, Wellington and one of the Maori centres' and help spread the growth of the NU game in the Dominion. It was also decided to send a delegate (Knox) to the NU in England to arrange a visit of an English team to NSW in 1910. The formation of an Australasian Rugby League was also mooted to ensure that all the areas playing the game could be represented by a controlling or governing body as required by the NU.[29]

The NSWRL was making tentative moves into regional areas. Letters began to arrive from country centres asking for rule books and visits. Meanwhile, the MRU's third grade competition was suffering greatly from a loss of younger players — one round in mid-July saw five of the ten scheduled matches abandoned because clubs were unable to field a team.[30]

The NSWRL appeared to have finally found some stability.

WALLABIES AND KANGAROOS TO BUMP?

The Sydney Sun, 11 August, 1909: 'Will the Wallabies and Kangaroos ever bump each other on the football field? Well, there are more improbable happenings, as well as more probable ones. Anyhow, a tussle between the two crack teams should draw a 45–50,000 gate easily.'

THE SHERIFF TACKLES THE MAORIS

Rugby league in Newcastle took a significant move forward when the local team defeated the previously unbeaten Maoris and South Sydney in the space of four days. Awakened by the 'athletic exploits of the Maoris in Sydney' a mid-week crowd of 4,000 attended the Show Ground to watch a game that included 'play rougher than ever' where the tackling was particularly heavy. Under the leadership of Stan Carpenter, Newcastle took a 7–6 victory over the Maoris.[31]

On the Saturday the premiership leaders, South Sydney, travelled up for the final round of the competition. In a reverse of the long journey the Newcastle men had been dealing with for two seasons, some of South Sydney's first choice players couldn't get away from work early enough to make the trip. Souths had only been defeated once in the League's first two seasons, to Easts in 1908, and most thought they would still scrape through. Another good crowd of 3,000 watched Newcastle take a 5–0 lead and then hold out Souths for the remainder of the game.[32]

The two wins dramatically lifted the interest in rugby league in Newcastle. A few weeks later it was reported that 'a great number of first grade players have signed over for next season.' Moves began to form a local League branch to handle the commencement of competitions in the district in 1910.[33]

The Sydney Sportsman lamented that despite Newcastle making the semi-finals 'they are just too far behind in competition points to have a chance' at progressing to the Final. For South Sydney, the loss to Newcastle meant that Balmain were now just two competition points behind and 'within striking distance.'[34]

The Balmain v Easts semi-final was scheduled for Wentworth Park, while Souths enjoyed home-field advantage against Newcastle at the Agricultural Ground. However, as neither Easts or Newcastle could progress even if they won, little interest was shown by the public or the players. Souths overran Newcastle 20–0 to avenge their loss the week before, while Balmain overcame Easts 15–8. Souths lobbied for the Final to be played at their home ground (the Agricultural Ground) 'as it is more central, and will suit League supporters more generally.' *The Sydney Sportsman* thought that Wentworth Park, located between the two districts, 'would be the best ground as it is a fair distance for both teams.'[35]

The Final was set down for two weeks later (Saturday, August 28). The newspapers offered that 'Balmain will want to train solidly for the Final with Souths, or else they will be admiring some pretty passing rushes from a distance and Souths will be piling up the points.' As far as they were concerned, 'on performances it looks the best of things for South Sydney.'

It was also pointed out that Balmain had to force a second Final to be played to have a chance to win the premiership: 'should Balmain win it will necessitate another match, as the clubs will then be equal on points.' It looked improbable that Souths could be beaten twice, particularly if the NSWRL held the Final(s) at the Agricultural Ground.[36]

Peter Burge was one of the Wallabies rumoured to be in discussions about playing in matches against the Kangaroos to end the 1909 season.

The interest in the Maoris' visit, though, delayed the Final. After Australia defeated the Maoris 23–16 (on Saturday, August 21, at the Agricultural Ground) the NSWRL and tourists agreed that a 'decider' was necessary as each team had won a 'Test' match in Sydney. The Maoris delayed their trip back to New Zealand while the League arranged a third Test match for August 28.

Meanwhile supporters of the Balmain club were aggrieved that the NSWRL selectors ignored the claims of their players for the NSW and Australian teams against the Maoris. The majority of the representative players came from Souths and Easts, even though the latter's season was already over.[37]

Australia won the third Test 20–13 with a 'fair' crowd of 10,000 present. The game almost didn't eventuate after Robert Jack, the man who had taken legal action against the Maoris in 1908, made another appearance. Jack still laid claim to a further £213 and secured a Court order against the nine Maoris who were part of the 1908 team. On the morning of the Test match, Sheriff officers descended upon the team's hotel and detained the players. Officials of the NSWRL were immediately informed of what was happening — faced with having to call the match off the League paid the amount (and a further debt of £121 owed to a Mr Marshall) to the Sheriff and the players were 'then left free.'[38]

However, as dramatic as the events surrounding the last day of the Maoris' tour were, they received little coverage in the press or amongst the sporting public. Some far larger news had broken a few days earlier: 'The Wallabies Stampede' was just one of the headlines.[39]

In what was quickly becoming a habit in rugby league matters, rumours were again becoming fact — the bulk of the Sydney players who comprised the 1908 Wallabies team had agreed to play in a series of professional rugby league matches against the Kangaroos.

CHAPTER FIFTEEN

KANGAROOS v WALLABIES

THE SIGNING OF THE WALLABIES

'The amazing part of it,' explained Dally Messenger, 'was that two such outstanding teams could be chosen from the ranks of Australian rugby. The Kangaroos were the old champions and the Wallabies the young champions. The Kangaroos were a great team, but there is no shadow of the doubt the Wallabies were also the goods.'

Of the thirty-one players involved in the Wallaby tour, fourteen signed to play in matches against the Kangaroos. As far as Messenger was concerned, the converts were the pick of the Wallaby team: 'The Union has lost its two best teams in the space of two years. You only have to look at the names to see the seriousness of the defection: William Dix, Edward Mandible, John Hickey, Charles Russell, Arthur McCabe, Chris McKivat, Charles McMurtrie, John Barnett, Kenneth Gavin, Robert Craig, Peter Burge, Albert Burge, Edward McIntyre and Paddy McCue.'[1]

Notwithstanding Messenger's assessment of the signings, the remaining Wallaby players that rejected, or were never made offers, were hardly the second-rate members of the tour party. Tom Richards, Norm Row, Ward Prentice, Philip Carmichael, Bede Smith, Syd Middleton, Danny Carroll, Fred Wood, Tom Griffin and the team's captain 'Paddy' Moran were all highly regarded and popular footballers. Of the Wallabies that defeated NSW in early June (20,000 attendance), half the players remained loyal to rugby union. The most telling point is that all the Wallabies who joined the League were working-class players, with most coming from Newtown, Glebe, and South Sydney.

Messenger attributed the signing of the Wallabies to Paddy McCue, the team's front-row forward from the Newtown club. 'Paddy did the spade work and brought over half the Wallabies with him,' said Messenger. Also convinced to sign-on were three other rugby union players: Bill Farnsworth, Viv Farnsworth, and S. Jubb. For John Hickey and Bill Farnsworth, it was their second attempt to join the League, having withdrawn at the last moment from the 1907 NSW professional All Blues team.

Some of the Wallabies always had a serious intention to switch to the League once they returned from England, and the NSWRU suspected as much even before they left Australia. John Hickey had already publicly demonstrated his interest and Chris McKivat contemplated the move during the tour. As a senior member of the team he had strong influence over other like-minded players.

Giltinan had suggested a Wallabies v Kangaroos style match in 1908, before the teams had left Sydney. His efforts in England may also have influenced the Wallaby players' intentions, but the moves to actually obtain the players' signatures were commenced in mid-May, 1909, by Bill Flegg, an Easts committee member and brother of 'Jersey' Flegg.

While the events of their tour to Britain had already convinced many of the Wallabies that their future more likely lay with League once the 1909 season was over, the ongoing battle between the NSWRL and the Unions made their loyalty a much more valuable commodity. Led by McKivat, the Wallabies went for the best possible deal by negotiating as a group and 'demanded three-figure sums of money' upfront. Bill Flegg explained,

> When the Wallabies and Kangaroos were touring England, I, as a follower of the League, was convinced that a series of matches could be arranged upon their return to NSW, which would not only place the League in the position to control rugby football in NSW, but at the same time give the Union a bump from which it would never recover. I broached the subject to some of the League officials, and they were of the opinion that the idea was a splendid one. They, however, thought the proposal impossible, otherwise they themselves would have tried to bring about the Wallabies-Kangaroos matches. The League at that time was not too financial, and whatever funds they had they did not care to risk, in view of the proposed visit of the British NU team to Australia.
>
> I then asked the League whether they would sanction my getting the finances privately, and running the matches as a private and business speculation. The officials of the League assured me that they would not only give me their sanction to do so, but would render every assistance towards bringing the Kangaroos and Wallabies together. My original proposal was to give each Kangaroo and Wallaby £10 per match, which, for the series of three matches, would have been a good week's pay.
>
> I was ready to approach the Wallabies with £500 in hand. I set about the undertaking, which was no easy one. I approached 15 of the Wallabies, and for no less a period than three months I was chasing to their homes, and wherever I could find them, in order to get them to fall in with the proposal. Those of the Wallabies who lived in the country I opened up correspondence with. Eventually, I was in a position to inform the League that 14 of the Wallabies were willing to play against the Kangaroos in three matches on certain terms.

My next move was to call a meeting at the League's rooms in Bridge Street (mid-August). The League's secretary (Ted Larkin), treasurer (Horrie Miller) and myself were the only Leagueites present. After considerable discussion, the meeting came to an abrupt termination, owing to one of the Wallabies talking of 'hundreds of pounds per man,' to play against the Kangaroos. I could see that it was all bluff on his part, and consequently I closed the meeting with the object of seeing each particular Wallaby again, and if possible, drop the Wallaby who was bluffing.

Next morning I was offered a position away from Sydney. I accepted it, and left the following afternoon. But before leaving I mentioned to Larkin and Miller that I would like to see George Ball and John Quinlan brought into the movement, as both of them had a good idea from me as to what was in train regarding the proposed matches. I felt certain they would keep the movement a secret — it was its secrecy that made it a success until the proposal had matured for the public knowledge. If the Union had divined what was going on before the proposal was ripe there is no doubt in my mind there would have been no defection of the Wallabies team. Two weeks after I left Sydney the Kangaroos and Wallabies played their first match.[2]

George [S.G.] Ball – one of the pioneer administrators of Australian rugby league.

Quinlan and Ball secretly met with Larkin. With the League unable to finance the upfront payments demanded by the Wallabies, and the end of the season fast approaching, the three men decided that Ball should propose to James Joynton-Smith that he might finance the signings.

Joynton-Smith, a well-known Sydney entrepreneur, had sold the Epping Ground to the MRU in 1907 which, evidently , was his closest involvement with rugby matters. However, Ball and Joynton-Smith were linked through the South Sydney community. In 1908, both had been elected into key positions at public meetings, Ball as secretary of the South Sydney rugby league club, and Joynton-Smith with the South Sydney Public Hospital.[3]

One of the problems faced by the League and Joynton-Smith was that paying large sums to the Wallabies just to turn a profit, would not be acceptable to the public. It would be seen as 'out and out professionalism,' probably a breach of the League's constitution, and an under-handed attack on the ranks of rugby union. However, if the profit were to be donated to a charity, that would be altogether different — and if the League gained the services of many fine footballers as a result of their being banned by the MRU, well that wasn't the League's doing.

Whether the three League men targeted Joynton-Smith because he possessed both the money and a favourite charity (the hospital) is not clear. Perhaps it was Joynton-Smith who first raised the charity option. More likely they chose Joynton-Smith because Ball had access to him. Within a matter of days the two men met and 'the interviewer was given a favourable answer to the question of financial support.'[4]

A meeting with most of the Wallabies involved in the negotiations then took place at the League's offices and signatures were taken. Bill Flegg was disappointed that the chief Wallaby inflating the sign-on fees (almost certainly Chris McKivat) was not left out.

> The bluffer I have referred to was included in the Wallabies team. It was dollars [sic] he was after, and it was dollars he got. He induced other Wallabies to follow his lead, and, ye gods, what substantial sums they got, whilst the Kangaroos, the real League players, did not get a single farthing.

> It was, no doubt, eagerness on the part of those who handled the trial stages of the negotiations that permitted the Wallabies to grab it all, and leave the Kangaroos without anything. McKivat (Glebe) received £200, McCabe (South Sydney) £150, McCue (Newtown) £150; the majority of the others £100 each.[5]

The meeting was probably on August 23 — the next day the morning papers broke the long-awaited news.

THE MAN BEHIND THE GUN

'It is understood that the "man behind the gun" is Mr J. Joynton-Smith,' reported *The Herald*. 'With so strong a man in that position' the newspaper pronounced that the matches were now 'within the range of probability, if not certainty. Three matches, possibly four, will be played for a charitable cause. Mr Joynton-Smith is president of the South Sydney Hospital, and the inference is, after putting two and two together, that the hospital will probably benefit to a very large extent by the matches. This movement is outside the League, but it is presumed that though that body is not behind it, its success will secure the imprimatur of the League, which will then gain by the transfer of the Wallabies to the League.'

Syd Middleton, one of the Wallabies said, 'I have not been approached, nor am I likely to be. Neither have Ward Prentice and Charles Hammand, and some more. I do not think anything will come of the proposal to play matches. Such a proposal for charity was made early in the season, and it came to nothing.' *The Herald* reported that 'Mr W. Hill, secretary of the NSWRU, said that he did not attach much importance to the rumours. He had heard them before, and they came to nothing.' Hill added that 'nothing tangible had come before the Union yet respecting any of the Wallabies closing with any offer. When it did it would be time for the Union to take action.'[6]

A FINANCIAL BAIT

Having been left out of the process, the chairman of the League's management committee, Alexander Knox, claimed that 'the executive of the League repudiated any knowledge of the suggested matches.' Incensed at what was occurring, he went on the attack, implying the proposals for the venture had been initiated by the Wallabies. 'Certain overtures,' said Knox, 'have been made by outside irresponsible parties, which are the outcome of a request by the Wallabies. The League players have not been approached at all.' He wanted the League to have no part of an action that induced a group of sportsmen to change their allegiances and potentially cause grave damage to another sporting body.

James Joynton-Smith, 'the man behind the gun' – provided the money needed to sign the Wallaby players for matches against The Kangaroos.

'I will not be a party to any movement,' continued Knox, 'having for its object the buying over in a body of a number of players — who are adherents of another association — by means of a bribe to bring over a number of men with a financial bait which is altogether wrong. The movement, as proposed, will bring about disruption to the League. As far as I am concerned, the League will do nothing that will cause the loss of prestige, or the gaining of prestige, by questionable financial means.'[7]

Ironically, Knox's reasoning may have been exactly why he was kept unaware of the negotiations with the Wallabies. There was no way the

NSWRL could pay the Wallabies money without suffering a major loss of credibility in the eyes of the public. But if an external party paid for and organised a private series of matches, the Wallabies would be disqualified by the Unions and have to play for the League (at nil cost to the League) or no one.

The last of the defectors was signed by the morning of the final Maoris v Australia match (August 28). Horrie Miller, the NSWRL's treasurer, told *The Herald* that 'an agreement has been signed, and the Wallabies are one of the contracting parties.' Miller wouldn't reveal any further details, primarily to ensure that the Wallaby players could turn out that afternoon for their clubs in the MRU competition. With no definite information about any particular player, the MRU could not take action against those involved, but they decided to hold an inquiry meeting on Wednesday, September 1, and required all Wallaby team members playing with Sydney clubs to attend.[8]

KNOCKOUT KNOX TRIES TO STOP THE VENTURE

Knox voiced his disapproval of the venture at the League's meeting to ratify the signing of the Wallaby players. Edward O'Sullivan, the League's president, also objected. The two men, who brought the NSWRL back from the brink of the disaster it faced through the first half of the season, were now completely at odds with the rest of the League's committee and supporters.

Knox and O'Sullivan felt that signing the Wallabies and organising the matches was not allowed under the League's constitution. Since the NSWRL's formation it had been battling to convince the public that all they were doing was providing players with a reasonable allowance to cover expenses and injuries — thus League players were still amateurs and no one could live off earnings from football. Paying the Wallaby players extraordinary amounts to play a series of matches was at odds with the League's position — it was clearly professionalism.

There were also others concerns. Signing the Wallabies had been conducted without any knowledge of the NSWRL committee; a speculator had provided the money, and the League and its Kangaroo players would get very little, if any, reward for their involvement (and the NSWRL had not authorised the Kangaroos participation).

The arguments put forward by Knox and O'Sullivan had plenty of support in the Sydney newspapers, particularly the 'buying of men over' to the League. Some questioned how the NU in England would view the League's behaviour, but as far as the rest of the committee were concerned, pulling the cream of the Union's talent into the League's ranks was reason enough to sanction the venture. Once the positive vote was taken, O'Sullivan bowed to the majority and declared he would do all he could to assist to make the Kangaroo v Wallabies matches a success.[9]

Knox stood his ground, telling *The Herald* that he would continue to fight against the vote.

> I am not surprised at the majority vote, as most members of the council do not understand or appreciate the far-reaching effect of their decision. Most of them have one thought in view, to obtain at any cost the Union players. The decision shows a weakness in the League and lays down a precedent, which if followed, might place the government of the League and the game entirely in the hands of a speculator. If we are going to allow the professional speculative element to enter into the League, then why not do it openly, and above board?

> If this League and its revenue are to be used to advertise this match for the purpose of finding a valuable purse for each of the Wallaby players, why not, in justice to the Kangaroos — who have thrown in their lot with us from the start — have them receive an equitable division of the spoils? The Kangaroo players will only be paid a bonus after the promoters have received theirs and all the expenses have been met.[10]

Horrie Miller, 'said that Mr Knox's action in flouting the League was resented by every other member there.' Larkin added that: 'These matches are not a private speculation at all. Mr Joynton-Smith is guaranteeing an amount sufficient to meet expenses. If there be any profit he will not participate in it; if there be any loss he will be the loser. He thinks there will be a profit, and by that profit he is afforded an opportunity for helping a worthy public institution — the South Sydney Hospital. The profits will be equally divided with the NSWRL. He has no interest in the League, but he does not mind the League profiting so long as the hospital receives an equal amount.'[11]

Joynton-Smith also took to Knox in the newspapers: 'I deprecate anyone stating that it is a private speculation. It is nothing of the kind. I do not get a postage stamp out of it. The matches will be played under the NSWRL which has given its assent to them. It strikes me as particularly bad taste that any member of the League, after being out-voted, should not bow to the inevitable. Three or four matches will be played on the Agricultural Ground.'[12]

Not done with, Knox then wrote a letter to Joynton-Smith setting out his claims that the League was acting outside its constitution. He stated that, since the League had sole rights to play football on the Agricultural Ground, all monies should be credited straight into the bank account of the NSWRL. Knox said he would be putting that proposal to the Royal Agricultural Society and the League. He concluded by revealing that 'a defence committee of members and citizens is being formed to find funds to carry this protest through the Equity Court if necessary.'[13]

The League did its best to quell Knox's public attacks — the newspaper space given to Knox was almost equal to news and speculation of the Wallabies themselves. At a committee meeting it was resolved, 'That Mr Knox be asked to take no further action, either by newspaper controversy or otherwise, and it is not doubted by his colleagues that actions hitherto taken have been carried out in what he conscientiously believes to the best interests of the League.'[14]

The Sydney Sportsman speculated that 'Knockout Knox' was creating the fuss 'because the Joynton-Smith syndicate got in ahead of another little "shindykate" [syndicate] — so there you are. As for what the NU will think — as soon as an amateur player in England shows any promise, he is immediately offered a price by the NU clubs to come over. Mr Knox never made such noise when England was giving fancy prices for Devereux, Deane, O'Malley, and a few others.'[15]

On August 31 *The Herald* reported that 'practically all the Wallabies who have been required by the League have signed the agreement to play against the League team. Meetings of Wallabies and Kangaroos were held last night. The latter decided to give the League all their support, they ask for nothing in the shape of remuneration. The Wallaby team will not include any of the Queenslanders. There is, however, a possibility of a match being played at Brisbane, in which case the League officials expect to have some Queenslanders in the Wallaby combination.'[16]

Faced with the inevitable, Alexander Knox announced that his resignation from the League's committee. His planned visit to England where he would meet with officials of the NU in the hope of organising a tour of Australia in 1910 was cancelled.[17]

ALAS POOR WALLABIES

As speculation continued over which Wallaby players were involved, the city's rugby union writers and supporters expressed their concerns. While the League and Joynton-Smith received the criticism they expected, the Wallaby players were also condemned. 'Alas poor Wallabies! The Scots may chuckle,' wrote *The Referee*, pointing out that the Scottish Rugby Union's accusation that colonial rugby supported professionalism now had more credibility.[18] 'We in Australia,' added *The Sydney Sportsman*, 'have taken exception to many adverse criticisms that have appeared in English and Scottish papers about our footballers and those of New Zealand, but I must admit that our critics have some cause for complaint.'[19]

Many felt the Wallaby players owed some loyalty to the NSWRU, and their hosts in England, Wales and the United States, who had provided them with the trip. 'Among the sports and games which cater for the public there is nothing purer, nothing more truly amateur than rugby union football,' wrote 'The Cynic' in *The Referee*.

> When 'The Wallabies' toured Great Britain and America they were strict amateurs, and welcomed as amateurs. At the Olympic Sports they competed as amateurs for the Olympic championship. They won it, and it was not their fault that the opposition seemed hardly worthy of the occasion. When the members returned from their tour they were welcomed with pride. Seemingly with pride most of them showed their Olympic medals.
>
> Now a number of the players are arranging, in return for a sum per man alleged to be £100, to make capital out of their membership of the famous team. Surely these men must be ignorant of the significance of the Olympic contest, ignorant of all that their Olympic symbols stand for. Further, those who have gone, or intend going over to the professional ranks, have no right to take with them the name of 'The Wallabies.' That name belongs to the Union amateur team. And if it be used by the professionals it will be insult added to injury, an insult not only to the game which has done so much for them, but insult to those other members of the same team to whom the lure is useless.
>
> The rugby union game in Sydney will, in my opinion, suffer little from the movement. It will do the League no good, and, in the end, probably no little harm. Some at least of the players are not suited to that game, and some are on the edge of the retiring period. But a few will be great players under the League rules if they join the movement.[20]

The editor of *The Herald* questioned whether it was fair to criticise the Wallaby defectors.

> Perhaps no member of the public would have a right of comment but for the recent English tour. A man has a right, it may be said, to adopt what profession, or to add to his earnings in any way, he pleases. But that answer is hardly open to the players who last year were enabled to enjoy the privileges of the amateur, and have taken this opportunity of playing for a fee.
>
> It is impossible for them to escape the imputation of disloyalty and the reproach of having given reason to such bodies as the Scottish Union to

suspect their countrymen of a breach of faith. It is tolerably certain that this adoption of professionalism will lower the reputation of Australian football abroad.[21]

As far as *The Bulletin* was concerned, the involvement of South Sydney Hospital was fanciful, claiming (without any proof) the institution was nothing more than a 'stalking horse' to hide Joynton-Smith's and the League's profits. The periodical also reflected upon the risky path the League was treading. 'It is reducing football to private enterprise and making it a wild scramble for cash. It is making the League merely a bogus sporting body whose premises will practically be an office where private syndicates will recruit footballers to play for fixed sums and portions of the gate; and the end will be the ruin of the League and its disappearance.'[22]

THE GLEBE POINT JELLY FISH

The MRU met to consider suspending the rugby union players (not just the Wallabies) who had agreed to play against the Kangaroos. Harrie Wood, MRU president, called each player in alphabetical order. 'Barnett and the Burges were first called, but were not there to answer their names,' reported *The Herald*. It was then apparent that only a handful of players were present at all. Apart from one, these men had all stayed loyal to the MRU.

When interviewed, the players revealed that they had first been made offers 'about three or four months ago.' It became clear that Paddy McCue and John Barnett had put offers to their Wallaby team mates, and that encouragement had been provided by 'some of the League players.' The Union officials at the meeting seemed incredulous at the amount of money the Wallabies were being offered. When Glebe's Tom Griffin admitted he had been promised £100, the meeting erupted in laughter.

The most detailed information presented at the meeting came from Griffin's team mate, S. Jubb, the only player present who had signed to play against the Kangaroos. While he was not a Wallaby, his eagerness to speak freely probably explains his presence at the MRU's meeting.

'I was down at Grace Brothers,' told Jubb, 'and I saw some of them [Wallabies] there, and went to the meeting' held at Jack Shearer's Hotel in Glebe. When asked which players were present Jubb replied, 'Barnett, McCue, Russell, Hickey, McKivat, A. Burge, McCabe, and myself.' Jubb told the meeting all the players, including himself, had signed to play against the Kangaroos.

However, it seems that in the interim Jubb had a change of heart about playing. He was set to play fullback, but the team subsequently secured the services of Test fullback William Dix. Jubb said, 'I could see they had a fullback — Dix. I saw them on the ground this afternoon, practising. Burges, Mandible and (Bill) Farnsworth were there.'

Jubb admitted that whether he was picked or not he was to receive £50, but now 'I would sooner play the amateur game.'

Wood asked him, 'You knew there were rules as to professionalism?'

I thought if I didn't take any money or didn't play,' replied Jubb, 'I could come out. I looked at John Hickey's case.'

At the end of the meeting the MRU announced that Jubb, together with all the players he had named (plus Bob Craig), were suspended.

The full details of the MRU meeting were published in the newspapers over the following days.[23] The Sydney Sportsman vilified Jubb for revealing the names of the players involved and other details: '"Jelly Fish" has got himself up as a lovely laughing stock for all the football world over his evidence before the Union inquiry. He reminded one of a big kid at school who pots his mates after wagging it with them in the hopes of getting a couple of cuts less. Glebe Point must be a good, warm spot for him just at present.'[24]

Two years had passed since the Hickey case and the MRU was not prepared to give Jubb the same treatment. With neither the League or the Union prepared to let him play, Jubb's football career was now in limbo.

ANOTHER CASE OF THE TEMPTER SUCCEEDING

The Wallabies' tour manager, James McMahon, offered his thoughts on the defection in The Sun. McMahon held back on criticising the actions of McKivat, and felt that in the face of such large offers the working-class Wallaby players could not withstand the lure before them.

When I was in England with the team Mr Giltinan, the manager of the Kangaroos, threw out some hints about probable defections. I also heard the same thing hinted at before the Wallabies went to England. But I must admit I was surprised when I learnt that the Wallabies had gone over to the League practically in a body.

There were players in the team who I thought were amateurs to the very core. The foremost of whom, in my opinion was Craig of Balmain, McCue was, I believed another staunch amateur.

But when sums as large as £200, £150 and £100 are flourished at young fellows the relative merits of amateurism and professionalism recede into insignificance for the time being. It is then a case of money talks.

I have not anything to say in disparagement of McKivat or any other player who was a member of the Wallabies. They all had earned their places in the team, they conducted themselves admirably whilst in Great Britain and their football record was an excellent one. I know the point has been emphasised that they were ungrateful to desert the body which had provided a trip abroad for them. Their action, no doubt, was unprecedented, in so far as a representative team was concerned, but it must not be forgotten that the majority of the team are working lads, and amounts like £200 and £150 represented a fortune to them. To some of them it meant working two years or more to save £150.

James McMahon, manager of The Wallabies on their 1908/09 tour – claimed that the men could not withstand the lure of the money.

I am sure I have no ill-will against any of them. Whilst I was in charge of them they were all a team could be as regards exemplary conduct and discipline. Having fulfilled their obligations to me I do not consider that they were amenable [agreeable] to me in any way. They decided to renounce amateurism. Well that was a matter purely for themselves to decide. Large sums of money were offered them and they accepted. It was another case of the tempter succeeding.[25]

That may have been situation, but it also appears that some of the Wallabies were ensuring they extracted all they could for their services.

KANGAROOS GET NOTHING BUT HARD KNOCKS

Contrary to the news reports, the League players were far from happy to play for nothing in the matches. 'The Kangaroos were very cranky about the big money paid to the Wallabies,' wrote one player. They were concerned that several of the Wallabies would become professional for these matches only, and 'then retire with the plum' — there was nothing in their agreement that required the Wallabies to stay on with the League in 1910.

The player continued, 'The Kangaroos had got nothing but hard knocks and hard times out of turning professional and pioneering the game. These men contended that they had done all the spade work in 1907 for free. They were not paid for turning pro., they turned down prospects of inclusion in the Wallabies team for the League's sake. In contrast, the Wallabies were paid. It was a very sore point.'[26]

The Kangaroos were given an allowance of £2/10/- for each match against the Wallabies. They were also promised a share of the profits at the end of the series.[27] In the end, the Kangaroos fell into line and agreed to play — short of calling the matches off and bringing more disruption to the League, they really had little choice but to hope the crowds rolled up in their tens of thousands.

THE GAME OF A CENTURY

The League announced that the first Wallabies v Kangaroos match would be played on the coming Saturday (September 4). Billed as 'The Game Of A Century' it would be followed up with further matches on the next Wednesday and Saturday. There was no news on the club Final.

On the Thursday before the first match, nineteen 'converts' were observed at Wentworth Park to be 'training and being coached for League matches.'[28] On the same day the NSWRL was shocked by the sudden resignation of O'Sullivan as its president. The revelations at the MRU inquiry about how the secret negotiations had taken place, and that League players were involved, was too much for O'Sullivan — he felt he could no longer support the NSWRL, saying,

> Some of the members of the League have been made very enthusiastic over the great success of their organisation, and are inclined to rush off and do things on their own. It now transpires from the replies given to questions put by members of the MRU that the whole of the movement to bring about a match between the Wallabies and Kangaroos was promoted by a few young men, who had no official authority for their action, and who (with one exception) would have had no responsibility in case of failure.

> With their friends in the League, and some of whom are apparently not fully acquainted with the terms of the agreement, they carried a motion to ratify an ambiguous letter bearing upon the matter. Though I voted against the ratification, I said I would help them to make the match a success. After the disclosures in the papers, however, I saw that would be a wrong thing to do, and therefore withdrew my support and resigned.

> I do not object to professionalism if it is properly controlled. As we have professional cricketers who play with amateurs, why not allow professional footballers to do the same? Some of the League players are wonderful footballers, with a vim and enthusiasm that carries them to victory; but in the matter of discipline, debate and procedure they are as innocent as babes, and as wild as zebras.[29]

O'Sullivan stuck to his principles — he felt that if the League was not going to conduct its operations following proper business practices and its own constitution, he could not be a part of it. The risk was that the NSWRL could easily lose the public's confidence or, worse still, the League could fall apart by putting itself at the mercy of speculators as a result of ill-considered decisions.

MIGHTY WALLABIES AND FAMOUS KANGAROOS

'Well, the miracle has come to pass, and the bringing together in football combat of the mighty Wallabies and the famous Kangaroos is an accomplished fact,' wrote *The Sydney Sportsman* after the first match. 'Despite the tremendous efforts of the Union, daily papers, and a section of the croakers, who are always trying to put a damper on any attempt to improve or advance a movement, sport or otherwise.'

Taking place at the Agricultural Ground the weather 'was more in favour of flannels than jerseys — delightful for the spectator to be out in the beaming sun, but the players felt the heat severely.' The attendance was over 18,000 and was far more than the crowd watching the MRU Final on the adjacent SCG.

'What should have proved the best Union attraction of the year,' commented *The Referee*, 'was only able to draw a few thousand, but the enticing sound from next door made a whole multitude forget their principles and to the Agra' they went.'

Concerns had been raised before the match that there would be trouble in the crowd. 'There has been a lot of rumours as to the match being interfered with by barrackers, and as a consequence the NSWRL has taken special precautions to prevent anything of the kind happening.' One report said that 'a terrible riot of bloodshed was promised.' As a result, the Inspector-General of Police ordered many more officers than normal to the ground.

'Seen in the dressing-room just before the start, the Wallabies were not a bit sure of the reception they were about to receive. The faces on a few of them showed that they were only just fully realising the seriousness of the steps they had taken.'

Said one player to McKivat, 'Chris, I'm glad you're skipper. You'll stop the first brick!'

'Where do we meet for dinner tonight boys?' asked another. A third player responded: 'Well, we can pay for our dinners now, lads, and be independent.'

As they walked into the field, they were relieved at the response from the audience. 'To see the long faces broaden into a grin was a treat when the roars of welcome went up from every throat, and without doubt, it was the finest reception that any team has ever received under the League banner,' reported *The Sydney Sportsman*.[30]

The two teams included men who had not been part of their English tours — the Wallabies had Bill Farnsworth in their three-quarter line, while the Kangaroos' backs included Webby Neill from Souths and Albert Broomham from Norths. Messenger, still not completely fit, made another return to the field for the big game.

Wallabies (Light Blue): W. Dix, E. Mandible, W. Farnsworth, J. Hickey, C. Russell, A.J. McCabe, C. McKivat(c), C. McMurtrie, J. Barnett, K. Gavin, R. Craig, P.H. Burge, A.B. Burge.

Kangaroos (Blue and Maroon): W. Neill, A. Broomham, H. Messenger(c), W. Heidke (Qld), F. Cheadle, A. Butler, A. Halloway, S. Pearce, A. Burdon, W. Noble, W. Cann, J. Davis, E. Courtney.

Once both teams were on the field, they faced each other and (in turn) gave their war-cry. The Kangaroos won the toss and defended the Randwick end of the ground. From the kick-off the Wallabies were able to keep the Kangaroos contained deep in their own half. The Kangaroos eventually made a break which, through some quick passing, resulted in Broomham crossing for the opening try. Messenger missed the relatively easy conversion.

Within two minutes the Wallabies had taken the lead. The Wallaby winger, 'Boxer' Russell, opened the way with a smart run before throwing a wild pass near the try line. The Wallaby forwards secured the ball and Barnett soon scored their first try, which Hickey converted. Wallabies ahead 5–3.

From a mark taken in centre-field, Messenger took a shot at goal and succeeded sending the ball between the posts amidst great applause, bringing the scores level at 5–5. Almost immediately after the kick-off, the Wallabies were again in possession at the Kangaroos end of the field. McMurtrie crossed over and the try was converted, taking the Wallabies to 10–5 lead. 'Considering the little experience the Wallabies had [with the NU rules] they were not making a bad showing,' wrote *The Herald's* reporter. 'Still, their mistakes were sometimes costly. A penalty was then awarded against them right in front of goal, and Messenger had no difficulty in raising the flags.' Wallabies 10 Kangaroos 7.

The game was very fast, and there were 'many interchanges of sparkling efforts bringing cheers from the crowd.' An attack by the Kangaroos met with success when the Wallaby fullback Dix failed to gather the ball being toed ahead by Courtney, who regained and scored a try. Messenger failed with the kick. 10–all.

The Kangaroos then took the ascendancy, 'running over the Wallabies' as Broomham scored another unconverted try. Again the

Wallabies were able to reply almost immediately. Farnsworth secured the ball, who passed to Hickey who ran toward the Kangaroos line. He gave the ball on to Mandible who skirted the touchline and defenders to score in the corner. Farnsworth and Hickey again combined to set up a try for Albert Burge, and the Wallabies were ahead 18–13. Halloway

After being absent for most of the 1909 rugby league season, Dally Messenger turned out for the Kangaroos in the matches against the Wallabies.

scored a Kangaroos try just before half-time, which Butler failed to convert. At the break the Wallabies were in the lead 18–16.

Early into the second half the Wallabies were penalised for not playing the ball with their foot after being tackled (though it appeared the Kangaroos were just as guilty of this offence on many occasions). Messenger kicked the penalty goal and scores were yet again level. The Kangaroo halves, Butler and Halloway, combined with some 'electrical flashes' that produced a try under the posts. With Messenger's conversion the Kangaroos were in front 23–18.

The Wallabies soon responded with a fine back-line movement that took play down to the Kangaroo goal line, ultimately resulting in Gavin scoring an unconverted try. Kangaroos 23–21. The Wallabies were quickly over the line again, but were called back by the referee for an infringement. Halloway collected another try for the Kangaroos and they seemed to be in control of the match at 26–21.

The Wallabies were struggling with the new rules: kicking out on the full and 'they were at a loss what to do in the scrums,' with the 3–2–1 scrum formation bewildering to them. The Kangaroo fullback, Webby Neill, put in a brilliant length-of-the-field run to put his side back on the attack, but they were unable to score. McCabe then snared a try for the Wallabies in a frenetic finish to the game. Hickey's conversion made the scores again level, 26–all, with time almost up.

The game now reached 'a most remarkable pace,' with great excitement amongst the crowd. Most of the spectators failed to notice a ring of fifty or so policemen encircling the ground as the game neared full-time — none of the expected trouble eventuated.

Messenger then put Cheadle into a gap and he ran along the touchline, evading the desperate dive of Mandible, to score for the Kangaroos in the corner. The goal was missed, leaving the full-time score Kangaroos 29, Wallabies 26.

After having pushed the Kangaroos in the first match, the opinion of most judges was that the Wallabies were going to take some beating in the remaining contests. The concern for the League and Joynton-Smith, though, was how many people would attend. *The Herald* wrote that despite the match providing exciting entertainment, 'the standard of play was not as high as the Maori-Kangaroo matches.' *The Referee* suggested that 30,000 should have been present at the first match, but 'the Sydney public is tired of football, and the sooner the League ends the season the better.'[31]

WEARING THE INSIGNIA OF YOUR COUNTRY

Away from the match itself, the League's officials basked in the moment — many saw it as the end for the MRU and NSWRU. Tom Peters, secretary of the South Sydney club penned his feelings in *The Sydney Sportsman*.

At last, the day of emancipation has arrived — and all honour to the gallant little band of twenty-two who started the [League] movement a little over two years ago. This little forlorn hope party were the recipients of threats, sneers and vituperation from all the snob followers of so-called amateurism in NSW. But they bore it all smilingly and battled quietly onwards — ever onwards, up till today.

And what a sudden change. Hosts of players in NSW, New Zealand and Queensland under NU rules, to mention nothing of wires of congratulations to the League from inland country districts and coastal towns as well, asking for affiliation. Secessions wholesale of junior [third grade] teams from the Union ranks, and dozens of prominent players from the Union already looking for places in the League ranks for next season.

It is very pleasing, brethren, to us all — men who have fought day and night for this movement. For we all had one ambition and one beacon light ever before us: 'To make the lot of the player a better one.' No inspired scribe can prejudice our cause, for this one little fact — the public are the sole arbiters of either League or Union, for upon their patronage we both either stand or fall.

There is not the faintest doubt in my mind that the NSW public — always with the battler — will next season support our movement for the one obvious reason: 'To help the player who provides the entertainment.' It is a strenuous life the footballer's, and you cannot last forever at it. So help the League movement along, and in doing so help yourselves. We have not much time, we workers in NSW, to prate [rave on about] amateurism. We are democratic here, brethren, and the majority of us have to hustle hard for a crust.

In conclusion, brethren, it is stated by inspired scribes that the Unions will doubtless alter the rules etc., for next season. Ahem! Yes, I do not doubt they will. They must do something, you know, to down these League Johnnies. 'Eh, what?' But I wonder what would have been the fate of any delegate a season ago who would have ventured such a proposal? His ultimate fate I shudder to contemplate.

So trusting to see you one and all in League teams next season, and wearing the insignia of your country, that is, The Kangaroo.[32]

THE CURTAIN SHOULD BE RUNG DOWN

As predicted, the Wallabies won the remaining two matches — and the crowds were not as strong as hoped for. The mid-week game was a 34–21 victory to the Wallabies, which they followed with a 15–6 win.

'The Wallaby team,' wrote *The Referee*, 'on the whole, was too heavy for the Kangaroos, and a bit too nippy. If well trained the Wallabies would take no end of beating. The Kangaroos put up a gallant fight trying to win the rubber, but had to acknowledge defeat by a better team. The Kangaroos have played with a great deal of genuine grit, but in my opinion their points in each of the two last games are flattering to their powers. They know much more about the tricks and points in the NU game than the Wallabies, but the latter as a body, are much superior as players as well as physique.'[33]

The crowds at the final two matches — 2,500 and 14,000 — meant that the gate-takings were not yet over £1,500. 'The gates on the whole are not quite up to expectations, and another match, if well patronised, will no doubt be very useful, seeing the conditions on which the Wallaby contingent entered into the arrangement. On this score, the arrangement of the match is quite reasonable.'[34] In other words, the

Wallabies should be made to play another game so that Joynton-Smith could recover the money paid to the players.

The possibility of the need for a fourth match had been incorporated into the agreement with the Wallaby players. As soon as the third game was over, and it was apparent that Joynton-Smith was still down £130, the move to play the fourth match the following Saturday (September 18) began. The League also wanted to recoup its advertising and incidental costs of £117 for jerseys, music bands and other items.[35]

The Sunday Sun reported, 'There is every probability that the Wallabies and Kangaroos will meet again next Saturday. Yesterday's losers expressed a keen desire to have another try against their victors, and a special League meeting is to be held tomorrow evening to consider the matter. The Final of the competition was down for decision next Saturday, but it is expected that this difficulty will be surmounted, and the big match played.'[36]

Few accepted the claim that a fourth match was brought about because the Kangaroos wanted to redeem themselves — in reality, it was their only hope of receiving a 'bonus' for their participation. The question was how interested would the public be in a fourth match that added another week to an already over-extended season?

The Referee was quick to offer the League a warning: 'The match will not meet with the approval of a great many supporters of the game. The club Final should be played and the curtain rung down.'[37]

CHAPTER SIXTEEN

THE BALMAINIACS FORFEIT
THE FINAL

A BRILLIANT DOUBLE EVENT

On the Monday evening the NSWRL convened a special meeting of the committee to set out the schedule for the remainder of the season. The first decision was to abandon the arrangements for a NSW (or Australian) team to visit New Zealand, owing to the extension of the season caused by the fourth Wallabies v Kangaroos contest.

The League intended playing this fourth contest and the club Final on consecutive Saturdays. However, faced with complaints that the Final should be played and the season brought an end, the League came up with a solution that it thought would satisfy everyone, and presumably deliver a larger crowd.

The NSWRL announced it would 'wind down the season with a big programme at the Agricultural Ground next Saturday. The early match will be the first grade Final between South Sydney and Balmain. The late match will be Wallabies v Kangaroos, and a very strong League team will represent the latter.' The League billed the day in newspaper advertisements as a 'Brilliant Double Event to Close Season!.'[1]

However, by mid-week the 'brilliant double event' was quickly losing its lustre.

The 'very strong League team' bore little resemblance to the Kangaroo teams that had played in England — in a 25–man squad announced for the game, just seven were from the 1908 tourists (though one was Messenger). While another four of the Kangaroos had been left out so they could appear in the club Final, the remainder were in England, retired, injured, or simply not interested in playing. Meanwhile the Wallabies called on the Farnsworth brothers to complete their team. The match was now a very watered-down version of the 'contest of a century.'[2]

Then the Balmain club took exception to the League's compromise. The NSWRL's constitution required that the proceeds from the club Final were to be divided between the 'ambulance associations' and the insurance fund for injured players. Balmain were adamant that they did not want the club Final to be played as a draw-card to help

Joynton-Smith and the League recover their expenses for the Wallabies
v Kangaroos matches.

Balmain announced that they would not be fronting-up and the
Final would not be played. Their opponents, South Sydney, appeared
to have no problems at all with the League's arrangements for the day.

Officials of the Balmain club went to the League's offices on the
Friday. They complained to NSWRL secretary Ted Larkin, 'that they
had been badly treated, and they should not be asked to play an early
match.' They asked for the Final to be played a week later, but there
was little time left and Larkin did nothing. The Final would go ahead
as scheduled. *The Herald* reported that 'the officials of the League state
that the Balmain club has no cause for complaint with regard to the
season's matches, and that if the club fails to turn up it will be a bad
case of disloyalty.'[3]

The Saturday newspapers carried the news that Balmain was intent
on not playing.[4] The day itself did not bode well for a good roll-up at
the gate; it was rainy and the playing field water-logged. The League's
run of good luck with sun-drenched days for big matches had finally
run out.

When the kick-off was due for the Final, Souths ran out onto the
field and stood waiting. Even though their players were at the ground,
Balmain stuck true to their word and did not send a team out. The
referee eventually asked South Sydney to kick-off. They chased the ball
down field, picked it up and scored a try. The referee then awarded
Souths the match, securing for them two points for the win, and with
it the premiership.

Earlier in the afternoon, as spectators were arriving, the Balmain
team had 'lined up outside the Agra' gates to let the public see they were
not going to play.' The crowd eventually totalled just 4,000, although

---

N.S.W. RUGBY LEAGUE

GREAT DOUBLE EVENT TO CLOSE SEASON.

AGRICULTURAL GROUND, NEXT SATURDAY.
WALLABIES V. KANGAROOS.

PRECEDED BY

SOUTH SYDNEY v BALMAIN,

FOR LEAGUE PREMIERSHIP AND MEDALS.

ADMISSION, 1/.

E. R. LARKIN, Sec.

---

weather conditions were so poor that sporting events across the city were cancelled or badly affected; the adjacent SCG hosted a soccer Final on what was described as 'treacherous ground conditions.' The gate-receipts were just enough for Joynton-Smith and the League to clear their debts.

To ensure the public still saw two matches as promised, Souths played a game against a 'Combined team' comprising players from various clubs, all of whom wore their team or training jersey. No one, on or off the field, took the game seriously. The final result was recorded as a win for Souths by 18–10.

As the Kangaroos made their final preparations for their match, it became apparent that their back-line players, Dally Messenger and 'Johnno' Stuntz, had decided not to turn up. *The Sydney Sportsman* accused them both of preferring to stay out of the rain. South Sydney's Tommy Anderson (a Kangaroo) and Arthur Conlin volunteered to play their second game of the day and take the place of the missing men. The team was now down to just four of the 1908 Kangaroos — Anderson, Pearce, Burdon and Courtney.

The ground was covered in parts by water, and included numerous 'muddy traps for the runners.' Considering the condition of the ground, 'it was a good game, played with great willingness. The men handled the slippery ball very well, and surprisingly good pace was shown by the forwards.'

The Kangaroos held on to win the match 8–6, with the Wallabies struggling to gain many penalties from their more experienced opponents. 'Pearce the willing, Burdon the silent, and Courtney the persistent, were the best of the Kangaroo pack.'[5]

The League's long season was now over — but off the field, Balmain's decision to not show up for the Final was long debated both in newspapers and at meetings called over the issue.

'SPORTS' DO YOU CALL THEM?

The Balmain club believed that they had saved the League from financial ruin in the early part of the 1909 season. While the other club matches failed to draw decent crowds, Balmain was attracting supporters by the thousands to Birchgrove Park. The NSWRL was practically living off the money returned to them from Balmain matches.

Balmain also felt strongly about the importance of local football — the treatment handed out to the Balmain community during the old MRU days was one of the principal reasons they were so staunchly behind the formation of the NSWRL. Their representative on the MRU committee, Pat McQuade, threatened to resign over the issue in 1906.

The club were often referred to in the press as the 'Balmainiacs.' *The Sydney Sportsman* even went so far as to say that wherever there was trouble with sport in the Balmain district, McQuade was sure to be found. He was now an official of the Balmain rugby league club.' Pat McQuade is bringing himself back into the limelight a lot over the Balmain affair. It is a strange coincidence that every committee he gets on, don't matter what the game is, there is always "something doing." It's time you took a tumble, Pat.'[6]

McQuade was Balmain's voice against the League's decision. They resented having the Final placed on the under-card to a perhaps more attractive match, but not a more important match. Having the funds from the day's takings used to finish off debt owed to Joynton-Smith, instead of the charities and insurance fund laid down in the League's constitution, made it all the less palatable.

Playing early wasn't of itself a problem. With only three grounds at its disposal since its inception, the League had been forced to schedule one match each round with a 2 p.m. kick-off. Work finished at mid-day, so players could easily reach the Agricultural Ground in time. News reports commented that the Balmain players were outside the ground well before the Final's kick-off time. The real objection by Balmain was that the match had been relegated to an under-card position, not what time it started.

Were these sufficient reasons to warrant forfeiting the Final? Surely they could see the benefit to the League of playing both matches as an attractive double-bill on this one-off occasion.

The League argued that Balmain had been well treated and ought to show some loyalty — in the ten club rounds Balmain were given nine at its home ground. South Sydney pointed out that both they and Wests were sent by the League to play club matches in Newcastle — both Sydney teams were forced to field weakened sides and were beaten.

Balmain had little support for their actions. *The Sydney Sportsman*, staunchly within the League camp since its inception, launched into the Balmain club.

Given a fine day, and had the Final been played, there would have been sufficient in the gate to have covered the lot, but as both Balmain and the weather jibbed, there was just enough to clear of Joynton-Smith's account. The Kangaroos got nothing, and charity and the assurance fund got the same amount.

Balmain have all season been booming themselves for the way they have stuck to the League and what good sports they were. The public believed

The Royal Agricultural Society's 'Challenge Shield' – donated to the NSWRL by the Society before the 1908 season, the shield was awarded to the winners of the club competition. The first club to win the premiership three times in a row would earn outright ownership of the shield.

them, and heartily appreciated their efforts, but the club has come down wallop from its high position in public esteem since its childish actions of last week.

Balmain have had all but two of their engagements [one a semi-final] on Birchgrove, and then, when asked to help to make up a big programme to finish up a successful season, and help rake in a few quid for the players [Kangaroos] who have been grafting for their state all the season, they turn turtle, and not only refuse, but run like a pack of kids with letters to the dailies, and use other efforts to prevent the crowd from rolling up to the fixture.

The final effort was for the team to line up outside the Agra' gates to let the public see they were not going to play. Sports do you call them?

The fact of the matter is they knew they were up against it when they met South Sydney, and thought their reputation would be saved by a back-out of this description. But, outside of their own following — and everyone knows what fanatics they are — there is not a single voice upholding the action of the club, and nothing but disgust is expressed for their despicable behaviour. The high-and-mighty wearers of the black-and-gold, flushed with the successes of a few wins on their own dunghill, want the world.[7]

The practically indisputable presumption was that Souths would win the Final and thus the season would end. An unlikely win by Balmain would have forced a second Final. Ironically, given the wet and muddy field, a number of judges thought that if Balmain had have played they could have produced the upset. The disgust expressed was not so much about the lack of a Final, but at Souths being denied their rightful honour to defeat the second-placed team and claim the premiership.

Balmain thought they had little to lose and much to gain by threatening to forfeit. They were trying to make the League publicly back down — forcing it to play the Final separately and distribute the gate-receipts under the terms expressed in the League's constitution.

However, it would also have meant the Wallabies v Kangaroos match would have had to attract a crowd in its own right, which could be difficult given the rapidly declining interest in these matches. Failure to gain the gate-receipts needed for Joynton-Smith would leave the NSWRL vulnerable to further public criticism. Claims were made that League treasurer Horrie Miller had underwritten Joynton-Smith to be personally liable for any short-fall.[8]

It was not clear what damage, if any, the officials of Balmain club were trying to wreak on the League or members of its committee by refusing to take part in the Final. The weeks immediately afterward revealed some of the architects behind the events and their motives — and they weren't all Balmain officials.

HIS ACTIONS NECESSITATED DISQUALIFICATION

The Balmain club organised a public meeting at the local town hall to protest the League's decisions and consider legal action. It was packed with supporters and officials (including McQuade), who were presumably eager to have the Final rescheduled. This would allow Balmain to continue their challenge for the premiership and ensure the gate-takings reached the charities and insurance fund.

However, that suggestion was not made.

All the discussions were about forcing the League to withhold paying off Joynton-Smith, and distributing the Final money in the constitutionally prescribed manner. They were solely concerned about the distribution of funds, not in resuscitating their premiership campaign. It practically confirms that Balmain forfeited the Final as a means to attack the League.

The first speaker at the meeting was not from the Balmain club, but North Sydney — it was Alexander Knox.

Knox came readily armed with a barrister's legal opinion stating that the League had 'distinctly acted contrary to the provisions of its by-laws.' Using the barrister's advice, Knox convinced the audience to vote in favour of taking legal action against the NSWRL. They would seek a Court injunction to prevent the League paying the proceeds of the day's takings to Joynton-Smith.

Two other North Sydney officials (Ernie Blue and Paddy Dunne) were also present. They successfully moved that a fund be set up to collect donations for the legal action and that all other clubs be given copies of the counsel's advice for their consideration.

The Sydney Sportsman attacked Knox and the other North Sydney officials who had attended the Balmain meeting, suggesting they 'would have shown a lot more block if they attended to the affairs of their own club, and left the squabbles of the other club alone.'

It is apparent that Balmain were influenced by Knox and other North Sydney officials to forfeit the Final. Balmain officials felt strong allegiance to Knox. Under his stewardship the League had allocated Balmain a home match every week bar one. Balmain often claimed the NSWRL (and before 1908 the MRU) was too influenced by Souths and Easts officials. If Knox could regain control of the League committee, then presumably Balmain would be in a more powerful position.

Balmain Rugby League Club's home ground – Birchgrove Park [Oval]. For most of the 1909 season it was the only ground earning money for the NSWRL. (Photographed here in the opening match of the 1910 season – Balmain v. South Sydney).

However, *The Sydney Sportsman* suggested that Knox was not just attempting to discredit the NSWRL, but seeking to build a rival League. 'The [Balmain] meeting finished up with an appeal to the public and other League clubs for sufficient dough to carry out the legal proceedings. Rumours are afloat of meetings to be held to form a new League, and out all the old officials, and a lot of other bunkum.'[9]

On the previous evening to the Balmain gathering, the NSWRL had held a meeting where there were calls by Quinlan, Miller, and others, to have Knox removed from the League's committee. The meeting was 'by no means a peaceful one' as arguments between the two sides raged. Miller argued that 'it was time they got rid of Mr Knox.' Blue said 'that in his opinion Mr Knox had done a good deal for the League.'

Knox was present at the meeting and pointed out that there was no rule under which the League could expunge his name and position. In the end, it was acknowledged that as Knox was representing his club, only the North Sydney members could remove him. Quinlan then said he 'would now leave it to Mr Knox's sense of decency whether or not he should resign.' The League eventually revisited the issue of how to deal with Knox and soon announced that it 'regrets that his actions necessitated his disqualification for life.'[10]

The proposed legal action by Balmain soon faded away. Their legal advice seemed to have overlooked that Balmain's forfeit meant no Final had been played — and the League could therefore dispose of the gate-receipts how it saw fit. Outside of the Balmain club, and some officials from North Sydney, no support could be found to pursue the matter any further.

Forfeiting the Final had achieved nothing.

THE UNIONS MUST WAKE UP

Amidst all the rumblings from Balmain and Knox, the League received a letter from Paddy McCue on behalf of the ex-Wallabies, including the Farnsworth brothers. It was read out at a NSWRL meeting where 'it was a great source of satisfaction to the delegates present — it set at rest a lot of reports flying around about the Wallabies next season. Paddy states all the men intend throwing in their lots with their various district clubs, while the countrymen are going to use their best endeavours to get the game going in their districts.'[11]

The Sydney Sportsman summed up the signing of the Wallabies as a great success for the League — and achieved at virtually no expense. The NSWRL finished the season with just £39 in the bank. Admittedly, it had cleared all its debts and met all its obligations to pay injured players, but there is clearly no way it would have been able to secure the Wallaby players (as long as they were demanding money for their crossing over) without the assistance of an outsider. 'It cost the League £117 for advertising for the whole fixtures,' wrote *The Sydney Sportsman*, 'but when it is considered that for the £117 they secured such star performers, and the chances of a large number of their club mates following them over next season, the League got a tip-top bargain, and one they would have been prepared to have paid a lot bigger price for.'[12]

Meanwhile the future of S. Jubb, the remaining convert, was less certain. Jubb, who didn't play in any of the four matches, continued to seek reinstatement to the MRU, but was rejected on each occasion.

The MRU and NSWRU recognised the problems they now faced. Restrained by the rules of the RFU in England, it was a frustrating time for many of their officials, players and supporters as they fought against the League. The two Unions had come through the 1909 season in a sound financial position, but the future was less certain.

The loss of the Wallaby players was in itself a blow, but the real danger would come from other players, and supporters, moving across to the League. Many, perhaps even the majority, had stayed loyal to the Unions in 1908 and '09 in hope that changes would occur from within. Improvement in player conditions had come, but the loss of the Wallaby players forced a crisis point and change in attitude. This was compounded by the ongoing debate over the need to modify the rules of rugby union to combat the growing public appeal of the NU rules in Sydney.

They wanted the Unions to act in the interest of local needs, not necessarily England's RFU. Their preference was for all rugby to unite again under the NSWRU — and their patience was running out.

'Wellwisher of the Union' was one of a number of letter contributors to *The Herald* in mid-September calling for significant change.

As a rugby union supporter I would like to make a few suggestions, which I think would benefit the Union if adopted. I, with many others, have noted with deep regret the split in our rugby ranks initiated some two years ago by the forming of the League. It was bound to come sooner or later, and the Union only have themselves to blame. The amateur status is altogether too finely cut for Australians. I am not favouring professionalism, but think it absurdly unfair for players who draw the crowds to be out-of-pocket by the sport. If a referendum were taken among rugby union players, a vast majority would, I am sure, favour the payment for loss of time.

'Wellwisher' then gave yet another example of the difficulties experienced by representative players having to travel away from home for weeks. 'The Union must wake up to these facts before it is too late.' He then argued that they should cut their ties with the RFU.

If the English Union declines to move, let us lead the way. Why not amend the rules, and make it possible for amateurs and professionals to play together. The Lord's of England do not object to playing on the same side as the labourer at cricket — why not in football? Australia is a working man's country, and I am feel sure New Zealand and Queensland would fall in line with this suggestion.

The matter is in the hands of the players. I trust that before the next annual meeting of the Union [early 1910], delegates will be elected who will insist on an alteration in the rules similar to the above, and also amend the laws of the game.[13]

WALLABIES ALLOWED BACK

To shore up their position, the MRU took some actions to counter both issues. They formed a sub-committee to look at altering the playing laws. Their brief was to examine all the proposed rule changes that had been made to the RFU by NSW and at the joint NSW-Qld-NZ rules conferences of 1903 and 1907 (the majority of which the RFU rejected).

In commenting on the MRU's initiative *The Referee's* rugby union writer 'hoped that the matter will not be unduly delayed.' He also observed that the NU game in Sydney 'generally produces many more passing movements, it is more exciting and attractive to the average man in the crowd. There would appear to be a great element of chance or luck in the new game.'[14]

The other change was a proposal put by E.S. Marks to amend the definition of an amateur. In short, Marks proposed 'to allow any player back into the Union fold who does not infringe his amateur status after March 1, 1910.'[15] In effect, those who had gone over to the NSWRL could return without punishment, provided that they joined a district club by the nominated date and committed no further acts of professionalism thereafter.

Marks and the MRU were ridiculed for their attempt to win back players (presumably the Wallabies in particular) by 'white-washing' them clean. Marks quickly responded in the newspapers, claiming that his proposal had been misconstrued by reporters. 'I have no intention of allowing any person who has been banned by the Union to again enter its ranks,' stated Marks.

He then went on to explain that his amendment would apply only to men found to be professionals in another sport, and who wanted to play rugby union. This definition would prevent the dramas that surrounded men such as Snowy Baker who, although a professional boxer, played rugby union for the Sydney club. The MRU's argument was that a man's status in another sport was irrelevant to his status as a rugby player. Conversely, this did not extend to rugby league players, because these 'professionals' breached the rules of the MRU — a man who was paid as a boxer did not.[16]

While Marks may have had no (public) 'intention' of allowing rugby league players to return to the ranks of the Union, to anyone who read his proposal it was allowable.

Clearly, the MRU and NSWRU were struggling with their position. The mood of the sporting public and press of Sydney was such that it was now quick to openly ridicule anything that it saw as attempts at deception or duplicity by the Unions, even well-intended ones. Finding and using 'imaginative' ways to satisfy the needs of players was going to be difficult in Sydney (though perhaps not in New Zealand). It was becoming apparent that the only real option for the NSWRU was to either break with the RFU or follow their amateurism rules absolutely.

THE TIME IS OPPORTUNE FOR A VISIT

At the same time the NSWRL was also looking to England for its future. The visit of English cricket and rugby union teams to Australia had (for the most part) been big money earners for the local authorities and garnered much public interest.

'With the very best material now under the command of the League,' an invitation was cabled from Sydney to England.[17] Would the NU send out a English team to Australia in 1910? A similar request was made by the NZRL. If the fledgling NU outposts — Sydney, Brisbane, Auckland and Newcastle — could be visited by an English team they could hope to make significant profits, particularly as the Unions were proposing no international visitors.

The Athletic News in England touched on the opportunities presently before the NU committee.

> The Australian League (NSWRL) have offered the same guarantee as the NU gave to the private enterprises of Messrs. Baskerville and Giltinan. To this the home Union (NU) has no objection. That the time is opportune for a visit even the most pessimistic official will admit. The NU has had convincing evidence from Colonial players now resident in England.

> Another point which will need consideration is that next season a NU team will be the only attraction in the Colonies. If the visit is postponed a season, what guarantee will the NU have that another team under rugby union rules — not necessarily English — may then provide an opposite attraction? The unrest in the Colonies may perhaps demand caution in the preliminary negotiations, but surely the NU authorities will not be found lacking in enterprise in this, the most important period in the history of professional rugby football.[18]

At the NU's committee meeting of 12 October the invitations from the NSWRL and NZRL were read out. A third cablegram had also been received — it was from Alexander Knox: 'Do not do anything until you receive my letter.' Presumably Knox wrote to inform the NU of the happenings surrounding the Wallabies signings.

The NU met again on 9 December but there was no discussion at all of Knox or further correspondence. It was resolved to set up a sub-committee to organise the tour arrangements — the English NU team were coming.[19]

CHAPTER SEVENTEEN

JACK IS NOW AS GOOD AS HIS MASTER

PLAYING THE GAME FOR THE GAME'S SAKE

'This is the third season under Northern Union rules in Sydney,' said *The Referee* in its preview of the 1910 season.

> This winter gives promise of being the most successful from the spectator's, the player's, and the financial standpoints. Enclosed grounds have been secured in Erskineville (Metters Oval), North Sydney (Oval) and Burwood (St Lukes Park) — which should help materially to push the game ahead in these districts. A new ground has also been secured at Newcastle, and latest reports from that centre are very encouraging to the League councillors.

> Additional interest has already been shown in the practice matches, and it may be taken as a good augury that the club games are to receive a larger share of patronage from the football public than has hitherto been the case.

> Though the NU code is practically in its infancy in this part of the globe, it is a sign of virility in the management that the visit of a powerful English team is to be made shortly. League officials are sanguine of the tour's success. It is to be hoped that the enterprise will be successful and lead to the game and its management winning the esteem and complete confidence of that wide section of the public which supports sport in Sydney who is prepared to patronise any rugby of a representative character.[1]

The dramas that surrounded the move of the Wallabies to the League were now in the past. The involvement of an outsider to fund the venture was viewed as a well-intended 'temporary lapse, in which the end is claimed to justify the means.' Joynton-Smith continued his involvement with the NSWRL, being elected president at the annual meeting in early 1910.[2]

Further offers from rugby union players were made to form a team to take on the League's best, no doubt following the cash trail of the Wallabies. The League considered, and then rejected the proposals. With a new found confidence, the NSWRL felt there was no gain to be made by repeating the Wallabies saga. 'If Union players wish to join the League,' said one official, 'let them come along and play trial matches.'[3]

Meanwhile the MRU (with Blair Swannell now its secretary) and the NSWRU made no moves of any significance in regard to changing the rules of rugby union or improving the conditions of players. The RFU listened to proposed modifications in the playing rules from Australia and New Zealand. *The Bulletin* reported that the NZRU had in fact asked the RFU 'to arrange a conference to discuss amendments of rugby rules — and then got a woodener in the eye in the shape of an intimation that the English [British] Unions would discuss the matter; but that "Colonials" could be allowed no voice in the matter.' The RFU subsequently adopted three minor amendments that were of little assistance in improving rugby union as a spectacle.[4]

At the NSWRU annual meeting, the committee men who had founded and led rugby in NSW since its inception (John Calvert, Monty Arnold, James Henderson and James McManamey), finally entered the debate over the rugby split. Members looking for reforms to stop the loss of players and supporters were disappointed at what they heard. The committee attacked those who wanted training expenses met, claimed the ex-Wallabies exhibited 'great ingratitude and their action should be condemned, especially as the Union had lost £1,400 on the tour,' and said it was 'almost useless to argue with the professional.'[5]

There was no hint of conciliation; the message was that changes were not coming. One Sydney rugby union club's captain berated his team mates for wanting improvements to the rules of rugby union to make it more like NU. He argued that they couldn't remain amateur if they improved the spectacle of rugby union. 'Amend the rules, make the game faster — and what then? You can't play it. It's the man who will step along and take his £3 a week who will be the football player then, and you or other fools will go on the bank [hill] and watch him.'[6]

The Unions believed that the best means to ensure their survival was to adopt the philosophy of 'playing the game for game's sake' and not competing for players by throwing better conditions or money at them. 'When men thought it better to get something out of the game, rather than giving something to the game, it was idle to argue,' said McManamey.[7]

Undoubtedly some were attracted by this approach, but many more wanted the benefits offered by the League. Footballers and spectators now knew exactly what each side offered. The result was record crowd and player numbers flocking to the League's opening matches. As long as there was confidence in the League's management, their success was now practically assured.

THEY LIKE TO SEE THEIR FAVOURITES WIN

The NSWRL club premiership for 1910 did not include Newcastle, who had now grown strong enough to conduct their own local competition. A new club, Annandale, joined in Newcastle's place. In a further example of how bitter Sydney's inter-suburban rivalry was, the Annandale players (who had come over from the Union) refused to join their district club Glebe. After gaining enough financial and community support to satisfy the NSWRL, Annandale was granted admittance to the competition.[8]

In the Juniors, the Munn Cup was replaced by the President's Cup (donated by Joynton-Smith) for contests between the representatives of each district. This now comprised Balmain, Souths, Easts, Norths, Wests, and St George as many young players joined the League.[9]

For the opening round of first grade matches, the League scheduled a re-match between Balmain and South Sydney, again at Birchgrove Park. A record club crowd of 5,000 surprised the League by its size. *The Referee* reported that only two turnstiles were open on the southern end of the ground (from where most patrons approach), 'whereas four, or even six, would not have been too many for the occasion. Some forty of fifty of the more impatient members [fans] got in by scaling the fence, and not the long arm of the law intervened, hundreds would have gone into the ground in a similar way.'

The match itself, not unexpectedly given the events that closed the 1909 season, was fiery. 'There were no beg-pardons in this game,' reported *The Referee*, 'everything that was given was well meant. It was fought out desperately and bitterly until the end. The local club placed a very solid vanguard [forward pack] in the field, while the backs, if not particularly resourceful, were reliable. South Sydney too placed its full strength in the field. The Balmain forwards jumped into the game from the outset, and in the first spell gave their opponents little peace — their tearaway rushes quite disconcerting the South Sydney rearguard. By no means attractive, the game kept the spectators deeply interested by reason of its pace and the strenuousness of the tackling. Play, in fact, was rough at times, as the casualties testify.'

For the most part, Balmain controlled the match. However, injuries to their captain 'Pony' Halloway (broken collarbone) and John Appolony (fractured jaw), gave Souths the advantage. In the last ten minutes the visitors scored two tries to take victory.

The Referee thought it necessary to praise the home crowd's conduct. 'Supporters of Balmain are to be congratulated on their behaviour, there being little to which anyone could take exception. Naturally they like to see their favourites win, and what district does not? In the present instance, however, their team had to play second fiddle, but as sports they took the defeat in good spirit, and liberally applauded the visitors.'[10]

RUGBY UNION FOOTBALL AS A WORLD GAME

The news that the NU had agreed to send an England team to tour Australia and New Zealand caused further concern for supporters of rugby union. *The Herald* reported many were 'wondering whether the NSWRU would take any steps towards putting up a programme of matches outside of the usual fixtures with Queensland and Country Week. Some Unionists fear that the NU team coming to play the League game will give the amateur rugby body a severe knock unless there is something like a visit from New Zealand to counteract the influence of the Northern [NU] team. Inquiries upon the matter have, however, elicited no information from Union officials. The officials are reticent.'[11]

The NSWRU had issued invitations to the Wales Rugby Union and the South African Rugby Board, but had been declined on both counts. Eventually it was announced that the All Blacks and a New Zealand Maori team would be visiting. Added to the calendar was a tour from an 'American Universities' team from the west coast of the United States.

One Union official praised the NSWRU for inviting the Americans: 'The NSW Union is to be congratulated on having made the arrangements for this tour, for it will be the first meeting of America and Australasians in either of the great national games on the soil of the Southern Hemisphere.' That the 'American' team was a combination of players from just two Universities, California and Stanford, didn't stem his enthusiasm. 'It is one more argument in favour of rugby union football as a world's game — a game which widens the horizons of its players and those interested in it.'[12]

THE CREAM OF THE OLD COUNTRY'S FOOTBALLERS

Through April and May crowds for the League continued to increase while MRU attendances began falling towards 2,000 for the biggest rugby union club matches. The first guide as to where the public's favour lay for the representative season came on May 28. A crowd of 10,000 went to watch the first rugby union inter-state game for 1910 between NSW and Queensland at the Sports Ground. Next door at the Agricultural Ground, the undefeated League competition leaders, Newtown and South Sydney, were clashing. Newtown won the match 12–7, but the NSWRL won the day; the crowd was a staggering 17,000.[13]

Present at the League match was the English NU team, who had just arrived in Sydney. They had been given an official welcome by the NSWRL at a function held a few days earlier at the Arcadia Hotel.

Said *The Referee*, 'A few very fine speeches were made, though several topics not pertinent to the occasion were elaborated upon. The large dining-room was packed and but one note permeated the proceedings — admiration for the new game.'

James Joynton-Smith gave the opening speech of welcome to the Englishmen, although he said very little about them and used the opportunity to attack the Unions. Any apparent disinterest for the rugby divide he exhibited during the controversy surrounding the signing of the Wallabies was now long gone.

> He spoke very ably, but his remarks were largely confined to the perennial topic of Union v League, or amateur v professional, and at that he applied it to [only] Sydney football. However, he said, the visit of the English NU team marked an epoch in Australian football. He regarded the team as the cream of the Old Country's football, and they would be opposed by the cream of Australian footballers, among whom would be members of both the Wallabies and Kangaroo teams which had toured England. Joynton-Smith then spent the remainder of his speech attacking the Unions for the money they had drawn from the people of NSW and asked 'what had become of these large sums?'

Fred Flowers (a member of NSW Parliament), who had become the League's patron, also made a speech welcoming the visitors. Flowers attributed the 'success of the NU game in Sydney largely upon by one matter — its spectacular interest for the public.' 'It is this, in the representative matches,' said Flowers, 'which has saved the League game here from its early mismanagement and dissension. Even the splendid work of Mr Larkin as secretary could not have pulled the League through without this strong asset.'

Flowers concluded by criticising the press. 'League football, like the party I represent in Parliament [Labor], received notices of about one inch, while the other fellows had columns written about them.' The remark elicited enthusiastic cheers and applause from the audience.

Joseph Houghton, joint manager of the England team (with John Clifford), responded on behalf of the visitors. Houghton had been the secretary of the NU for many years, and was the current NU president. One of the Kangaroos wrote in *The Referee* that 'while we were in England, Mr Houghton was the great supporter of our scheme for an early tour' to Australia. Significantly, two of his sons [who had played for the St Helens NU club] were in the New Zealand rugby league team that visited NSW in 1909. One was now running the operations of the Auckland Rugby League, while the other was on the committee of the North Sydney club. Whether the Houghtons had provided any assistance to Baskerville in 1907 remains unclear.

Houghton said that, unlike those who had preceded him, he was not an orator. He preferred to talk only of football matters and developing the game in Australia and New Zealand. 'The Northern Union regards this as a missionary tour,' he explained, 'and is prepared to lose £1,000 over it. It would have been easy to have sent out a weaker combination at a much smaller cost. But the Northern Union spared no expense in getting together the most powerful team possible. I think you will all agree with me that the combination is a brilliant one.'[14]

The NU might not have 'spared any expense,' but it ensured that the financial terms of the tour were in its favour: a guarantee of £3,000 and 60 per cent of the gross takings at each match. This would leave the local League only 40 per cent, from which they would have to pay for ground rent, players' expenses, and match expenses, including advertising. The risk to the NSWRL seemed minimal, as anticipation that there would

ENGLAND v. N.S. WALES

NEXT SATURDAY,
JUNE 11.
Agricultural Ground

ADMISSION, 1s; GRANDSTAND, 1s EXTRA; SUTTOR STAND, 1s 6d EXTRA; CHILDREN, HALF-PRICE.

NEWTOWN BAND.

E. R. LARKIN, Secretary.

be big crowds drawn to the England matches was very high. Even the trustees of the SCG 'were desirous of securing some of the fixtures of the NU team — but a clause in the agreement with the NSWRU made it impossible.'[15]

The Referee commented that apart from a few of the Kangaroos who had seen the players in England, the NU men '...are little known here, save by repute.' Captain of the 1908 Kangaroos, Dinny Lutge, said that 'the team is most formidable; in fact, he goes the length to say that it will be found to be the strongest NU combination that ever stepped on a football field.'[16]

John Stuntz, now at St Helens, told NU supporters in *The Athletic News* (reproduced *The Referee*): 'Your team should win, for the form of your leading players has surprised me, and they will do even better in Australia — of that I am convinced. They will play with a rather smaller ball, which is more easily held and more conventionally carried.' Stuntz concluded by advising the NU tourists to practice taking the ball on a hard surface. 'Overcome this difficulty and prolific scoring should result.'[17]

The 'England' team included seven players from Wales and one from Scotland. The deeds of James Lomas, Billy Batten, Albert Avery, James Leytham and others had been reported in the Sydney newspapers in the lead up to the tour. With so much being said about the talents of the visitors, 'one almost imagines he has seen them in action' noted one League columnist. 'But that pleasure is in store for next Saturday.'[18]

THE GAME WAS AS FAST AS THE WIND

'The Englishmen filed in to the arena first in hooped jerseys of red and white, led by a stalwart — deep-chested and massive-limbed — in the person of James Lomas,' reported *The Referee*. To many in the 33,000 strong crowd at the Agricultural Ground, 'a record for Northern Union football,' the team's appearance reminded them of the 1888 British tourists who were dominated by 'Northern men' in the forwards.

'These knobby Englishmen,' continued *The Referee*, 'were preceded by a lean, gaunt stage lion, a striking antithesis of the "noble beast," and a peculiar physical contrast with the men its wake. The NSW team marched in headed by a real, if small, kangaroo surcingled in blue and driven or yanked along by a once famous New Zealand forward. This tomfoolery amused the crowd for a few moments.'

The match marked the first combined representative team of the former Kangaroos and Wallabies, with four from each selected in the NSW side.

NSW: W. Neill, A. Broomham, J. Hickey, H. Messenger, C. Russell, W. Farnsworth, C. McKivat, W. Cann, J. Barnett, E. Courtney, W. Spence, W. Noble, C. Sullivan.

England: F. Young, J. Bartholomew, J. Lomas, B. Jenkins, F. Farrar, J. Thomas, F. Smith, F. Webster, R. Ramsdale, W. Jukes, W. Winstanley, F. Boylen, G. Ruddick.

A mere ten days off the ship, the six weeks sea voyage took its toll on the English team during the game. The 'game was fast as the wind' and the 'local men were seemingly as fresh as paint.' Unfortunately, the visitors had no answer to the Blues' performance, losing 28–14. One reporter claimed, 'It was one of the finest displays by forwards and backs ever given by a NSW representative team, and quite the best ever exhibited by a League combination in Sydney.'

The combination of Wallabies and Kangaroos in the backs proved a great success. 'The three-quarters played quite at their top,' wrote *The Referee*, 'with Messenger and Hickey standing out by their daring and clever running and kicking. They were both champions. McKivat and Bill Farnsworth, as connecting links with the three-quarters line, were in excellent fettle — McKivat shooting the ball out to the five-eighth with wonderful accuracy. Several times, when the defence was on top of Farnsworth, McKivat took the situation in a at a glance, slung the oval [ball] high and hard over the five-eighth's head to Hickey, a manoeuvre often successful in getting the backs on the move goal-wards.'[19]

A second match was played between the teams two days later, a holiday Monday. Again the League enjoyed a huge crowd, a further 33,000. The result was the same on the field as well, with NSW winning 27–20. The Englishmen again struggled — two converted tries late in the contest brought the scores closer together but questions were starting to be asked about the visitors' ability. *The Referee* offered: 'It is to be hoped they will improve, and perform in keeping with what English experts pronounced them to be, viz., The Cream of English Northern Union football.'[20]

After finally coming to terms with the hard and fast surface of the Agricultural Ground, and gaining improved fitness, the Englishmen swept aside NSW 23–10 with another 30,000 spectators in attendance at the third match. *The Sydney Sportsman* declared: 'Among the visitors, Lomas stood alone, and in the game quite played up to his reputation.'[21]

The League was buoyant at the gate-takings — almost 100,000 patrons had witnessed the three opening games of the tour. On the adjacent SCG, a NSW v New Zealand rugby union match passed with little attention. From the 52,000 that attended in 1907, the same contest drew 16,000 in competition with the League.

THE BUSTLING TACTICS OF THE BRAWNY ENGLISH

The following Saturday saw the first Test between the League teams. Against it was scheduled a NSW v Maoris rugby union game. The gap in public support widened even further when the Test was '...played before the largest assemblage which has gathered at a rugby league match in any part of the world — 39,000 people.' Barely 10,000 went to the rugby union international.[22]

'The League officials never anticipated such a huge crowd, attractive and all as the programme was,' reported *The Referee*. 'The takings amounted to over £1,700, so the success of the tour is financially assured.' *The Sydney Sportsman,* apt to overestimate the League's success, claimed the crowd topped 40,000. Combined with the NSW matches, the Englishmen's share of the profits now exceeded the £3,000 guarantee given by the NSWRL.[23]

Despite Dally Messenger kicking five goals and scoring a try, the English defeated Australia. The home team (wearing blue and maroon jerseys) led 12–11 at half-time in a contest where 'the pace had been a

Albert 'Opai' Asher (Australasia) attempts to fend away England's Billy Batten. The two wingers had a 'butting bout' at every opportunity when they opposed each other. Both were also adept at hurdling over tacklers.

cracker.' However, the Australian team fielded a lighter 'six-pack' than the tourists and 'the bustling tactics of the brawny English pack had a telling effect.' In the second half 'the game was now too fast for the local men, whose stamina was clearly inferior to that of the Englishmen.' With charges down the field by Billy Batten and James Lomas, backed up their forwards no less, England scored sixteen points without reply from Australia.

The 'Blue and Maroons' scored late tries to close the gap, but were eventually defeated 27–20. The last Australian try came with barely seconds left in the game. Messenger had an easy kick from in front of the posts to bring the home team within five points of the English. However, according to *The Referee*, with time effectively over, Messenger short-kicked the conversion, 'his mind being on securing the ball as a momento of the match.'[24]

The newspaper had now changed its opinion of the visitors: 'Having seen every English team play in this country (since 1888), one is certain that a stouter-hearted set has never invaded Australia than those in the present combination. They are men of the bulldog breed.'[25]

After just two weeks of matches in Sydney, the visit of the English team was already a resounding success for the League. The NU and NSWRL's primary purpose for the tour had been to give the Unions a blow from which they could not recover. They were well on their way to achieving that objective.

However, 'the most important match of the rugby league season,' according to its title, England v Australasia' at the Agricultural Ground was still yet to come.[26] The Sydney public would have to wait a further three weeks for that much awaited contest, while the Englishmen visited Newcastle and Brisbane.

Supporters of the League in those cities hoped the visit of the England team would achieve the success it had in Sydney. In Auckland too, anticipation began to rise. Already there were indications a very big crowd, well over 15,000, would attend the Test match against New Zealand near the end of the tour.[27]

AUCKLAND R.U. AWARE OF THE APPROACHING EVIL

It was a difficult battle for rugby league to establish itself in New Zealand. 'In Auckland there is no disguising the fact that the NU game is gradually getting a foothold, and if their rules were modified to allow a 5 or 10 yards throw-in, rugby union as played presently, from a spectator point of view, would have to take a back seat,' offered *The Auckland Star* newspaper. 'The Auckland officials are well aware of the approaching evil, and it is to combat it that they are so anxious to brighten up the rugby game.'[28]

Auckland was '…practically the only place in the Dominion in which it has a footing at present. The NU competition has six teams engaged and amongst the players are S. Riley, W. Tyler, Dunning, Doran, Asher, Harrison, Mackrell and Long, all of whom have been Auckland rugby union reps at one time or another. During the past season or two the cream of Auckland's rugby talent — and the Dominion's for that matter — has, unfortunately for the amateur game, gone over to the rival code.' The effect of this, along with the Ponsonby club's domination, saw a collapse of the Auckland Rugby Union's district club scheme.[29]

Unfortunately for the NU enthusiasts in Auckland, they could not capitalise on the problems faced by the local rugby union administrators. Many of the footballers seeking to play NU bypassed the rugby league competition in Auckland and went to England or Sydney.

The North Sydney club seemed to have a never-ending stream of New Zealanders crossing the Tasman hoping to play in the NSWRL premiership. The two most notable additions were Con Sullivan and T. Houghton, both members of the New Zealand Test team in 1909 (the latter did not play for Norths, becoming involved as an official).

T. Houghton's brother, Samuel, was secretary of the Auckland Rugby League (ARL). He appears to have been unable to stop the departure of New Zealand players in any way at all. Many players (of both codes) accepted offers directly from NU clubs, on the advice of fellow New Zealanders already playing in England. Others simply tried their luck, arriving with a 'letter of introduction' from a colleague. Charles Grey (to St Helens) and Charlie Seeling (to Wigan) both joined NU clubs by this method.[30]

The recently formed Council for the NZRL, also based in Auckland, eventually managed to gain a concession from the NU that would only allow players to join English clubs with the approval of their New Zealand rugby league club.[31] Of course, this did nothing to prevent New Zealand rugby union players joining NU clubs instead of a local rugby league club.

Plans were put in place for an Auckland team to make a nine-match tour of the North and South Islands in September. Newspaper advertisements were placed during the lead up to attract players to oppose Auckland. This tactic was also used across the Dominion as preparations were being made for the visit of the English team: 'Players who are anxious for representation against the proposed touring NU team are requested to lose no time in nominating, so that the team can be selected in time for coaching.'[32]

316

Aware of the transformations occurring in Sydney football, some amongst the New Zealand rugby union community feared a sudden change could take hold in the Dominion just as easily. When the Canterbury Rugby Union president exhorted New Zealanders to support their counterparts in Sydney to keep the amateur game pure, *The Referee's* New Zealand correspondent suggested they never mind Australia, but look at the whole of the North Island of New Zealand.[33]

Meanwhile in Brisbane the QRU was in rapid decline, as interest in watching the state team dropped away. The QRU started the 1910 season with just £4/7/- in the bank (down from £92 the previous year), forcing it to advise the NSWRU that it could not afford to host any matches against the visiting New Zealand amateur All Blacks. Not that there was much money to made from hosting state and international matches in Brisbane, but the Queensland Rugby League did well enough from the 1909 visits (New Zealand Test and Maoris teams) to start 1910 with £70 in credit.[34]

New Zealand's Albert 'Opai' Asher played for the Australasian rugby league team in matches against the touring England team in 1910.

When the English NU team arrived in Brisbane, sporting interest was focused upon rugby league. After a crowd of 8,000 attended the first Queensland v England match (won by the visitors 33–9 at the Exhibition Ground on June 25), the QRU recognised that all attention the following Saturday would be centred upon the Test match and immediately cancelled the Final of the Hospital Cup until a week later to avoid the clash.[35]

THE KANGAROOS BENEFIT MATCH

'When it became known on Friday morning that Monday (June 27) was to be a public holiday, the NSWRL communicated with the Englishmen in Brisbane by telegraph. It was suggested that a party of the visitors should return to Sydney and play the Kangaroos. With prospects of a big gate, the English managers agreed,' reported *The Referee*. By first train on the Saturday night a 'strong team' was despatched to Sydney, arriving on Monday morning. After having played on the Saturday afternoon against Queensland, and then travelled (over 700 miles) direct to Sydney 'the Englishmen were courting defeat.'[36]

The match was arranged as a benefit game for (some of) the Kangaroos who had played against the Wallabies at the end of the 1909 season. It was also a necessary counter attraction to the second rugby union Test between Australia and New Zealand, which had also been hastily arranged for the Prince of Wales Birthday holiday. The first Test, played just two days earlier, attracted a healthy crowd of 30,000 to the SCG (though significantly lower than the comparable match in 1907).

On a fine and bright afternoon, the Kangaroos v England match drew 28,000 to the Agricultural Ground, while the rugby union Test could muster only 8,000. *The Referee* attributed the enormous drop in attendance to the quality of the football exhibited in the opening rugby union Test which 'was not an entrancing display from the point of view of the man who pays his shilling to witness passing bouts ad lib.'[37]

In the League contest the English team held a half-time lead. However, as expected after such a long rail journey, they faded in a 22–10 loss to the home team. The Kangaroo players who took part each received a payment of £15 — not bad for an afternoon's play, but hardly comparable to what the Wallaby players received. The other Kangaroos received nothing.[38]

Meanwhile the English players, after earning another £500 towards the tour profits, were back on the train for Brisbane an hour after the match. Five of them would be needed to play on Wednesday afternoon in the second match against Queensland.

BRISBANE'S GROUND PACKED TO OVERFLOWING

In Brisbane, match reports describe some of the Englishmen still lethargic after the journey to Sydney and back, but the team was still too strong for the Maroons.[39] The English scored five unconverted tries to defeat Queensland 15–4.

The Australian team for the second Test included seven Queenslanders, with Bundaberg's Bill Heidke appointed captain. Again at the Exhibition Ground, the expected large crowd flocked to the match. On an unseasonably warm day, the attendance reached 18,000, which was a record for a football match of any code in Brisbane. 'Both grandstands were packed to overflowing, and the crowd round the ring and on the hill was very densely packed,' reported *The Referee*.[40]

Australia, wearing maroon and blue in Brisbane for the first time, raced out to an 11–0 lead inside the first twenty minutes with tries to Barnett, Messenger and McKivat. Lomas then ignited the visitors as they responded with two converted tries, finishing the half just one point behind. The Lions continued on their way in the second half, at one point extending their lead to 22–11. Australia scored two late consolation tries but the game, and the rubber, belonged to England (winning 22–17).

The Englishmen's week-long visit to Brisbane greatly boosted the Queensland Rugby League, with around 30,000 watching the three games. The gross proceeds amounted to £391, which left the QRL in a very healthy position on which to build. Its first action was to complete arrangements for a tour of the NSW 'Blues' to Brisbane in early August, with three matches against Queensland.[41]

At the same time the League Test was being played in Brisbane, the third and deciding rugby union Test was being held in Sydney. The NSWRU was again hit with a poor attendance and, most dishearteningly, with no League contest up against it. *The Referee* wrote that, 'Football interest was expected to concentrate on this, in a sense, unique rugby contest. The NSWRU officials anticipated a record attendance for this reason, but they were disappointed, only 15,000 assembling. The Union has undertaken so many liabilities in connection with visiting teams that a large attendance at this, the greatest event of the year, was essential in order these diverse undertakings should not entail financial embarrassment or, at the very least, unduly press upon its resources.'[42]

On and off the field, the NSWRU had banked on the deciding Test match being a success. The Australian team was thrashed 28–13 in an eight-try rout by the All Blacks. The poor gate-takings left the Union unable to compete financially with the NSWRL.

THE MEETING OF THE GIANTS

'Fresh from their second victory over Australia, the Englishmen arrived in Sydney from Brisbane on Monday morning,' reported *The Referee*. 'The manager reports all hands well, and are pleased with their short sojourn in the northern capital. The whole party is looking forward to the match of the tour against Australasia next Saturday at the Agricultural Ground. A stirring struggle should be witnessed and the biggest crowd of the season should be the outcome.'[43]

The Herald described the upcoming match as 'the northern against southern hemisphere at Rugby League football'; the combination of representative footballers from New South Wales, Queensland and New Zealand into an Australasian side, opposed against those from England and Wales. The bringing together of representatives from the former colonies as 'Australasia' occurred in the 1908 Olympic Games

Former Wallaby Chris McKivat on the attack for Australasia [rugby league] in 1910 against the visiting English 'Northern Union' team.

and was used in tennis for the Davis Cup. 'This is the first time the representation has been as wide in football,' wrote *The Herald*.[44]

The public had wanted such a contest back in 1899 when the Reverend Mullineux's British team had visited — but it failed to eventuate due to the dispute between the NSWRU and NZRU. As far as everyone was concerned, this was the premier contest of the tour. That the bulk of the players came from NSW didn't seem to matter. As in all representative matches, the home state provided most of the players. The popular New Zealand Maoris, 'Opai' Asher and Riki Papakura, made yet another visit to Sydney to take part. Also included was dual New Zealand and Australian Test player Con Sullivan. Queensland's sole representative was former Easts player Herb Brackenreg.

Australasia (blue, maroon and black hoops): R. Papakura (NZ), A. Asher (NZ), H. Messenger (NSW), V. Farnsworth (NSW), A. Broomham (NSW), W. Farnsworth (NSW), C. McKivat (NSW), E. Courtney (NSW), S. Pearce (NSW), R. Craig (NSW), H. Brackenreg (Qld), W. Cann (NSW), C. Sullivan (NSW).

England (red and white hoops): J. Sharrock, W. Batten, B. Jenkins, J. Leytham, J. Thomas, T. Newbould, A. Avery, W. Jukes, R. Ramsdale, H. Kershaw, F. Webster, W. Winstanley, J. Lomas.

The NSWRL expected the public interest to rival the 39,000 that attended the recent Test match against England. They underestimated.

'For hours before the "meeting of the giants" just one continuing stream of people flowed through the clinking turnstiles,' reported *The Sydney Sportsman*, 'and the silver pattered into the League moneyboxes. The faces of the secretary Larkin and the League officials fairly beamed with joy and gratification. The barrackers for the new game were jubilant, and took every opportunity of drawing the attention of all Union barrackers they happened to tumble across to the magnificent turn-up. It was like rubbing it in, but seemingly they were unable to resist the opportunity.'[45]

On a perfectly fine winter's afternoon, the attendance reached over 42,000. (£18,000 taken at the gate). *The Herald* noted the crowd was the largest seen at a football match since the visit of the New Zealand amateur team in 1907. The newspaper added that had the match been held in the comfort of the SCG, it is likely the 52,000 record set during 1907 would have been broken.[46]

With crowds at the Union representative matches rapidly falling away, the League could now say that it had usurped the Union as the city's preferred rugby code — barely three years after coming into existence.

The English team, travelling by a horse-drawn drag, reached the edge of Moore Park where they were welcomed by a hundred 'blue-jackets' from visiting British naval ships in port at the time. The sailors removed the harnesses from the horses, tied ropes to the drag, and pulled the team towards the ground's entrance.

A [brass] band (which the League ensured was present for all big matches) were cajoled into leading an impromptu parade. With the band playing a marching tune in front, the sailors swung out onto the race track around the perimeter of the ground, pulling the English team behind them 'amidst tremendous cheering and shouts of applause — it was an inspiring spectacle.' With no place left in the ground to accommodate them, the 'blue-jackets' sat on the track in front of the eastern stand.[47]

The match was described by *The Herald* as 'a great one.' The highlights were some spectacular runs by Messenger, and 'a terrific butting bout' between opposing wingers, 'Opai' Asher and Billy Batten, as each tried to leap over the other at every opportunity. England staged a dramatic comeback from 13–5 down, to snare a 13–all draw with a late converted try. As soon as the referee called full-time, the British sailors rushed the ground and hoisted Lomas on their shoulders, carrying him to the dressing rooms in the Suttor Pavilion.[48]

British 'Bluejackets' [sailors] dragging the English team into the Agricultural Ground for their rugby league match against Australasia.

ALL WERE IN A FEARFUL GOOD HUMOUR

After the Australasia v England match, the League hosted a banquet for the two teams, officials, guests and 'the press' at Sargent's Café in Market Street. *The Sydney Sportsman* noted 'all were in a fearful good humour, and made the chicken, roast duck, and lager fly away in a phenomenal fashion — it was very festive.'

Apart from music provided by a band, the evening also included numerous thank you speeches from the representatives of the four Leagues involved.

They all reflected upon the success of the day and the position of strength that rugby league now enjoyed. Joynton-Smith said the League was proud that its men were receiving allowances for their expenses out in the open, 'whereas the others took it under the table.' He then lauded the efforts of the Australasian team and 'finally sat down with a beaming smile' amidst much applause.

Lomas and the two English team managers also made speeches. John Clifford said, 'The general public has shown its unmistakable preference to the League game by rolling up to the game in such great numbers.' He also praised the efforts of the local team saying, 'Jack is now as good as his master.'[49]

His comment was a good summation of the League's position. On the field, the players had demonstrated they were the equals of the highly rated exponents from England and Wales. Off the field, the men were now openly receiving money for their efforts. On both counts, the standing of the working-class footballers was now where they had wanted it to be. In terms of their football lives, they were their own masters.

SENTIMENT WILL NOT PAY THE UNION'S EXPENSES

In the wake of the Australasian match, the press and supporters of the Unions reflected upon the future of the amateur game. Idle threats made when the League first appeared, that the Unions would rather play to empty stands than jeopardise their amateur status, now had more than a sense of reality to them. *The Referee* wrote that,

> The rugby union game is not regaining its popularity. Matches which formerly attracted from 13,000 to 25,000 people now coax from 1,000 to 2,500. The empty benches are not minimising the keenness of players, but the sight of them is not elevating rugby unionists.
>
> Football enthusiasm in Sydney is as keen as it ever was, but the schism has hit the old game desperately hard. Some of the controllers of rugby union football may not yet be able to thoroughly realise this. Nevertheless, they

are now facing a problem which time may swell from a small hill to a towering mountain.

The favour with which the NU game has been received by the public has provided the League with the sinews of war and, in turn, the sinews of war are keeping the pulse of play going serenely by the swill of the fresh talent, as rugby union develops it.

The future of the rugby game in this country may be brilliant, or it may be checkered. It will, I believe, depend very largely on the moral fibre of the NSWRL controllers. Thus far in many matters they lose nothing in a comparison with the organisers of the Union, and in some have been more progressive. They are handling a game better suited to the Australian sporting mind than the old game, and also more thoroughly provided for in its controlling side on the field of play [by easier playing rules to interpret and apply].

There are features in this NU game and its control, for which the heart of the Australian who plays and the Australian who looks on has cried [after] for years. Tradition, associations, and other sentimental influences cry out to remain firm in the allegiance to the old rugby union game as England, Ireland, Scotland and Wales dispenses it and as we knew it in the days of rugby's past. The sentiment is good, but sentiment will not pay the Unions' expenses.

The Referee then commented about further proposals being brought before the MRU and NSWRU to bring their playing rules more closely in line with those of the NU.

If the Unions of NSW be not prepared to move in accordance with public opinion, which, in this case, is merely that held for many years, they must be prepared to sink back into minor bodies, healthy enough in their way, but exercising little sway. Even now, if the Unions do make the changes in the laws, there is no certainty that the position will be regained early, for at present the League has secured many of players who are best known, and whose abilities command the support of the crowd, as well as practically all the grounds it needs. But to this one may say, it is never too late to mend.[50]

I RECENTLY STOOD AT A STREET CORNER

By mid-August Lewis Abrams decided he had could wait no longer for the Unions to ensure rugby union maintained some semblance of popularity and importance in Sydney. He called a meeting at the A.B.C. Café to form an action group to overthrow the MRU. Approximately fifty men turned up, including a number of senior officials, most notably Monty Arnold.

'The object in calling this meeting,' Abrams told the gathering, 'is to get an expression of opinion as to whether it would be wise for the Rugby Union [the MRU and NSWRU] to alter its method of playing the game.'

> I have proposed almost similar motions at the MRU, but the delegates of that body thought differently to me and the proposals were defeated. I decided to call a meeting of footballers, with a view to getting some alteration made.

> The difficulty is that the NSWRU is too conservative and will not hear of any innovation. Many years ago there was only one Union, but now there are two bodies — the MRU and the NSWRU. I have always held that this was a mistake, and the MRU [i.e., Sydney clubs] should carry on the game in this state.

Dally Messenger in action for Australasia at the Agricultural Ground

> If we want to keep the game alive we must alter the rules. I recently stood at a street corner and asked twenty passers-by which game they preferred, the Rugby Union or the Northern Union. Fifteen out of the twenty stated that they were in favour of the latter.

> There are certain parts of the game that want altering to suit Australian conditions. Queensland has already launched out on their own account and introduced new rules — and New Zealand is contemplating following suit. Amateur clubs cannot carry on without money, and the recent international matches have shown which game the public prefer [to pay for]. If the players do not have the crowds watching them they will not go into the game with the same enthusiasm.

Abrams then proposed,

> That, in the opinion of this meeting of rugby footballers and supporters, it is imperative that in order to retain the interest of the players and the public of the state and competition matches, the MRU should play the game next season with such improvements to the rules as are necessary and suitable

for the condition of Australian and New Zealand players and public, and control the game on an amateur basis in NSW.[51]

In supporting Abrams' proposal, Mr Burleigh 'stated that alterations had for some time been suggested by the MRU, but they had been overruled by the NSWRU. The constitution of the two Unions was wrong as the majority of the members of the head body [NSWRU] were representatives of country Unions.'

Monty Arnold took a position that neither supported or condemned Abrams. 'Although the League game is the more attractive to the spectators,' he said, 'the rugby union game is the more attractive to the players. I suggest that the meeting approach the NSWRU.'

A vote was taken and Abrams' proposal was adopted unanimously. Also adopted was a proposal calling for an increase in the NSW players' daily allowance to 10s per day. It was agreed that all the footballers present would return to their clubs and hold meetings to elect representatives on the MRU committee who would vote to make the necessary changes.[52]

The following Saturday produced a further decline in the crowds at rugby union club matches. *The Referee* suggested the Unions' biggest problem was not a matter of keeping star players, but rather the public preference's for the League game itself: 'The emptiness of the SCG last week was a striking contrast to the appearance at the Agricultural Ground where nearly 12,000 people assembled to see the rugby league match (Newtown v Souths). It is a rare change for the rugby union players accustomed in former years to many thousands of spectators. The change is all the more striking in view of the rugby league clubs in several cases being comprised of inferior players. This should set the rugby union fathers thinking.'[53]

ITS PERMANENCY IS ASSURED

Within weeks Abrams and his supporters received their final answer. The Unions rejected making changes to the playing rules or improving the player allowances. The NSWRU reasoned that to play a game the same or similar to NU rules would only serve to send the Unions broke. There was no point in the Unions wasting their already rapidly dwindling financial reserves in trying to be a semi-professional version of the League.

From where the Unions stood, they felt that the League could not take any more players. Those who wanted to play by those principles could go there if they wished. 'The League has secured some very able players from the Union this year,' wrote *The Referee*, 'but as each League club is able to put only 13 men into each match, the recruiting for at least some of the clubs cannot continue as active in the near future as it has been within the last two years.'[54]

With the money seekers having all left for the League, and the Unions' financial reserves gone, the amateur ideal was all that was left as a motivating force. The means to secure a future for rugby union in Australia was to fully embrace amateurism — appeal to a group of footballers, officials, and supporters who were not tempted by the money nor a version of rugby modified for the thrill of the crowd. Those who remained with rugby union would play as pure amateurs — no tricks, no under-the-lap payments, just for the love of the game.

The Unions banned professionals — no matter which sport — from playing rugby union. *The Referee* reported, 'This was done to ensure the principles of amateurism are applied and bring the game into line with the views of the bulk of the players and the game's supporters.'[55]

'The stringent amateurism to be recognised will tend to safeguard the playing strength of the Union from the recruiting inroads of the League clubs,' offered *The Referee's* rugby union correspondent. 'Players who take up rugby union will belong to a class who are amateurs at heart and in principle and are less likely to listen to the golden voice of the tempter.'[56]

The declaration would take rugby union in Australia to a level of pure amateurism it had never been to before (except perhaps in the 1870s). It would become as pure as the Irish and Scottish Unions had demanded. Yet it had come at a price. Australian rugby union was now cleansed of the 'evil of professionalism,' but it had lost the bulk of its players and supporters in the process.

As for rugby league in Australia and New Zealand, they were now confident that they were here to stay.

'Some thought,' observed *The Referee*, 'that with the departure of the British players attendances at League games would dwindle, and that the supporters of the opposition body who had just come over to see what the NU game was all like, would return to their first love, but such has not been the case. The turn of the tide in favour of the 13–a-side game has been so pronounced that its permanency is assured. Clean government is all that is now required to further increase the popularity of the game.'[57]

Asked for his thoughts on the Unions, Joynton-Smith replied: 'The League's position is now so strong that we do not want to say anything of the other fellow.'[58]

'We will simply go along quietly and mind our own business.'

AUTHOR'S NOTE AND ACKNOWLEDGEMENTS

The journey that led to the writing of The Rugby Rebellion began with a meeting I had with Len Smith in 1998. Len had the hard luck to twice be denied a footballing tour of Britain. In 1939 he arrived in England with the Wallabies, only to find WW2 had been declared. In 1948, he was captain-coach of the Australian rugby league team in home Tests against the Kiwis. In what remains a mystery to this day, the national selectors then chose to leave him out of the Kangaroos squad for England. I was embarrassed that, as a former Union player and a fan of League, I had never heard these stories and decided to do something about it. This led to the creation of RL1908.com and my career as a sports writer and historian. The more I looked at the early history of both rugby codes in Australia, the more I felt the real story had never been told, and certainly not in any great detail. In February 2004, I began an exhaustive study of old newspapers, books, and the archives of the NSWRL and ARU. The result, some 14 months later, was The Rugby Rebellion.

I would like to thank the following — without them there may have been no book, or its scope may not have been so complete.

My family — Luanne, Annelise and Matthew, for their unwavering support and encouragement. Michael O'Malley for providing me with the means and opportunity. Helen Elward (Best Legenz) for bringing the end product into reality. Kim Dixon for editing the text and restoring photographs. Ian Heads for his guidance, direction and encouragement. Pat Walsh (grandson of 'Nimmo') for providing family anecdotes, photographs, and additional newspaper clippings. Tony Collins, for uncovering information from sources in England, and for answering my questions about the Northern Union and early rugby. Geoff Armstrong for assistance in regard to the early history of Australian cricket. David Thomas for reviewing and interpreting the 'All Golds' agreement. Also thanks to Judy Macarthur (ARU Archivist), Terry Williams (NSWRL), Bob Luxford (NZ Rugby Museum), and David Middleton. And thanks to the newspaper writers and publishers of a century ago.

Sean Fagan
Winter, 2005

Photograph credits (page numbers in brackets):
The family of Pat Walsh (80, 97); New Zealand Rugby League Ltd (184); Auckland Rugby Football Union [digital archive developed by Online Business Management Ltd www.obm.co.nz] (92, 94, 112, 154); Australian Rugby Union Archives (52, 132); New South Wales Rugby League (176); Peter Sharpham (134, 286); Ian Heads (front cover [action], rear cover [Broomham], 137, 140, 146, 196, 226, 230); The National Museum of Australia / George Serras (front.rear cover [background], 298). All other photographs are from the author's collection.

For more information on The Rugby Rebellion visit:
www.RugbyRebellion.com

To read other work by Sean Fagan visit:
www.RL1908.com

MATCH RESULTS AND PLAYER REGISTERS

RESULTS OF TEST MATCHES 1899–1910
Test Matches: 1899–1907

Date	Played at	Result	Opponent	Points	Crowd
24.6.1899	Sydney	won	Great Britain	13 to 3	28,000
22.7.1899	Brisbane	lost	Great Britain	11 to 0	15,000
5.8.1899	Sydney	lost	Great Britain	11 to 10	16,000
12.8.1899	Sydney	lost	Great Britain	13 to 0	7,000
15.8.1903	Sydney	lost	New Zealand	22 to 3	30,000
2.7.1904	Sydney	lost	Great Britain	17 to 0	34,000
23.7.1904	Brisbane	lost	Great Britain	17 to 3	15,000
30.7.1904	Sydney	lost	Great Britain	16 to 0	24,000
2.9.1905	Dunedin	lost	New Zealand	14 to 3	3,000
20.7.1907	Sydney	lost	New Zealand	26 to 6	48,677
3.8.1907	Brisbane	lost	New Zealand	14 to 5	17,000
10.8.1907	Sydney	drawn	New Zealand	5 to 5	29,000

Test Matches — Rugby Union: 1908–1910

Date	Played at	Result	Opponent	Points	Crowd
12.12.1908	Cardiff	lost	Wales	9 to 6	30,000
9.1.1909	Blackheath	won	England	9 to 3	18,000
25.6.1910	Sydney	lost	New Zealand	6 to 0	30,000
27.6.1910	Sydney	won	New Zealand	11 to 0	8,000
2.7.1910	Sydney	lost	New Zealand	28 to 13	18,000

Test Matches — Rugby League: 1908–1910

Date	Played at	Result	Opponent	Points	Crowd
9.5.1908	Sydney	lost	New Zealand	11 to 10	20,000
30.5.1908	Brisbane	lost	New Zealand	24 to 12	6,000
6.6.1908	Sydney	won	New Zealand	14 to 9	13,000
12.12.1908	London	drawn	England	22 to 22	2,000
23.1.1909	Newcastle	lost	England	15 to 5	22,000
15.2.1909	Birmingham	lost	England	6 to 5	9,000
12.6.1909	Sydney	lost	New Zealand	19 to 11	6,000
26.6.1909	Brisbane	won	New Zealand	10 to 5	6,000
3.7.1909	Sydney	won	New Zealand	25 to 5	6,000
18.6.1910	Sydney	lost	England	27 to 20	39,000
2.7.1910	Brisbane	lost	England	22 to 17	18,000

RESULTS OF RUGBY LEAGUE REPRESENTATIVE MATCHES 1907–1910

Date	Result	Played at
17.8.1907	New Zealand 12 d. N.S. Wales 8	Agra' Grd Syd.*
21.8.1907	New Zealand 19 d. N.S. Wales 5	Agra' Grd Syd.*
24.8.1907	New Zealand 5 d. N.S. Wales 3	Agra' Grd Syd.*
22.4.1908	New Zealand 53 d. Newcastle 6	Newc. Show Grd*
25.4.1908	New Zealand 37 d. Newcastle 8	Newc. Show Grd
2.5.1908	N.S.Wales 18 d. New Zealand 10	Agra' Grd Syd.
6.5.1908	N.S.Wales 13 d. New Zealand 10	Agra' Grd Syd.
9.5.1908	New Zealand 11 d. Australia 10	Agra' Grd Syd.
16.5.1908	New Zealand 34 d. Queensland 12	Exhib. Grd Brisb.
20.5.1908	New Zealand 43 d. Metropolitan 10	Exhib. Grd Brisb.
23.5.1908	Queensland & New Zealand 12-all	Exhib. Grd Brisb.
30.5.1908	New Zealand 24 d. Australia 12	Exhib. Grd Brisb.
6.6.1908	Australia 14 d. New Zealand 9	Agra' Grd Syd.
8.6.1908	N.S.Wales 18 d. Maoris 9	Agra' Grd Syd.
13.6.1908	N.S.Wales 30 d. Maoris 16	Agra' Grd Syd.
17.6.1908	Maoris 23 d. Metropolitan 20	Wentworth Pk Syd.
20.6.1908	Maoris 15 d. Newcastle 2	Newc. Show Grd
27.6.1908	Maoris 19 d. Queensland 16	Exhib. Grd Brisb.
1.7.1908	Maoris 13 d. Queensland 5	Exhib. Grd Brisb.
4.7.1908	Queensland 6 d. Maoris 5	Exhib. Grd Brisb.
7.7.1908	Queensland 11 d. Maoris 9	R.A.S. Grd Toowoomba
8.7.1908	Queensland 23 d. Maoris 14	Queens Pk Warwick
11.7.1908	Maoris 30 d. Newcastle 16	West Maitland
11.7.1908	N.S. Wales 43 d. Queensland 0	Agra' Grd Syd.
15.7.1908	Metropolitan 37 d. Queensland 8	Agra' Grd Syd.
18.7.1908	N.S. Wales 12 d. Queensland 3	Agra' Grd Syd.
18.7.1908	Australia 20 d. Maoris 10	Agra' Grd Syd.
22.7.1908	Maoris 34 d. Metropolitan 13	Birchgrove Pk Syd.
5.5.1909	Kangaroos 34 d. N.S. Wales 8	Agra' Grd Syd.
8.5.1909	Kangaroos 43 d. N.S. Wales 10	Agra' Grd Syd.
5.6.1909	N.S. Wales 26 d. New Zealand 21	Agra' Grd Syd.
7.6.1909	N.S. Wales 27 d. New Zealand 20	Agra' Grd Syd.
9.6.1909	Metropolitan 27 d. New Zealand 18	Birchgrove Pk Syd.
12.6.1909	New Zealand 19 d. Australia 11	Agra' Grd Syd.

16.6.1909	New Zealand 6 d. Newcastle 3	Newc. Show Grd
19.6.1909	New Zealand 40 d. Queensland 25	'Gabba Brisb.
23.6.1909	New Zealand 27 d. Queensland 19	'Gabba Brisb.
26.6.1909	Australia 10 d. New Zealand 5	'Gabba Brisb.
30.6.1909	New Zealand 20 d. N.S.Wales 8	Wentworth Pk Syd.
3.7.1909	Australia 25 d. New Zealand 5	Wentworth Pk Syd.
24.7.1909	Maoris 24 d. N.S. Wales 21	Agra' Grd Syd.
28.7.1909	Maoris 14 d. N.S. Wales 11	Agra' Grd Syd.
31.7.1909	Maoris 16 d. Australia 14	Agra' Grd Syd.
4.8.1909	Newcastle 7 d. Maoris 6	Newc. Show Grd
7.8.1909	Queensland 21 d. Maoris 11	'Gabba Brisb.
11.8.1909	Maoris 36 d. Queensland 25	'Gabba Brisb.
14.8.1909	Australia 16 d. Maoris 13	'Gabba Brisb.
21.8.1909	Australia 23 d. Maoris 16	Agra' Grd Syd.
25.8.1909	Maoris 12 d. N.S. Wales 8	Wentworth Pk Syd.
28.8.1909	Australia 20 d. Maoris 13	Agra' Grd Syd.
4.9.1909	Kangaroos 29 d. Wallabies 26	Agra' Grd Syd.
8.9.1909	Wallabies 34 d. Kangaroos 21	Agra' Grd Syd.
11.9.1909	Wallabies 15 d. Kangaroos 6	Agra' Grd Syd.
18.9.1909	Kangaroos 8 d. Wallabies 6	Agra' Grd Syd.
4.6.1910	N.S. Wales 28 d. England 14	Agra' Grd Syd.
6.6.1910	N.S. Wales 27 d. England 20	Agra' Grd Syd.
11.6.1910	England 23 d. N.S. Wales 10	Agra' Grd Syd.
15.6.1910	England 34 d. Metropolitan 25	Agra' Grd Syd.
18.6.1910	England 24 d. Northern Districts 8	Hamilton
18.6.1910	England 27 d. Australia 20	Agra' Grd Syd.
22.6.1910	England 40 d. Newcastle 20	Newcastle
25.6.1910	England 33 d. Queensland 9	Exhib. Grd Brisb.
27.6.1910	Kangaroos 22 d. England 10	Agra' Grd Syd.
29.6.1910	England 15 d. Queensland 4	Exhib. Grd Brisb.
2.7.1910	England 22 d. Australia 17	Exhib. Grd Brisb.
9.7.1910	Australasia & England 13-all	Agra' Grd Syd.
13.7.1910	Australasia 32 d. England 15	Wentworth Pk Syd.
20.7.1910	England 29 d. Maoris 0	Victoria Pk Auck.
23.7.1910	England 52 d. Auckland 9	Victoria Pk Auck.
27.7.1910	England 54 d. Rotorua 18	Rotorua
27.7.1910	N.S. Wales 37 d. Newcastle 5	Newcastle

30.7.1910	England 52 d. New Zealand 20	Domain, Wellington
30.7.1910	N.S. Wales 40 d. Queensland 21	'Gabba Brisb.
3.8.1910	N.S. Wales 32 d. Queensland 18	'Gabba Brisb.
6.8.1910	N.S. Wales 19 d. Queensland 3	'Gabba Brisb.
6.8.1910	England 50 d. N.S. Wales 12	Agra' Grd Syd.

* played under rugby union rules

INTER-COLONIAL MATCHES V NEW ZEALAND: 1882–1907

Year	Venue	Won By	Against	Points
1884	Sydney	New Zealand	N.S. Wales	11 to 0
1884	Sydney	New Zealand	N.S. Wales	21 to 2
1884	Sydney	New Zealand	N.S. Wales	16 to 0
1893	Sydney	New Zealand	N.S. Wales	17 to 8
1893	Sydney	N.S. Wales	New Zealand	25 to 3
1893	Brisbane	New Zealand	Queensland	14 to 3
1893	Brisbane	New Zealand	Queensland	36 to 0
1893	Sydney	New Zealand	N.S. Wales	16 to 0
1894	Christchurch	N.S. Wales	New Zealand	8 to 6
1896	Wellington	New Zealand	Queensland	9 to 0
1897	Sydney	New Zealand	N.S. Wales	13 to 8
1897	Sydney	N.S. Wales	New Zealand	22 to 8
1897	Brisbane	New Zealand	Queensland	16 to 5
1897	Brisbane	New Zealand	Queensland	24 to 6
1897	Sydney	New Zealand	N.S. Wales	26 to 3
1901	Wellington	New Zealand	N.S. Wales	20 to 3
1903	Sydney	New Zealand	N.S. Wales	12 to 0
1903	Sydney	New Zealand	N.S. Wales	3 to 0
1903	Brisbane	New Zealand	Queensland	17 to 0
1903	Brisbane	New Zealand	Queensland	28 to 0
1905	Sydney	New Zealand	N.S. Wales	19 to 0
1905	Sydney	Draw	N.S. Wales	8 to 8
1907	Sydney	New Zealand	N.S. Wales	11 to 3
1907	Sydney	N.S. Wales	New Zealand	14 to 0
1907	Brisbane	New Zealand	Queensland	23 to 3
1907	Brisbane	New Zealand	Queensland	17 to 11

N.S.WALES v QUEENSLAND MATCHES: 1882–1907

| Overall: | NSW 48 | QLD 21 | Drawn 3 |
| Series: | NSW 14 | QLD 3 | Drawn 9 |

Year	Venue	Won By	Points
1882	Sydney	N.S. Wales	28 to 4
1882	Sydney	N.S. Wales	18 to 0
1883	Brisbane	Queensland	12 to 11
1883	Brisbane	N.S. Wales	13 to 0
1884	Sydney	N.S. Wales	17 to 4
1884	Sydney	N.S. Wales	26 to 0
1885	Brisbane	Queensland	14 to 0
1885	Brisbane	N.S. Wales	12 to 2
1886	Sydney	Queensland	4 to 2
1886	Sydney	N.S. Wales	25 to 4
1887	Brisbane	Queensland	9 to 8
1887	Brisbane	N.S. Wales	4 to 0
1888	Sydney	N.S. Wales	15 to 13
1888	Sydney	N.S. Wales	9 to 2
1889	Brisbane	N.S. Wales	19 to 12
1889	Brisbane	N.S. Wales	13 to 10
1890	Sydney	N.S. Wales	15 to 3
1890	Sydney	Drawn	Nil
1891	Brisbane	Drawn	9 to 9
1891	Brisbane	Queensland	11 to 0
1892	Sydney	Queensland	12 to 0
1892	Sydney	Queensland	19 to 9
1893	Brisbane	N.S. Wales	14 to 6
1893	Brisbane	Queensland	11 to 6
1894	Sydney	N.S. Wales	4 to 3
1894	Sydney	N.S. Wales	20 to 12
1895	Brisbane	Queensland	26 to 16
1895	Brisbane	N.S. Wales	11 to 8
1896	Sydney	Queensland	13 to 7
1896	Sydney	N.S. Wales	15 to 9
1897	Brisbane	N.S. Wales	26 to 8
1897	Brisbane	N.S. Wales	16 to 12
1898	Sydney	N.S. Wales	13 to 5

1898	Sydney	Queensland	18 to 16
1898	Brisbane	Queensland	14 to 5
1898	Brisbane	Drawn	3 to 3
1899	Sydney	N.S. Wales	9 to 2
1899	Sydney	N.S. Wales	16 to 3
1899	Brisbane	N.S. Wales	11 to 5
1899	Brisbane	Queensland	13 to 3
1900	Sydney	N.S. Wales	11 to 10
1900	Sydney	N.S. Wales	11 to 9
1900	Brisbane	Queensland	8 to 0
1900	Brisbane	Queensland	20 to 0
1901	Sydney	N.S. Wales	17 to 10
1901	Sydney	N.S. Wales	11 to 8
1901	Brisbane	Queensland	17 to 11
1901	Brisbane	Queensland	15 to 6
1902	Sydney	N.S. Wales	24 to 13
1902	Sydney	N.S. Wales	13 to 8
1902	Brisbane	Queensland	16 to 11
1902	Brisbane	N.S. Wales	13 to 8
1903	Sydney	N.S. Wales	11 to 6
1903	Sydney	N.S. Wales	11 to 8
1903	Brisbane	N.S. Wales	11 to 3
1903	Brisbane	N.S. Wales	12 to 5
1904	Sydney	N.S. Wales	11 to 6
1904	Sydney	Queensland	11 to 7
1904	Brisbane	N.S. Wales	10 to 6
1904	Brisbane	N.S. Wales	8 to 0
1905	Sydney	N.S. Wales	24 to 9
1905	Sydney	N.S. Wales	22 to 4
1905	Brisbane	Queensland	8 to 6
1905	Brisbane	N.S. Wales	15 to 3
1906	Brisbane	N.S. Wales	11 to 9
1906	Brisbane	N.S. Wales	8 to 6
1906	Sydney	N.S. Wales	25 to 3
1906	Sydney	N.S. Wales	14 to 8
1907	Sydney	Queensland	11 to 6
1907	Sydney	N.S. Wales	11 to 3

| 1907 | Brisbane | N.S. Wales | 18 to 3 |
| 1907 | Brisbane | N.S. Wales | 6 to 3 |

RUGBY UNION INTER-STATE MATCHES: 1908–1910

Year	Venue	Won By	Points
1908	Brisbane	N.S. Wales	13 to 8
1908	Brisbane	Drawn	9 to 9
1908	Sydney	N.S. Wales	17 to 10
1908	Sydney	N.S. Wales	21 to 6
1909	Sydney	N.S. Wales	37 to 0
1909	Sydney	N.S. Wales	21 to 11
1909	Brisbane	N.S. Wales	8 to 3
1909	Brisbane	N.S. Wales	13 to 6
1910	Sydney	N.S. Wales	13 to 3
1910	Sydney	Queensland	8 to 6
1910	Brisbane	N.S. Wales	11 to 7
1910	Brisbane	N.S. Wales	21 to 8

RUGBY LEAGUE INTER-STATE MATCHES: 1908–1910

Year	Venue	Won By	Points
1908	Sydney	N.S. Wales	43 to 0
1908	Sydney	N.S. Wales	12 to 3
1910	Brisbane	N.S. Wales	40 to 21
1910	Brisbane	N.S. Wales	32 to 18
1910	Brisbane	N.S. Wales	19 to 3

AUSTRALIAN TEST REPRESENTATIVE REGISTER 1899–1907

Name	State	Opponents	Tests*
Anlezark, E. 'George'	N.S.W.	N.Z., 1905	1
Baker, R. 'Snowy' J.	N.S.W.	G.B., 1904	2
Barnett, John,	N.S.W.	N.Z., 1907	3
Barton, Roger	N.S.W.	G.B., 1899	1
Boland, Sine	QLD	G.B., 1899 ;N.Z., 1903	3
Bouffier, Robert G. F.	N.S.W.	G.B.,1899	1
Boyd, Arch	N.S.W.	G.B., 1899	1
Burdon, Alec	N.S.W.	N.Z., 1903, 1905; G.B., 1904	4
Burge, Albert B.	N.S.W.	N.Z., 1907	1
Burge, Peter	N.S.W.	N.Z., 1905, 1907	3
Canniffe, Bill	QLD	N.Z., 1907	1
Carew, Patrick J.	QLD	G.B., 1899	4
Carmichael, Philip	QLD	G.B., 1904; N.Z., 1907	2
Carson, J 'Jum'	N.S.W.	G.B., 1899	1
Challoner, Robert	N.S.W.	G.B., 1899	1
Clarken, James	N.S.W.	N.Z., 1905	1
Cobb, Walter	N.S.W.	G.B., 1899	2
Colton, Alfred	QLD	G.B., 1899	2
Colton, Thomas	QLD	G.B., 1904	2
Corfe, Arthur C.	QLD	G.B., 1899	1
Currie, Ernest	QLD	G.B., 1899	1
Davis, Walter	N.S.W.	G.B., 1899	3
Dix, William	N.S.W.	N.Z., 1907	3
Dixon, Ernest	QLD	G.B., 1904	1
Dore, Edmund	QLD	G.B., 1904	1
Dore, Mickey	QLD	N.Z., 1905	1
Ellis, Charles	N.S.W.	G.B., 1899	4
Evans, Llewellyn	QLD	N.Z., 1903; G.B., 1904	3
Evans, William T.	QLD	G.B., 1899	2
Fihelly, Jack	QLD	N.Z., 1907	1
Finley, Francis G.	N.S.W.	G.B., 1904	1
Flanagan, Peter	QLD	N.Z., 1907	2
Futter, Francis C.	N.S.W.	G.B., 1904	1
Graham, Charles S.	QLD	G.B., 1899	1

Gralton, Austin	QLD	G.B., 1988; N.Z., 1903	3
Griffin, Thomas	N.S.W.	N.Z., 1907	2
Hardcastle, Bill	N.S.W.	N.Z., 1903	2
Henry, Albert	QLD	G.B., 1899	1
Hindmarsh, John	QLD	G.B., 1904	1
Hirschberg, William	N.S.W.	N.Z., 1905	1
Hughes, James	N.S.W.	N.Z., 1907	2
Joyce, James E.	N.S.W.	N.Z., 1903	1
Judd, Harold A.	N.S.W.	N.Z., 1903, 1905; G.B., 1904	5
Kelly, Alexander J.	N.S.W.	G.B., 1899	1
Larkin, Ted R.	N.S.W.	N.Z., 1903	1
Lucas, Basil	QLD	N.Z., 1905	1
Lutge, Dinny	N.S.W.	N.Z., 1903; G.B., 1904	4
Mandible, Edward	N.S.W.	N.Z., 1907	2
Manning, John	N.S.W.	G.B., 1904	1
Marks, Hyram	N.S.W.	G.B., 1899	2
Maund, John W.	N.S.W.	N.Z., 1903	1
McCue, P. 'Paddy'	N.S.W.	N.Z., 1907	2
McCowan, Robert	QLD	G.B., 1899	3
McKinnon, Alex	QLD	G.B., 1904	1
McKivat, Chris	N.S.W.	N.Z., 1907	2
McLean, Doug J.	QLD	G.B., 1904; N.Z., 1905	3
Meibusch, John	QLD	G.B., 1904	1
Messenger, Dally	N.S.W.	N.Z., 1907	2
Miller, Sidney	N.S.W.	G.B., 1899	1
Nicholson, Frank	QLD	N.Z., 1903; G.B., 1904	2
O'Donnell, Ignatius C.	N.S.W.	G.B., 1899	2
Oxenham, H. B.	QLD	G.B., 1904; N.Z., 1907	2
Oxlade, Allen	QLD	G.B., 1904; N.Z., 1905, 1907	4
Parkinson, Esmond	QLD	N.Z., 1907	1
Penman, Arthur P.	N.S.W.	N.Z., 1905	1
Redwood, Charles	QLD	N.Z., 1903; G.B., 1904	4
Richards, Bill	QLD	G.B., 1904; N.Z., 1905, 1907	5
Riley, Sidney	N.S.W.	N.Z., 1903	1
Rosewell, John	N.S.W.	N.Z., 1907	2
Row, Frank	N.S.W.	G.B., 1899	3
Row, Norm	N.S.W.	N.Z., 1907	2

Russell, C. 'Boxer'	N.S.W.	N.Z., 1907	3
Sampson, James	N.S.W.	G.B., 1899	1
Smith, F. Bede	N.S.W.	N.Z., 1905, 1907	4
Smith, Lancelot M.	N.S.W.	N.Z., 1905	1
Spragg, Stephen A.	N.S.W.	G.B., 1899	4
Street, Norman	N.S.W.	G.B., 1899	1
Swannell, Blair I.	N.S.W.	N.Z., 1905	1
Tanner, William H.	QLD	G.B., 1899	2
Verge, John	N.S.W.	G.B., 1904	2
Walsh, Pat	N.S.W.	G.B., 1904	3
Ward, Peter	N.S.W.	G.B., 1899	4
Ward, Thomas	QLD	G.B., 1899	1
Watson, George	QLD	N.Z., 1907	1
Webb, William	N.S.W.	G.B., 1899	2
White, Charles	N.S.W.	G.B., 1899, 1904; N.Z. 1903	3
White, James	N.S.W.	G.B., 1904	1
Wickham, Stanley	N.S.W.	N.Z., 1903, 1905; G.B., 1904	5
Wood, Fred	N.S.W.	N.Z., 1907	3

*as at the end of the 1907 season

AUSTRALIAN RUGBY UNION TEST PLAYERS 1908–1910

Name	State	Opponents	Tests*
Barnett, John,	N.S.W.	E., 1908; W., 1909	2
Burge, Albert B.	N.S.W.	E., 1908	1
Campbell, John	N.S.W.	N.Z., 1910	3
Carmichael, Philip	QLD	E., 1908; W., 1909	2
Carroll, Danny	N.S.W.	E., 1908	1
Clarken, James	N.S.W.	N.Z., 1910	3
Craig, Bob	N.S.W.	E.,1908	1
Dix, William	N.S.W.	W., 1909	1
Dunbar, Alfred	N.S.W.	N.Z., 1910	3
Dwyer, Lawrence	N.S.W.	N.Z., 1910	3
Farmer, E.H.	QLD	N.Z., 1910	1
Gavin, Kenneth	N.S.W.	W., 1909	1
George, H.W.	N.S.W.	N.Z., 1910	3
Gilbert, Herb	N.S.W.	N.Z., 1910	3
Griffin, Thomas	N.S.W.	E., 1908; N.Z., 1910	3
Hammand, Charles	N.S.W.	E., 1908; W., 1909	2
Hickey, John	N.S.W.	E., 1908; W., 1909	2
Hodgens, Charles	N.S.W.	N.Z., 1910	3
Mandible, Edward	N.S.W.	E., 1908	2
McArthur, Malcolm	N.S.W.	W., 1909	1
McCabe, Arthur	N.S.W.	W., 1909	1
McCue, P. 'Paddy'	N.S.W.	E., 1908; W., 1909	2
McKivat, Chris	N.S.W.	E., 1908; W., 1909	2
Middleton, Syd	N.S.W.	W., 1909; N.Z., 1910	4
Moran, H. 'Paddy'	N.S.W.	E., 1908	1
Murphy, Peter	QLD	N.Z., 1910	3
Prentice, Ward	N.S.W.	E., 1908; W., 1909; N.Z., 1910	5
Reynolds, Lionel	N.S.W.	N.Z., 1910	2
Richards, Tom	QLD.	E., 1908; W., 1909	2
Row, Norm	N.S.W.	W., 1909; N.Z., 1910	4
Russell, C. 'Boxer'	N.S.W.	E., 1908; W., 1909	2
Slater, Stephen	N.S.W.	N.Z., 1910	1
Stuart, Robert	N.S.W.	N.Z., 1910	2
Timbury, Fred	QLD	N.Z., 1910	2
Wood, Fred	N.S.W.	N.Z., 1910	3

*as at the end of the 1910 season

Australian Rugby League Test Players
1908–1910

Name	State	Opponents	Tests*
Abercrombie, Jim	N.S.W.	E. 1908/09	2
Anderson, Tommy	N.S.W.	N.Z. 1908	1
Anderson, Vic	QLD	N.Z. 1909	1
Anlezark, E. 'George'	QLD	E. 1909	1
Baird, Edward	QLD	N.Z. 1908	1
Barnett, John	N.S.W.	E. 1910	2
Bolewski, Mick	QLD	E. 1908/09; N.Z. 1909	4
Brackenreg, Herb	QLD	N.Z. 1909; E. 1910	3
Broomham, Albert	N.S.W.	N.Z. 1909; E. 1910	4
Buckley, Edward	QLD	E.1910	1
Burdon, Alec	N.S.W.	E. 1908/09	2
Butler, Arthur	N.S.W.	E. 1908/09; N.Z. 1909	3
Cann, Billy	N.S.W.	N.Z. 1908, 1909	3
Cheadle, Frank	N.S.W.	N.Z. 1908, 1909	5
Conlon, Albert	N.S.W.	E. 1909; N.Z. 1909	3
Courtney, Tedda	N.S.W.	E. 1908/09, 1910; N.Z. 1909	6
Craig, Bob	N.S.W.	E.1910	2
Davis, James	N.S.W.	N.Z. 1908, 1909	3
Deane, Sid	N.S.W.	E. 1908/09	2
Devereux, Jim	N.S.W.	N.Z. 1908; E. 1908/09	5
Dickins, Harold	QLD	N.Z. 1909	1
Dore, Mickey	QLD	N.Z. 1908, 1909	3
Duffin, George	QLD	N.Z. 1909	1
Farnsworth, Bill	N.S.W.	E. 1910	2
Frawley, Dan	N.S.W.	E. 1909; N.Z. 1909	3
Frawley, Mick	N.S.W.	N.Z. 1909	1
Graves, Bob	N.S.W.	N.Z. 1908, 1909; E. 1909	6
Halloway, A. 'Pony'	N.S.W.	N.Z. 1908, 1909; E. 1908	4
Hardcastle, Bill	QLD	N.Z. 1908	2
Hedley, Charlie	N.S.W.	N.Z. 1908; E. 1909	3
Heidke, Bill	QLD	E. 1909, 1910; N.Z. 1909	4
Hennessy, Arthur	N.S.W.	N.Z. 1908	2
Hickey, John	N.S.W.	E. 1910	2
Jones, Lou	N.S.W.	N.Z. 1908	1

Leveson, Jack	N.S.W.	N.Z. 1909	1
Lutge, Dinny	N.S.W.	N.Z. 1908	3
McCabe, Tom	N.S.W.	E. 1909	1
McGregor, Dugald	QLD	N.Z. 1909; E. 1910	2
McKivat, Chris	N.S.W.	E. 1910	2
McLean, Doug	QLD	N.Z. 1908	1
Messenger, Dally	N.S.W.	N.Z. 1908; E. 1908/09, 1910	7
Morton, Andy	N.S.W.	E. 1908/09	1
Nicholson, Robert	QLD	N.Z. 1909; E. 1910	2
Noble, Bill	N.S.W.	N.Z. 1909; E. 1910	4
O'Malley, Larry	N.S.W.	N.Z. 1908, 1909; E. 1908/09	6
Pearce, Sid	N.S.W.	N.Z. 1908, 1909; E. 1908/09	6
Rosenfeld, Albert	N.S.W.	N.Z. 1908; E. 1909	4
Rosewell, John	N.S.W.	N.Z. 1908	1
Russell, C. 'Boxer'	N.S.W.	E. 1910	1
Spence, Bill	N.S.W.	E. 1910	1
Sullivan, Con	N.S.W.	E. 1910	1
Tubman, Bob	QLD	N.Z. 1908; E. 1910	2
Walsh, Pat	N.S.W.	E. 1908/09	3
Watson, George	QLD	N.Z. 1908	1
Woodhead, Charlie	QLD	N.Z. 1909; E. 1910	4
Woolley, Fred	N.S.W.	N.Z. 1909	2

*as at the end of the 1910 season

AUSTRALIAN DUAL 'INTERNATIONALS' (TESTS)
1908 –1910

Name	State	League Debut	Union/League* Tests
Dore, Mickey	QLD	9 May, 1908	1/3
Lutge, Dinny	N.S.W.	9 May, 1908	4/3
McLean, Doug J.	QLD	9 May, 1908	3/1
Messenger, Dally	N.S.W.	9 May, 1908	2/7
Rosewell, John	N.S.W.	9 May, 1908	2/1
Hardcastle, Bill	QLD	30 May, 1908	2/2
Watson, George	QLD	30 May, 1908	1/1
Burdon, Alec	N.S.W.	12 Dec., 1908	4/2
Walsh, Pat	N.S.W.	12 Dec., 1908	3/3
Anlezark, E. 'George'	QLD	15 Feb., 1909	1/1
Barnett, John	N.S.W.	18 June, 1910	2/2
Craig, Bob	N.S.W.	18 June, 1910	1/2
Hickey, John	N.S.W.	18 June, 1910	2/2
McKivat, Chris	N.S.W.	18 June, 1910	2/2
Russell, C. 'Boxer'	N.S.W.	18 June, 1910	2/1

*as at the end of the 1910 season

BIBLIOGRAPHY

BOOKS/MAGAZINES

Andrews, Malcolm *ABC of Rugby League*, ABC (1992)

Armstrong, Geoff *The Greatest Game*, Ironbark Press (1991)

Aust. Society for Sports History *Sporting Traditions*, (1984-)

Baskerville, Albert H. *Modern Rugby Football, New Zealand Methods* (1907)

Boucher, David *Steel, Skill and Survival: Rugby in Ebbw Vale and the Valleys 1870-1952*, Ebbw Vale RFC (2000)

Collins, Tony *Rugby's Great Split*, Cass (1998)

Diehm, Ian *Red! Red! Red! The Story of Queensland Rugby*, Playright (1997)

Dixon, George H. *The Triumphant Tour of the New Zealand Footballers 1905*, Geddis & Blomfield (1906)

Ellison, T.R. *The Art of Rugby Football*, Geddis & Blomfield (1902)

Encyclopaedia Britannica (1911)

Gallaher, D. & Stead, W.J. *The Complete Rugby Footballer*, Methuen & Co. (1906)

Gate, Robert *Rugby League - An Illustrated History*, George Weidenfeld & Nicolson (1989)

Gate, Robert *The Struggle For The Ashes*, Robert Gate (1986)

Growden, Greg *Gold, Mud 'N' Guts* (Tom Richards), ABC (2001)

Growden, Greg *The Snowy Baker Story*, Random House Australia (2003)

Haigh, Gideon *The Big Ship: Warwick Armstrong and the Making of Modern Cricket*, Aurum Press (2002)

Haynes, John *From All Blacks to All Golds*, Ryan & Haynes (1996)

Heads, Ian *Saints: The Legend Lives On*, Playright Publishing (2001)

Heads, Ian *The Kangaroos*, Lester-Townsend (1990)

Heads, Ian *True Blue: The Story of the NSW Rugby League*, Ironbark (1992)

Hickie, Thomas *The Game For The Game Itself*, Sub-District Rugby Union (1982)

Hickie, Thomas *They Ran With The Ball*, Longman Cheshire (1993)

Howell, Max *They Came to Conquer - International Rugby Union Tours to Australia*, Focus (2003)

Howell, Max & Reet *The Greatest Game Under the Sun (History of Rugby League in Queensland)*, Beddington for the QRL (1990)

Jenkins, Peter *Wallaby Gold*, Random House (1999)

Jones, Lloyd *The Book of Fame*, Penguin Books (2000)

Lester, Gary *Clouds of Dust, Buckets of Blood (Western Suburbs RLFC)*, Playright Publishing (1995)

Lester, Gary *The Story of Australian Rugby League*, Lester-Townsend (1988)

Macklin, Keith *The History of Rugby League Football*, Stanley Paul (1962)

Messenger, Dally R. *The Master*, Angus & Robertson Publishers (1982)

Moore, Andrew *The Mighty Bears!*, Macmillan (1996)

Moorhouse Geoffrey *A People's Game: The Official History of Rugby League*, Hodder & Stoughton (1995)

Moran, Herbert 'Paddy' M. *Viewless Winds*, Peter Davies (1939)

Pollard, Jack *Australian Rugby, The Game and the Players*, Angus & Robertson Publishers (1984)

Ryan, Greg *Forerunners of the All Blacks*, Canterbury University Press (1993)

Sewell, E.H.D. *The Book of Football*, J.M. Dent & Sons (1911)

Sharpham, Peter *Trumper: The Definitive Biography*, Hodder & Stoughton (1985)

Sharpham, Peter *The First Wallabies*, Sandstone (2000)

Thomson, A.A. *Rugger My Pleasure*, Sportsman's Book Club (1957)

NEWSPAPERS/PERIODICALS
Australia
The Arrow
The Australasian
The Australian Field
The Australian Star
The Bulletin
The Courier (Brisbane)
The Daily Telegraph
The Evening News
The Melbourne Age
The Newcastle Morning Herald
The Northern Star
The Observer
The Referee
The Rugby League News

The Sun
The Sunday Sun
The Sydney Mail
The Sydney Morning Herald
The Sydney Sportsman
The Town & Country Journal
The Truth

New Zealand

Otago Daily Times
The Canterbury Times
The New Zealand Herald
The New Zealand Times

Great Britain

The Athletic News
The Yorkshire Post

FOOTNOTES

a)   Primary sources only are identified
b)   For full title of abbreviated titles see Bibliography
c)   Refer also to www.RugbyRebellion.com

Chapter One (pages 1 to 20)
1.   *SMH*, 6.1.1908; *They Ran With The Ball.*
2.   *Tom Brown's Schooldays.*
3.   *The Book of Football.*
4.   *Rugger My Pleasure.*
5.   *Sydney Mail*, 11.7.1874; refer also to R.F.U. laws (var. dates/ amend.); *Auckland RU Annual 1892.*
6.   *They Ran With The Ball.*
7.   *Sydney Mail*, 1.9.1877.
8.   *They Ran With The Ball; Sporting Traditions*, 11/1987.
9.   *They Ran With The Ball; Sporting Traditions*, 11/1987; *Sydney Mail*, 27.4.1878.
10.   *They Ran With The Ball.*
11.   *They Ran With The Ball; Sporting Traditions*, 11/1987.
12.   *Red! Red! Red!*
13.   *Sun*, 22.7.1906.
14.   *Red! Red! Red!*
15.   *Sun*, 22.7.1906.
16.   *They Came To Conquer.*
17.   *Rugby's Great Split; Referee*, 17.4.1901.
18.   *They Came to Conquer; Forerunners of the All Blacks; Rugby's Great Split.*
19.   *Sporting Traditions*, 11/1997.
20.   *Rugger My Pleasure; Sun*, 22.7.1906; *Referee*, 4.4.1900; *Complete Rugby Footballer.*
21.   *N.S.W.R.U. Minutes*, held by A.R.U. Archives; *Red! Red! Red!*
22.   *Complete Rugby Footballer.*
23.   *Rugby's Great Split.*
24.   *Rugby's Great Split.*
25.   *Referee* - various articles, e.g., 14.2.1900.

Chapter Two (pages 21 to 37)
1.   *SMH*, 18.4.1896.
2.   *SMH*, 2.5.1896.
3.   *Referee*, 22.4.1896.

4. *Referee*, 5.5.1897 & 27.9.1899.
5. *The Game for the Game Itself.*
6. *SMH*, 24.4.1896 & 15.5.1896.
7. *Rugby's Great Split; Referee*, 8.4.1987; R.F.U.'s *'Regulations Relating to Insurance'* (1886 & var. amendments thereafter).
8. *Referee*, 8.4.1897.
9. *SMH*, 8.4.1897; *Daily Telegraph*, 8.4.1897.
10. *Rugby's Great Split.*
11. *Referee*, 4.8.1897.
12. *Referee*, 4.8.1897.
13. *Referee*, 4.8.1897 & 16.5.1898.
14. *Referee*, 4.8.1897.
15. *Referee*, 4.8.1897.
16. *Referee*, 11.8.1897.
17. *Referee*, 11.8.1897.
18. *Telegraph*, 16.4.1898; *SMH*, 16.4.1898.
19. *N.S.W.R.U. Minutes.*
20. *SMH*, 29.4.1898.
21. *SMH*, 6.5.1898.
22. *Telegraph*, 15.4.1898.
23. *SMH*, 2.5.1898.
24. *SMH*, 27.4.1898.
25. *SMH*, 25.7.1898; *Rugby League News (RLN)*, 20.4.1940.
26. *Referee*, 24.3.1897 & 20.4.1898.
27. *The Game for the Game Itself.*
28. *SMH*, 6.5.1899.
29. *RLN*, 27.4.1940; *Bulletin*, 16.7.1898.
30. *Bulletin*, 16.7.1898; *SMH*, 16.5.1898.
31. *SMH*, 137.1898 & 18.7.1898.
32. *Referee*, 4.8.1897; *SMH*, 23.7.1898.

Chapter Three (pages 38 to 50)
1. *Referee*, 12.4.1899.
2. *Referee*, 11.8.1897 & 6.5.1899; *SMH*, 11.5.1899.
3. *SMH*, 11.5.1899.
4. *SMH*, 21.4.1899.
5. *SMH*, 20.4.1899; *Referee*, 19.4.1899.
6. *Referee*, 12.4.1899.
7. *Referee*, 21.6.1899; *SMH*, 8.4.1899.
8. *SMH*, 26.4.1899.
9. *N.S.W.R.U. Minutes.*
10. *SMH*, 8.4.1899 & 20.5.1899; *Referee*, 10.5.1899.

11.   *Referee*, 10.5.1899.
12.   *N.S.W.R.U. Minutes; SMH*, 12.5.1899.
13.   *Referee*, 28.6.1899.
14.   *Referee*, 28.6.1899.
15.   *Referee*, 20.9.1899; *N.S.W.R.U. Minutes*.
16.   *Referee*, 27.9.1899.
17.   *Field*, 26.8.1899.
18.   *Field*, 26.8.1899.
19.   *Field*, 26.8.1899.
20.   *Field*, 26.8.1899.
21.   *Field*, 9.9.1899.
22.   *Field*, 23.9.1899.
23.   *Referee*, 27.9.1899.
24.   *Field*, 23.9.1899.
25.   *Red! Red! Red!*.
26.   *Encyclopaedia Britannica*.

Chapter Four (pages 51 to 69)

1.   *SMH*, 11.9.1899.
2.   *Referee*, 3.5.1899.
3.   *SMH*, 22.4.1899.
4.   *Referee*, 16.5.1900.
5.   *Referee*, 27.9.1899.
6.   *Referee*, 27.9.1899.
7.   *Referee*, 14.2.1900.
8.   *Referee*, 14.2.1900.
9.   *Referee*, 22.8.1900.
10.   *SMH*, 9.3.1900, 10.3.1900 & 12.3.1900; *Referee*, 14.3.1900.
11.   *Referee*, 16.5.1900.
12.   *SMH*, 28.3.1900.
13.   *SMH*, 17.3.1900 & 21.5.1900; *Referee*, 16.5.1900.
14.   Colours appear to originate from the cardinal waratah (the 'red-fern'). See reference to Souths R.U. Club (*Referee*, 3.11.1909) and the Redfern Cricket Club (*Sportsman*, 6.1.1909). The 1908 Wallabies also wore a red-and-green band around their boater hats - the colours of their waratah badge (see *Gold, Mud 'N' Guts*). Interestingly, that team were originally called 'The Rabbits'.
15.   All contemporary reports refer to Birchgrove Park, not Birchgrove Oval.
16.   *Rugby's Great Split*.
17.   *Encyclopaedia Britannica*.
18.   *SMH*, 12.3.1900.

19.   *SMH*, 12.4.1900 & 15.8.1900; *Referee*, 26.9.1900.
20.   *Sunday Sun*, 12.4.1908.
21.   *Referee*, 16.5.1900.
22.   *SMH*, 21.5.1900.
23.   *Referee*, 18.4.1900 & 2.5.1900.
24.   *Referee*, 22.8.1900 & 5.9.1900.
25.   *Referee*, 18.4.1900.
26.   *Referee*, 29.8.1900.
27.   *Referee*, 29.8.1900; *SMH*, 27.8.1900.
28.   *Referee*, 26.9.1900; *Book of Football*.
29.   *Referee*, 29.8.1900.
30.   *Referee*, 15.8.1900.
31.   *Northern Star*.
32.   *Snowy Baker Story*.
33.   *SMH*, 29.4.1901.
34.   *The Game for the Game Itself*; *RLN*, 27.4.1940.
35.   *SMH*, 29.4.1901 & 25.4.1903.
36.   *Viewless Winds*.
37.   *Truth*, 21.4.1940; *RLN*, 1.6.1940.
38.   *SMH*, 11.5.1901, 19.3.1902 & 17.5.1902.

Chapter Five (pages 70 to 85)

1.   *Referee*, 17.4.1901.
2.   *SMH*, 13.8.1907.
3.   *Referee*, 22.7.1903.
4.   *Referee*, 19.8.1903.
5.   *Referee*, 22.8.1903.
6.   *RLN*, 8.6.1940.
7.   *SMH*, 23.3.1903 & 31.3.1903.
8.   *SMH*, 23.3.1903.
9.   *SMH*, 29.4.1903.
10.   *Snowy Baker Story*; *Australia R.U. - The Game & the Players*.
11.   *RLN*, 17.6.1940.
12.   *Snowy Baker Story*.
13.   *SMH*, 25.3.1904 & 29.8.1907.
14.   *Sporting Traditions*, 11/1987; *Melbourne Age*, 'Unearthing Roots of Harbour City Talent', 3.8.2003.
15.   *SMH*, 9.4.1904.
16.   *SMH*, 30.3.1904 & 11.4.1904.
17.   *NZ Times*, 7.4.1904.
18.   *SMH*, 13.4.1904.
19.   *SMH*, 7.5.1904.

20. *Town and Country*, 7.9.1904.
21. *Viewless Winds*.
22. *Mail*, 137.1904; *Sportsman*, 13.7.1904.
23. *Sportsman*, 29.6.1904; *Newcastle Herald*, 7/1904 (undated clipping); *SMH*, 1.8.1904; *Referee*, 7.9.1904; *Town and Country*, 18.7.1904.
24. *Snowy Baker Story*.
25. *Snowy Baker Story*.
26. *RLN*, 26.7.1941.
27. *Town and Country*, 7.9.1904.
28. *Referee*, 7.9.1904.
29. *RLN*, 17.6.1940.
30. *SMH*, 1.4.1905.
31. *SMH*, 25.3.1905.
32. *SMH*, 6.4.1905, 21.4.1905 & 29.4.1905.

Chapter Six (pages 86 to 107)

1. *SMH*, 29.4.1905.
2. *Referee*, 8.8.1906.
3. *The Triumphant Tour*.
4. *Observer*, 24.6.1905.
5. *Courier*, 3.7.1905.
6. *Newcastle Herald*, 8.7.1905.
7. *Arrow*, 8.7.1905.
8. *Arrow*, 22.7.1905.
9. *RLN News*, 17.8.1940.
10. *The Triumphant Tour*.
11. *SMH*, 10.7.1905.
12. *SMH*, 10.7.1905.
13. *Yorkshire Post*, 13.11.1908.
14. *Referee*, 2.8.1905.
15. *Newcastle Herald*, 31.7.1905.
16. *Arrow*, 12.8.1905; *Newcastle Herald*, 19.8.1905.
17. *Sportsman*, 16.8.1905.
18. *Town and Country*, 16.8.1905.
19. *Referee*, 30.8.1905.
20. Discussion between the author and Pat Walsh's grandson, Pat Walsh; *Australasian*, 25.11.1905.
21. *N.S.W.R.U. Minutes*. Photograph of the team (provided by Auckland R.U. Archives).
22. *N.S.W.R.U. Minutes*.
23. *Referee*, 13.9.1905.

24. *Canterbury Times,* 20.9.1905.

25. *Referee,* 20.9.1905; *Wallaby Gold.*

26. *Referee,* 13.9.1905 & 20.9.1905.

27. *Referee,* 13.9.1905; *Truth,* 21.4.1940.

28. *Referee,* 20.9.1905.

29. Discussion between the author and Pat Walsh's grandson, Pat Walsh; *Australasian,* 25.11.1905.

30. *Referee,* 1.11.1905.

31. *Referee,* 6.12.1905.

32. Northern Union Annual General Meeting, 1906 (minutes held by the Rugby Football League archives) - All Blacks playing style avoided scrummaging and mauling wherever possible.

33. *The Triumphant Tour.*

34. *Book of Football.*

35. *The Triumphant Tour; Book of Fame.*

36. *Book of Football.*

37. *The Triumphant Tour.*

38. *All Blacks to All Golds.*

39. Interestingly, Fred Cooper won the 100 yards championship at the 1898 AAA British championships. It suggests the possibility that Smith and Cooper met at some time as a result of their common interests. For Smith's profile visit www. rugbymuseum.co.nz.

40. *www.dnzb.govt.nz.*

41. *SMH,* 28.6.1907.

42. *The Triumphant Tour.*

43. *True Blue.*

44. *Rugby's Great Split.*

45. *Referee,* 2.5.1906; 9.5.1906 & 15.5.1906.

46. *Referee,* 15.5.1906.

47. *Trumper: The Definitive Biography.*

48. *SMH,* 6.2.2004, *The Ton That Stopped a Nation; The Big Ship.*

49. *Bulletin,* 2.9.1909.

50. *Bulletin,* 2.9.1909.

51. *Referee,* 27.9.1905; *SMH,* 4.4.1906.

52. *SMH,* 4.4.1906.

53. *Referee,* 15.5.1906.

54. *Referee,* 15.5.1906.

55. *Referee,* 6.6.1906.

56. *Referee,* 6.6.1906.

57. *Referee,* 6.6.1906.

58. *Referee,* 21.3.1906.

59.   *Newcastle Herald*, 24.4.1906.
60.   *NZ Herald*, 5.5.1906.

Chapter Seven (pages 108 to 128)

1.   *Referee*, 11.7.1906.
2.   *Referee*, 11.7.1906.
3.   *Referee*, 11.7.1906.
4.   *Sunday Sun*, 15.7.1906.
5.   *RLN*, 24.8.1940; *Sportsman*, 8.4.1908.
6.   *Viewless Winds.*
7.   *Australian Star*, 10.8.1907.
8.   *Referee*, 30.5.1906.
9.   *Truth*, 28.4.1940.
10.   *Referee*, 18.7.1906.
11.   *Sunday Sun*, 15.7.1906.
12.   *Sunday Sun*, 15.7.1906.
13.   *SMH*, 16.7.1906.
14.   *Referee*, 25.7.1906; *Yorkshire Post*, 13.11.1908.
15.   *Greatest Game Under the Sun.*
16.   *Referee*, 8.8.1906.
17.   *Wallaby Gold.*
18.   *Viewless Winds.*
19.   *Sportsman*, 8.9.1909.
20.   *Referee*, 25.7.1906; *SMH*, 19.7.1906.
21.   *Referee*, 25.7.1906.
22.   *Referee*, 1.8.1906.
23.   *Referee*, 8.8.1906.
24.   *Referee*, 1.8.1906.
25.   *Referee*, 25.7.1906.
26.   *Referee*, 25.7.1906.
27.   *SMH*, 13.9.1909.
28.   *Referee*, 22.8.1906.
29.   *Referee*, 25.7.1906.
30.   *Referee*, 1.8.1906.
31.   *SMH*, 6.8.1907.
32.   *Truth*, 5.5.1940; *Sportsman*, 8.9.1909.
33.   Sheldon, Peter *In Division is Strength: Unionism Among Sydney Labourers 1890-1910.*
34.   *Referee*, 1.8.1906.
35.   *Referee*, 22.8.1906.
36.   Thanks to Tony Collins for McCabe's playing record.
37.   Fox, S., *'Tom McCabe - Our First Kangaroo' (www.widnesvikings. co.uk).*

38. McCabe wrote articles for *The Referee* during the Kangaroos' tour of 1908/09.
39. Northern Union Annual General Meeting, 1906 (minutes held by the Rugby Football League archives) - All Blacks playing style avoided scrummaging and mauling wherever possible.
40. *Rugby's Great Split.*
41. Macklin, K., *The History of Rugby League Football.*
42. R.F.U.'s *Laws of the Game; Referee*, 15.9.1909.
43. Northern Union Annual General Meeting, 1906 (minutes held by the Rugby Football League archives) - All Blacks playing style avoided scrummaging and mauling wherever possible.
44. *Referee*, 8.8.1906.
45. *Referee*, 22.8.1906.
46. *SMH*, 7.8.1907.
47. *Referee*, 22.8.1906.
48. *Sunday Sun*, 24.6.1906.
49. *Referee*, 8.8.1906.
50. *Referee*, 30.5.1906 & 8.8.1906.
51. *The Game for the Game Itself.*
52. R.F.U.'s *Laws As To Professionalism.*
53. *SMH*, 4.4.1907.
54. *SMH*, 21.3.1907.
55. *SMH*, 4.4.1907.
56. *SMH*, 29.3.1907.
57. *Referee*, 26.6.1907.
58. *The Insurance and Banking Record*, July, 1906.
59. *Bulletin*, 2.9.1909.
60. *True Blue*; Biography at *www.parliament.nsw.gov.au* (refer to 'Former Members' section).
61. *Truth*, 5.5.1940.

Chapter Eight (pages 129 to 146)

1. In all but a few contemporary documents his name is spelt as Baskerville (including his own book). See *All Blacks to All Golds* which states the birth spelling is Baskiville. A NZ article reproduced in *Referee* (1.7.1908) claimed his first names were Arthur Herbert. His contemporaries all called him Bert or Bertie.
2. *Modern Rugby Football.*
3. *Complete Rugby Footballer.*
4. *Otago Daily Times*, 10.12.1907.
5. *Otago Daily Times*, 10.12.1907.
6. *True Blue.*

7.   *Otago Daily Times,* 10.12.1907.

8.   *Otago Daily Times,* 10.12.1907.

9.   *"New Zealand All Black Rugby Football Team" Agreement* (dated 24.8.1907) - copy provided to the author by New Zealand Rugby League.

10.   *All Blacks to All Golds; NZ Herald,* 13.8.1907.

11.   *SMH,* 6.5.1907.

12.   *Sunday Sun,* 26.5.1907.

13.   *SMH,* 18.5.1907.

14.   *Sunday Sun,* 19.5.1907; *SMH,* 1.5.1907.

15.   *Rugby League News,* 25.4.1940 & 14.6.1941.

16.   *Rugby League News,* 14.6.1941.

17.   *Rugby League News,* 14.6.1947; *Truth,* 5.5.1940.

18.   *Truth,* 5.5.1940.

19.   *Bulletin,* 2.9.1909.

20.   *Truth,* 5.5.1940.

21.   *True Blue.*

22.   *Referee,* 21.8.1907.

23.   *SMH,* 8.8.1907.

24.   *SMH,* 6.8.1907.

25.   *Rugby's Great Split.*

26.   *Australian Star,* 10.8.1907.

27.   *Sunday Sun,* 26.5.1907.

28.   *SMH,* 31.5.1907.

29.   *SMH,* 31.5.1907 & 1.6.1907.

30.   *SMH,* 31.5.1907; *All Blacks to All Golds.*

31.   *SMH,* 25.6.1907.

32.   *SMH,* 3.6.1907.

33.   *Australian Star,* 10.8.1907.

34.   *Sportsman,* 5.6.1907.

35.   *SMH,* 6.6.1907.

36.   *SMH,* 13.7.1907.

37.   *SMH,* 8.6.1907 & 10.6.1907.

38.   From 1900 onwards a four-match series was played (1882-'99 used a two-match series).

39.   *SMH,* 10.6.1907 & 13.6.1907; *Sunday Sun,* 16.6.1907.

40.   *SMH,* 14.6.1907 (note this incorrectly states the N.S.W.R.U. purchased the ground).

41.   *SMH,* 6.8.1907.

42.   *Sunday Sun,* 23.6.1907.

43.   *SMH,* 6.8.1907.

44.   *SMH,* 6.8.1907 & 10.8.1907.

45.   *SMH*, 14.6.1907 & 17.6.1907.
46.   *Sunday Sun*, 26.6.1907 & 3.7.1907.
47.   *SMH*, 19.6.1907.
48.   *Truth*, 28.4.1940 & 5.5.1940.
49.   *Northern Star*, 2.7.1907 & 8.7.1907.
50.   *SMH*, 28.6.1907.

Chapter Nine (pages 147 to 171)

1.   *SMH*, 3.7.1907; *Northern Star*, 27.7.1907.
2.   *Australian Star*, 11.7.1907.
3.   *SMH*, 12.7.1907.
4.   *SMH*, 13.7.1907 & 15.7.1907.
5.   *SMH*, 15.7.1907, 16.7.1907 & 18.7.1907.
6.   *SMH*, 17.7.1907.
7.   *Sportsman*, 3.7.1917 & 17.7.1907; *SMH*, 16.7.1907 & 17.7.1907.
8.   *SMH*, 10.6.1907 & 26.6.1907.
9.   *SMH*, 20.7.1907; *Northern Star*, 22.7.1907.
10.   *True Blue*; *Northern Star*, 22.7.1907 & 27.7.1907.
11.   *SMH*, 20.7.1907.
12.   *Sunday Sun*, 21.7.1907.
13.   *SMH*, 22.7.1907.
14.   *SMH*, 22.7.1907.
15.   *SMH*, 22.7.1907.
16.   *SMH*, 22.7.1907; *Australian Star*, 23.7.1907.
17.   *Australian Star*, 27.7.1907.
18.   *SMH*, 22.7.1907.
19.   *SMH*, 8.8.1907; *Arrow* of 3.8.1907 claimed that All Blacks Seeling and 'Massa' Johnston assisted Baskerville and 'Bumper' Wright to select the professional NZ team.
20.   *SMH*, 25.7.1907.
21.   *Truth*, 28.4.1940; *Sportsman*, 25.3.1908.
22.   The R.F.U.'s *'Rules As To Professionalism'* .
23.   *St George Call*, 17.8.1907; also *Sportsman*, 25.3.1908.
24.   *SMH*, 5.8.1907; *Newcastle Herald*, 7.8.1907.
25.   *Arrow*, 3.8.1907.
26.   *Newcastle Herald*, 3.7.1907.
27.   *Australian Star*, 7.8.1907; *Telegraph*, 7.8.1907.
28.   *SMH*, 5.8.1907.
29.   *SMH*, 5.8.1907.
30.   *SMH*, 6.8.1907.
31.   *SMH*, 6.8.1907.
32.   *SMH*, 6.8.1907.

33.   *SMH*, 6.8.1907.
34.   *SMH*, 6.8.1907.
35.   *Referee*, 21.8.1907.
36.   *SMH*, 6.8.1907.
37.   *SMH*, 7.8.1907.
38.   *SMH*, 6.8.1907.
39.   *Australian Star*, 7.8.1907; *SMH*, 7.8.1907.
40.   *Sportsman*, 7.8.1907.
41.   *Northern Star*, 9.8.1907.
42.   *Australian Star*, 8.8.1907.
43.   *Newcastle Herald*, 8.8.1907.
44.   *Northern Star*, 9.8.1907; *SMH*, 10.8.1907.
45.   *Wallaby Gold; Red! Red! Red!; Sydney Mail*, 14.8.1907.
46.   *Northern Star*, 9.8.1907; *Arrow*, 21.8.1907.
47.   Due to the impact of rugby league and World War One, rugby union practically disappeared from Queensland from 1920 to 1929.
48.   *Sydney Mail*, 14.8.1907; *Australian Star*, 8.8.1907.
49.   *SMH*, 10.8.1907.
50.   A search of *The Sun* and *The Sunday Sun* failed to confirm the evidence of the article referred to in *The Rugby League News*, 16.6.1941.
51.   *Australian Star*, 10.8.1907.
52.   *Sunday Sun*, 12.4.1908.
53.   *SMH*, 12.8.1907.
54.   *Sydney Mail*, 14.8.1907.
55.   *SMH*, 12.8.1907.
56.   *SMH*, 12.8.1907.
57.   *SMH*, 26.3.1908.
58.   *SMH*, 12.8.1907.
59.   *Australian Star*, 14.8.1907.
60.   For example, *Australian Star*, 14.8.1907 & *SMH* 14.8.1907.
61.   *True Blue; The Story of Australian Rugby League*.
62.   *Truth*, 5.5.1940 & 12.5.1940.
63.   *The Master*.
64.   *SMH*, 13.8.1907.
65.   *Australian Star*, 10.8.1907 & 12.8.1907.

Chapter Ten (pages 172 to 194)

1.   *SMH*, 13.8.1907.
2.   *SMH*, 13.8.1907, 14.8.1907 & 17.8.1907.
3.   *Sydney Mail*, 14.8.1907.

4. *Australian Star*, 14.8.1907.
5. *Sportsman*, 14.8.1907.
6. *SMH*, 16.8.1907 & 17.8.1907.
7. See team photograph.
8. *SMH*, 16.8.1907 & 17.8.1907; *Sydney Mail*, 21.8.1907.
9. *NZ Herald*, 13.8.1907.
10. *Referee*, 4.9.1907.
11. *SMH*, 14.8.1907; *Star*, 15.8.1907.
12. *SMH*, 16.8.1907.
13. *Sydney Mail*, 21.8.1907; *Newcastle Herald*, 29.8.1907.
14. *RLN*, 27.9.1941.
15. *Sydney Mail*, 21.8.1907.
16. *Referee*, 21.8.1907.
17. *SMH*, 19.8.1907.
18. *Sportsman*, 21.8.1907.
19. *SMH*, 21.8.1907 & 22.8.1907.
20. *RLN*, 14.6.1907.
21. *SMH*, 21.8.1907.
22. *SMH*, 22.8.1907.
23. *SMH*, 24.8.1907.
24. *SMH*, 24.8.1907.
25. N.Z.R.L. Archives.
26. *Referee*, 28.8.1907; *SMH*, 24.8.1907.
27. *SMH*, 24.8.1907; *Referee*, 28.8.1907.
28. *SMH*, 24.8.1907 & 26.8.1907; *Sunday Sun*, 25.8.1907.
29. *Referee*, 28.8.1907.
30. *Referee*, 28.8.1907.
31. *Herald*, 26.8.1907.
32. *Herald*, 29.8.1907.
33. *Herald*, 29.8.1907; *True Blue*.
34. *RLN*, 5.7.1941 & 2.8.1941.
35. *Herald*, 10.8.1907; *Referee*, 4.9.1907; *Sportsman*, 25.3.1908.
36. *Yorkshire Post*, 24.9.1907.
37. *Yorkshire Post*, 24.9.1907.
38. *Referee*, 2.10.1907 & 23.10.1907.
39. *Referee*, 4.9.1907.
40. *A People's Game*.
41. *All Blacks to All Golds*; *Referee*, 23.10.1907.
42. *A People's Game*; *All Blacks to All Golds*; *Referee*, 23.10.1907.
43. *Referee*, 8.1.1908.
44. *All Blacks to All Golds*.
45. *Referee*, 11.12.1907.

46.   *Referee*, 20.11.1909.
47.   *Referee*, 24.12.1907.
48.   *Steel, Skill & Survival.*
49.   *Referee*, 15.1.1908.
50.   *Truth*, 12.5.1940.
51.   *Truth*, 12.5.1940.
52.   For example, *SMH*, 25.3.1908; *Referee*, 8.4.1908; *All Blacks to All Golds.* (Note - the profit taken varies between sources.).
53.   *All Blacks to All Golds*; additional information from Tony Collins. *The Referee* (4.12.1907) refuted claims that Jim Gleeson had been a medical student at Sydney University.
54.   *All Blacks to All Golds.*

Chapter Eleven (pages 195 to 214)

1.   For example, *SMH*, 15.1.1908 & *Sportsman*, 25.3.1908.
2.   *SMH*, 10.1.1908; *Referee*, 15.1.1908.
3.   Refer to *SMH* and *Referee* throughout this period. *SMH* (15.1.1908) & *Referee* (22.1.1908) both state Newtown formed on 14 January. See also *True Blue, Story of Australian Rugby League* & various club history books.
4.   *Clouds of Dust* (Wests R.L. club history).
5.   *Saints: The Legend Lives On.*
6.   *SMH*, 17.3.1908.
7.   *Evening News*; *SMH*, 27.3.1908.
8.   *Sportsman*, 15.4.1908; *Arrow*, 11.4.1908.
9.   *Sportsman*, 22.4.1908.
10.   *SMH*, 24.1.1908.
11.   *SMH*, 9.3.1908.
12.   *Sunday Sun*, 12.4.1908.
13.   *Sportsman*, 25.3.1908.
14.   *SMH*, 9.3.1908.
15.   *True Blue.*
16.   *SMH*, 25.4.1908; *Sportsman*, 29.4.1908.
17.   *Sportsman*, 26.2.1908.
18.   *Sunday Sun*, 26.4.1908; *Sportsman*, 8.4.1908.
19.   *Referee*, 8.1.1908.
20.   From club meetings reported in *SMH* and *Referee*, January-March, 1908.
21.   *SMH*, 24.2.1908; *True Blue.*
22.   *SMH*, 18.4.1908.
23.   *Sportsman*, 25.3.1908; *SMH*, 18.4.1908.
24.   *Sportsman*, 25.3.1908 & 15.4.1908.

25.   *SMH*, 31.3.1908.
26.   *SMH*, 9.3.1908, 26.3.1908 & 31.3.1908.
27.   *Referee*, 28.1.1908.
28.   *Sportsman*, 22.4.1908.
29.   *Greatest Game Under the Sun; Sportsman*, 8.4.1908; *Referee*, 15.4.1908 & 13.5.1908.
30.   *Greatest Game Under the Sun.*
31.   *SMH*, 20.4.1908 & 21.4.1908.
32.   *True Blue; SMH*, 6.4.1908.
33.   *All Blacks to All Golds, SMH*, 21.4.1908; *True Blue.*
34.   *Referee*, 18.4.1908; *Sportsman*, 15.4.1908.
35.   *Sportsman*, 15.4.1908.
36.   *SMH*, 21.4.1908; *Referee*, 22.4.1908; *True Blue.*
37.   *Sportsman*, 22.4.1908; *Sunday Sun*, 26.4.1908; *True Blue.*
38.   *SMH*, 23.4.1908 & 27.4.1908; *Newcastle Herald*, 25.4.1908.
39.   *Sunday Sun*, 26.4.1908.

Chapter Twelve (pages 215 to 234)

1.   *SMH*, 4.5.1908.
2.   *Sunday Sun*, 3.5.1908.
3.   *Sportsman*, 13.5.1908; *Referee*, 13.5.1908.
4.   *SMH*, 8.5.1908; *Sportsman*, 13.5.1908.
5.   *SMH*, 11.5.1908; *Sportsman*, 13.5.1908; *Referee*, 13.5.1908. (The *SMH* incorrectly identified the Australian try-scorers.)
6.   *SMH*, 12.5.1908 & 14.5.1908.
7.   *Sportsman*, 13.5.1908.
8.   *Referee*, 13.5.1908, 27.5.1908 & 12.8.1908; *SMH*, 18.5.1908; *Courier*, 18.5.1908; *Sportsman*, 20.5.1908. (Why the New Zealanders travelled by sea instead of train could not be determined.)
9.   *Greatest Game Under The Sun; SMH*, 23.5.1908 & 25.5.1908.
10.   *Greatest Game Under The Sun; SMH*, 25.5.1908; *Sportsman*, 3.6.1908.
11.   *SMH*, 30.5.1908; *Sportsman*, 3.6.1908.
12.   *SMH*, 1.6.1908; *Sportsman*, 3.6.1908.
13.   *Referee*, 10.6.1908 & 1.7.1908; *SMH*, 15.6.1908.
14.   *SMH*, 9.6.1908; *Sportsman*, 10.6.1908.
15.   *Sportsman*, 22.7.1908.
16.   *SMH*, 24.6.1908.
17.   *SMH*, 15.6.1908 & 18.6.1908; *Sportsman*, 17.6.1908 & 24.6.1908.
18.   *SMH*, 18.6.1908; *Sportsman*, 24.6.1908.
19.   *Sportsman*, 8.7.1908 & 22.7.1908.

20.   *SMH*, 24.6.1908.

21.   *Sportsman*, 15.7.1908 & 22.7.1908.

22.   *Northern Star*, 9.6.1908 & 3.7.1908; *SMH*, 29.6.1908.

23.   *Greatest Game Under The Sun*; *SMH*, 6.7.1908; *Referee*, 8.7.1908.

24.   *Greatest Game Under The Sun*; *SMH*, 8.7.1908; *Referee*, 15.7.1909; *Sportsman*, 29.7.1908.

25.   *Referee*, 12.8.1908.

26.   *SMH*, 5.8.1908 & 10.8.1908; *Sportsman*, 8.7.1908 & 19.8.1908.

27.   *Arrow*, July 1908; *SMH*, 5.6.1908 & 18.7.1908.

28.   *Referee*, 10.6.1908.

29.   *Sydney Sportsman*, 7.7.1908 & 15.7.1908.

30.   *Referee*, 8.7.1908.

31.   *SMH*, 13.7.1908.

32.   *SMH*, 18.7.1908 & 21.7.1908; *Newcastle Herald*, (undated) 1908; *Sportsman*, 22.7.1908.

33.   *NZ Herald*, 8.7.1908 & 15.7.1908.

34.   *SMH*, 20.7.1908 & 23.7.1908.

Chapter Thirteen (pages 235 to 257)

1.   *Sportsman*, 22.7.1908; *SMH*, 4.8.1908 & 7.8.1908.

2.   *SMH*, 21.7.1908 to 4.8.1908; *Sportsman*, 12.8.1908.

3.   *SMH*, 9.7.1908; R.F.U.'s *'Rules As To Professionalism'*.

4.   *SMH*, 18.7.1908 to 4.8.1908.

5.   *Referee*, 26.8.1908.

6.   *Newcastle Herald*, (undated) 1908.

7.   *Referee*, 9.9.1908; *SMH*, var 8/1908.

8.   *Sportsman*, 12.8.1908; *SMH*, 10.8.1908.

9.   *SMH*, 10.8.1908.

10.   *SMH*, 17.8.1908 & 24.8.1908.

11.   *SMH*, 27.3.1908; *Referee*, 21.4.1908 & 13.5.1908.

12.   *Sporting Traditions*, 11/2000.

13.   *SMH*, 27.3.1908; *Sporting Traditions*, 11/2000.

14.   *Referee*, 16.12.1908; *Sporting Traditions*, 11/2000.

15.   *Referee*, 23.12.1908; *Sporting Traditions*, 11/2000.

16.   *Referee & SMH*, 8/1908.

17.   *SMH*, 13.8.1908; *Sportsman*, 19.8.1908.

18.   *Sportsman*, 19.8.1908 & 26.8.1908.

19.   *SMH*, 21.7.1908; *Sunday Sun*, 6.9.1908.

20.   *SMH*, 24.9.1908.

21.   *Sportsman*, 1.8.1908.

22.   *Referee*, 9.9.1908.

23.   *SMH*, 29.8.1908; Stradbroke Is. confirmed as war-cry's origin by

Referee (26.8.1908) & *Sunday Sun* (30.8.1908).

24.   *SMH*, 29.8.1908 & 31.8.1908.

25.   *Sportsman*, 2.9.1908.

26.   *Referee*, 26.8.1908.

27.   *Sportsman*, 26.8.1908.

28.   *Sporting Traditions*, Nov. 2000.

29.   *Gold, Mud 'N' Guts*.

30.   *Gold, Mud 'N' Guts*.

31.   *Viewless Winds*.

32.   *Telegraph*, 8.4.1897; *Referee*, 26.9.1900.

33.   Aust. National University (Australian National Dictionary Centre); see also poetry by Henry Lawson, e.g., 'On The Wallaby' (1891).

34.   *SMH*, 24.7.1908; *Northern Star*, 13.5.1908.

35.   *Referee*, 30.9.1908.

36.   *The Master*.

37.   *The Master*.

38.   *Truth*, 19.5.1940.

39.   *Referee*, 14.10.1908.

40.   *Truth*, 19.5.1940.

41.   *SMH*, 23.4.1909.

42.   *Yorkshire Post*, (undated) 1909.

43.   News clippings held by family of Pat Walsh.

44.   News clippings held by family of Pat Walsh.

45.   *The Master*.

46.   *Referee*, 28.7.1909 & 11.8.1909.

47.   *SMH*, 23.4.1909.

48.   *Gold, Mud 'N' Guts*.

49.   *SMH*, 21.4.1909.

50.   *Sporting Traditions*, 11/2000.

51.   *Sporting Traditions*, 11/2000.

52.   *Viewless Winds*.

53.   *Gold, Mud 'N' Guts*; *Yorkshire Post*, 2.11.1908; *Yorkshire Evening Post*, 2.11.1908.

54.   *Book of Football*.

55.   *Sporting Traditions*, 11/2000.

56.   *Sporting Traditions*, 11/2000.

57.   *Referee*, 16.12.1908; *Sporting Traditions*, 11/2000.

58.   *Viewless Winds*.

Chapter Fourteen (pages 258 to 274)

1.   *Sportsman*, 21.4.1909.

2.   *True Blue; The Story of Australian Rugby League; SMH & Referee,* 3/1909.
3.   *True Blue; The Story of Australian Rugby League; SMH & Referee,* 3/1909.
4.   *SMH,* 22.4.1909.
5.   *SMH,* 23.4.1909.
6.   *SMH,* 22/23/24.4.1909 & 2.6.1909.
7.   Review of *SMH & Referee* during 1909 season.
8.   *Sportsman,* 2.6.1909.
9.   *Sportsman,* 2.6.1909.
10.   *Sportsman,* 26.5.1909; *Referee,* 4.8.1909.
11.   *SMH,* 22.5.1909.
12.   *SMH,* 6.5.1909, 7.5.1909 & 10.5.1909.
13.   *SMH,* 13.5.1909.
14.   *Sportsman,* 5.5.1909.
15.   *Referee,* 19.5.1909.
16.   *Greatest Game Under The Sun.*
17.   *Sportsman,* 9.6.1909.
18.   *Sportsman,* 9.6.1909; *SMH,* 8.6.1909.
19.   *SMH,* 10.6.1909.
20.   *SMH,* 5.7.1909.
21.   *A People's Game.*
22.   *SMH,* 16.7.1909.
23.   *SMH,* 17.7.1909; refer to team photo.
24.   *SMH,* 19.7.1909.
25.   *SMH,* 26.7.1909.
26.   *Sunday Sun,* 1.8.1909; *SMH,* 2.8.1909.
27.   *SMH,* 3.8.1909.
28.   *Referee,* 4.8.1909.
29.   *SMH,* 10.8.1909; *Referee,* 11.8.1909.
30.   *SMH,* 17.7.1909.
31.   *Referee,* 11.8.1909.
32.   *Sportsman,* 11.8.1909.
33.   *Sportsman,* 6.10.1909; *Referee,* 18.8.1909.
34.   *Sportsman,* 11.8.1909.
35.   *Sportsman,* 18.8.1909; *Referee,* 18.8.1909.
36.   *Sportsman,* 18.8.1909.
37.   *Sportsman,* 25.8.1909; *SMH,* 23.8.1909.
38.   *SMH,* 30.8.1909; *Referee,* 1.9.1909; *Sportsman,* 1.9.1909.

Chapter Fifteen (pages 275 to 293)
1.   *Truth,* 2.6.1940.

2. *Sun, 30.8.1910; First Wallabies; True Blue.*

3. *Referee, 22.1.1908; SMH, 2/1908,* James Joynton-Smith's surname has been hyphenated for clarity. He was rarely referred to as 'Mr Smith' alone, mostly 'Mr Joynton Smith.'

4. *True Blue.*

5. *Referee, 22.1.1908; SMH, 2/1908.*

6. *SMH, 24.8.1909.*

7. *SMH, 25.8.1909.*

8. *SMH, 28.8.1909.*

9. *SMH, 28.8.1909.*

10. *SMH, 28.8.1909.*

11. *SMH, 30.8.1909.*

12. *SMH, 30.8.1909.*

13. *SMH, 31.8.1909.*

14. *Referee, 1.9.1909.*

15. *Sportsman, 1.9.1909.*

16. *SMH, 31.8.1909.*

17. *SMH, 2.9.1909.*

18. *Referee, 1.9.1909.*

19. *Sportsman, 1.9.1909.*

20. *Referee, 1.9.1909.*

21. *SMH, 2.9.1909.*

22. *True Blue.*

23. *SMH, 2.9.1909.*

24. *Sportsman, 8.9.1909.*

25. *Sun, 2.9.1910; First Wallabies.*

26. *Truth, 2.6.1940.*

27. *Truth, 2.6.1940.*

28. *SMH, 3.9.1909.*

29. *SMH, 3.9.1909.*

30. *Sportsman, 8.9.1910.*

31. *Sportsman, 8.9.1910; Referee, 8.9.1910; SMH, 6.9.1909.*

32. *Sportsman, 8.9.1910.*

33. *Referee, 15.9.1909.*

34. *Referee, 15.9.1909.*

35. *Referee, 15.9.1909.*

36. *Sunday Sun, 12.9.1909.*

37. *Referee, 15.9.1909.*

Chapter Sixteen (pages 294 to 305)

1. *SMH, 18.9.1909.*

2. *SMH, 18.9.1909 & 20.9.1909.*

3.   *SMH*, 18.9.1909.
4.   *SMH*, 18.9.1909.
5.   *SMH*, 20.9.1909.
6.   *Sportsman*, 29.9.1909.
7.   *Sportsman*, 22.9.1909 & 29.9.1909.
8.   *SMH*, 25.9.1909.
9.   *Sportsman*, 6.10.1909.
10.   *Referee*, 9.3.1910.
11.   *Sportsman*, 6.10.1909.
12.   *Sportsman*, 29.9.1909.
13.   *SMH*, 16.9.1909.
14.   *Referee*, 15.9.1909.
15.   *SMH*, 6.9.1909.
16.   *SMH*, 7.9.1909.
17.   *Referee*, 15.9.1909.
18.   *Referee*, 29.9.1909.
19.   N.U. Minutes held by R.F.L.

Chapter Seventeen (pages 306 to 326)

1.   *Referee*, 20.4.1910.
2.   *Referee*, 9.3.1910 & 20.4.1910.
3.   *Sportsman*, 20.4.1910.
4.   *Bulletin*, 26.8.1909; *SMH*, 22.3.1910.
5.   *SMH*, 5.4.1910; *Referee*, 6.4.1910.
6.   *Referee*, 23.3.1910.
7.   *SMH*, 5.4.1910.
8.   *SMH*, 18.3.1910.
9.   *SMH*, 23.4.1910; *Sportsman*, 20.4.1910.
10.   *Referee*, 4.5.1910.
11.   *SMH*, 11.3.1910.
12.   *Referee*, 16.3.1910.
13.   *Referee*, 1.6.1910.
14.   *Referee*, 1.6.1910.
15.   *Referee*, 20.4.1910.
16.   *Referee*, 11.5.1910.
17.   *Referee*, 23.3.1910.
18.   *Referee*, 1.6.1910.
19.   *Referee*, 8.6.1910.
20.   *Referee*, 8.6.1910.
21.   *Sportsman*, 15.6.1910.
22.   *Sportsman*, 22.6.1910; *Referee*, 22.6.1910.
23.   *Sportsman*, 22.6.1910; *Referee*, 22.6.1910.

24.   *Referee*, 22.6.1910.
25.   *Referee*, 22.6.1910.
26.   *Referee*, 13.7.1910.
27.   *Referee*, 3.8.1910 (17,000 attended).
28.   *Referee*, 26.1.1910.
29.   *Referee*, 15.6.1910.
30.   *Referee*, 2.3.1910; *SMH*, 13.4.1910.
31.   *Referee*, 11.5.1910.
32.   *Referee*, 31.8.1910 & 5.10.1910.
33.   *Referee*, 13.4.1910.
34.   *Referee*, 13.4.1910.
35.   *Referee*, 29.6.1910 & 6.7.1910.
36.   *Referee*, 29.6.1910.
37.   *Referee*, 29.6.1910.
38.   *Sun*, 30.8.1910; *Referee*, 29.6.1910; *SMH*, 9.7.1910.
39.   *Referee*, 6.7.1910.
40.   *Referee*, 6.7.1910.
41.   *Referee*, 20.7.1910.
42.   *Referee*, 6.7.1910.
43.   *Referee*, 6.7.1910.
44.   *SMH*, 9.7.1910 & 11.7.1910.
45.   *SMH*, 11.7.1910; *Sportsman*, 13.7.1910.
46.   *SMH*, 11.7.1910.
47.   *Referee*, 13.7.1910.
48.   *SMH*, 11.7.1910; *Referee*, 13.7.1910.
49.   *SMH*, 11.7.1910; *Referee*, 13.7.1910.
50.   *Sportsman*, 13.7.1910; *Referee*, 7.9.1910.
51.   *SMH*, 11.8.1910.
52.   *SMH*, 11.8.1910.
53.   *Referee*, 17.8.1910.
54.   *Referee*, 14.9.1910.
55.   *Referee*, 24.8.1910.
56.   *Referee*, 14.9.1910.

INDEX

a) Pages in italics refer to a photograph
b) Names may be abbreviated to surname only in the text
c) + indicates first name/initial could not be determined
d) Names inside [ ] brackets are modern name
e) Where a range of page no.s is given (e.g. 120-34), the person/subject
   will be found on most pages

A

B

C

D

E

F

G

H

I

J

M

N

O

P

S

U

V

W

X

Y

Z

Sub-Headings Directory

Chapter 5: What the Devil is That For?

Chapter 6: Messenger & Co.

Chapter 7: The Great Reunion

Chapter 8: The Mirage of Professionalism

Chapter 9: A Professional League is Now a Certainty

Chapter 13: Our Colonial Footballers in England

Chapter 14: Dead to the World

Chapter 15: Kangaroos v Wallabies

Chapter 16: The Balmainiacs Forfeit the Final

Chapter 17: Jack is Now as Good as His Master

* * * * * * * * * *

FOR MORE INFORMATION ON THE RUGBY REBELLION VISIT:
www.RugbyRebellion.com

TO READ OTHER WORK BY SEAN FAGAN VISIT:
www.RL1908.com